Business Regulation and Public Policy

INTERNATIONAL STUDIES IN ENTREPRENEURSHIP

Series Editors:

Zoltan J. Acs
George Mason University
Fairfax, VA, USA

David B. Audretsch
Max Planck Institute of Economics
Jena, Germany

Other books in the series:

Hansen, T., Solgaard, H.S.
New Perspectives in Retailing and Store Patronage Behavior
Davidsson, P.
Researching Entrepreneurship
Fornahl, D., Audretsch D., Zellner, C.
The Role of Labour Mobility and Informal Networks for Knowledge Transfer
Audretsch D., Grimm, H., Wessner, C.
Local Heroes in the Global Village
Landstöm, H.
Pioneers in Entrepreneurship and Small Business Research
Lundström, A., Stevenson, L.
Entrepreneurship Policy: Theory and Practice
Elfring, T.
Corporate Entrepreneurship
van Stel, A.
Empirical Analysis of Entrepreneurship and Economic Growth
Fritsch, M., Schmude, J.
Entrepreneurship in the Region
Reynolds, P. D.
Entrepreneurship in the United States
Congregado, E.
Measuring Entrepreneurship: Building a Statistical System
Acs, Z., Stough, R.
Public Policy in an Entrepreneurial Economy: Creating the Conditions for Business Growth
Aydogan, N., Chen, Y.P.
Social Capital and Business Development in High-Technology Clusters: An Analysis of Contemporary U.S. Agglomerations
André Nijsen, John Hudson, Christoph Müller, Kees van Paridon, Roy Thurik
Business Regulation and Public Policy: The Costs and Benefits of Compliance

André Nijsen · John Hudson · Christoph Müller · Kees van Paridon · Roy Thurik
Editors

Business Regulation and Public Policy

The Costs and Benefits of Compliance

Springer

Editors
André Nijsen
Adviser Regulatory Reform,
Schoonhoven
The Netherlands
nijsena@xs4all.nl

John Hudson
University of Bath
Somerset, UK
j.r.hudson@bath.ac.uk

Christoph Müller
University of Sankt Gallen
Switzerland
christoph.mueller@unissg.ch

Kees van Paridon
Erasmus University
Rotterdam
The Netherlands
vanparidon@fsw.eur.nl

Roy Thurik
Erasmus University
Rotterdam
The Netherlands
thurik@few.eur.nl

ISBN 978-0-387-77677-4 e-ISBN 978-0-387-77678-1
DOI 10.1007/978-0-387-77678-1

Library of Congress Control Number: 2008940858

Printed on acid-free paper

springer.com

Contents

Introduction: The World of Regulation and Compliance

André Nijsen, John Hudson, Kees van Paridon, Christoph Müller, and Roy Thurik

Abstract This book tries to answer the most relevant questions about how to tailor regulations in such a way that businesses are able and willing to comply with government regulations. It brings together a number of diverse contributions from leading experts in their related fields. The book is written to mark the retirement of André Nijsen in February 2008.

It explains how the authors were getting fascinated by the issue of business effects of regulations. For years, businesses are complaining about regulations and compliance costs. On the other hand, society is becoming aware of more and more risks for the well being of people, nature and planet. Regulating seems to be one of the answers to safeguard against these risks. How can we deregulate and regulate at the same time, without bargaining our public goals and acting as a brake on economic growth? That is the key question to be answered in this book.

One of the basic conditions for such a policy is the availability of clear concepts and unquestionable information about compliance effects. The question is which perspective do we need to create transparency about business effects of regulation? Do we need the classic business perspective or could a public policy perspective be more useful to take away or avoid unnecessary compliance costs? The business perspective appears to be important as a starting point but to improve the quality of regulation we need to change this perspective into a public policy one. One of the strongest arguments to favor a policy to reduce compliance costs is that compliance costs are regressive in nature. They are especially burdensome for the small businesses.

1 Introduction

The concept of compliance costs, part of which is the administrative burden, can be traced back at least as far as Adam Smith (Smith 1966). In recent years, it has become increasingly important and increasingly 'in fashion'. This recent rise in interest, both academic and political, is due in no small part to the enduring contributions of André Nijsen to this policy domain. In fact, with his SCM-model he has been the principal architect of this development. Together with the work done in the Netherlands, not of course unlinked to André Nijsen and the SCM model, this has provided information on the extent of 'the problem' and also a demonstration of what is practicable to achieve in terms of tackling that problem. In doing so, it has set an example which other EU member states and countries across the globe are following. This is André Nijsen's true legacy.

This book tries to answer the most relevant questions about how to tailor regulations in such a way that businesses are able and willing to comply with government regulations. It brings together a number of diverse contributions from leading experts in their related fields. It is written to mark the retirement of Andre Nijsen in February 2008 whose pioneering work in developing the Standard Cost Model in the Netherlands has played such a crucial part in the revolution in attitudes and approach which is currently underway in Europe and also the rest of the World. André Nijsen's first pioneer steps on the road to the development of SCM – at that time named Mistral® – were taken in 1991. The crowning glory was his PhD in January 2003, of which Mistral® was a substantial part (Nijsen, 2003).

Getting fascinated by a subject like business effect of regulations seems to be a contradiction in terms. Nevertheless it is what happened to all the authors of this book. The fascinating thing is not business effects as such, but the whole field of influence of which business effects are parts of. Business effects are one of the exponents of the way government is dealing with society. The simple fact that government interferes with daily business routines is a nuisance to many entrepreneurs, but the manner in which the governments are doing this makes it even worse. Until recent times, governments were hardly aware of these types of nuisances. As a consequence, the quality of many regulations and the level of compliance are suboptimal. In the end, this has a negative effect on the realization of the public goals.

Getting involved with the subject business effects of regulations implies getting in touch with many ministries, many enforcing governmental institutions, and different types of enterprises. Then, it appears, there are a lot of conflicting interests in dealing with business effects of regulations. How to deal with these conflicts of interests by optimizing benefits for society and costs for businesses is the major subject of this book.

This chapter is structured as follows: In the next section, we will present the problem description while in the following section it will be shown that business effects are two sides of a coin. We will continue in the next section with discussing what the problem with compliance costs is. The chapter will be continued with a presentation of some anticipating thoughts about what is at stake in the World of Regulation and Compliance. The central issues are 'Better regulation as a learning curve' and the highlighting of possible developments which may facilitate the reduction of unnecessary compliance costs. Finally, in the concluding section, the structure of the book will be presented.

2 Problem Description

For years, businesses have been complaining about regulations and compliance costs (Grilo and Irigoyen, 2006 and Grilo and Thurik, 2008). Deregulation seems to be the most appropriate reaction to that. But at the same time, society is becoming more and more aware of increasing risks for the well being of people, nature and the planet. Regulating seems to be one of the answers to safeguard against these risks. How can we deregulate and regulate at the same time, without bargaining away our public goals and acting as a brake on economic growth? (Capelleras, Mole, Greene and Storey, 2007).

The simple fact that businesses are complaining about regulations is not a sufficient argument to skip regulation, because of the necessity to safeguard the related public goals. That is why many regulations, and this holds true especially for regulations stemming from public administration law, definitely are after forcing businesses to behave in a less rational way from the business economic perspective, at least in the short term. Dumping garbage in the canal is generally much cheaper for the firm than the processing of waste in a correct manner. Nevertheless, there is enough evidence that most entrepreneurs are willing to produce in an environmentally friendly way and under safe working conditions. That is why much attention is needed from the side of the policy makers and law makers to avoid or to take away unnecessary compliance costs to businesses. Unnecessary or avoidable compliance costs mostly originate from a lack of tailoring in the policy making or the law making process. Such a lack of tailoring leads to low quality laws from the perspective of those who have to comply with these laws, the norm addressees or the business sector.

Nowadays, many instruments are available to assess the effects of laws. The so-called regulatory impact assessment (RIAs) is a well known example and applied mostly in case of new or planned regulation. The RIA system is flexible and contains a set of different instruments like cost/benefit analysis, cost-effectiveness analysis, risk analysis and cost assessments. Each of those instruments have their own strengths and weaknesses. However, most of these instruments have in common their focus on the public goals to be achieved, and not on those who are being addressed by the laws, the addressees. In this context, the businesses are the addressees. The position that we want to put forward is, that public goals will be achieved better if compliance costs of the addressees, the businesses, are as low as possible. Our argument is that businesses will comply more and in a better way in case of low(er) compliance costs. After all, complying with legal obligations in a satisfactory way is the first and most necessary step to reach the related public goals. The avoidance of unnecessary compliance costs implies a win-win situation for all involved parties, the business sector, and government and, as a consequence, the society as a whole.

Most regulations are focusing on businesses and to a lesser degree on civilians. Regulating is regulating businesses (Cranston, 1979: pp. 1–4).

Therefore, there is the need for a stronger position of a special kind of RIA, the so-called business impact assessment (BIA). The argument is not that the classic type of RIA, being cost/benefit analysis, should be replaced by the BIA. But the argument is that regulating businesses should start with a BIA to assure that businesses that are willing to comply also are in the position to comply. In the end, compliance is a function of the preparedness and the ability to comply. If government is striving in a systematic way to improve the ability of businesses to comply by avoiding unnecessary compliance costs, the preparedness of businesses to comply will increase. That is what we have called a win-win situation for all involved parties, including society as a whole.

3 Business Effects: Two Sides of a Coin

Effective debates about compliance effects require high awareness about the two sides of the coin that exist. On the one hand, there is the business side and, on the other hand, the government side.

From the perspective of the business side, the process of complying is different for nascent versus established businesses (van Stel, Storey and Thurik, 2007); also the priorities of young versus established businesses are different (Grilo and Thurik, 2008), while new businesses are concerned about raising capital and establishing a position in the marketplace, established businesses are focused on maximizing profits and maintaining or increasing market share and their relationships with government will be different. For this reason, this book will provide some commentary on the particular opportunities and challenges that entrepreneurial businesses face and how they can most effectively navigate these.

From the perspective of government – policymakers, lawmakers and inspectors – it is important to illustrate how governments can be responsive in order to promote business creation and stimulate economic growth by making high quality business regulation (Audretsch, Grilo and Thurik, 2007). This implies a deep knowledge of the relevant characteristics of businesses in different sectors, size, classes, and life cycles. Our argument is, if governments want to regulate businesses in an effective way – and that's what governments need to do in order to guarantee public goals – legal obligations will have to be tailored to the relevant characteristics of the business sectors.

For that reason, we will in part focus on the determinants of business effects which can be influenced by government – policy makers, law makers and inspectors – rather than on the determinants which can be influenced by the entrepreneurs themselves. This implies that we assume, competition will force businesses to comply in a cost effective or efficient way. It will be demonstrated that this major assumption has consequences for definitions and methodology.

4 What's the Problem with Compliance Costs?

There are many reasons to discuss the issue of compliance costs (Nijsen 2003), viz.:

- Compliance costs are hidden costs.
- Unnecessary compliance costs are a brake on economic growth.
- Compliance costs are regressive in nature: the burden is relatively most heavy for small businesses.
- Strong political field of influence.
- Confusion of perspectives.

4.1 Hidden Costs

Apart from the direct financial costs like taxes, premiums etc., the compliance costs incurred by businesses (and citizens) are, in fact, hidden costs. No explicit account of information compliance costs (administrative burden) and substantive compliance costs can be found in any administration kept by businesses. Even more serious is the fact that the compliance costs for businesses are not included when compiling the National Budget.

Officials who are responsible for designing new legislations and regulations are generally badly informed about the "off budget" effects of regulations. Apart from taxes, premiums etc. again, estimates of costs and benefits of legislations and regulations are limited to the consequences for the National Budget ("on budget" effects) usually. In this respect, Van der Bij refers to internal and external regulation costs (Van der Bij, 1994, pp. 227 ff). Regulation costs, which are included in the National Budget, are termed internal regulation costs, the remaining regulation costs, which remain outside the budget,[1] are termed external regulation costs. Consequently, when estimating the budget, calculations are usually based on considerably low budgetary price and thereby little incentive for reduction of costs of regulation is left.

Nowadays, this problem is internationally recognized. The perceived intrusiveness of government regulation in many OECD countries could be detected only through anecdotal information, partial indicators and general impressions. Systematic efforts to track and account for regulatory effects are uncommon despite recognition that the scope of regulation is broad indeed." (Hopkins, 1997, p. 274).

---

[1] Van der Bij gives the example of what he terms external regulation costs, those connected with pay roll tax administration and compiling annual tax report.

4.2 Compliance Costs Are Regressive in Nature

Compliance costs place a relatively heavy burden on medium and small sized businesses. For this reason, policies are being developed, both nationally and internationally, to aim at eliminating or preventing unnecessary compliance costs – in particular for small and medium sized businesses (OECD, 1997; EIM/ENSR, 1995). Sandford argues that tax compliance costs have undesirable distributional effects. They are capricious in their incidence, regressive and fall with disproportionate severity on small firms in particular. Moreover, small firms suffer from a disadvantaged position being created by the state. Additionally, tax compliance costs fall much more heavily on the self-employed than on employees (Sandford, 1995, p. 95). Table 1 presents the disadvantaged position of small firms.

From Table 1 it appears that administrative burdens of small firms (1–9 workers) are 9.5% of value added, and only 1.1% for businesses with 100 or more workers. The main reasons for this regressiveness are administrative burden being fixed cost mainly and the low value added of small firms. Small Dutch firms (1–9 workers) create about 20% of the total value added, but incur almost 70% of the total administrative burden. The comparable figures for businesses with 100 and more workers are respectively 50% of the total value added and only about 16% of all the administrative burdens (Boog, Jansen and Tom, 2002).

To understand the problems of starting businesses and what happens thereafter, Table 2 presents some figures.

Table 1 Administrative burden as a percentage of value added for the Dutch private sector, according firm size; 2000

Industry	1–9 workers	10–99 workers	100 and more workers	total
		percentages		
Agriculture, hunting, forestry, fishing	9.0	0.7	0.5	7.2
Mining	1.1	0.1	0.0	0.1
Manufacturing	8.3	2.6	1.1	2.2
Public utilities	9.0	0.9	0.4	0.5
Building	9.6	2.7	1.5	4.0
Trade and reparation and trade	10.5	2.2	1.6	4.4
Hotel and catering industry	11.2	4.5	2.1	7.0
Transport, storage and communication	7.1	2.1	0.9	1.9
Financial sector	6.2	1.6	0.6	1.3
Business-to-business services	10.3	0.8	1.4	2.7
Health care and welfare	9.0	2.1	1.5	3.0
Culture, sport, broadcasting	13.6	2.0	1.1	6.9
Total	9.5	1.8	1.1	3.0

Source: Boog, Jansen and Tom, 2002

Table 2 Administrative burdens in euros according to life event for a sandwich bar and a painting business: The Netherlands 2007

Life event	Sandwich bar: One-off costs	Sandwich bar: Structural costs	Painting business: One-off costs	Painting business: Structural costs
Start business	241	1,898	146	1,553
Hiring first employee	830	486	742	486
Hiring 4 additional employees	480	140	480	140
From one-man business to a private limited company	788	4,514	781	4,514
Total life events all in one year	2,339	7,038	2,149	6,693
Additional, when starting from a benefit situation	216	0	216	0

Source: Tom, Suyver, and Boog, 2007

The situation for these two cases was even worse in 1998. From 1998–2007, the one-off cost went down by about 24–27% and the structural costs with 8–9% as a consequence of reduction policy (Tom et al., 2007). Too high an administrative burden for starting a business and hiring the first employee might have a negative effect on the total number of starters and employment.

The Global Entrepreneurship Monitor reports too provide indications for differentiation into young and established businesses for over 40 countries. Of the 13 individual factors of the GEM reports, the following factors with regulation reference are particularly relevant for young businesses (GEM Report, 2006):

- Protection of intellectual property
- Policy 2: Regulation and taxes
- Market Openness 2: Market entry barriers
- Market Openness 1: Market changes

Legal protection for intellectual property, free enterprise, low-hindrance regulations and low market entry barriers are basic prerequisites for the development of founding companies. In relation to these three factors, the countries to the fore of the GEM ranking should be particularly highlighted as positive examples: USA, Singapore, United Arab Emirates, Iceland, Belgium, Finland and Australia. For established companies, it is more important to defend their market positions, to be able to erect high market entry barriers against newcomers and to impose high compliance costs on young companies by setting high regulation standards. The GEM Report therefore comes to the conclusion, in relation to industrial countries, that countries with better (poorer) structural conditions tend to present a higher (lower) founding quota (GEM Report, 2006, p. 27).

4.3 Brake on Economic Growth

The hidden costs of regulation in general should not be underestimated. Businesses take measures to comply with the regulations imposed upon them by the government. Such measures are accompanied by significant costs. To an increasing extent, it is becoming recognized that unnecessary compliance costs may have adverse effects on economic growth and employment.

Which mechanism is causing the negative effects of unnecessary compliance costs on economic growth in general and small businesses especially? Compliance costs are primary costs for businesses. Businesses will have a direct cost-reduction if their compliance costs decrease. This cost-reduction leads to higher profits and, by consequence, to more investment. Besides, the cost-reduction will be passed partially in prices. Lower prices will improve the competitive position. As a consequence, exports will grow. Finally, trade unions will succeed in taking part of the profits to increase wages. The increased wages will lead to a higher consumption. In the end, the production of businesses will increase, due to all these factors: higher investments, more export and more consumption. In the short term, employment of clerically jobs could decrease slightly. However, in the longer term, this job loss could be compensated by other jobs. In the long run, the effect on employment is expected to be zero (De Wit and Nijsen, 2002).

4.4 Ideologically Charged Policy Discussions

Generally speaking, policy discussions about compliance costs are characterized, on the one hand, by their highly practical content and, on the other, by their very ideological content. The "Leitmotiv" for many discussions can be best described by mottos such as "cut the red tape burden" and "Bürokratieüberwälzung".

One illustration of the tone of the political debates on this subject in the US is revealed by the remarks made by Senator John Glenn: "...Together, I believe, these expanded agency requirements provide the greatest opportunity for progress in the war against red tape".[2] The focus is often one-sided, aiming to reduce the costs of compliance, but paying little attention to the benefits for

---

[2] Floor remarks of Senator John Glenn, 141 Cong. Rec. S 5276 (April 6, 1995) in: The Paperwork Reduction Act of 1995: Implementing Guidance for OMB Review of Agency Information Collection, Office of Information and Regulatory Affairs, Office of Management and Budget, June 1999, page 54

society. Another aspect is that, through the ties with the compliance costs the political objectives and the regulation itself have become, indirectly, the subject of discussion.

As a result of the above one-sided approach, policy aiming at reducing compliance costs, now unnecessarily finds itself in a political field of influence. This is an adverse effect on the effectiveness of the policy.

4.5 Confusion of Perspectives

The main problem is perhaps the confusion of concepts related to compliance costs caused by an unclear mix of two different perspectives. The most dominant perspective in the literature is the business perspective; the other, the public policy perspective. Our position is, we need the policy perspective to reduce, avoid or take away unnecessary compliance costs successfully.

The dominance of the business perspective is easy to understand. Compliance costs are cost of businesses. However, only a minor part of these costs can be influenced by businesses and it is to be expected that businesses will do their utmost to keep the cost of compliance as low as possible by complying in an efficient way. Competition will force them to do so. This is what we call the endogenous part of compliance costs. It does not make sense to integrate the endogenous part of compliance costs in reduction policies. The core of the business perspective is that compliance costs are the costs that would disappear if there was no legal obligation. Of course, this argument makes sense. However, it appears very difficult to measure compliance costs from this perspective. To calculate the business economic costs of complying with legal obligations, it is necessary to reckon all the different specific conditions of the regulated businesses. For instance, we should know about the relevance of legal information obligations as management information for the businesses themselves. Or, we should know about the benefits of complying for the businesses themselves. Or, we should know which part of compliance costs are avoidable from the perspective of the law, e.g. asking for tax advice or inefficient compliance. Or, we should know the opportunity costs of complying with the law. For instance, if an entrepreneur would comply with his legal information obligations during underloaded hours, his compliance costs would be zero.[3]

The most important question, however, is about the value added of answering these questions from the perspective of an efficient policy addressed at taking away or avoiding unnecessary compliance costs. The origin of compliance costs is the public sector. So we need information about the exogenous

---

[3] Some argue, opportunity costs will never be zero, because alternative opportunities will always be there, like product innovations or working upon the market.

determinants, from the perspective of the businesses, of compliance costs. That's the very reason why the Standard Cost Model (SCM) standardizes the way of compliance of businesses into a 'normally efficient way of compliance'. To stress the business perspective (endogenous determinants of compliance costs) might be even counterproductive. This could give the public sector which is responsible for business regulation, an argument to lean back, saying it is entrepreneurs' responsibility first to keep compliance costs as low as possible. The public sector should give the business sector the optimum exogenous framework conditions regarding compliance costs, which enables the businesses to keep the endogenous part of compliance costs as low as possible. This should be one of the cornerstones of high quality regulation.

5 What's at Stake in the World of Regulation and Compliance?

It is an important area. Businesses are the lifeblood of the economy. Independent of government, they respond to market signals in a far more efficient manner than central planning ever can achieve. Increasingly too, private business is carrying out tasks which were previously in the province of the public sector. But simply because they are independent of government, this does not mean they are independent of society. They need to be regulated as well as to act as government agents in certain cases. Both of these aspects impose costs on business, costs that reduce the size of the potential national cake available for consumption and investment, and, in an increasingly global market place, could reduce the competitiveness of business in their market place. Reducing the business burden is not simply about pandering to the special pleas of an enclave within society: it is about significantly increasing the prosperity and welfare of society in general. Similarly the move to better regulations is not simply about reducing the business burden: it is also about getting better, more effective regulation which achieves the intended purpose at a minimum cost. The essence of this book is the lower the level of unnecessary compliance costs, the higher the degree of compliance!!!!

5.1 Doing Things Better

In this book, we have attempted to describe this process, to look at the problems involved, to forecast its future developments and to derive relevant policies. These insights are intended as a resource for those engaged in forming regulations in all countries, particularly those involved with reducing the compliance costs. The contributors are all leading experts in the field, many of whom have direct policy experience, while others are academics. Interest in reducing the compliance costs is not simply limited to countries in Europe nor even advanced market economies. It has become, as we have said, a global issue. But simply because it is an idea whose time has come, it does not mean that all countries are treading the same path, nor that they should tread this same path. Different countries are at different stages of development, have different regulatory regimes and different depths of such regimes. Arguably, many countries do not need less, but more regulation. It must be clear from the outset that simply reducing the level of the business burden has never really been the goal of those concerned with this activity. It is about doing things better. That whatever burden is imposed should be administered in the most efficient way and, in particular, with respect to the compliance costs it puts on firms, but also on individuals. It is also saying, yes regulation is important, but so too is business. There is a trade off to be made. At times, this means reducing the business burden; at times, it may mean increasing it. But, it will always mean regulating as efficiently as possible, where the impact on business is part of the calculus.

5.2 *Where Do We Stand?*

This is why the movement for better regulation is at differing stages in different countries. At the forefront is the EU and certain countries within the EU, who are committed to controlling, and initially at least, reducing the business burden. Central to this process is the measurement of the business burden, being the costs of the regulated businesses. A high degree of compliance of the regulated businesses is the first and indispensable step towards the achievement of the public goals. As the book has emphasized, this is then the trigger for an examination of the whole policy making process, from conception to implementation. Some countries have, temporarily at least, simply skipped the measurement stage. In many cases, as emphasized, this is appropriate and the move to better conception and implementation of policies is welcome. Indeed, such is the importance of this not just to firms but to the whole of the country, that it seems to us a valid focus for development aid which has to date met with rather limited success in promoting developing countries economic growth and poverty reduction. Such is the quality of regulation in many developing countries as described in this book, that it should be possible to substantially increase the extent to which the regulation achieves its intended purpose, whilst at the same time, substantially reducing the regulatory burden and perhaps simultaneously substantially reducing the size of the shadow economy. Nonetheless, at some stage, it becomes necessary to measure the administrative burden. If you are trying to travel from Copenhagen to Barcelona, then in the initial stages of the journey, just heading south may be sufficient, but after a point, a map with distances and locations becomes essential. Here, it seems likely that the methodology being developed by the EU will eventually become the template for other countries across the world.

5.3 Better Regulation as a Learning Curve

What is more, the SCM methodology and the move towards better regulation has been both a learning curve to administrators and a reawakening for them as to the importance of business and the entrepreneur. The administrators have been forced to put themselves in the shoes of the person bearing the administrative burden, in modeling step by step all aspects of that burden. Because of this, it becomes apparent that traditional obligations placed on firms and individuals can be organized better. This is why, at this stage of the process, it is feasible to focus on cost reductions which to a considerable extent can be achieved by getting rid of 'regulatory slack', i.e. doing existing tasks more efficiently and removing parts of the administrative burden which no longer have relevance, or at least, sufficient relevance to warrant their continued existence. This is the archetypal win-win situation, but it is a stage with a finite life. Thereafter, a stage will come at which easy cuts in the administrative burden can no longer be made, but rather such costs will entail the abandonment of regulation that fulfils a genuine purpose or substantive obligations with related substantive compliance costs which are very close to the public goal to be achieved itself. At that stage, it will need to be asked more specifically whether the gains from reducing compliance costs further outweigh the welfare costs from reducing regulations, i.e. a cost-benefit analysis.

Nor does this necessarily imply government simply targeting an administrative burden of a certain magnitude, with regulation unchanging. The world changes, the need for regulation changes, much of the impetus is in an upward direction. Increased prosperity brings with it increased concerns for health, safety, environment and the general standards of product quality. New products are continually appearing on the market, at an increasing rate. These products, as with Genetically modified foods and mobile phones, are technology driven, with new technologies about which, in many cases, we are not yet in the possession of full information as to their full effects. These products need to be regulated. Increasing concerns with the environment require governments to ensure that business behaves in accordance with a code of practice which is likely to become increasingly stringent. But this does not mean that it is inevitable that the compliance costs are set to rise at some point in the future, nor even that further reductions in this burden are impossible.

That's exactly where the instrument of Regulatory Impact Assessment (RIA) can be very helpful. RIA being a tool by which governments integrate benefits and costs of public policy into a balance that achieves the country's priorities. RIA has evolved into a framework for public-private cooperation that can greatly improve the relationship between public and private sectors in effective and efficient public policy. The private sector should ensure that it is a constructive partner in this consultation process.

5.4 How to Facilitate Reduction of Compliance Costs?

The book has highlighted several possible developments which may facilitate reduced compliance costs or, more specifically, administrative burden. The first of these is IT and, more generally, technology. The administrative burden is in a large part about the costs of providing information and, above all, IT has facilitated the flow of information and will continue to do so in the future. But, even amongst firms, and especially amongst ordinary citizens, IT skills are not evenly spread and care needs to be taken to ensure that future developments do not further disadvantage those on the wrong side of the digital divide. Here, education is important.

Secondly, there is the possibility that what are current obligations with current reporting flows could become voluntary, depending upon the goodwill of firms and citizens and also social pressure to ensure that they are complied with. Corporate Social Responsibility (CSR) or self-regulation are key words in this context. There are obvious problems with this and if some firms choose not to comply, this may trigger a race to the bottom. But in addition, many obligations carry information valuable to the consumer, or, in the case of intermediate goods, to other firms. This information will still need to be conveyed to the purchaser and simply stating the information on the packaging may not be a sufficiently credible signal. This is why firms invest in IS09000 and ISO14000 to signal their management quality or environmental credentials. These are expensive accreditations to acquire, but for many firms in many markets, these accreditations are far from optional, and even now, they too in a sense are part of the compliance costs imposed on business by semi-public organizations.

Thirdly, we emphasize again that this is a dynamic process and we now focus on several dimensions of this process. Firstly, increasingly in the age of globalization, much of the regulatory burden placed on business stems from international treaties and organizations. There are two particular dangers here: (i) That there may be the temptation to move to a one-size-fits-all approach, which is not applicable to a world as diverse as ours at the beginning of the 21st century; and (ii) International agents concerned with this process are divorced from the process of implementing the regulation and, to an extent, divorced from the impact on and the needs of business. Hence, they may not care as much as entrepreneurs and supporters of better working markets would like. There is also the Lucas critique which implies that when we change the policy environment, economic agents will behave in ways which could not be predicted from their past behavior (Lucas, 1976). In other words, there will be unexpected consequences of the move to better regulation. Many are likely to be beneficial, e.g. the literature argues that excessive regulation is a factor pushing business into the shadow economy. Will the move to better regulation cause a reduction in the size of the shadow economy? But to paraphrase Rumsfeld, what is there we don't know that we do not know?

Fourthly, it has to be emphasized once more how important the policy environment is. However relevant all theoretical insights are, however useful the SCM method and other approaches, without sufficient and enduring support at the political level, it will not work. In this book, it was demonstrated on several occasions that the way any country or group of countries (as in the EU) is dealing with this issue strongly depends on the intensity and willingness of politicians to make the issue of compliance costs and of the administrative burden central in their overall policies. The better this link is realized, the better also the results that can be expected. Furthermore, the multilevel aspects have become better known, both upward and downward. Initially, the orientation was strongly national, but now, the relevance of this approach both at the supranational level like the EU and at the local and regional level (municipalities) has become much clearer. In the near future, this multilevel situation should get more attention.

Finally, as mentioned earlier, the current approach to better regulation even in, e.g. the Netherlands where it is fairly advanced, will continually evolve and this includes our approach to measuring the regulatory impact. This is, in part, because of the changing environment in which business and government operates in as noted above. But it is also because we will be moving closer to our target of reducing the regulatory burden towards its optimal level and, as we approach Barcelona, moving south will no longer be sufficient as a strategy. At some stage, it will become necessary to consider not just the regulatory burden but also the regulatory advantage, i.e. a cost-benefit approach. Nonetheless, it remains our view that the SCM will continue to provide the best foundation for evaluating regulations and thus will be the foundation for regulatory impact analysis in the foreseeable future.

6 Structure of the Book

The book is structured as follows: After this Introduction, we will continue in *Chapter 1* with the issue that today, compliance costs of businesses are part of the political agendas of many countries from the EU, the OECD and even developing and transition countries. It will be demonstrated that this has not been the case always by highlighting the major phases between the first recognition by professionals about 200 years ago until the establishment of monitoring systems in the beginning of this century.

Chapter 2 will focus on the increasing number of countries which have been starting policies to reduce administrative compliance costs. Also, at the level of the EU, such initiatives have been taken. This chapter puts in picture an international comparison of mainly European countries regarding administrative compliance costs and reduction policies. The focus will be on the compliance costs for the business sector.

To get a full understanding of the phenomenon of compliance costs, a theory about origin and functionality of regulations is being presented in *Chapter 3*. Only if we understand where businesses regulation is coming from and what we want to achieve and by which means, can we combat unnecessary compliance costs of businesses in an effective way.

There are a considerable number of techniques and models for estimating the level of impact of regulations as will be demonstrated in *Chapter 4*. Cost benefit analysis is considered particularly important for regulatory analysis. However, there is no definition of compliance costs that has gained wide acceptance. Disagreement exists about whether certain elements should be included in the calculation of compliance costs. This chapter offers a critical explanation of a variety of techniques that are in common use and then summarizes those that are adopted by governments around the world.

How to measure compliance costs is the issue of *Chapter 5*. Adequate measurement needs sound definitions. The container concept 'compliance costs' will be analyzed in this chapter. In this chapter, the Standard Cost Model (SCM) will be explained. Also, a new module of the SCM to measure substantive compliance costs will be introduced. One of the crucial aspects of the understanding of SCM is to discuss for which target group the results are. Is it the entrepreneur to help him/her reduce his/her own compliance costs? Or, is it the politician or the law maker to facilitate improving the quality of law by avoiding or taking away unnecessary compliance costs? The answer to this question has a big impact on how to measure compliance costs.

In the USA there is a longstanding experience with reducing compliance costs as will be illustrated in *Chapter 6*. Many consider regulatory relief for small business and implementing regulatory objectives a zero-sum game. The U.S. Regulatory Flexibility Act (RFA) of 1980 directly challenges the zero-sum game proposition by requiring regulatory agencies to search for non-zero-sum solutions for regulations having a significant impact on a substantial number of small businesses. This chapter evaluates the Regulatory Flexibility Act.

Chapter 7 presents the case of Tanzania. Tanzania's dilemma of poverty in the midst of plenty is captured in the concept of the "missing middle", featuring failure of micro firms to graduate into small and medium enterprises that would create a demonstration effect of the benefits of formalization. Tanzania needs efficient mechanisms for contract enforcement to stimulate economic linkages and encourage commercial bank lending. Tanzania needs an efficient labor market, focusing on skills improvement and competence rather than mandatory legislation as the basis for higher returns to labor. Tanzania, and countries with similar problems, need more efficient systems of information on the business sector and registration of movable and immovable property. Implementation of the program for Business Environment Strengthening for Tanzania addresses these problems. This chapter highlights the hassles and vicissitudes of change management in a regulatory reform process in a developing country environment, and the instruments that are available to handle the challenges involved.

Chapter 8 stipulates the opposite developments of globalization and 'Europeanizing on the one hand, and the need for customized regulations on the other. The average citizen and entrepreneur is afraid that the most essential part of the regulation, the flexibility and the content, based on his own responsibility, will be under threat. There is no doubt whatsoever that there are great efficiency benefits to be reaped there. It would be wise to harvest these. Time will learn with what speed and to what extent this change will have to be made. It will be necessary to reduce the burden of regulations, but in doing so, to pay attention not only to quantitative but also qualitative objectives.

Laws and regulations have their limitations will be the issue of *Chapter 9*. In abundance, they might become futile, particularly due to regulatory capture. Business Impact Assessment is called for to reduce costs of doing business in Dubai and to improve the quality of regulations. Corporate social responsibility (CSR) is also viewed to improve the general business environment. This chapter highlights the impact of regulations on businesses in Dubai and the situation of CSR in the market environment. The chapter calls for CSR (self-regulation) and argues that when fitted in sound public–private partnership framework could achieve general improvement of the business environment in Dubai.

Chapter 10 discusses government regulation and the consequent compliance costs for the private sector from the perspective of transaction cost economics. In many cases, government regulation is shaped as legally binding standards. In order to comply with these standards, private sector firms meet various types of transaction costs, such as the bonding costs that the principal/agent relationship of government regulation brings about. On the other hand, good standards may reduce transaction costs. Therefore, optimal design of government regulation requires the design of standards with the lowest possible transaction costs. Due to network externalities and economics of scale, and in order to guarantee a level playing field, good coordination and unifying standards within the EU can be beneficial. This chapter provides examples of such standards.

Chapter 11 focuses on regulatory reform from the perspective of developing countries in general. Many countries today have placed regulatory reform programs at the core of their governance and microeconomic strategies. Within those reforms, regulatory impact assessment (RIA) has become a prominent tool by which governments integrate benefits and costs of public policy into a balance that achieves, over time, the country's development priorities. The spread of RIA into less developed countries is largely due to intense pressures to stimulate growth, particularly pro-poor growth. Although RIA began as a set of analytical methods, RIA has evolved into a framework for public-private cooperation that can greatly improve the relationship between public and private sectors in effective and efficient public policy. Yet business representatives have not, in general, built capacities to assess proposals from governments, nor the capacities to collect relevant and timely information that can support the process of discovering the right solution. The private sector should ensure that it is a constructive partner in the consultation process by supplying timely, relevant, and reliable information through the consultation process.

The reasons for giving special treatment to enterprises, compared with other stakeholders, are extensive and will be the central issue of *Chapter 12.* This chapter is from a Swedish perspective. Companies and entrepreneurship, as such, enjoy no special status. Instead, what counts is the sum total of direct and indirect repercussions of political decisions. This is what dictates their being given special treatment, in terms of the consequences of new and amended business regulations. Business owners are a political minority and will most certainly remain so and few politicians know what everyday life in business is, although many politicians mean well. The politicians' main concern is, of course, the budget but what is self-evident when the state is a stakeholder is deemed by decision-makers to be less obvious where other stakeholders, such as business, are concerned. In a market economy, it is necessary to ensure that companies can compete on equivalent terms. This is why an early RIA is so important. It should be an analysis that, in the initial phase, is confined to direct effects on companies but is used to assess the effects on society as a whole in the subsequent phase.

In *Chapter 13,* the public policy process is viewed as a continuous source of compliance costs. Explanations are sought for the phenomenon that a substantial part of these costs could have been evaded or prevented and for the fact that it is an arduous task to expel unnecessary (or unwanted) compliance costs afterwards. Main drivers behind unnecessary compliance costs are described per stage in the policy process. The key factor for improving policies and reducing compliance costs is adequate information.

Regulation matters, is the device of *Chapter 14.* It organizes markets and societies and is, therefore, a cornerstone of freedom and welfare. But regulation may also cause problems, unnecessary burdens, unintended side-effects and costs. The aim of this chapter is to give evidence that – and how – regulatory systems can be built to become more effective than most of them are today. With a heuristic approach, this chapter is looking for successful measures and trying to identify patterns. The conclusion is, that a regulatory system should be built on evidence-based solutions, acceptance within the businesses by consultation, the monitoring and steering of the regulatory process, independent scrutiny and legitimacy and a political program to make the cross cutting issues powerful.

Chapter 15 describes the institutions for cutting administrative burdens in the Netherlands, based on the following criteria: measurement, reduction targets, coordinating minister, and incorporation in the regulatory process. The chapter examines how the institutions helped to change the policy culture. Moreover, it is argued that the institutions can effectively be applied in other countries and for a broader scope of better regulation including administrative burdens for citizens and substantive compliance costs.

ICT solutions to reduce administrative burdens will be the central issue of *Chapter 16.* The paper based functional hierarchy appears to be one of the important origins of the administrative burden. In such a functional hierarchy, the knowledge of the professionals on the one hand and the information of the clients on the other are two important resources. Both resources need to be managed for the organization to be effective and efficient. Two trends are witnessed. First, ICTs create an interorganizational information infrastructure that is becoming interoperable. Second, professional knowledge is becoming modularized, with organizations starting to share their professionals and their knowledge in focusing on core competencies, outsourcing all other activities (and the relevant knowledge) and creating shared service centers. This results in a radical transformation of organizations. This transformation of the organization results in potentially high levels of reduction of the administrative burden, without reducing the number and the level of norms and regulations. But to achieve such a transformation, we need a breakthrough comparable with the digging of the Canal of Suez.

Chapter 17 examines the contemporaneous relationship between the exchange rate regime and structural economic reforms over a period of 30 years for a broad "world sample" and an OECD country sample. The central question is whether structural reforms are complements or substitutes for monetary commitment in the attempt to improve macroeconomic performance. The empirical results, on the base of panel data techniques, suggest that, on average, an exchange rate rule positively correlates with the overall structural reforms and trade liberalization in particular. On the other hand, no significant and robust impact of exchange rate commitment on labor and product market reform was found. The results are similar for both the wider, more heterogeneous world sample and the panel of OECD economies. They contradict the hypothesis that exchange rate commitments may have slowed down the pace of structural reform, but neither provide robust evidence that losing the possibility of an exchange rate adjustment promotes labor and product market reforms.

Finally, in *Chapter 18,* a new developed RIA coordination system will be presented. Measuring compliance costs of businesses e.g. administrative burden is hot stuff, from scientific view point as well from policy praxis. Also, the number of persons involved has increased considerably from a small inner circle of scientists and ministerial experts to rather larger numbers of politicians, public officers and private consultants, specialized in public advisory. Almost by consequence, the debate about concepts, definitions and methodology starts again, every time new participants join the debate. In these debates, there are mostly two key questions. First, are there arguments to introduce the public goals of regulations in the measurements or could the measurement be restricted to the costs of the regulated parties (businesses, citizens etc.) only? Second, which methodology is most appropriate to measure benefits and costs of regulations? This chapter tries to bring more transparency in order to stimulate a more impartial discussion about the topic deregulation and its consequences. Important elements of this transparency are an adequate categorization of the separate cost and benefit effects, a systematic evaluation of these cost and benefit effects, and finally, an evaluation of the available techniques/methodologies. Such transparency could be guidance for all who are involved in the law making process and the measurement of compliance effects.

References

Audretsch, D.B., I. Grilo and A.R. Thurik (eds), (2007) *The Handbook of Research on Entrepreneurship Policy*, (Edward Elgar Publishing Limited, Cheltenham, UK and Northampton, MA, US,)

Bij, van der, J. (1994), Kosten van regelgeving, (Costs of Regulations), in: Regelmaat, ff. 227

Boog, J.J., M. Jansen and M.J.F. Tom (2002), Monitor Administrative Lasten Bedrijven 2001 (Monitor Administrative Burden Businesses 2001), EIM, Zoetermeer

Capelleras, J-L., K.F. Mole, F.J. Greene and D.J. Storey (2007), Do more heavily regulated economies have poorer performing new ventures? Evidence from Britain and Spain, *Journal of International Business Studies* 38, 1–17.

Cranston, R. (1979), Regulating business: law and consumer agencies, Macmillan Press, London and Basingstoke

GEM Report (2006), Authors: Sternberg, R., Brixy, U., Hundt, C., Global Entrepreneurship Monitor – Unternehmensgründungen im weltweiten Vergleich, Länderbericht Deutschland 2006, Hannover / Nürnberg, März 2007

Grilo, I. and A.R. Thurik (2008), Determinants of entrepreneurial engagement levels in Europe and the US, *Industrial and Corporate Change.*

Grilo, I. and J.M. Irigoyen (2006), Entrepreneurship in the EU: to wish and not to be, *Small Business Economics*, 26(4): 305–318

Hopkins, Th.D. (1997), Developing general indicators of regulatory costs, in Regulatory Impact Analysis; Best Practices in OECD countries, OECD, Paris

EIM/ENSR (1995), The European Observatory for SME's, Third Annual Report

OECD/PUMA (1997), Regulatory Impact Analysis, Best Practices in OECD countries

Lucas, R. (1976), "Economic Policy Evaluation: A Critique", Carnegie-Rochester Conference Series on Public Policy 1: 19–46

Nijsen, A.F.M. (2003), Dansen met de Octopus; Een bestuurskundige visie op informatieverplichtingen van het bedrijfsleven in de sociale rechtsstaat (Dancing with the Octopus; Information obligations of enterprises in the social constitutional state from a public policy perspective), Eburon/EIM, Delft/Zoetermeer (diss.)

Sandford, C. (1995), The rise and rise of tax compliance costs, in Tax Compliance Costs Measurement and Policy, Ed. by C. Sandford, Fiscal Publications in association with the Institute for Fiscal Studies, Redwook Books, Trowbridge Wiltshire

Smith, A. (1966) *Inquiry into the Nature and Causes of the Wealth of Nations,* Book 5, Chapter 2. See e.g. Smith, pp. 307–309

Stel, A. van, D. Storey and A.R. Thurik (2007), The effect of business regulations on nascent to young business entrepreneurship, *Small Business Economics*, 28(2–3): 171–186.

Tom, M., F. Suyver and J. Boog (2007), Kleine ondernemers, hoge lasten; Regeldruk voor een broodjeszaak en een schildersbedrijf in 1998 en 2007 (Small entrepreneurs, high burdens; Bureaucracy for a sandwich bar and a painting business in 1998 and 2007), EIM, Zoetermeer

Wit, de, G. and A.F.M. Nijsen, Administratie tot last van het algemeen, in: Economisch Statistische Berichten, Volume 86, nr. 4353, March 29 2002, pp. 248–250

Contributors

1 Editors

John Hudson is a professor of economics at the University of Bath. He has written almost 80 papers for leading economic journals in Europe and North America, including the Economic Journal, Journal of Economic Perspectives and the Journal of Public Economics, as well as three books and numerous chapters to edited books. His work has included analyses of regulation, development economics, taxation, wellbeing and bankruptcies. He has also published widely in leading political and social science journals. In recent years, he has been a member of the Panel of Economic Advisors for the South West Regional Development Agency (SWRDA) and conducted research for the Welsh Assembly and SWRDA, particularly on firm productivity. He has also worked for the Department for International Development, advised the Commonwealth Scholarship Commission and been on the organizing committees of numerous international conferences in North America and Europe. For further detailed information see: http://staff.bath.ac.uk/hssjrh. e-mail: J.R.Hudson@bath.ac.uk

Christoph Müller, Prof. Dr., (1968), has studied Business Administration and Economics at the University of Hohenheim (Stuttgart, Germany) from 1988–1992, then he started at the University of Sankt Gallen in Switzerland with doctoral degree courses and worked from 1993–1995 at his doctoral thesis about the 'strategic management of medium-sized European companies – exemplified by the tool making industry' and achieved the award of the degree of Dr. oec. in 1995. From 1997–2001, he wrote his habilitation about '(De-) Regulation and Entrepreneurship: An economic, political, historical analysis and model development' (concerning an SME-test for reducing administrative burden). In 2001, he was awarded the degree Privatdozent at the University of

Sankt Gallen. Since 2002, he has owned the endowed chair of entrepreneurship at the University of Hohenheim and he was chairman of the center of entrepreneurship. In 1998, he published his first study about 'Administrative burdens on SMEs – An international and inner-Swiss comparison' for the Ministry of Economic Affairs in Switzerland. Together with the president of the Sankt Gallen – Appenzell Chamber of Industry and Commerce, he developed a more advanced version of the SME-test in 2001. In 2005, he developed a concept for the measurement of costs of regulation on the basis of an international survey of methods for the German Bertelsmann-Foundation, which was one of the initial starting points for the development of SCM – handbooks and studies in Germany. He is also member / vice-president / president of advisory boards of SMEs in Germany and Switzerland. From October 2008 on, he works again as a professor for SME and start-ups at the University of Sankt Gallen and for a technological entrepreneurship project with universities in the Baden-Württemberg region. For further detailed information, see www.unipreneur.de and www.kmu.unisg.ch. e-mail: christoph.mueller@unisg.ch

André Nijsen (1943) graduated in sociology, specialization research and methodology, from the Catholic University Tilburg, the Netherlands in 1969. From 1969 until 1978, he was with the Netherlands Central Bureau of Statistics (CBS). His specialization was labor market statistics and wage statistics. During this time, he represented CBS as national expert in EUROSTAT conferences and meetings in Brussels and Luxembourg. From 1979 onwards, he worked at EIM Business and Policy Research in Zoetermeer, the Netherlands, the largest, private small business research institute in the world. He started as a labor market researcher. From 1982 until 2001, he was manager of the Department Social Policy. From 2001 until 2004, he was member of the board of directors of EIM Business and Policy Research and from 2004 until his retirement in February 2008, he was one of the directors of EIM Group, in 2005 renamed as Panteia Group, The Netherlands. From February 2008 onwards, he is an independent adviser in the area of regulatory reform. In January 2003, he obtained his PhD at the Erasmus University Rotterdam. The title of his thesis is: "Dancing with the Octopus; Information obligations of enterprises in the social constitutional state from a public administrative point of view." Mistral®, of which André Nijsen is the founding father, is one of the cornerstones of this thesis. Mistral® is the forerunner of the Standard Cost Model (SCM).

In 2005-2006, he developed a new instrument to measure the compliance costs of substantive obligations for enterprises, called SIROCCO, Scanning Instrument on Regulations for Other Compliance Costs. André Nijsen has a lot of (inter)national experience as an adviser in the field of regulatory reform. He advised national governments and ministries in the Netherlands, Denmark, Sweden, South-Africa, Belgium, Slovenia, Dubai, Luxemburg, Germany and Austria. He was also adviser on behalf of the European Commission, EUROSTAT, the OECD and the World Bank Group. e-mail: nijsena@xs4all.nl

Kees van Paridon (1952) is since 1999 professor of economics at the Department of Public Administration (Faculty of Social Sciences) of the Erasmus University, Rotterdam. Currently, he is head of the department of public administration. He studied at the economics department of that same university, and also got his PhD there (1987). He worked, from 1979 to 1987, as assistant professor at the Faculty of Social Sciences. Thereafter, he worked (1987–1989) with CPB Netherlands Bureau for Economic Policy, the official economic forecasting agency of the Dutch government, and then (1989–1999) with the Scientific Council for Government Policy. He was professor for Dutch-German economic relationships (1992–2002). He published extensively on labor market, social security, economic policy and competitiveness, on the Dutch, German and European economy. He worked at IIASA (Austria) and MIT, and was visiting professor in Münster. He has lectured inside and outside the university and has been advisor for ministries and national and international organizations. For detailed information, see http://www.eur.nl/fsw/staff/homepages/paridon/. e-mail: vanparidon@fsw.eur.nl

Roy Thurik is Professor of Economics and Entrepreneurship at Erasmus University, Rotterdam and Professor of Entrepreneurship at the Free University in Amsterdam. He is scientific advisor at EIM Business and Policy Research in Zoetermeer, the Netherlands, the largest, private small business research institute in the world. He is Research Professor of Entrepreneurship, Growth and Public Policy at the Max-Planck-Institut für økonomik (Max Planck Institute of Eco-nomics) in Jena, Germany. He is a Research Fellow at two renowned Dutch research schools: The Tinbergen Institute for Economic Sciences and the Erasmus Research Institute for Management. Roy's research focuses on the role of small firms in markets, the role of business owners in firms, industrial organization and policy, nascent entrepreneurship and the consequences and causes of entrepreneurship in economies. His research has been published in over one hundred and fifty articles in leading academic journals. He is associate editor of Small Business Economics: an Entrepreneurship Journal and Journal of Small Business Management. He is on the executive committee of the European Council for Small Business. He is Ameritech research scholar of the Institute for Development Studies of Indiana University. He consulted with many firms and (international) institutions. For detailed information, see http://www.thurik.com. e-mail: thurik@few.eur.nl

2 Authors

Ansgar Belke is currently Full Professor of Macroeconomics (W3) at the University of Duisburg-Essen (Campus Essen) since April 2007. Until March 2007, he was Full Professor of International Economics (C4) at the University of Hohenheim since August 2001. He has been Full Professor of Economics at the University of Vienna and Assistant Professor at the University of Bochum. He received his PhD in 1995 and finished his habilitation thesis in 2000 at the Ruhr University of Bochum (supported by the German Research Foundation) with a double venia legendi ('right to lecture') for Economics and Econometrics. He has been visiting researcher at the CentER for Economic Research, Tilburg, the Centre for European Policy Studies (CEPS), Brussels, the Kiel Institute of the World Economy (IfW) and the Oesterreichische Nationalbank (OeNB), Vienna. Until March 2007, he was Head of the "Research Center for European Integration" and a Board member of the "Eastern European Center", University of Hohenheim. He is also active as a member of the group "ECB Observer", of the Euro Area Business Cycle Network (EABCN), of the Scientific Advisory Council of the IAW, Tübingen, as a member of the Committees for Economic Policy and International Economics within the German Economic Association and as Member of the Council of the "Arbeitskreis Europäische Integration" (AEI). Since 2004, he is also a Research Fellow at the Institute for the Study of Labor (IZA), Bonn. He serves as a co-editor of Empirica, and as an Associate Editor of Economics (Kiel Institute of the World Economy). He has published widely in refereed international journals and in a number of international newspapers on a regular basis. His main research interests are: International Macroeconomics, Monetary Economics, Public Choice and European Integration. e-mail: ansgar.belke@uni-due.de

Frank A.G. den Butter (1948) studied econometrics at the University of Amsterdam and obtained his PhD from Erasmus University, Rotterdam. From 1973–1988, he worked at the Netherlands Central Bank where he was involved in economic modelling, policy analysis and research management. Since 1988, he is professor of economics at the Free University Amsterdam and founded the research team ALERT (Applied Labor Economics Research Team). From 1989–1996, he was a director of the Tinbergen Institute, the Economics Research

Institute and Graduate School of the Amsterdam and Rotterdam Universities. From 1998–2002, he was member of the multidisciplinary Scientific Council for Government Policy (WRR) at the Prime Minister's office in The Hague. His report on "The Netherlands as a trading nation" initiated the founding of the Research Institute for Transaction Management (RITM). Moreover, he has been chairman of the Royal Netherlands Economic Association (the oldest economists' association in the world) from 1997–2003 and was member of the Central Statistical Committee (the supervisory committee of the Central Bureau of Statistics) from 1998–2004. He is chairman of the supervisory committee of the Economic Institute for the Building Industry. Outside the Netherlands, he has been member of the board of European Association of Labor Economists and acted as consultant for OECD, ILO, the World Bank, the government of Ethiopia and the IAB. Frank den Butter published about 15 books and 300 articles, both in the main international and in policy oriented academic journals in the Netherlands. e-mail: fbutter@feweb.vu.nl

Francis Chittenden, MBA, PhD, FCCA, ACIS. Francis Chittenden is ACCA Professor of Small Business Finance at Manchester Business School, University of Manchester, UK. Before becoming an academic, Francis Chittenden was a practising accountant whose work experience had also encompassed manufacturing, distribution, retailing and banking. During this time, he founded or co-founded four businesses. Francis lectures, publishes and consults internationally on raising and managing finance, and the impact of tax and regulation on small and medium-sized enterprises (SMEs). He is a member of Council of the Association of Chartered Certified Accountants (ACCA), chair of ACCA's SME Committee and a member of their Tax Committee. Professor Chittenden is Vice Chair of the SME / SMP Working Party of FEE, the European Federation of Accountants. He is actively involved in, or has recently completed, research projects with ACCA, the British Chambers of Commerce, the Enterprise Directorate, Eurochambres, the Institute of Chartered Accountants in England and Wales and the Institute for Economic Affairs. Professor Chittenden's current research interests include raising finance, capital investment decisions, and the impact of the tax and regulatory regime on SMEs. e-mail: francis.chittenden@mbs.ac.uk

William J. "Denny" Dennis, Jr. is a Senior Research Fellow at the NFIB Research Foundation in Washington, DC, and directs the Foundation's activities. He has held positions with the Foundation, affiliated with the National Federation of Independent Business, the largest small business advocacy organization in the United States, for over 32 years. In his tenure, he has prepared and delivered numerous testimonies and presentations for official bodies of the United States Congress and various State Legislatures, administered and co-authored the first longitudinal study on new business in the United States (New Business In America: The Firms & Their Owners), was an original member of the Panel Study on Entrepreneurial Dynamics (PSED I), co-authored Small Business Economic Trends for over 20 years, and founded and edited the National

Small Business Poll. He is a former President of the International Council for Small Business (ICSB). The U.S. Small Business Administration (SBA) presented him the 1998 Special Advocacy Award for Research and the Academy of Management, Entrepreneurship Division, honored him with its 2006 Advocacy Award. Dennis has served on two panels for the National Research Council of the National Academies of Science and is a member of the National Advisory Group for the State of the USA initiative. e-mail: denny.dennis@nfib.org

Frank Frick is Director of the new program on "Good Governance" at the Bertelsmann Stiftung, dealing with "Better Regulation" and "Optimizing Political Reform Processes". Before this, Frank Frick led the Agenda Modern Regulation program at the Bertelsmann Foundation, since it began in 2005. He coordinated the overall program which focuses on designing better regulation concepts and strategies and streaming German employment law. Frank Frick studied Political Science at the University of Bonn and at Berlin's "Free University", where he received his degree in 1991. He then began his career as scientific assistant at the Institute of Work and Technology. Since joining the Bertelsmann Stiftung in 1994, he has worked in the fields of employment and labor market policies, social policy and social market economy. e-mail: Frank.Frick@Bertelsmann.de

Peter van Hoesel graduated in 1970 in organizational psychology and research methodology. In the first half of the 1970s, he was assistant professor in Research Methods at the University of Leyden. From 1976 until 2000, he was manager with several Dutch policy research institutes. Since 2001, he is general manager of EIM Group, in 2005 renamed as Panteia, a leading Dutch company in policy research and market research. Since 2002, he is also part-time professor in Public Administration at the Erasmus University of Rotterdam. His dissertation in 1985 was devoted to methods of programming policy research. He is main author of a book about policy research in the Netherlands, published in 2005. His list of publications counts about 200 titles. He took part in many international, national and regional policy studies, amongst others in the following areas: labor market, working conditions, education, youth, small business, innovation, science. He was policy advisor for some departments of the European Committee, for nearly all ministries of the Dutch government, for several regional and local authorities in the Netherlands, and for several Dutch trade organizations. e-mail: p.van.hoesel@panteia.nl

Stefano Iancich is an MBA graduate at Manchester Business School. He collaborated with the British Chambers of Commerce analyzing the Better Regulation policies for the EU and UK and their impact on economic competition. He graduated at the University of Trieste in Italy, gaining the title of Doctor in Economics and Trade. He has extensive experience in the IT industry and has been a member of the board of directors of Rean Elettronica Industriale, Italian leader in Business Technology Solutions. e-mail: Stefano.Iancich@mba.mbs.ac.uk

Scott H. Jacobs, Managing Director of Jacobs and Associates, is among the leading international experts on regulatory reform, with over 20 years of experience in the field. He has advised governments of over 80 countries and many international institutions on regulatory reform strategies. He developed and directed the Program on Regulatory Reform in the Paris-based Organization for Economic Co-Operation and Development (OECD) from 1991 to 2001. His work in regulatory reform began in 1985 in the U.S. Office of Management and Budget in the Office of the President. Since 2001, he has managed Jacobs and Associates, an international firm specializing in regulatory reform with headquarters in Dublin and Washington, D.C. He has written 22 books and many articles. He received his graduate degree from Princeton University in the United States. e-mail: scottjacobs@regulatoryreform.com

Shivant Jhagroe (1983) studied Public Administration and History at the Erasmus University, Rotterdam. He has conducted (and assisted) researches at several Dutch departments in 2005–2007 (decision making processes and network management) and at the U.S. Department of Transportation in 2007 (safety policy from a systems-theoretical perspective). He has also conducted discourse analyses of modern Surinamese political history. Furthermore, he has been a secretary of a Dutch Red Cross District Board since 2005. His main areas of interest are complexity, political theory/philosophy, social epistemology and institutional (re)arrangements. After being a student assistant for over a year (2005–2007), at the moment, he is a lecturer in Public Administration at the Erasmus University Rotterdam. e-mail: jhagroe@fsw.eur.nl

Robin Linschoten is the chairman of the Dutch Advisory Board on Administrative Burden (Actal) since 2000. In November 2007, he was appointed by the European Commission as a member of the High Level Group of Independent Stakeholders on Administrative Burdens. Robin Linschoten is a former state-secretary of Social Affairs. He is a crown member of the Social Economic Council (SER), which is the main advisory body to the Dutch government and the parliament on national and international social and economic policy. He is owner of Vemako Consultancy Ltd. and Associate of the Dutch Group Captive Ltd. Besides, he holds numerous positions in advisory committees, boards, e.g.: Chairman of the board of supervisory directors PsyQ Nederland; Chairman of the board of supervisory directors ProgreSZ School of Social Security; Chairman of the board of supervisory directors Vitago Ltd.; Member of the board of supervisory directors Guarantee Fund Owner Occupiers; Member of the board of supervisory directors DSB Bank; Member of the board of supervisory directors DSB Insurances; Member of the board of supervisory directors Menzis Care and Income; Member of the advisory council Foundation Institute GAK/ Industrial Insurance Board. e-mail: info@actal.nl

Bede Lyimo is an Economist specializing in trade and development issues with considerable experience on legal and regulatory reforms. He has more than 20 years of experience as an Economist in the Ministry of Industry and Trade.

For two years, he served as Assistant Director responsible for Multilateral Trade Programs, including participation in negotiations on the Doha Development Agenda. In 2006, he left the civil service, on sabbatical leave, to work as a consultant on a World Bank and Donor funded program supporting major legal and regulatory reforms, coordinating support for capacity building for better government service delivery in four areas: Business registration and regulation; land administration; labor laws as well as commercial dispute resolution reforms. He holds an MBA from the Catholic University of Leuven, Belgium and is currently a member of the Board of Directors of CRDB Bank Limited. e-mail: bedelyimo@fastmail.fm

Jeroen Nijland (1965) is currently director of the Regulatory Reform Group, a joint organization of the Ministry of Finance and Ministry of Economic Affairs. This organization is established in 2007, and responsible for delivering the targets the present government set for easing regulatory burdens for businesses. The work of the group covers reducing administrative burdens, substantive compliance costs, easing processes for obtaining business permits, business impact assessments and improving the quality of services delivered to businesses. The Regulatory Reform Group is a merger of the administrative burden task force, which was situated in the Ministry of Finance and three project groups dealing with business regulation in the Ministry of Economic Affairs. Before heading the Regulatory Reform Group, Jeroen was leading the administrative burden task force as of its founding in 2003. Prior to that, he worked for a consultancy firm and for the Ministry of Economic Affairs. Jeroen studied Political Science and Economics at Nijmegen University. e-mail: j.c.m.nijland@rr.nl

Lennart Palm has been counselor to the Board of Swedish Industry and Commerce for Better Regulation since 2006. From 2001 to 2006, he was president of the Board. Before joining the Board of Swedish Industry and Commerce, Lennart Palm worked for the Swedish Employers' Confederation as head of the Competition/Public Sector and Deregulation section and as senior political adviser in the Ministry of Trade and Commerce. He was vice chairman of the Governance Committee in the Business and Industry Advisory Committee to the OECD (BIAC) from 2003 to 2008. He also served as secretary for Economic Policy, vice president and vice president of Legal Policy from 1974 to 1991at the Swedish Federation and Association of Free Enterprises. His professional experience also includes the chairmanship of the Board for Social Affairs at the University of Stockholm. Lennart Palm has a degree in law. e-mail: lennart.plm@telia.com

Belaid Rettab worked since 2001 as advisor to the UAE Ministry of Labor and Social Affairs, and from 2003 to 2007 Executive Director Business Research at Dubai Chambers, where he established a full fledged research department serving the research needs of the country. In 2007, he restructured the Centre for Responsible Business from which he contributes to changing behaviors of businesses in the region towards business ethics and social corporate responsibility, and since 2008, Senior Executive Director at Dubai Chamber. Belaid Rettab accumulated 20 years of outstanding achievements in research and advisory work in Western and Eastern Europe, Africa and Asia. He assisted the European Union, UN, WB, and several national governments with the implementation of several economic development programs. He published dozens of articles and research reports directly relevant to policy makers in the fields of Economics and International Management, entrepreneurship, international trade, public administration and business ethics. He graduated from the Economic Faculty (FEW) of Erasmus University Rotterdam (EUR), where he worked from 1987 to 1998 as researcher and later as senior consultant at the Foundation for Economic Research, Rotterdam. He defended his Doctorate thesis partially funded by the Netherlands Scientific Research Organization's (N.W.O) in 1995at the EUR-FEW, and in 1998, he moved to EIM Policy Research where he worked as International Consultant. e-mail: belaid.rettab@dcci.ae

Frank Robben graduated in law and post graduated in legal informatics, computer auditing and business administration. Frank is general manager of the Belgian Crossroads Bank for Social Security (CBSS), an institution he conceived and founded. The CBSS elaborates the eGovernment strategy within the Belgian social sector and coordinates the eGovernment projects in that sector. The CBSS received the first Belgian eGovernment Champion Award in 2004, a prestigious United Nations Public Service Award for eGovernment in 2006 and a European Public Service Award in 2007. Frank is also co-founder of the Belgian eHealth-platform and strategic advisor at Fedict, the Belgian federal public service for eGovernment. In that function, he developed the concept of the electronic identity card and worked out the general information security and privacy protection policy of the Belgian federal government. Furthermore, Frank is a member of the Belgian Privacy Commission and the steering committee of the Belgian public service for administrative simplification. He is also the Belgian representative in various commissions and working groups of the EU relating to eGovernment, ICT and social security. Finally, Frank Robben is co-founder of and researcher at the Interdisciplinary Centre for Law and Information Technology at the University of Leuven and lectures on business administration. He wrote more than 100 publications relating to eGovernment, management, ICT law and social security. Frank Robben was elected Flemish public manager of the year 2005. e-mail: Frank.Robben@ksz-bcss.fgov.be

Jaap Sleifer (1972) is a senior policy advisor at the Dutch Advisory Board on Administrative Burden (Actal) since 2005. He studied at the University of Groningen and graduated in (economic) history and also in law. In 2003, he completed his PhD thesis at the Faculty of Economics (University of Groningen). The commercial edition of his thesis, “Planning Ahead and Falling Behind: The East German Economy in Comparison with West Germany

1936–2002", was published in 2006. For this book, Jaap Sleifer was awarded the René Kuczynski Prize 2007. After completing his PhD thesis, he worked at the Centre for German Studies (CDS) of the University of Nijmegen. Jaap Sleifer is a participant at the Groningen Growth and Development Centre (GGDC). e-mail: j.a.sleifer@actal.nl

Brian Sloan is a Visiting Researcher at Manchester Business School where he is involved with modelling small and medium sized business taxation and compliance costs. This work is an extension of Brian's PhD, which he completed at the School in 2007. This extension involves the ex ante evaluation of enterprise policy initiatives. Brian writes mainly on tax policy issues and has presented a series of reports that have appraised the impact of the UK Chancellor's Budget Statements on small and medium sized businesses that also included proposals for alternative policy responses to small business tax issues; co-authored with Professor Francis Chittenden. Brian also consults for the British Chambers of Commerce on economics, tax and pensions policy issues, along with conducting the BCC's prestigious Quarterly Economic Survey; the largest economic confidence survey of its kind in the United Kingdom. Brian was previously involved with change management and the introduction of lean manufacturing during a successful engineering career that saw him achieve Chartered Engineer status before changing career path. e-mail: BSloan@dom01.mbs.ac.uk

Leo G.M. Stevens (1944) graduated in 1971 from the Catholic University Tilburg (now Catholic University Brabant) in economic science, specialization fiscal-economy. After working for 4 years in the Internal Revenue Service he was appointed at the Erasmus University Rotterdam. Until December 8 2006, he chaired the Department Fiscal Economy and the Foundation for European Fiscal Studies which offers postgraduate education. At the same time, he chaired the Advisory Board of the Institute of Financial Planning, attached to the Erasmus University. Leo Stevens obtained his doctorate in 1980 with a thesis concerning 'Ability to Pay'. In 1984, he was decorated with the Professor Hofstra-Medal. He was appointed as professor Fiscal Economy at the Erasmus University Rotterdam in 1986. Leo Stevens published innumerable articles, reports and books, along with several textbooks about Income Tax and Tax Law. In 2006, Leo Stevens was given emeritus status. Besides his academic activities, Leo Stevens was coordinating editor at Kluwer Publisher and a member of several editorial boards. Among others, he was crown-appointed deputy member of the national Social Insurance Council and still is a member of several commissions of the national Social Economic Council. Recently he chaired the state commission Regulatory Reform, installed by the Dutch Cabinet, also called 'commission Stevens'. e-mail: lgm.stevens@wxs.nl

Arre Zuurmond works at the University of Delft, where he lectures, on information and communication technologies (ICT) in public administration. His research interests include organizational development, the process of informatization, and evaluation of public service delivery. Professor Zuurmond has also published on organizational reform. He is one of the founders of the Kafka brigade, a group of scientists, practitioners, and consultants who help citizens overcome bureaucratic deadlock. Before joining academia, Professor Zuurmond was Managing Director of an information technology firm. In 2000, he started a consultancy firm, Zenc. He holds a cum laude Ph.D. in public administration and has studied political science in Amsterdam. e-mail: arre.zuurmond@zenc.nl

Chapter 1
Historical Review: 1750–2000

André Nijsen

Abstract Today, compliance costs of businesses are part of the political agendas of many countries from the EU, the OECD and even developing and transition countries. This has not always been the case. It was good old Adam Smith who said in 1778 "Every tax ought to be so contrived as both to take out and to keep out of the pockets of the people as little as possible over and above what it brings to the public treasury of the state."

From that time on, it took more than 200 years before a systematic monitoring of the development of only a part of the compliance costs, e.g. the compliance costs of information obligations started at the end of the 20th century. This chapter highlights the major phases between the first recognition by professionals until the establishment of monitoring systems. The more recent developments from 2000 onwards will not be illustrated in this but in the following chapters.

1.1 Introduction

Since the eighties of last century, interest in compliance costs has increased reasonably in EU and OECD countries. From 2000 onwards, interest increased also in developing and transition countries. Most attention has been paid to the field of fiscal legislation because this area is responsible for a substantial part of the total costs. It appears to be plausible then to assume that the conclusions drawn in literature concerning the increasing awareness regarding cost of complying in the fiscal area will, on the whole, also apply to other areas of legislation.

Pope (1989) distinguishes five phases in the recognition of information transfer compliance costs for Australia:

- Recognition by professionals (economists, tax consultants etc.)
- Quantifying the scope
- Recognition by politicians: the subject is placed on the political agenda

A. Nijsen (✉)
Adviser Regulatory Reform, Schoonhoven, The Netherlands
e-mail: nijsena@xs4all.nl

A. Nijsen et al. (eds.), *Business Regulation and Public Policy*,
International Studies in Entrepreneurship 20, DOI 10.1007/978-0-387-77678-1_1,

- Development of policy measures aiming at lightening the burden of compliance costs
- Monitoring the developments.

It seems plausible that these various stages of consciousness are recognizable in more countries than Australia (Allers 1994). The five stages that have been distinguished will be dealt with one by one later in this chapter. First of all, general comments will be made for each of the above listed stages. Subsequently, attention will be paid to the experience in EU and OECD countries until about 2000. The other chapters will focus on more recent developments.

1.2 Phase 1: Recognition by Professionals (1750–1935)[1]

The issue of compliance costs started to draw serious attention since the second half of the 18th century. However, professionals have been familiar with this issue for a longer time. As early as 1778, in his Wealth of Nations, Adam Smith reported four theories concerning the levying of taxes: Equity, Certainty, Convenience and Economy that referred to compliance and compliance costs (Smith 1966). Economic theory refers most directly to the compliance costs of information obligations: "Every tax ought to be so contrived as both to take out and to keep out of the pockets of the people as little as possible over and above what it brings into the public treasury of the state".

His theory of Equity received by far the most attention as far as policy is concerned and only lip service was paid to the other three (Sandford et al. 1989). Accordingly, this remained so until the second half of the 20th century (Allers 1994)[2].

As far as recognition by professionals is concerned, there is nothing special to report about the EU and OECD countries, which entered the picture much later.

1.3 Phase 2: Quantification (1935–1995)

Since the recognition of the compliance costs by professionals, it took two centuries before the first concrete steps were taken towards the quantification thereof.

The first step involved the compliance costs for levying taxes in the United States and Canada, the Netherlands, Germany, Switzerland, the United

---

[1] These and following dates in the headings of sections are only approximate dates.

[2] Allers 1994, p. 8. Allers gives one exception; McCulloch (1975) first published in 1845, pages 38 and 399 who emphasizes that the last three theories mentioned are actually the most important. He even provides some estimates of administrative costs as examples of taxes that offend against these rules, In France, for example, 120 million livres were spent to acquire 30 million (net) in taxation.

Kingdom and Ireland. The initial investigation in this field took place in 1930 (United States). In Europe, the first studies on this subject were carried out in the forties (the Netherlands), to be followed in the fifties and sixties by Germany and Switzerland and by England and Ireland in the seventies and eighties.[3]

Except the legislation, which regulates the transfers (taxes/premiums and social benefits/subsidies) between government on the one hand and citizens and businesses on the other, no quantification of compliance costs took place up to the nineties.

In the EU and OECD, the first attempts to quantify compliance costs were made in the middle of the nineties of last century. For example in 1995, a comparative study was carried out in all the Member States of the EU about the extent of compliance and possible policy strategies to reduce the compliance costs (EIM/ENSR 1995).

1.4 Phase 3: Recognition by Politicians (1985–1995)

Once the substantial amounts involved in complying with information obligations became commonly known – in the eighties and beginning of the nineties – politicians in the various countries became able to place this subject on the political agenda.

Nevertheless, political consciousness, as regards the issue of compliance costs of information obligations for businesses, increased considerably within the European Union in the eighties and nineties.

At the European Union level, the general principle is to prepare European legislation in the form of directives to be implemented in national legislation allowing it to fit better with the existing practical execution in the member states. As far as the Union's own legislation is concerned, it is worthwhile mentioning that the process of "regulatory reform in the European Union" has paid attention to compliance costs. This program consists of the following elements:

- "Better Lawmaking", based on the principles of subsidiarity and proportionality. The final objective is the simplification, consolidation and improvement of transparency of European legislation. In the meantime, the Commission has issued a progress report (European Commission 1997).
- The Single Market Program, the most important EU legislation program for business. The completion of the Common Market itself had considerable influence on regulatory reform. This included:

[3] To obtain a complete review of a great many Dutch, German and English studies in this field, refer M. Allers, Administration and Compliance Costs of Taxation and Public Transfer in the Netherlands. Groningen University 1994, Appendix B, Review of earlier studies on operating costs.

- the revoke, simplification and standardization of legislation in almost 300 areas of legislation;
- the revoke of thousands of laws and regulations at national, Member State, level;
- replacing these with new laws and regulations which regulate many aspects of business behavior;
- the SLIM-initiative, Simpler Legislation for the Internal Market, with, as subject, the existing legislation of the Common Market itself.

- The EU Small and Medium sized Enterprise Policy (SME Policy), which includes special attention to be paid to the application of the regulatory reform in order to simplify and improve the administrative and regulatory environment
- Development of analysis tools, such as a tool for business impact assessment, to estimate the cost effectiveness of proposed measures (ex-ante appraisal of legislation). In 1985, the Commission adopted the principle that every Commission's proposal for legislation sent to the Council must be accompanied by an assessment of its impact on business, SMEs in particular, and on job creation. The procedure became operative on June 1, 1986. In carrying out the assessment, the Directorate-General has to take into account compliance costs and the potential administrative burden for business.[4]
- Working Parties (Molitor Group and BEST, the Business Environment Simplification Task Force), Conferences (the Birmingham conference on simplification in 1992, the conference in the Hague in 1997 on the quality of European and national legislation in relation to the Internal Market).
- European Business Panel, to introduce the direct experience of enterprises into the review of this area of legislation.

At that time (1985–1995), there were also indications for increasing consciousness within the individual Member States of the EU. The aforementioned EIM/ENSR comparative study on compliance costs, which covered the several Member States, showed that there was still a considerable degree of variation in the strategies, policies, and measures adopted in the different countries and that in some countries, the reduction of administrative burdens just started (see also Table 1.1 below) (EIM/ENSR 1995).

The fourth report (EIM/ENSR 1996) noted that a similar pattern was emerging in the responses at a national level to the problem of administrative burdens. Most countries had established a committee to analyze the status quo, and to make recommendations on how and where burdens could be reduced.

---

[4] For more references on this topic, see European Communities (1993). Bulletin of the European Union, EC 10-1993, page 128, European Commission (1994/1996) Integrated Program in favour of SMEs and the Craft Sector 1994, Com (94) 207 final, and Com (96) 329 final., and The European Parliament (1997) Report *on Strengthening the Business impact Assessment System*, no. A4-0413/96 of 24th April 1997.

Table 1.1 Strategies, policies and measures to reduce administrative burdens in the different European countries, 1995

Country	Research	Information / advice	Forms / reporting requirements	Administrative procedures	Special rules for SMEs	Replacement existing laws	Possible burdens of new legislations
Austria	■	■		■	■		■
Belgium	■		■	■			
Denmark		■	■	■	■	■	■
Finland	■			■		■	
France	■	■	■	■	■		■
Germany	■	■				■	
Greece			■	■	■	■	
Ireland			■		■		■
Italy				■	■		
Luxembourg	■	■	■	■			
Netherlands	■	■		■	■	■	■
Norway	■	■	■	■		■	
Portugal	■	■		■		■	■
Spain		■					■
Sweden	■		■		■	■	
United Kingdom	■	■	■	■	■	■	■

Source: EIM (1995) The European Observatory for SMEs, The Third Annual Report, Theme Study Administrative Burden, chapter 14, EIM, The Netherlands, Zoetermeer.

Most had also taken the "first steps" of introducing systems to review proposals for new legislation and of modifying the systems for collecting taxes. The fifth report (EIM/ENSR 1997) confirmed this picture. In the period 1996–1997, in almost all Member States, with the exception of Greece and Ireland, actions to reduce the compliance cost for business, in the various European countries, were undertaken or being planned to be undertaken.

Even in many other OECD countries, there is an increasing consciousness of regulatory costs for business, including information compliance costs. The following excerpt illustrates that "Improving the empirical basis for regulatory decisions through impact analysis of new regulatory proposals is a popular reform strategy in OECD countries. By 1996, more than half the OECD countries had adopted Regulatory Impact Analysis (RIA) programs, up from one or two in 1980, and an increasing proportion of laws and other regulations affecting citizens (and businesses) are being shaped in part by various forms of RIA. In 1995, governments in all OECD countries agreed to use techniques such as RIA to improve the quality of new regulations (OECD 1997)."

1.5 Phase 4: Effective Policy Measures (1990–2000)

Until 1994, no country was in Pope's fourth and fifth stages, taking effective policy measures and monitoring. Allers refers to this as follows: "All in all, we must conclude that, although policy recognition has been on the increase lately, the last two phases of Pope, i.e. implementing effective policy measures and continual monitoring of operating costs, have not yet been reached in the Netherlands nor indeed in any other country" (Allers 1994). This situation changed in the second half of the nineties of last century. Policy making applying to the field of compliance costs of information obligations started to improve and has become adapted for action. One important reason for this is presumably, that in the first half of the nineties, the result of surveys carried out into the quantifying of the extent of the costs of complying with information obligations resulted in a shock effect among politicians in the various countries. Probably that new possibilities in the field of ICT have also played a positive part in the realization of effective policy measures.

A study carried out in 1998 in nine countries (Australia, Canada, Denmark, Germany, England, Norway, the United States, Sweden and New Zealand) has assessed several projects in the field of ICT and administrative burdens. This study – charged by the Dutch Ministry of Economic Affairs – has resulted in the identification of 56 projects all having the same objective namely, to reduce the compliance costs of information obligations for businesses (Ministry of Economic Affairs 1998). Most of these projects were based on electronic data exchange, proactive service (e.g. one counter), unique identification number, authentic data management and basic registration. This study showed that there are significant similarities in the ideas and initiatives developed in the field.

For the purpose of illustration, a number of examples of policy measures, being taken at that time in OECD countries, are given below (Snellen 1999).[5]

In the *United Kingdom,* the following initiatives have been taken to reduce compliance costs of information obligations by using ICT. These are mainly important for small businesses:

- Direct Access Government is a "one stop shop" or a "single counter" facility for businesses; a project initiated by the Cabinet office to offer entrepreneurs the opportunity to use interactive forms to be completed and submitted through Internet.
- The Small Business Service, a project managed by the DTI (Department of Trade and Industry) since May 1, 1999. This initiative aims to give the small scale entrepreneur a say within the government. Possibly, this Service will become a "single electronic gateway" for small businesses. The service

[5] Information taken from country reports, reports of fact-finding missions which Prof. I Th. Snellen has compiled on the instructions of the Committee for administrative burdens. These refer to the United States. The United Kingdom, Denmark, Norway and Sweden, July–September 1999

became operational in November 1999. It is expected that, possibly, this service will take over the above mentioned one (Direct Access Government).
- The INFOSHOP, a pilot project at local level aiming at providing enterprises with a review of all the applicable variations of legislation and measures applying in the region through a single window. Many laws made by central government are implemented at local or regional level in the United Kingdom.

In *Denmark,* the following ICT applications aiming to reduce the cost of information compliance are worth mentioning:

- Within the Ministry of Trade and Industry, a special agency is responsible for reducing the costs of information transfer compliance; this is the Ehrvervs- og Selskabsstyrelsen. This Agency is assigned to copy all governmental forms on to the Internet. In due course, this is expected to lead to a certain amount of unification.
- Ideas are being developed to offer small businesses the possibility to outsource to administration offices all contacts with the government involving the exchange of information and the accompanying legal obligations.

In *Norway*, there is a Central Co-ordinating Register of Legal Entities Bronnoysundregistrene, which exists since 1980 and aims at reducing compliance costs. This Register is an agency belonging to the Ministry of Justice and manages registers for various other ministries. The objective of the agency is to promote trustworthy relationships in society. One of the agency's responsibilities is to encourage efficiency in the traffic between the public and private sector and to avoid the same information being stored many times. In 1997, a new Register of Administrative Regulations was established to contain a record of all forms that regulate the traffic between businesses and the Government. The legal tasks of this register are to coordinate existing and new information regulations, act as an information center for business and government, organize hearings for the legislator and also to work out definitions for data collection by public authorities.

Finally, the *Netherlands*. One of the first definite initiatives, aiming at the reduction of the compliance costs of information obligations in the Netherlands, was the establishment of the Foundation for Enlightening Administrative Burdens of Small and Medium Sized Businesses (Stichting Administratieve Lastenverlichting Midden- en Kleinbedrijf, SALM) in 1990. The initiative was a combined venture involving the association of entrepreneurs, enforcement authorities, the business community and the government (the Ministry of Economic Affairs). SALM was mainly preoccupied with the reorganization of the infrastructure for information transfer between businesses and enforcement agencies by external integration. Electronic data and one central collection point were major key words for this initiative.

Another significant initiative in the Netherlands was the appointment of the van Lunteren Committee in 1994, a committee named after its chairman, the Director-General of the Taxation Authorities. The objective of the committee was to reduce the compliance costs of information obligations in the field of taxation. The initiative was taken by the Ministry of Finance to create a platform for structural discussions between the Ministry and business associations. The subject of discussion was the execution models of information obligations in the field of taxation. So, it was not taxation itself that was under discussion but the method by which this was levied. In 1995, this committee was converted by the Secretary of State for Finance into a permanent consultative body for the business organizations and the Tax authorities. One of the items placed on the agenda of this consultative body concerned the development of a tool to measure the costs of complying with fiscal information transfer regulations for businesses the Standaardkostenmodel Fiscale Verplichtingen (A Model of the Standard Cost of Tax Regulation), developed by EIM as a special module of Mistral (Measuring InSTrument Administrative Loads).

The statement of the first Kok Cabinet, during its government period 1994–1998, to reduce the compliance costs of information obligations for business by 10%, had a significant impact on policy making in the Netherlands. The Ministry of Economic Affairs was responsible for coordinating the actions required to achieve this goal. The Cabinet regularly informed the Lower House about the progress and results of this policy[6]. During the period 1994–1998, a total of 69 definite amendments were made to the legislative regulations concerning information transfer from businesses to the government. The majority of these amendments originated from the explicit objective to reduce compliance costs by 10% (Boog et al. 1999). Also, the second Kok Cabinet has decided to reduce the information transfer compliance costs by another 15% during its second period in government.

In the Netherlands in 1998, there were about 53 projects with a common goal to reduce the compliance costs of information obligations by using ICT (Zijden, van der et al. 1998). Most of these projects were based on electronic data exchange, proactive service (e.g. one counter) unique identification number, authentic data management and basic registration.

1.6 Phase 5: Monitoring from 1999 Onwards

By monitoring, we mean following the annual developments of the compliance costs of information obligations systematically and in separate fields of legislation. This is the area where the situation in the Netherlands differs from the United States. In the US, monitoring is more general in nature.

---

[6] Lower House, *Towards fewer administrative burdens*, 27 June 1995; Lower House, *Progress in the reduction of administrative burdens for businesses*, 14 July 1997; Lower House, *Present state of affairs of the project to reduce administrative burdens*, 14 April 1998; Lower House, *Report of general discussions on the lightening of administrative burdens for businesses*, 26 August 1998.

So far, the available literature suggests that the Pope's final phase – monitoring the administrative burdens- was reached at the end of the 20th century only in the Netherlands and to a lesser extent in the United States.

In the Netherlands, the initial results on the subject of monitoring the compliance costs of information obligations appeared in 1999; these covered the period 1993–1998. From 2000 onwards, there are annual reports of the developments in compliance costs of information obligations for Dutch businesses.

In the United States, attempts were being made to monitor the entire costs of regulation for businesses. Compliance costs of information obligations are an especially recognizable part. These costs are measured in hours. As far as is known, there are data available for the period 1977–1998 (Hopkins 1992 and 1996).

1.7 Summary and Conclusions

More than 200 years passed after Pope's first phase, consciousness of professionals, before the final phase, monitoring, was reached. Figure 1.1 shows the total overview. The periods cannot be distinguished exactly – there is some overlapping.

It is striking that recognition by politicians has taken so long; approximately 60 years after the initial quantification of the compliance cost of information obligations. From that time onwards, more attention has been paid to this issue. This development could be explained by at least five reasons:

1. One is the density of regulations. The extent of social regulations to protect consumers, employees and the environment increased significantly in the last

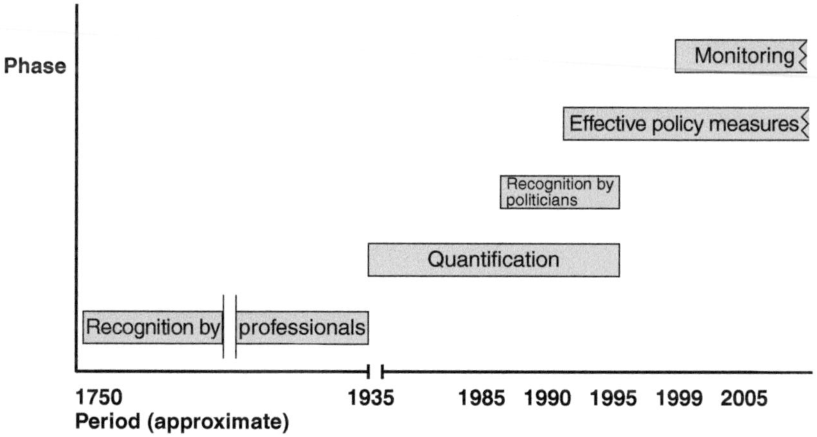

Fig. 1.1 Phases of increasing awareness of compliance costs for businesses

ten years or so. Previously, information regulation was more economic oriented and general in nature, especially taxation was dominant.
2. Another reason is the increasing interest of politicians to enhance information technology use in reducing compliance costs.
3. The fast development of communication technology.
4. The pulling back behavior of governments as a result of growing democratization.
5. Finally, the globalization and accompanied world wide competition.

References

Allers, M. (1994) *Administrative and Compliance Costs of Taxation and Public Transfers in the Netherlands,* Wolters-Noordhoff, RUG, Groningen, p. 7

Boog J.J. et al. (1999), *Monitoring Administrative Burdens for Businesses; Checking the Objective of the First 'Purple' Government*, EIM, Zoetermeer, p. 37

European Commission (1997), *Better Lawmaking,* Com(97) 626 final

EIM/ENSR (1995) *The European Observatory for SME's, The Third Annual Report, Theme Study, Administrative Burden, Chapter 14,* EIM, The Netherlands, Zoetermeer

EIM/ENSR (1996) *The European Observatory for SME's, The Fourth Annual Report,* EIM, The Netherlands, Zoetermeer

EIM/ENSR (1997) *The European Observatory for SME's, The Fifth Annual Report,* EIM, The Netherlands, Zoetermeer

Hopkins T. D. (1992), *The Costs of Federal Regulation,* Journal of Regulation and Social Costs, Vol. 2, No. I, March 1992, pp. 5–31

Hopkins, T. D. (1996), *Regulatory Costs in Profile,* Policy Study No. 132, centre for the Study of American Businesses, Washington University, St. Louis, Missouri, August 1996

Ministry of Economic Affairs of the Netherlands (1998), *Eindrapport "ICT en administratieve lasten",* Ministry of Economic Affairs of the Netherlands , The Hague, 12 November 1998

OECD (1997), *Regulatory Impact Analysis, Best Practices in OECD Countries,* OECD, Paris, p. 13

Pope, J. (1989) *The Compliance Costs of Personal Income Taxation – a Review of the Lessons,* Discussion Paper 89.03, Nedlands: Department of Economics, University of Western Australia, pp. 2–7

Sandford, C.T., M.R. Godwin, P.J.W. Hardwick (1989), *Administrative and Compliance Costs of Taxation,* Fiscal Publications, Bath

Smith, A. (1966) *Inquiry into the Nature and Causes of the Wealth of Nations,* Book 5, Chapter 2. See e.g. Smith, pp. 307–309

Snellen, I.Th.M. (1999) *Report Visit to the UK,* on behalf of the *Commissie Administratieve Lasten,* 15 July 1999, The Hague

Zijden, van der, H. et al. (1998), *Final report "ICT and administrative burdens",* Ministry of Economic Affairs. The Hague, 12 November 1998

Chapter 2
Reduction of Compliance Costs: An International Perspective

Kees van Paridon and Shivant Jhagroe

Abstract In an increasing number of countries, policies have been started to reduce administrative compliance costs. Also, at the level of the EU, such initiatives have been taken. This chapter puts in picture an international comparison of mainly European countries regarding administrative compliance costs and reduction policies. We focus here on compliance costs for the business sector. In this chapter, we describe the reduction policies and compliance costs, and explain this with the role of the regulatory state and the role of the market and institutions.

Data on these issues is hard to find. We have used several proxy data to analyze the relative position of mostly EU-member countries regarding compliance costs and reduction policies and its development over time. We reflect on these data, and relate them to certain theoretical notions on welfare state arrangements and institutional change. Finally, concluding and contemplative remarks will be made.

2.1 From More Towards Less Government: An Overview

For a long time, the importance of the public sector has increased considerably. A crude indicator like the expenditure quote or the tax quote, in both cases normalized against the country's GDP, showed an increase in all western economies. Mainly due to differences in the size and importance of social security arrangements, these quotes did range from low 30s in certain Anglo-Saxon countries security arrangements till almost 60% for some Scandinavian countries. After 1990, many countries showed a certain decline of these quotes, mostly as a consequence of their policies to trim the social security system.

K. van Paridon (✉)
Department of Public Administration, Faculty of Social Sciences, Erasmus University Rotterdam, Rotterdam, The Netherlands
e-mail: vanparidon@fsw.eur.nl

A. Nijsen et al. (eds.), *Business Regulation and Public Policy*,
International Studies in Entrepreneurship 20, DOI 10.1007/978-0-387-77678-1_2,

A similar pattern of rise and decline occurred with regard to regulation and compliance costs. As André Nijsen wrote in his dissertation (2003), a modern social constitutional state means that a government has to perform in many domains, from social security and health care to safe labor conditions and a clean environment.[1] To realize these demands, the government was in need of more information regarding the regulation of the behavior of its citizens and firms.

To measure the administrative costs and the possible reduction because of deliberate policies, Christoph Müller (2006) investigated what approaches have been used so far in the different countries.[2] He could discern 24 different approaches, 10 with a microeconomic orientation, 5 with a macroeconomic orientation and 9 with a macro-micro approach. Of these 24 approaches, only one reached the highest level of quality regarding its methodology, precision and political influence, namely the Standard Cost Model (SCM).

The SCM, developed in the early 1990s in the Netherlands, is a method to quantify the administrative costs on account of information demands by government and governmental agencies. This approach has been applied thoroughly in the Netherlands (see Paragraph 2.3), initially by measuring the extent of the administrative costs. Subsequently, based on these calculations, reduction policies were formulated and implemented. It became clear that EU-regulation did play an important role. The Dutch government used the EU presidency to export this approach to other countries and to the Commission level. That initiative got a great response. In the meantime, a whole array of European countries has adopted this approach to measure and subsequently reduce the administrative costs. This includes Austria, Finland, Germany, Ireland, Latvia, Luxembourg, the United Kingdom, Norway, Sweden, Denmark, Belgium, Flanders (Belgium), the Netherlands, France, Hungary, Italy, the Czech Republic, Poland and Estonia (OECD, 2006a). The SCM also allows cross-country comparisons. They can also be used as a tool to highlight the impact of international legislation, especially EU regulation.

Also at the supranational level, initiatives were taken to measure and reduce the administrative costs. In September 2004, the OECD's Working Party for Regulatory Management and Reform decided to give highest priority in its 2005–2006 Program of Work to activities on administrative simplification. Therefore, the OECD launched the Red Tape Scoreboard project, which aimed at developing a methodology measuring, comparing and analyzing and consequently policy recommendations.[3] The OECD also

---

[1] See Nijsen, A. (2003) Dansen met de octopus. Een bestuurskundige visie op de informatieverplichtingen van het bedrijfsleven in de sociale rechtsstaat (Dancing with the octopus. A public administrative vision at the information requirements of the private sector in a social state), Delft: Eburon.

[2] See Christoph Müller (2006), Bürokratiekostenabbau – internationaler Methodenvergleich und das Niederländische Erfolgsrezept, Die Volkswirtschaft, number 1–2, pp. 27–31

[3] Website SCM Network: www.administrative-costs.com

chose, albeit in a modified form, to apply the SCM method for its 'Red Tape Scoreboard' in 2005, in order to measure administrative costs across OECD countries.[4]

The European Commission announced to launch an Action Program to measure and reduce administrative costs generated by EU legislation in the 'EU25'. In October 2005, the EC proposed a common EU methodology for measuring administrative costs imposed by legislation – both existing and planned legislation, based on the Dutch SCM. Adapted to EU needs and resources, this EU SCM approach takes into account the fact that EU legislation often replaces 25 different national legislations and thus decreases operating costs at the EU level. The 'European Commission's Better Regulation Strategy' is aimed at measuring and reducing administrative costs. According to estimates, it would be feasible to reduce administrative costs by as much as 25% by 2012. This would have a significant economic impact on EU economy – an increase in the level of GDP of about 1.5% or around € 150 billion.[5] In 2007, the EC launched a pilot project which also explored how the SCM tool can best be applied for cross-country measurement and the EC would refine the European version of the SCM model so that it can be used for ex-post measurement in all EU member states.[6]

A majority of EU countries has developed explicit plans or commitments to reduce the administrative costs.[7] Many of them do want to apply the SCM approach, but their ambitions, plans and consequent implementations are not really synchronized yet. A number of countries have announced to complete or to undertake a full baseline measure program. These countries are Austria, the Czech Republic, Denmark, Germany, the Netherlands, Norway and the UK. Other countries, like Belgium and Poland, have planned to measure a significant portion of sectors. Some national regulatory reform plans (e.g. 'Agenda 2010' in Germany (OECD, 2004)) are linked to the SCM method, making the overlap and interdependencies of institutions more complex. These national plans and ambitions can be seen as an unintentional differentiation of regulatory reforms across EU countries, with the SCM model as an instrument to bring about a minimum level of convergence with regard to the methodology applied and the results realized. Currently, countries still vary in the SCM

---

[4] The OECD has published widely on (reducing) administrative costs, also relevant (by us used) background documents for this chapter. See in general on regulatory reforms: OECD, 2002, 2003b, 2005, 2006c, 2007d; Gönenç, R., Maher. M and Nicolcti, G. 2000. More specific on administrative burdens see: OECD 2003a, 2006b, 2006c, 2007b, 2007c.

[5] Website EC: www.ec.europa.eu

[6] For more relevant and (by us used) background documents of the European Commission on administrative costs see: Boeheim, M., Renda, A., Leo, H., Weijnen, T., Unterlass, F., Coletti, P. and Schratzenstaller, M, 2006; European Commission, 2005a, 2005b, 2006a, 2006c.

[7] See for instance Dutch (EIM, 2002; IOO, 2007; IPAL, 2003; Regioplan Beleidsonderzoek (Region policy research), 2002; Research voor beleid (Research for policy), 2007; TILT, 2006) or Flemish reports (Flemish Government, 2006).

Table 2.1 SCM-network countries and reduction targets[8]

Country	Targets
Australia – Victoria	15% reduction over three years and 25% reduction over 5 years.
Austria	25% reduction by the year 2010
Belgium	No specific target or not available
Czech Republic	20% reduction by the year 2010
Denmark	25% reduction by the year 2010.
Estonia	No general reduction target approved by the government in Estonia (yet)
France	No specific reduction targets or not available
Germany	A reduction target has been set in 2007 after the baseline assessment was finished.
Italy	25% reduction by the year 2012.
Latvia	No specific reduction target or not available.
The Netherlands	25% reduction by the year 2007.
Norway	No specific targets, however 'considerable reductions' are planned by autumn 2009.
Poland	Neither deadline for baseline assessment nor reduction target has been decided (yet).
Spain	25% reduction by the year 2012.
Sweden	25% reduction by the year 2010.
UK	25% reduction by the year 2010.
Slovenia	25% reduction by the year 2010.

measure techniques applied, but also due to the SCM network there is a trend towards more sophisticated techniques allowing a more detailed comparison of administrative costs among countries. In 2005, 19 of the 22 countries reporting had a government program to reduce administrative costs; 14 had established a system for measuring costs and 9 had quantitative reduction targets (OECD, 2006a).

So far, every country has its own specific agenda. For instance, in France and Latvia no overall target has been set, whereas the Dutch government had the ambition to reduce administrative obligations by 25% by 2007.[9] Table 2.1 gives an overview. Multiple strategies to reduce the administrative costs can be observed, all with specific aims, commitments and time stringency. The Netherlands and Denmark are examples of countries that have high ambitions combined with measurable results, whereas Italy and France have less 'enthusiastic' and also less concrete plans. Some countries face some practical problems of incomplete data of their assessment, which makes the planning and consequent implementation of the administrative compliance costs policy problematic.

[8] Website SCM Network: www.administrative-costs.com

[9] See European Commission (2006b), Pilot Project on Administrative Costs. Prepared by WiFo and CEPS for the European Commission, DG Enterprise, December 2006 Costs

Table 2.2 Compliance costs, as a percentage of GDP[10]

	2001	2002	2006	2007
United Kingdom	–	–	1.16%	–
Denmark	2.59 %	–	1.37%	–
Netherlands	–	3.6%	–	2.38%

Interestingly but unfortunately, at this moment (early 2008), only a small group of countries can genuinely be assessed in terms of compliance costs and their progress in reducing the quantity of red tape. The Netherlands, Denmark and the United Kingdom are a few of the countries that have (available) measured results. Table 2.2 provides data on the level of compliance costs of the GDP of these three countries, on a comparable base.

It is of importance to note that only Denmark and the Netherlands have measured the total costs of administrative costs and also conducted an assessment after implementing a reduction policy. A significant reduction of the compliance costs can be noticed in both the Netherlands and Denmark.

This paragraph has made clear that the issue of reducing administrative costs has become a major economic policy issue, both in individual countries and for supra- and international organizations. In many countries, it is now a prominent goal, although countries differ in their level of aspiration. Furthermore, by opting for the SCM-approach, a minimum level of standardization seems to have been realized, for measuring the level and development over time of the administrative costs. The available data, however, are still so scarce that international comparisons remain very difficult. Later in this chapter, we will try to make that comparison, based on alternative indicators. But first, we concisely deal with some more theoretical issues that can explain recent developments of administrative costs policies in European countries.

2.2 Theoretical Notions on the Welfare State and Institutions

We have seen that the domain of administrative compliance costs is quite complex and rather problematic to grasp because of its internal and external economic and political characteristics as well as institutional developments. In this paragraph, two theoretical notions will briefly be discussed, namely (1) the welfare state and (2) institutional change. The aim is to have a better understanding of the development of policy ambitions, level of administrative costs and level of adoption.

Esping-Andersen (1990) laid out three general types of welfare states, which have their own logic of social policy: (1) The social-democratic welfare state; (2) The conservative-corporatistic welfare state; and (3) The liberal welfare state. The criteria for this classification are: (1) The possibility to retain a reasonable level of welfare, independent of the participation of the labor market (decommodification

[10] Source data derived from databanks of the WBG and the IMF

score); (2) The role of institutions of social security; and (3) The level of preservation or dissolvement of social stratification and inequalities. In the social-democratic or Scandinavian model (Denmark, Sweden and Norway), individualism and universalism are central elements. Market dependency is highly important as well as reducing inequality by state intervention. The conservative-corporatistic model (Germany, France, Austria, Switzerland, Italy, Belgium, and the Netherlands) has ideological ties with both catholic social philosophy and labor syndicalism. The family as a social institution forms the cornerstone. Sector-based social security as a result of agreements of social partners leads to social economic policy. The liberal or Anglo-Saxon model (UK, US, Canada and Australia) believes in the market as a social mechanism. However, there is a minimum set of social security for people who fall outside the 'social span of control' of the market. An example of the social mechanism of the market is the idea that labor market problems for lower educated laborers can be solved by low paid jobs. Social partners have a relatively minor voice in social-economic policy in the liberal welfare state model. Methodologically, we conceptualize the three criteria of the Esping-Andersen's classification of welfare states. In order to conduct an interesting analysis, the criteria will be related to the more abstract notions of (1) role of the regulatory state and (2) the role of the market and the consequent questions: (3) to what degree does the state intervene, how and why?

Related, but theoretically separate is the paradigm of institutional economy. We cannot discuss all nuances of this paradigm here,[11] so we will only pay attention to the theoretical paradigm of institutionalist political economy (IPE) (Chang, 2002; Hodgson, 1998). Chang (2002) argues that politics and economics can theoretically not be divided (since the market is a political construct). His analyses of the market, the state and politics encompass the idea that the role of the state is per definition a 'subjective referee' and there are de facto no (strict) ideological boundaries between the state and the market. Second, Chang argues that all institutions have a 'constitutive role' (Chang and Evans, 2000). Third, political and public institutions therefore operate with ideological language within a neo-liberal oriented constitution. As a consequence, institutions shape people's motivations, perceptions and political action. Thus, the role of institutions is that they do not constrain factors of human behavior, but institutions constitute them. The interest of the institutions as such is essentially imposed upon individuals (citizens, politicians, etc.) through institutionalization in 'institutional contact'. Methodologically, we again conceptualize the two indicators (1) the role of the regulatory state; and (2) the role of the market, and additionally (3) the role of (national or inter- or supranational) institutions. The consequent question is as follows: How are these entities' related?

[11] For other relevant and interesting work on political and institutional economics see: Aoki, M., 2001; Bardhan, P.K., 2005; Bowles, S., 1998; Featherstone, K. and Radaelli, M., 2003; Hamilton, W.H., 1919; Hodgson, G.M., 1988; North, D.C., 1990; Przeworski, A., 2004; Rutherford, M., 2001; Schmid, A.A., 2005; Samuels, W.J., 1971.

We have put forward two theoretical concepts which deal with the role and characteristics of the state and some institutional dimensions of political economy. In Paragraph 2.4, we will try to explain the recent developments regarding the reduction of administrative costs in European countries.

2.3 International Comparisons

In Section 2.1, it became clear that a majority of countries are willing to accept the SCM-approach as their standard for measuring the administrative costs and also to use it as a yardstick for their reduction policies. However, the actual application has been still very limited. Only Denmark, the UK, the Czech Republic and the Netherlands have published detailed results using this approach. So far, no other standardized results are available that allow a detailed comparison of the relative size and development of the administrative costs in different countries. Yet, that is one of the most intriguing questions there is regarding this subject. In this paragraph, some alternative measures are used to gain more insight into these issues.

These authors are not the first to have tried to create such an alternative measure. During the EU presidency of the Netherlands, the Dutch CPB published an estimate of the total administrative costs for EU countries.[12] This analysis started with data of Djankov cs. regarding the start-up costs of firms.[13] Using detailed Dutch material, taking into account differences in economic structure and detailed data for each EU member state on firm start-up costs, Kox was able to present low and high estimates on the total administrative costs for 19 EU member states.[14] The differences were remarkable. Whereas Sweden, Finland and the UK showed administrative costs as a percentage of GDP between 1.2 and 1.5%, Greece and Hungary saw a percentage somewhere between 5.4 and 6.8%. Table 2.3 shows the results for the individual countries. In more general terms, it can be observed that Anglo-Saxon and Scandinavian countries do show low estimates, that Mediterranean countries are on the high end and the Continental countries do score in the middle.

---

[12] Industrial Policy and Economic Reforms Papers No. 1, The new Lisbon Strategy – An estimation of the economic impact of reaching five Lisbon Targets by George M.M. Gelauff and Arjan M. Lejour (CPB Netherlands Bureau for Economic Policy Analysis), January 2006, based Kox, H., 2005.

[13] See S. Djankov, R. La Porta and A. Shleifer (2002), The regulation of entry, Quarterly Journal of Economics, vol. 117 (1), pp. 1–37.

[14] See H. Kox (2005), Intra-EU differences in regulation-caused administrative costs for companies, CPB Memorandum, nr. 136 Rev. 1, Table 5.1

Table 2.3 Administrative costs for 18 EU countries in 2003, and the long term effects on GDP of a 25% reduction policy[15]

	Kox –low estimate	Kox –high estimate	LT effects on GDP
Finland	1.2	1.5	1.2
Sweden	1.2	1.5	1.1
UK	1.2	1.5	1.0
Denmark	1.5	1.9	1.2
Ireland	1.9	2.4	1.3
Belgium	2.2	2.8	1.4
Czech Republic	2.6	3.3	1.8
France	2.9	3.7	1.8
Germany	2.9	3.7	1.7
Netherlands	2.9	3.7	1.6
Slovenia	3.3	4.2	1.8
Austria	3.6	4.6	2.0
Italy	3.6	4.6	1.9
Portugal	3.6	4.6	1.9
Slovak Republic	3.6	4.6	2.5
Spain	3.6	4.6	1.8
Greece	5.4	6.8	2.2
Hungary	5.4	6.8	2.6

In later EU publications, the high estimate was taken as an approximation of the administrative costs.[16] Subsequently, the CPB calculated the short- and long-term effects on GDP. In the table, the long-term effects of a 25% reduction of the administrative costs for each country are presented. These effects are one-time increases in the level of GDP. The impact on the EU in total of such a reduction policy would be an increase in the level of GDP by 1.5%. Tang and Verwey, using Dutch data and working with the CPB World Scan model, made clear that a 25% reduction in administrative costs, a similar decline as the Dutch had selected as policy goal for the period 2003–2007, would lead to a 1.7% increase in real GDP for the European Union.[17] In the long run, the impact was even higher. The gains were slightly bigger with a coordinated reduction strategy instead of a unilateral reduction. The higher the administrative costs, the higher also the impact of reduction strategies on the pace of economic development. These data do describe the situation in 2003, but do not allow tracking possible changes over time.

---

[15] Source: Kox (2005) and Tang and Verweij (2004)

[16] See G.M.M. Gelauff and A.M. Lejour (2006), Less red tape in Europe, in: G.M.M. Gelauff and A.M. Lejour, Five Lisbon Highlights. The economic impact of reaching these targets, CPB document 104, chapter 8, and Commission of the European Communities (2007), Impact Assessment accompanying the « Action Program for Reducing Administrative Costs in the European Union », Staff working document SEC (2007) 84

[17] See P. Tang and G. Verweij (2004)

These authors have used two other sources that could be used for calculating approximate estimates of regulation costs and charting changes over time. The OECD has collected data on product market regulation for 1998 and 2003.[18] At several levels of aggregation, data are collected, among which are data on 'regulatory and administrative capacity' and 'administrative costs start-ups'.[19] Based on extensive questionnaires, data were collected for 16 so-called low level indicators, ranging from the level of public ownership to regulatory barriers to trade and investment. These data were then aggregated into 3 mid-level indicators, and then finally in one overall indicator for product market regulation. We call these data the OECD PMR data.

The World Bank started in 2003 a major project, called Doing Business.[20] For 10 phases, representing the several stages of business's life, from starting to closing a business, indicators for 178 economies are collected. The data collection started in 2003. Yearly, these data are published. The latest data are from 2007.[21] These data are called WB DB.

Both sources have been used here as approximations for the relative size of the administrative costs in different countries, and of changes in those costs between 1998 and 2003 respectively 2003 and 2007. Where necessary, the data are standardized. For each variable, the minimum and maximum value is traced. Then for each country, the relative distance to the minimum level, as compared with the maximum distance (i.e. between minimum and maximum) is calculated.[22] In Table 2.4, for 18 countries data are presented, distilled from these three different sources, namely the Kox estimates, the OECD PMR data and the WB DB data.[23]

Even at first view, clear similarities in the relative ranking of the countries mentioned are observable. Using simple correlation statistics, the correlation coefficient between Kox and OECD PMR 2003 is 0.69 and between Kox and WB DB 2003 B 0.62. So, the relative position of countries regarding their administrative costs, as calculated by Kox, corresponds quite well with the relative position of these countries using two different indicators of (product market) regulation.

---

[18] See http://www.oecd.org/document/1/0,3343,en_2649_34323_2367297_1_1_1_1,00.html, the Product Market Regulation homepage. The data are to be find at http://www.oecd.org/dataoecd/25/10/34634740.xls

[19] All data were standardised with values between 0 and 5.

[20] See http://www.doingbusiness.org/

[21] During that period, it was possible to broaden the selection of indicators and to fill in many till then missing values. For the Western countries, the data set showed relatively few missing values.

[22] In formula, if Vmin is the minimum value found in any country for a particular indicator, Vmax is the maximum value in any country for that same indicator, and Vi the value of that indicator for country I, then the score of this country is ((Vi – Vmin)/ (Vmax – Vmin)). The minimum value is 0, the maximum value is 100. The outcome changes if the country's value changes, or if the minimum and/or maximum value changes.

[23] Starting point were the 19 countries for which Kox (2005) presented data. Because the OECD did not provide data for the Slovak Republic, that country was removed. For the remaining 18 countries, data from the sources mentioned were collected and partly calculated.

Table 2.4 Relative levels of administrative costs in 18 countries, according to different sources

	Kox	OECD PMR		WB DB			
				2003	2007	2007	2007
	2003	1998	2003	A	B	C	D
Finland	1.4	2.07	1.32	33.5	31.1	13	31.4
Sweden	1.4	1.80	1.23	39.1	38.1	14	32.5
United Kingdom	1.4	1.15	0.92	29.3	28.3	6	36.9
Denmark	1.7	1.46	1.12	21.8	18.1	5	22.6
Ireland	2.2	1.47	1.12	31.8	28.4	8	35.7
Belgium	2.5	2.05	1.37	30.8	23.3	19	40.9
Czech republic	3.0	3.03	1.75	42.5	44.3	56	46.9
France	3.3	2.48	1.70	37.8	32.8	31	39.9
Germany	3.3	1.90	1.43	44.8	45.2	20	39.9
Netherlands	3.3	1.79	1.37	42.0	39.2	21	35.7
Austria	4.1	1.81	1.38	37.7	39.8	25	36.5
Italy	4.1	2.78	1.87	44.4	54.0	53	54.3
Portugal	4.1	2.13	1.56	57.0	45.8	37	47.0
Slovak Republic	4.1		1.39	42.4	39.8	32	46.1
Spain	4.1	2.33	1.61	60.3	59.8	38	51.8
Poland	4.5	3.91	2.76	43.7	48.7	74	53.0
Greece	6.1	2.79	1.83	51.0	53.3	100	46.6
Hungary	6.1	2.46	2.02	39.3	33.4	45	43.4

Sources: Kox (2005), average from low and high estimate.
OECD Product Market regulation (see footnote 23).
World Bank Doing Business (see footnote 25), with
A: Calculated value (method described in footnote 24) on the basis of 18 indicators
B: Calculated value (method described in footnote 24), using the same indicators as under A
C: Position in the overall list 'Easy doing business' for 178 countries
D: Calculated value (method described in footnote 24) on the basis of 42 indicators

Regarding the development over time, the OECD PMR data for 2003 are lower for all countries than for 1998, indicating a reduction of the administrative costs. After 2003, there is less clarity. Taking 2003 A and 2007 B as comparable indicators, because they are using the same indicators, the results are mixed. For 12 countries, a decline in the relative level can be observed between 2003 and 2007, while for 6 countries an increase can be detected. The last two indicators, indicated as 2007 C and 2007 D, do take into account all available indicators in 2007. Over the years, more and more indicators are taken into account.[24] With some reluctance, it can be concluded that over the period 1998 till 2007, in a majority of the 18 countries analyzed here, a reduction of the relative administrative costs could be realized.

---

[24] In 2003 the World Bank used 18 indicators, in 2007 it was 42. Started with 4 groups of indicators in 2003, in 2004 two new groups were added, and in 2005, another 4. The World Bank expects to include new indicators on Infrastructure and Transparency in the Doing Business 2009 report.

Table 2.5 Relative levels of administrative costs in 5 aggregated groups of countries, according to different sources

	Kox	OECD PMR		WB DB			
				2003	2007	2007	2007
	2003	1998	2003	A	B	C	D
Scandinavian countries	1.7	1.7	1.2	29.1	25.9	8.6	29.9
Anglo-Saxon countries	1.8	1.3	1.3	30.6	28.3	7.0	36.3
Continental countries	3.3	2.0	1.5	38.6	36.1	23.2	38.6
East-European countries	4.4	2.4	2.0	42.0	41.5	51.8	54.6
Mediterranean countries	4.6	2.5	1.7	53.2	53.2	57.0	53.8

Source: For the country groupings, see footnote 27. For an explanation of the indicators used, see Table 2.4.

In Table 2.5, aggregated data are presented, for five groups of countries,[25] using the earlier mentioned Esping-Andersen categorization. These data do show that countries with more or less similar welfare state arrangements also do have quite similar relative levels with regard to their administrative costs. The Scandinavian and Anglo-Saxon countries do show relative low levels in their administrative costs, and they also show a substantial reduction over time, especially the Scandinavian countries. The Continental countries have a position about average. They do show a reasonable decline over time. Finally, the East-European and Mediterranean countries do show much higher relative levels of administrative costs and a slower decline after 2003.

2.4 Welfare State, Institutions and Beyond

The previous paragraphs have provided us with quantitative and qualitative data on the policies of reducing compliance costs of European countries. What did we find?

Based on Esping-Andersen's categorization, significant differences in the relative level of administrative costs can be observed. However, for a number of other indicators and developments, explanations for the Esping-Andersen models do seem to be less relevant. First, we clearly see significant convergence of government policy and national institutions (departments and other public institutions) in terms of assessment, willingness and reduction of administrative costs. Second, the 'leading group' countries (the Netherlands, Denmark, United Kingdom and the Czech Republic), leading in terms of having measured the compliance costs in order to have a quantified plan de campagne, do represent different models (Anglo-Saxon, Scandinavian, Continental and even East-European countries).The Esping-Andersen typology does not discriminate. That is also the case with examining the willingness and ambitions of countries on reducing

[25] The regular groupings are used, namely Scandinavian (Denmark, Finland and Sweden), Anglo-Saxon (Ireland and United Kingdom), Continental (Austria, Belgium, France, Germany, and Netherlands), Eastern European (Hungary, Poland, and Slovak Republic) and Mediterranean countries (Greece, Italy, Portugal and Spain).

compliance costs. Countries as different as Austria, Czech Republic, Denmark, Italy, the Netherlands, Spain, Sweden, UK and Slovenia have set quantitative reduction targets with a minimum of 20% reduction of administrative compliance costs before the year 2013. Also, here, these models do not discriminate. Finally, all countries (again multiple welfare state models are represented) do show a (reasonable) decrease in the level of administrative costs emanating from their 'traditional' historic socioeconomic policy, even though the level of administrative costs and the degree of reduction is not totally synchronized.

For a more institutionalist explanation for the convergence process, we turn to Chang. The elements of convergence, according to Chang, are a result of constitutive institutionalization of the market ideology. The fact that governments are willing to utilize the SCM model and have set ambitions, and even that some countries with different institutional histories have reduced significant percentages of administrative costs, are indications of a general acceptance of neo-liberalism as an ideology (worldview, moral codes, etc.). Thus, the role of the market as a vital indicator of neo-liberalism (as a political-economic philosophy), is decisive and, in fact, the very frame of reference. This includes all the related instrumental policy issues, such as creating a level playing field and an attractive fiscal climate and unmistakably reducing compliance costs. Consequently, the role of the regulatory state, political institutions (e.g. parliament) and public organizations (e.g. departments) is also facilitative. There is no boundary between politics and market, and since (mostly) political and administrative institutions comprise the state, the state is the constituted facilitator of the market. Furthermore, supranational institutions (OECD, WB, EU) have a constitutive role as well, disseminating the SCM model and stimulating EU countries to reduce administrative costs. The degree of implementation and its success in several countries are additional indicators (of future data), which will learn to what extent this paradigm is explanatory.

As a result, we find Esping-Andersen's categorization and Chang's IPE notions helpful to understand and relate the complex development and interaction of financial instrumental incentives and a political-economic ideology along the lines of the role of the regulatory state, the market and institutions on different levels.

2.5 Concluding Remarks

In this chapter, the issue of administrative compliance costs is analyzed from an international perspective. The reason is obvious; one after another, countries have taken up initiatives to deregulate their economy, also by reducing the level of administrative compliance costs. Some started earlier, some did it with more vigor, but in all countries, the direction is the same. A majority of EU countries have (politically) embraced the reduction policy including the application of the SCM method. However, a minority of the countries has actually used the SCM method yet. Also, a small minority of countries has implemented the reduction policy as such. Furthermore, a set of supranational institutions try to stimulate, coordinate and align the political agendas, ambitions and policy implementation processes.

Consequently, we can formulate four conclusions. These conclusions are based on two pillars: (1) A development of convergence which is related to normative institutionalism; and (2) Dissimilarity which is related to historical institutionalism. First, institutions (OECD, WB, EU and some national political institutions) are constitutive. They comprise the 'engine' for policy (re)orientation. These institutions constitute values with instrumental tools (SCM method). Evidently, political autonomy enables national parliaments and governments to reject these influences, however in a globalizing economy, in which fiscal climate and a level playing field are increasingly important; it is not very easy to stop the influence at the country border. Second, the convergence of national political agendas, ambitions and policy goals has been the result of a (further) reorientation of the role of the market. This is a consequence of institutions that promulgate the (implicit) underlying ideological motives. Third and consequently, the role of the regulatory state is therefore facilitative. Hence the increasing number of countries adopting the SCM, having political (-economic) ambitions. Fourth, the difference between Southern and Eastern European states on the one side, and other regions (i.e. based on Esping-Andersen models and legislative and regulative path dependency) on the other, is not only an issue of convergence or not, but also a relatively trivial issue of the instrumental fine-tuning of the SCM method and reduction strategy per country.

Finally, we see three interesting and intertwined questions that arise, which can only be answered by the forthcoming research. One, will the difference in policy and especially concrete levels of administrative costs between North-Western and South-Eastern European countries increase or decrease, and if so, by what determinants? Two, is this political-economic institutional convergence merely another (familiar) pendulum swing, or a policy change with a structural character? Three, what will the role be of the EC (and other institutions) as a symbolic, political, regulatory and legislative institution, in a competitive global economy in which national and supranational authorities will not just evaporate?

References

Aoki, M. (2001) *Towards a Comparative Institutional Analysis.* Cambridge: MIT Press.

Bardhan, P. K. (2005) *Scarcity, Conflicts, and Cooperation: Essays in the Political and Institutional Economics of Development.* Cambridge, MA: MIT Press.

Boeheim, M., Renda, A., Leo, H., Weijnen, T., Unterlass, F., Coletti, P. and Schratzenstaller, M. (2006) WiFo and CEPS for the European Commission, Final Report. *Pilot Project on Administrative Costs.* Vienna/Brussels.

Bowles, S. (1998) Endogenous Preferences: The Cultural Consequences of Markets and Other Economic Institutions. *Journal of Economic Literature.* March, vol. 36, pp. 75–111.

Chang, H-J. (2002), Breaking the Mould – An Institutionalist Political Economy Alternative to the Neo-Liberal Theory of the Market and the State, *Cambridge Journal of Economics*, vol. 26, no. 5.
Chang, H-J. and Evans, P. (2000) *The Role of Institutions in Economic Change*, paper presented at the workshop on 'The Other Canon in Economics', 15–16 August, Oslo, Norway.
CPB Netherlands Bureau for Economic Policy Analysis (2004), Reducing the administrative costs in the European Union. August 2004.
EIM (2002) Administrative lasten. Strategisch akkoord 2002. EIM. September 2002.
Esping-Andersen, G. (1990) *Three Worlds of Welfare Capitalism*. Princetonn NJ: Princeton University Press.
European Commission (2005a), Impact assessment guidelines, June 2005.
European Commission (2005b), Implementing the Community Lisbon program: A strategy for the simplification of the regulatory environment, October 2005.
European Commission (2006a), First progress report on the strategy for the simplification of the regulatory environment, November 2006.
European Commission (2006b), Pilot project on administrative costss. prepared by WiFo and CEPS for the European Commission, DG Enterprise, December 2006.
European Commission (2006c), Strategic review of better regulation in the European Union, November 2006.
European Commission (2007), Action Program for Reducing Administrative Costs in the European Union, Brussels.
Featherstone, K. and Radaelli, M. (2003) *The Politics of Europeanization*. Oxford: Oxford University Press.
Flemish Government (2006), The development of indicators for regulatory management. Dienst Wetmatigheid (Flemish Governmental agency). 2006.
Gelauff, G.M.M. and Lejour, A,M. (2006) A. Industrial Policy and Economic Reforms Papers No. 1, *The New Lisbon Strategy – An Estimation of the Economic Impact of Reaching Five Lisbon Targets* (CPB Netherlands Bureau for Economic Policy Analysis), January 2006, based Kox, H., 2005.
Gönenç, R., Maher, M. and Nicoletti, G. (2000), The Implementation and the Effects of Regulatory Reform: Past Experience and Current Issues, *OECD Economics Department Working Papers*, No. 251, OECD Publishing. Paris, doi:10.1787/413754754615.
Hamilton, W. H. (1919) The Institutional Approach to Economic Theory. *American Economic Review*. March, vol. 9, pp. 309–318.
Hodgson, G. M. (1988) *Economics and Institutions: A Manifesto for a Modern Institutional Economics*. Philadelphia, PA: University of Pennsylvania Press.
Hodgson, G. M. (1998) The Approach of Institutional Economics. *Journal of Economic Literature*, vol. 36 (March), pp. 166–192.
Interdepartementale Projectdirectie Administratieve Lasten (Interdepartmental Direction on administrative costs) (2003), Meten is Weten. Handleiding voor het definiëren en meten van administratieve lasten voor het bedrijfsleven., December 2003.
IOO (Institute for Research on Governmental expenditures) (2007), Verinnerlijking administratieve lasten. Overkoepelend rapport meting 2006. March 2007.
North, D. C. (1990) *Institutions, Institutional Change and Economic Performance*. Cambridge: Cambridge University Press.
Nijsen, A. (2003) *Dansen met de octopus. Een bestuurskundige visie op de informatieverplichtingen van het bedrijfsleven in de sociale rechtsstaat (Dancing with the Octopus. A Public Administrative Vision at the Information Requirements of the Private Sector in a Social State)*, Delft: Eburon.
OECD (2002) *OECD Reviews of Regulatory Reform Regulatory Policies in OECD Countries. From Interventionism to Regulatory Governance*. Paris: OECD.
OECD (2003a) *From Red Tape to Smart Tape. Administrative Simplification in OECD Countries*. Paris: OECD
OECD (2003b) *The Political Economy of Regulatory Reforms: Telecoms in the Southern Mediterranean*. Paris: OECD Development Centre, November.

OECD (2004) *OECD Reviews of Regulatory Reform. Germany. Consolidating Economic and Social Renewal.* Paris: OECD.
OECD (2005) *Economic Policy Reforms. Going for Growth 2005.* Paris: OECD, 2005.
OECD (2006a) *Cutting Red Tape. National Strategies for Administrative Simplification.* Paris: OECD.
OECD (2006b) *Better Regulations – Simply Explained.* Brussels: European Commission.
OECD (2006c) *Economic Policy Reforms. Going for Growth* 2006. Paris: OECD.
OECD (2007b) *Cutting Red Tape. Comparing Administrative Costs across Countries.* Paris: OECD.
OECD (2007c) *Cutting Red Tape. Administrative Simplification in the Netherlands.* Paris: OECD.
OECD (2007d) *Economic Policy Reforms. Going for Growth 2007.* Paris: OECD.
Przeworski, A. (2004) *Some Historical, Theoretical, and Methodological Issues in Identifying Effects of Political Institutions.* New York: Department of Political Science, New York University.
Regioplan Beleidsonderzoek (Regioplan policy research) (2002) Impact-onderzoek Actal. October.
Research voor beleid (Research for Policy) (2007) Inventarisatie regeldruk coalitieakkoord Balkenende IV. May.
Rutherford, M. (2001) Institutional Economics: Then and Now, *The Journal of Economic Perspectives*, vol. 15, no. 3 (Summer), pp. 173–194.
Schmid, A. A. (2005) An Institutional Economics Perspective on Economic Growth, Paper was Prepared for the Seventh International Workshop on Institutional Economics, University of Hertfordshire, UK, June 22–24.
Samuels, W. J. (1971) The Interrelations Between Legal and Economic Processes. *Journal of Law and Economics*. vol. 14, October, pp. 435–50.
Tang, P., and Verweij, G. (2004), Reducing the administrative costs in the European Union, CPB Research memorandam 93.
TILT (2006) Verschillen tussen de WBP en Richtlijn 95/46/EG en de invloed op de Administratieve lasten-en Regeldruk. TILT – Centrum voor Recht, Technologie en Samenleving Universiteit van Tilburg. June 2006.

Websites

Website Dutch Ministry of Finance www.compliancecosts.com (visited September 2007–January 2008)
Website SCM Network: www.administrative-costss.com (visited September 2007–January 2008)
Website EC: www.ec.europa.eu (visited September 2007–January 2008)
Website International Monetary Fund: www.imf.org [visited December 2007–January 2008]
Website World Bank: www.worldbank.org [visited December 2007–January 2008]

Chapter 3
Origin and Functionalities of Regulation

André Nijsen

Abstract To get a full understanding of the phenomenon of compliance costs, we need a sound theory about origin and functionality of regulations. Only if we understand where businesses regulation is coming from, what we want to achieve and by which means, we can combat unnecessary compliance costs of businesses.

A theoretical model about business regulation can be very helpful to understand and answer these questions about origin and functionality. From this model, it appears that different actors are playing an active role in this process of law making, each from their own perspective.

3.1 Introduction

To understand compliance costs from a business perspective, we need to understand the origin of regulation and the role of businesses within the constitutional state. To understand the business effects of regulation, we need to know about the different functionalities of legal requirements. This understanding will allow constructing a theoretical model about regulating businesses.

The major questions to be answered in this chapter are the following: Why is there regulation? Why is a certain degree of regulation of society, including regulation of businesses inevitable? Why does the tendency exist to create so much regulation?

This chapter is structured as follows: We will start with a clarification of the origin of regulation and the role of businesses within the constitutional state in Section 3.2. Section 3.3 describes the functionalities of regulations. Finally, we will present a theoretical model about regulating businesses (Section 3.4) and the chapter will conclude with summary and conclusions (Section 3.5).

A. Nijsen (✉)
Adviser Regulatory Reform, Schoonhoven, The Netherlands
e-mail: nijsena@xs4all.nl

A. Nijsen et al. (eds.), *Business Regulation and Public Policy*,
International Studies in Entrepreneurship 20, DOI 10.1007/978-0-387-77678-1_3,

3.2 The Origin of Obligations

3.2.1 'Le contrat social'

By asking *'L'homme est né libre, et partout il est dans les fers. Qu'est- ce qui peut le rendre légitime?'*[1] Rousseau started in 1762 his debate about legitimacy to develop his ideology of democratic identity based on the hypothesis of the voluntarily accepted agreement of social behavior, the 'contrat social' (Rousseau 2001). This agreement would involve the acceptance of general laws and regulations, ideally by common intent but in reality, through the vote of the majority (Friedrich 1963). The principle of political democracy can now be considered to be the dominant legitimacy principle in the 20th century of developed Western society (Westle 1989; Hoogerwerf et al. 1993).

The principle of the political decision-making process, through which public goals are set, is based, therefore, on the participation of citizens who, as members of a political society fulfill a double role: on the one hand, that of the free citizens who govern and, on the other hand, that of the subjects who are governed. Aristotle defines a citizen as the one who is able both to govern and be governed and actually does so. Prior to the existence of the social constitutional state, not everyone was able to fill this dual role. In ancient Greece, for example, only those who were head of their own household – an 'oikos' – were citizens. This home base gave them the independence – the time and the means – to act as citizens in the public sphere. Later, it was possible to obtain citizenship through the ownership of other things. In the social constitutional state, the 'oikos' of many citizens is maintained by the provision of social security benefits, rent subsidies, child allowances, educational grants, etc. The 'oikos' on which citizenship is based is now guaranteed by that same state in which the citizens, whose independent judgment is not possible without the 'oikos', also participate, critically, in government (Van Gunsteren 1994).

In the modern social constitutional state, the active participation of free citizens in political decision making – as a member of a political party, for example – is no longer a matter of course. Only a limited share of the electorate is a member of a political party and this number is declining rapidly. In the 13 old Western-European democracies, the number of party members as a percentage of the electorate dropped from 9.8 in 1980 to 5.7 at the end of the 1990s. And, of the remaining loyal members, according to optimistic estimates, only 20% are active within the party. There are signs that the representative democracy is changing to become a 'spectator's democracy' (De Beus and van Praag 2001).

3.2.2 Administrative Law

The period within which the 'contrat social was, particularly, intended for the defence of national borders is now far behind. In a social welfare state, citizens

[1] 'Man is born free, however he is handcuffed everywhere. What is it that legitimizes that?'

expect the government to provide social security, friendly environment, and good working conditions. Citizens also require adequate provisions of health care, education, infrastructure etc.

To finance such public services, the government should be entitled, by law, to levy taxes. The wishes of citizens become thus explicit in the process of political democracy. Through this process, the government is assigned several tasks (responsibility) and being provided several instruments/tools (authority) to be able to meet the abovementioned expectations. Such responsibility and authority of the government are clearly specified in the rules of the Administrative Law. Administrative law, being part of Public Law, is about regulation of the relations between governments on the one hand and, citizens and businesses on the other hand. Private Law is ruling the relations from businesses to businesses, from citizens to citizens and from businesses to citizens.

Administrative Law entails obligations and burden for governments, citizens as well as the business community. The objective of this law is first, to guarantee the compliance of citizens and businesses with the stipulated law and provide the necessary information regarding their behavior and the result of this behavior; and, second, to meet their expectations with respect to public services, such as social security, sound environment, etc. Apart from the stipulations of imperative law, Private Law does not entail obligations and burdens for government, citizens and businesses comparable to Administrative Law. This implies, only Administrative Law and imperative law can be the origins of compliance costs as referred to in this book. The obligations stemming from Administrative Law and imperative law do generally govern the behavior of citizens and businesses: 'thou shalt or thou shalt not'. The regulations affecting businesses and the related compliance costs are the subject of this book.

3.2.3 Businesses and the Constitutional State

What about the involvement of businesses in the process of achievement of the public goals of a constitutional state? That's not what businesses are for, is an often heard saying in the business community. However, the processes of production and service in businesses are an integrated part of the whole social process of the constitutional state. The business community is not an enclave within the society but strongly intermingled with it. 'For aside from governments and government agencies, more and more it is corporations that are effectively the sectors in our society . . . Corporations have long since become, for better and for worse, the most effective "private" forces to do both widespread good and widespread harm. For this reason, to solve society's problems is, in no small measure, to come to grips with the corporation problem (Stone 1975).'

Industries and trades are a subsystem of the whole society. Most citizens earn their primary incomes by working in industries and trades.[2] Safety, health and wellbeing of citizens depend to a high degree on the quality of work places in businesses. There is an important role for employers in the redistribution process of primary incomes to secondary incomes by deducting pay roll taxes and premiums on the gross wages of their employees and transferring this money to the tax authorities. Citizens spend a big part of their incomes on products and services which originate from businesses. The quality of the environment of citizens is highly influenced by the processes of production and service of the business sector.

The lives of citizens are closely interwoven with processes within businesses. This implies that not only the behavior of citizens is of relevance for the achievement of the public goals of the constitutional state, but business behavior as well. In other words, government needs the cooperation of businesses to achieve a certain part of the public goals. That's why government – by making use of Administrative Law – imposes rules and obligations on businesses.

It is expected in a constitutional state that the number of regulations especially in the social domains will expand. The reason is the increasing social abundance and the need for social protection (Kip Viscusi 1997).

3.3 The Functionalities of Legal Obligations

3.3.1 Three Types of Functionalities

To get a profound understanding of the effects of legal obligations for those who are obliged to comply with, it appears very helpful to look at the functionalities of the different types of obligations. In addition, it will appear that an effective policy to reduce regulatory costs – compliance costs and enforcing costs – requires knowledge about the functionalities of the different types of legal obligations.

The functionality of an obligation to inform government, for example the tax authority, differs very much from the functionality to safeguard working conditions during the production process. The obligation to inform the tax office about revenues related to the corporate tax to be paid, has a very different impact on the business process and the process of the tax office, compared to the obligation to guarantee safe working conditions in a chemical factory. The same holds for the obligation to inform government about unusual or suspect money transfers of clients, compared to the obligation to inform consumers about the health risks of products. Figure 3.1 illustrates the different categories of business effects caused by the compliance with legal obligations.

[2] It goes without saying that – mutatis mutandis – the same holds for citizens who earn their salaries by working as a public officer in the public sector as well as for the citizens who consume collective goods and services. In this context, government being an employer and producer is comparable to industries and trades.

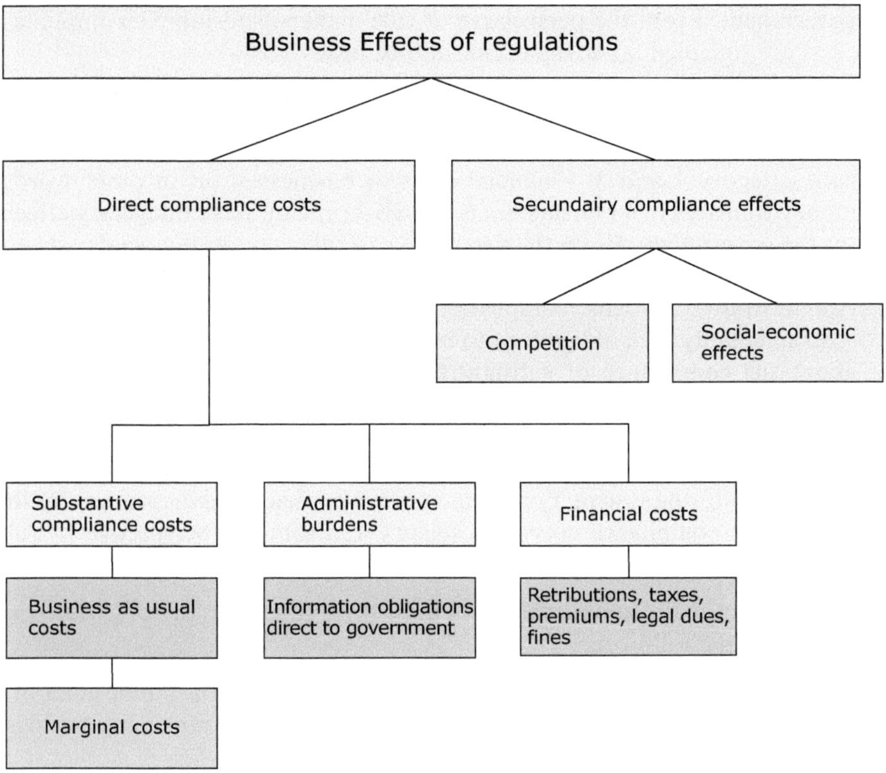

Fig. 3.1 Business effects of regulations

Firstly, there are primary and secondary effects of regulations. The primary effects are the direct compliance costs for the businesses who are – in the strict juridical sense – obliged to comply with the legal obligations. We call them the addressees of the regulation. Almost every specific regulation has its own categories of addressees. As a result of their compliance, there might be secondary effects for competition (lower or higher prices can cause more or less turnover) and for the economy as a whole (economic growth or decrease in terms of value added or employment).

The concept compliance costs covers three different categories of compliance costs (see Fig. 3.1):

1. Substantive compliance costs: All costs to comply directly with legal standards and norms in order to achieve the related public goals. For instance, investments of businesses in buildings, machines or products in order to safeguard working conditions or environment. Or, so-called third party disclosure like product information to protect consumers, and putting price tags on consumer products, etc. Substantive compliance costs originate from substantive obligations and don't have any budgetary effects for

government. From the perspective of rule makers, substantive compliance costs are so-called off-budget costs of businesses.
2. Financial compliance costs: All payments or transfers of retributions, taxes, premiums, legal dues and fines to government or related authorities. Financial costs originate from financial obligations, but there is a major difference with category 1 and 3. Financial costs of businesses, or, in other words, money transfers from businesses to the government, have budgetary effects for the government. From the perspective of rule makers, financial costs are on-budget costs of businesses.
3. Administrative burdens (compliance costs of information obligations): All costs to comply with obligations to inform government or related authorities about the compliance of substantive obligations (category 1) and of the financial costs (category 2). In addition, there are administrative burdens originating from statistical information obligations. Administrative burdens are micro-monitoring costs of the businesses. Official statistics are part of a macro monitoring system. For administrative burdens hold the same as for the substantive compliance costs of category 1. From the perspective of rule makers, administrative burdens are off-budget costs of businesses.

With respect to the functionalities of these three categories of obligations, we can conclude the following:

1. The functionality of substantive obligations is to achieve the public goals in a direct way by keeping up with legal standards and norms in the business processes.
2. The functionality of financial obligations is to contribute to the budget of state or to redistribute primary incomes.
3. The functionality of information obligations is to monitor compliance of substantive and financial obligations, and to provide statistical information.

Looking from the perspective of the functionalities of obligations is also very useful to separate the marginal costs of regulations, viz. that part of regulatory costs that would disappear in case there would be no regulation, from the business-as-usual-costs. It is easy to understand that there are relatively more marginal costs involved in sending information to government or paying tax, compared to safeguarding working conditions. For that reason, Figure 3.1 shows 'business as usual costs' being part of substantive compliance costs only. In other words, administrative burden (costs of informing government) and financial costs (taxes etc.) do not include 'business as usual costs'. That's why we need clear concepts and definitions to prevent measuring of compliance costs being just a matter of perception only.

3.3.2 A *'ménage á trois'*

In the previous section, it was explained that there are three types of legal obligations, viz. substantive obligations, financial obligations and information obligations. Not only businesses are influenced by these obligations, but citizens and government and related institutions as well. The related public domain is a 'ménage á trois'. How does it work?

The fact that government requires businesses and citizens to comply with substantive, financial and information obligation also incurs costs for the government. Take, for example, the cost of monitoring whether businesses or citizens actually comply with these regulations. Such costs are called enforcing costs. In this way, four types of costs could be distinguished:

- Substantive compliance costs, directly applying to the content of the public goal itself for the account of the business or citizens
- Financial compliance costs applying to the payment and transfers of money from businesses and citizens to the government and related authorities
- Information compliance costs related to the transfer of information to government or governmental bodies, again for the account of businesses or citizens
- Enforcing costs incurred by the government.

It is however important to recognize that the enforcing costs incurred by the government and the information compliance costs incurred by businesses or citizens are often communicating vessels. Van Lunteren, the former General-Director of Dutch Tax Department speaks of a 'ménage á trois', in which all the interested parties join in the game of 'passing the buck'.

The government may reduce its enforcing costs – for example, those connected to keeping records – by insisting that businesses use a book keeping system so that the government needs only to receive the results. The government makes considerable use of banks; in particular, to provide information that enables the government to monitor to what extent the clients comply with law. Examples of such regulations are reporting about interest and dividend but also about extraordinary transactions, e.g. money laundering. The banks are required, annually, to inform the Tax Department about any interest or dividend earned by individual account holders or deposit holders. This is to facilitate the Income Tax Authorities in claiming the correct amount of income tax.

3.4 Theoretical Model About Regulating Businesses

3.4.1 Introduction

To integrate the foregoing insights about origin and functionalities of regulations, we need a theoretical model about regulating businesses. This model is the central issue of this section. Such a model allows for answering the most central questions about regulating businesses. Important questions are thereby, where does this regulation come from? What is its origin? How is it legitimized? How is it designed and enforced?

In this model, relevant insights on the position and nature of the determinants of the costs of complying are provided (see below for a figure of the model). The cohesion in the model between the several components will be discussed and explained, but in general terms.

The regulations governing the behavior for businesses and the cost of complying with these regulations is the main subject of this book. To be able to present a complete picture of the relevant cohesion in the model, it is necessary to give the citizen, as individual actor, a place in the model (Section 3.4.2).

Businesses within a social constitutional state have to behave in a certain way or have to refrain from certain behavior to make it possible for the government to safeguard public goals. Such rules of behavior applying to businesses have been called substantive and financial obligations. To allow implementation, monitoring and enforcement businesses have to inform the government about their behavior. Such obligations have been called information obligations. Information obligations imposed on businesses are, therefore, an integrating component of the social constitutional state. Without this information from businesses, the government cannot succeed in achieving its public goals (Section 3.4.3).

Information and the exchange of information play an essential part throughout this process. This is two-way information. Greatly simplified the process is as follows. See Figure 3.2

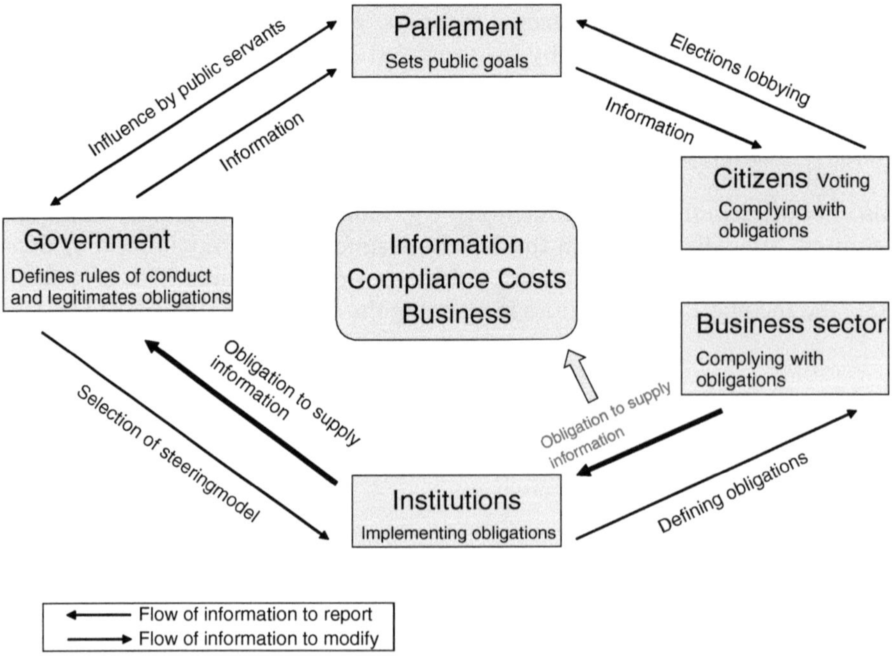

Fig. 3.2 Theoretical model of regulating businesses and compliance costs
Source: Nijsen 2003

3.4.2 Actors and Instruments

Five interconnected actors form the skeleton of the theoretical model. The first two individual actors are citizens and businesses; they operate within the private domain. Two other actors are parliament and government, both positioned in the public domain. Finally, there are the institutions, which operate partly in the public domain, for example the Tax Authorities, and partly in the private domain e.g. Safe Working Conditions Authorities or Health Cost Insurance Companies.

The individual actors have, as far as regulations are concerned, a mutual structural relationship. These structural relationships are maintained through the instruments utilized in this model. The contacts between civilians/businesses and parliament are mainly realized through the instrument election/business lobby. Parliament and government interact through the instrument legislation. The government maintains contact with institutions through the steering instrument. Last but not least, the relationship between the institutions and businesses or civilians is maintained through the design instrument of the substantive, financial and information obligations. Citizens and businesses have therefore their role to play; at the beginning of the process, they have the right to state their preferences by way of elections or business lobby, while at the end of the process, they have the duty to comply with substantive, financial and information obligations.

At the beginning of the process of regulating, citizens have, in a democratic state, the right to speak so as to determine the social values that they may consider important. Similarly, at the end of the process, these persons have to be obedient and cooperate in the execution of the government policy and comply with the laws and other regulations. This implies, the civilians are turning into the subjects of the state.

Citizens, actor 1, have personal preferences with respect to social values such as safety, environment, labor conditions, health, social security and equity. Citizens indicate social preferences at the elections by voting for the political party whose program corresponds best to their preferences. In an ideal situation, the elected parliament, actor 2, is then a reflection of the sum of the individual preferences of those citizens who have made use of their right to vote. The relationship between citizens and parliament comes into being via the election instrument.

Noticeable is that businesses, being legal entities, have no personal role to play within the instrument of elections. Of course, businesses are private cooperations of citizens, but have as such no voting rights, because that is a personal privilege.

However, the involvement of citizens in businesses can take many forms and may vary from extremely strong involvement to no involvement at all. A citizen could, for example, be the director-owner of a company but he could also be a shareholder or manager. In addition, a citizen could be an (ex) employee, customer or supplier of a business. The ultimate form of involvement is the independent entrepreneur who, as private person, runs a business without corporate rights.

For the self-employed, the role of citizen and business merges. In western social welfare states, most citizens have, either directly or indirectly, some sort of relationship with one or more companies. Many citizens are also stakeholders. This implies that preferences of individual citizens are always represented, to some extent, in individual companies. Naturally, this does not apply to the same extent to all citizens and all businesses. It is also common practice that organized business uses political lobbies to make its preferences known to members of parliament. For that reason, we added business lobby as a separate element to instrument 1. The preferences of organized business circles are not always identical to the preferences of citizens. Mostly, business lobbies try to mitigate the policy effects of preferences of citizens. Apart from this, regulation helps businesses to create more transparency about markets, processes e.g. the processes of how to build houses, and standardizations. Regulation can also be useful for businesses when facilitating economic transactions like exporting or innovations. Regulation can also protect businesses from unfair competition. For the rest, businesses are prepared to accept social responsibility more and more.

Parliament, actor 2, sets social goals and objectives taking into account the preferences expressed by the majority electorate. The 'contract social' is agreed in parliament and the citizen transfers part of his/her individual rights to collectivization (De Swaan 1993). Parliament passes the responsibility for executing these policies to the government, actor 3. The government then compiles laws and regulations, the determination of standards and values in behavioral patterns, which will regulate the behavior of the citizens and businesses in such a way that the specified goals and objectives can be achieved. In addition to the determination of behavioral patterns, the legitimization of legislation is essential, not only in the relationship between parliament and the government (formal legitimization), but certainly in the relationship between government/institutions and citizens/businesses (material legitimization) too. From this perspective, it is relevant to understand that a decision-making authority in a constitutional state is allowed to act on the basis of a law/regulation only. This is what is called the legality principle. Besides, there is also the specialty principle: a decision-making authority is allowed to be enforced only within the context of the empowering law. The combination of the legality principle and the specialty principle is – besides the overcharging citizens and politicians – one of the origins of the enormous numbers of laws in the constitutional state.

The government draws up a budget to finance all the relevant activities required to achieve these objectives. Parliament supervises by either approving or rejecting proposed legislation and regulations and the budget itself. The relationship between parliament and the government comes into being primarily through the process of legislation, instrument 2.

The government, actor 3, chooses the suitable policy instruments for achieving its social objectives (public goals). In principle, the government has a choice out of three steering models to influence the behavior of the citizens and enterprises: the communicative model (persuasion), the economic model (levy or subsidy) and the legal model (enforcement). For each type of steering model, there is a specific type of institution, actor 4, which is responsible for the execution of the law or regulation applying to behavioral control (with respect to obligations).

Agreements are made between the government and the institutes to defray the institutes' execution costs. These costs incurred by the institutes are, in principle, an item in the National Budget (on budget). There are exceptions to this rule, in case of (privatized) institutes, which operate outside the public domain, for example, in the Netherlands, the Safe Working Condition Authorities. Here, the cost is borne by businesses (off budget), which can be legally obliged to be associated with such an authority. For businesses, these are the costs of complying with legislation and regulations. The relationship between the government and the institutes is governed by instrument 3, the choice of steering models.

Actor 4, the institute, applies the chosen instrument to businesses (actor 5), and to civilians (actor 1), but then, in their role as subjects. Regulations are imposed on both businesses and citizens to steer social behavior in desired direction. As soon as the institute wishes to be informed about the effects of this behavioral manipulation, then the aspect of the obligation of businesses or citizens to transfer information comes into picture. Whenever monitoring the substantive and financial obligations is involved, the institutes enforce the information obligations. Such information obligations enforced by the institutes result in information compliance costs (administrative burdens) for businesses. From the point of view of businesses, both endogenous and exogenous determinants play a part in determining the extent of the compliance costs. We will come back to this later while discussing problems in measurement of compliance costs.

In addition to the actual cost of complying, the psychological costs are also significant. These are determined to a great extent by the business's degree of acceptance of the obligations. The nature of the relationship between the institutes and citizens/businesses, which ensues from this obligation, is determined via instrument 4, the design of the substantive, financial and information obligations.

3.4.3 Data Flow as Feedback

The relationships described in the model begin by actor 1 (the citizen) and proceed through parliament (actor 2) to the government (actor 3). The government gives instructions to the institutes (actor 4) that impose regulations on businesses (actor 5) and citizens (actor 1). Then, the circular flow is complete. The objective of the processes set in course is to enforce/ensure the required social behavior.

For the actors in the public domain, it is essential to have access to information about the extent of compliance by businesses and citizens in the private domain with the socially desired behavior. The actors in the public domain need this information to be able to assess whether the required objectives have been achieved or not, and, if not, to what extent they need to be adjusted. In the model, the flow of information concerning the compliance with legislation and regulation is shown by arrows marked information, which move counter-clockwise. The flow starts by the one who is deemed to comply with the information obligations: the businesses and citizens (as subjects) and ends at the citizen. The conclusion of the 'contrat social' should be that the citizen is informed about the effectiveness of collectivization. What has he/she received in return for sacrificing part of his/her personal freedom to collectivization? To what extent have the desired social objectives – good social security, good health care, the fair distribution of income etc. actually been achieved?

The compliance of businesses with substantive and financial obligations and the obligation to transfer information to the institutions, and the accompanying compliance costs form the core of this book. Information exchange concerns the reports of individual businesses to the institutes. Government funds the compliance costs of neither businesses nor citizens anyway. Compliance costs of businesses and citizens are no part of the National Budget. That's why we call them 'off budget' costs. Other information flows – from the institutes to the government, from the government to parliament and from the parliament to the electorate and the executive costs of the public sector – are in principle the responsibility of the National Budget ('on budget'). The latter information flows, executive activities and related on budget costs will not be dealt with further.

One flow of information originates from the free citizens. They inform the politicians – via the elections – of their preferences. The politicians chosen to be Members of Parliament inform the government about the democratically selected public objectives. The government then informs the implementing institutions about the regulations to be implemented and how these are to be enforced. The implementing institutions, in turn, inform businesses (and citizens, now in the role of subjects) about the rules and regulations with which they have to comply when running their businesses. This type of obligation is called the substantive obligation and reflects the actual behavior or absence of such behavior or state of affairs.

The second flow of information follows the same path but in the opposite direction. It starts with the businesses (and subjects) that have to inform the authorities about the way in which they have complied with substantive and financial obligations. Such obligations are called information obligations and they report the behavior of or conditions in a business. Implementing institutions have, in turn, to report to the government about business compliance with the regulations. The government then informs parliament about the extent to which public objectives have been achieved. The parliament has final accountability to the electorate, the free citizens.

It is essential to recognize that each of the information flows has its own specific function. The main objective of the flow of information that originates from the citizen and ends by businesses is to change the behavior of, or conditions in businesses to meet the requirements of public goals. It starts with (citizens-parliament) influencing political opinions and policymaking, following that (parliament-government) exerting influence on the process of policymaking and regulation. Then (government-implementing institution) the accent within the information flow shifts to the direct modification of behavior by, and conditions within businesses for the implementation and enforcement of the regulations. This flow of information is called the modifying flow. The second information flow – from businesses to the free citizen – primarily provides feedback about the extent to which public objectives have been achieved. A second important function of this flow of information is to supply input for the working processes of implementing institutions, in particular, for those institutions responsible for the transfer of income and capital. This second information flow is called the reporting flow.

Another significant difference between the two flows is the following: The modifying information flow commences when individual citizens with the right to vote form their own political opinions and these are concentrated in parliament and become public goals at macro level. These public goals are then – via implementation and regulation – disaggregated again to become rules of behavior for individual businesses. This flow runs from macro public goals to micro-rules of behavior. The reporting flow, on the contrary, runs in exactly the opposite direction: from reports from individual enterprises – the micro-level – to aggregated reports concerning sectors or the entire business world, the macro level.

3.5 Summary and Conclusions

Why is there regulation? Why is a certain degree of regulation of society, including regulation of businesses inevitable? Why does the tendency exist to create so much regulation? This chapter tries to answer these questions.

The 'contrat social' and the principle of political democracy can be considered to be the dominant legitimacy principles in the present time of developed Western society. Nevertheless, the active participation of free citizens in political decision making is no longer a matter of course. There are signs that the representative democracy is changing to become a 'spectator's democracy'.

The period during which the state was particularly intended for the defence of the national borders is now far behind. Today, citizens expect the government to provide social security, friendly environment, and good working conditions. Citizens also require adequate provisions of health care, education, infrastructure etc. It is expected that the number of regulations especially in the social domains will expand. The reason is the increasing social abundance and the need for social protection.

To finance such public services, the government should be entitled, by law, to levy taxes. The wishes of citizens become explicit in the process of political democracy. Through this process, the government is assigned several tasks (responsibility) and being provided several instruments/tools (authority) to be able to meet the abovementioned expectations. Such responsibility and authority of the government are clearly specified in the rules of the Administrative Law. Administrative law, being part of Public Law, is about regulation of the relations between governments on the one hand and, on the other hand, citizens and businesses. Private Law is ruling the relations from businesses to businesses, from citizens to citizens and from businesses to citizens. The obligations stemming from Administrative Law do generally govern the behavior of citizens and businesses.

From the perspective of functionality, there are three different types of legal obligations for businesses: substantive, financial and information obligations. The functionality of substantive obligations is to achieve the public goals in a direct way by keeping up with legal standards and norms in the business process. The functionality of financial obligations is to contribute to the budget of state or to redistribute primary incomes. The functionality of information obligations is to monitor compliance of substantive and financial obligations, and to provide statistical information. It is very important to distinguish these three different types of obligations when drawing up programs to reduce compliance costs for businesses.

The relations between citizens, parliament, government, institutions and businesses are described in a theoretical model about business regulation. There exist two fundamentally different information flows between these five actors in the model. The first flow, called the modifying flow, starts with the free citizens and ends with the businesses (and the citizens being a subject). The primary function of the modifying flow is to change the behavior of or conditions in business to meet the requirements of public goals. The second flow called the reporting flow starts with the businesses and ends with the free citizens. The primary function of that the reporting flow is to provide feed back about the extent to which the public goals have been achieved (monitoring function).

Compliance costs originate from a complex process of political democracy. There are many actors involved in this process of law making. It has been indicated that we can expect more regulations in the future, especially in the social domain. It is also important to be aware of the different types of legal obligations of businesses, depending on the functionalities. The drawing up of effective programs to reduce the compliance costs of businesses needs transparency about these functionalities.

References

De Beus, J., and Ph. van Praag (2001), De wedergeboorte van de politieke deelname; in De Volkskrant, Reflex, January 6, p. 21R

De Swaan, A. (1993), In Care of the State, Health Care, Education and Welfare in Europe and the USA in the Modern Era, Polity , Cambridge

Friedrich, C.J. (1963), Man and his Government: An Empirical Theory of Politics, McGraw-Hill, New York/San Francisco, pp. 234

Hoogerwerf, A., M.J. Arentsen, and P.J. Klok (1993), Om een aanvaardbaar beleid: Een studie over de maatschappelijke acceptatie van overheidsbeleid, Centrum voor Bestuurskundig Onderzoek en Onderwijs, Faculty Political Science, University of Twente, Enschedé, p. 18

Kip Viscusi, W. (1997), Improving the analytical basis for regulatory decision-making, in: Regulatory Impact Analysis, Best Practices in OECD Countries, OECD/PUMA, Paris, p. 178

Nijsen, A.F.M., (2003), Dansen met de Octopus; Een bestuurskundige visie op informatieverplichtingen van het bedrijfsleven in de sociale rechtstaat (Dancing with the Octopus. Vision from a Public Administration Perspective at the Information Requirements of the Private Sector in a Constitutional State), Eburon/EIM, Delft/Zoetermeer (diss.)

Rousseau, J.J., (2001) Du Contrat Social ou Principes Du Droit Politique, par Bruno Bernardi, GF Flammarion, Paris

Stone, C.D., (1975) Where the Law Ends: The Social Control of Corporate Behavior, Harper and Row, New York, pp. xi, xii

Van Gunsteren, H.R.(1994), Culturen van besturen, Boom, Meppel, pp. 8–9, 21

Westle, B. (1989), Politische Legitimität: Theorien, Konzepte, empirische Befunde, Nomos, Baden-Baden, pp 22–25

Chapter 4
Techniques Available for Estimating the Impact of Regulations

Francis Chittenden, Stefano Iancich, and Brian Sloan

Abstract There are a considerable number of techniques and models for estimating the level of impact of regulations. Cost benefit analysis is considered particularly important for regulatory analysis. However, there is no definition of compliance costs that has gained wide acceptance. Disagreement exists about whether certain elements should be included in the calculation of compliance costs (e.g. "psychological costs" that are difficult to measure and quantify). This chapter offers a critical explanation of a variety of techniques that are in common use and then summarizes those that are adopted by governments around the world. A pre-requisite for any method is that relevant data should exist (or be collected) and that this data must be assembled in the most appropriate way. In the absence of these requirements, even the most suitable techniques will be subject to criticism.

4.1 Introduction

A dynamic private sector, where companies make investments, create jobs, and improve productivity, promotes growth and expands opportunities for people.[1] Improving and simplifying the business environment is considered to be of the highest priority, as the level of regulation imposed by governments is claimed to be one of the major obstacles to business success (UNICE 1995). Whilst no society can exist without the state providing some kind of order, reducing the burden of regulation on business is entirely consistent with the objective of increasing the international competitiveness of any economy.[2]

[1] OECD.

[2] Chittenden F, Kauser S and Poutziouris P, 2002, The Regulatory Burdens of small Business: A Literature Review, Manchester Business School.

F. Chittenden (✉)
Manchester Business School, University of Manchester, Manchester, UK
e-mail: francis.chittenden@mbs.ac.uk

A. Nijsen et al. (eds.), *Business Regulation and Public Policy*,
International Studies in Entrepreneurship 20, DOI 10.1007/978-0-387-77678-1_4,

According to the Office of Management and Budget (OMB) in the U.S.A.[3], the three main areas of government policy where regulation plays a significant role are social, process and economic regulations. Social regulations address benefits to society such as health and safety, transport, employment, environmental, and other similar benefits. Process regulations address the mechanics of governments, such as administration and paperwork, government forms for taxation, immigration, procurement and the collection of statistics. Economic regulations seek to alter the commercial and financial frameworks and markets. They are usually intended to promote fair competition, for example, by imposing restrictions on prices or on firms entering or exiting lines of business in a way that might cause harm to the economic interest of other businesses or consumers.

This chapter critically discusses different techniques available for estimating the impact of regulations on businesses, including social, process and economic regulations. The development and diffusion of these methods are part of a broader strategy that several OECD countries are implementing to deliver a "Better regulation agenda". Section 4.2 introduces the concept of "Better regulation policy" and explores the main initiatives undertaken by government to improve the quality of regulation. Section 4.3 contains a detailed consideration and evaluation of different techniques available for measuring the impact of regulation with a particular focus on compliance costs. Sections 4.4 and 4.5 present an overview of the current burden reduction programs around the world. Section 4.6 introduces alternative studies of compliance costs to emphasize the practical drawbacks of these methods, and Section 4.7 draws together the final lessons to be learnt.

4.2 Better Regulation Agenda

Policies addressing the regulatory agenda have been gaining momentum in developed nations for around 30 years.[4] For example, in the USA, Congress embarked on regulatory reform by passing the Regulatory Flexibility Act of 1980. In the EU, early notions of regulatory reform were articulated at the 1992 Edinburgh Council.[5] At the time, the issue of improving regulations was closely linked to three main drivers of EU regulatory concerns: competitiveness, good governance and sustainable development. Subsequently, at the 2000 Lisbon European Council, competitiveness came to the fore of European thinking.[6]

---

[3] Supra, n. 4.

[4] Chittenden F, Ambler T and Xiao D, 2007, Impact Assessment in the EU, in Better Regulation, Weatherill S (editor) Hart Publishing , Oxford.

[5] R E Lofstedt, 'The Swing of the Regulatory Pendulum in Europe: From Precautionary Principle to Regulatory Impact Analysis' 28:3 The Journal of Risk and Uncertainty 237.

[6] F Vibert, 'The Limits of Regulatory Reform in EU' 26 Journal of Institute of Economic Affairs 3, at 17–21.

The 2006 EU Work Program, which is constructed around a number of key themes, emphasizes the crucial role of "Delivery and Better Regulation". Effective policy delivery is central to the credibility and legitimacy of the European Union. But it is not only about what policies are chosen: how policies are developed and how they are implemented is equally important. In 2005, the Commission stepped up its existing work on better regulation to ensure that the regulatory framework in the EU meets today's requirements. This aims to reinforce the contribution from better regulation to growth and jobs while continuing to take into account the social and environmental objectives and good governance.

4.3 Overview of the Techniques Available for Estimating the Impact of Regulations

One of the central aims of better regulation is to ensure that governments refrain from issuing regulation which is not strictly necessary and/or impacts disproportionally on businesses.[7]

A variety of approaches can be adopted to estimate the impact of regulations. The most widely recognized technique is cost-benefit analysis (Froud et al 1998; Pearce 1998).

Cost-benefit analysis examines the trade-offs in terms of the costs and benefits of a policy. This method is recognized as particularly important for improving regulatory analyses. However, it has been criticized because of the perceived difficulty of identifying and quantifying the costs and benefits of regulations (Hahn 1999; Kenneth et al 1996; Moyle 1999; Morrison et al 1998). Despite this criticism, supporters of cost-benefit analysis claim that it is the best available technique to inform policy decisions and so improve economic efficiency (Pearce 1998; Lutter 2000; Hahn 1998; Hahn and Litan 1998).

Hahn and Hird (1991) describe five general approaches to estimating the costs of regulation:

- Econometric studies: Typically measure output markets directly or use production and cost functions to assess the impact of regulatory change. Econometric studies are a potentially powerful means of measuring the impact of regulations. However, their disadvantage is that substantial amounts of data are required in order to conduct the statistical calculations.
- Expenditure evaluations: Typically rely on surveys of businesses to determine compliance costs. While such surveys provide quantifiable data, there are a number of problems. Firstly, respondent biases, e.g. a firm may provide inflated estimates of costs, in the hope that politicians will consider regulatory relief. Second, a counterfactual cannot be specified, e.g. an automobile

[7] See Better Regulation Task Force, "Less is More: Reducing Burdens, Improving Outcomes", 2005.

company may choose to install stronger bumpers in response to consumer demand without a regulation forcing it to do so. To include the total cost of such bumpers would overstate the impact of the regulation.
- Engineering approaches: Estimate the cost of installing equipment directly in order to comply with a regulation. However, this approach does not take account of adjustments that may occur as a result of a regulation, such as changes in consumer preferences. For example, consumers would be expected to prefer cars with good safety features (e.g. stronger bumpers). Regulation might hasten the adoption of these safety features, but it would be inappropriate to attribute the cost of the installation to regulations for an indefinite period. Thus, like expenditure evaluations, engineering studies may be ineffective in determining the counterfactual.
- Productivity studies: Estimate the difference between observed changes in productivity over time and those that would have occurred in the absence of a regulation.
- General equilibrium models: Used to examine how a perfectly competitive market responds to a new policy, e.g. through a change in the levels of output or employment as a result of a new regulation. This approach requires substantial data but it may provide an improved representation of regulatory effects.

The benefits of regulations can be measured using two main approaches:

- Asking people what they are willing to pay for changes in regulatory standards.
- Inferring from observed behavior the amount actually paid by individuals for such changes (e.g. the value that workers place on safety is assumed to be the wage premium received by those working in more dangerous circumstances).

There are also a variety of general approaches to valuing the burdens of environmental regulations (Hahn and Hird 1991; Hazilla and Kopp 1990; Robinson 1995; Ruteledge and Vogan 1995). Approaches not already mentioned above include the following:

- Actuarial techniques: Involve the statistical analysis of historical data on the costs that can lead to environmental liabilities such as accidents and adverse health outcomes.
- Professional judgement: Draws upon the expert opinions of engineers, scientists, lawyers and environmental specialists. For instance, scientific judgement may be used to assess the hazardous effects of substances released into the environment and the potential responses of animals, humans and ecosystems.
- Decision analysis techniques: Techniques such as probability distributions, level of confidence etc. are used in structuring expert judgment, in order to quantify environmental liabilities.
- Valuation approaches: A variety of legal and economic techniques for putting monetary values on environmental consequences (usually used for the purposes of assessing compensation).

Alternative approaches which can be adopted to estimate the impact of regulations include cost-effectiveness analysis and risk assessment.

According to Viscusi,[8] "... *Cost-effectiveness measures provide an index of the relative cost to society of various options for promoting a particular objective (usually expressed as cost per unit of benefit). Within the context of risk regulation, for example, the task of this approach is to ascertain which policies minimize the cost of eliminating a given risk"*. A major difference between cost-effectiveness and benefit-cost tests is that, for the former, benefits need not be valued explicitly, thus eliminating the difficult task of attempting to value them. However, the main limitation of this approach is based on the assumption that the policy objectives and the benefits that should be achieved are not questionable.

Risk assessment methodologies are typically more limited in scope than other policy approaches discussed above. In fact, they focus on only one aspect of policy effects, i.e. the risks that will be reduced. It means that there is neither assessment of the costs incurred to achieve the risk reduction nor consideration of social interests in achieving policy objectives.

4.4 Deregulation: The Case of UK

One of the most common complaints from business and citizens in OECD countries is the number and complexity of government formalities and paperwork.[9] This reflects the fact that formalities are among the most visible of the regulatory burdens imposed on business by governments, while their importance to the achievement of substantive regulatory objectives is often not clearly apparent. Administrative requirements are presently estimated to amount to 3.5% of GDP in the EU[10] and 1.5% of GDP in the UK.[11]

In March 2005, the UK government accepted the Better Regulation Task Force's Less is More Report which set out eight recommendations for reducing the burdens on business of complying with regulation.[12] In May 2005, the government began implementing the recommendations through the Administrative Burdens Reduction Program. The government's aim is to improve the UK business environment by: ensuring that regulation is used only when necessary; simplifying and removing unnecessary regulations; and making

[8] Viscusi, W. (1997), Improving the analytical basis for regulatory decision-making, in: Regulatory Impact Analysis, Best Practices in OECD countries, OECD/PUMA, Paris, 1997.

[9] See Better Regulation Task Force, "Less is More: Reducing Burdens, Improving Outcomes", 2005.

[10] European Commission, "Action Program for Reducing Administrative Burdens in the European Union", COM (2007)23 final.

[11] Measuring administrative costs and reducing administrative burdens in the EU, MEMO/06/425, Brussels, 14th November 2006.

[12] NAO, "Reducing the Costs of Complying with Regulations: the Delivery of the Administrative Burden Reduction Program", 2007.

sure that EU law is not gold-plated when transposed into UK law. The ultimate objective is to achieve a faster rate of productivity growth in the UK.[13] Two main measurement exercises were carried out between September 2005 and May 2006. The Better Regulation Executive (BRE) employed PricewaterhouseCoopers (PwC) to measure the administrative costs imposed on business by 16 departments and their agencies, based on the Standard Cost Model (SCM). The cost of the consultancy contracts was £17 million. Staff costs incurred by departments were not recorded, but must have been significant.

The consultants conducted interviews and held focus groups with a small sample of businesses to establish the time and resources they spent carrying out the activities each year. The estimated costs of these administrative activities were then added together for each regulation. This allowed government to estimate the aggregate administrative burdens imposed on business. The results showed that the administrative burden of regulations in the UK was just under £20 billion as at May 2005.[14]

Eighteen UK government departments and agencies have committed to reducing administrative burdens on business by at least 25% by May 2010. Due to the specialist nature of tax regulation, the Chancellor of the Exchequer set separate targets for HMRC to: reduce the cost to business of complying with tax forms by 10%, and the cost to compliant businesses of complying with audits and inspections by at least 15% by 2010–2011. If all these targets are achieved, they represent total potential aggregate savings for business of approximately £4 billion per annum. These targets involve a net reduction in administrative burdens. Departments should, therefore, estimate the administrative burdens imposed by regulations introduced between May 2005 and May 2007 in order to update their baselines. In May 2007, the Better Regulation Executive (BRE) introduced a revised Impact Assessment process, requiring departments to record the estimated administrative burdens of new, or changes to existing, regulations.

Particular consideration was given to the so-called ‘Business as usual’ costs. These are costs of activities that business would continue to do even if the regulation did not exist. For example, companies are required to file annual accounts via Companies House, but also need this information for their own business purposes.[15] It is argued that there would be little benefit in removing the information obligations that companies would carry on complying with, as this would not lead to a change in behavior or reduced costs for business. ‘Business as usual’ costs have, therefore, been excluded from the calculations of ‘administrative burdens’ in the UK. Each department’s baseline is based on administrative burdens so that measures taken to reduce costs are focused on areas where businesses will feel a difference. The total administrative costs

---

[13] Budget 2005, Chapter 3, Meeting the Productivity Challenge.

[14] NAO, op. cit.

[15] Ibid.

measured in the UK were approximately £31 billion. After 'business as usual' costs had been taken out, the administrative burden was estimated to be just under £20 billion as at May 2005.

In March 2008, the UK government announced that it would introduce a system of Regulatory Budgets that departments of government would have to comply with from 2009-2010. This innovation represents acceptance of another element of the "Less is More" Report issued by the Better Regulation Task Force in 2005, although the idea had originally been proposed in the UK by the British Chambers of Commerce some four years earlier. Discussions within government on how Regulatory Budgets could work are being led by the Department for Business Enterprise and Regulatory Reform and will be followed by a public consultation, prior to implementation.

4.5 Deregulation: The Case of EU and OECD

An important part of the administrative costs countries face has an origin in European legislation. According to the UK government (Pre-Budget Report, 2004), half of all significant new regulations affecting UK businesses originate in EU law. The European Movement claims this to be a gross exaggeration with a figure of only 8% of UK regulations originating with the EU. More recent evidence (Ambler et al. 2005) shows that the true figure for the UK, by value and volume, is roughly in the middle. If the UK is typical then the EU may account for around one quarter of all new regulations enacted by member states.

EU law making seeks uniformity across member states but the differing national legal codes make that difficult, if not impossible. The EU tries to overcome this issue by using four different types of legislation, at least for the time being.[16] Regulations, which are directly applicable and binding in all EU Member States without, in theory, the need for any national implementing legislation. Directives, which bind Member States as to the objectives to be achieved within a certain time limit while leaving national authorities the choice of form and means to be used. Decisions, which are binding for those to whom they are addressed. Decisions do not require national implementing legislation. A Decision may be addressed to any or all Member States, to enterprises or to individuals. Finally, Recommendations and Opinions, which are not binding.

As a consequence of Directives being implemented in national legislation in accordance with the procedures of the individual EU states, it has been suggested that some member states are quite efficient at translating the requirements into national law whilst other governments "gold-plate" EU Directives adding to the compliance burdens placed on businesses (Ambler et al. 2004). In

[16] Web site of the European Commission Representation in the United Kingdom, www.cec.org.uk/info/pubs/bbriefs/bb37.htm.

order to test this popular assertion, Ambler at al. developed a metric called the Transposition Ratio (TR) that is based upon the word-length of national legislation divided by the word-length of the EU directive. The TR is then calculated and compared for France, Germany, Portugal and the UK for Directives that came into force during 1998–2002.

The TRs for the 87 directives considered are given in Table 4.1. The first data row shows the averages across all 87 directives studied, but that is open to challenge since only 17 directives were transposed in the five year period in all four countries. Table 4.1 shows that the pattern for these common directives is similar to all of the Directives implemented, and the UK "gold plates" much more than France or Portugal and slightly more than Germany.

The authors acknowledge that the TR is a less sophisticated measure than comparing compliance costs between member states. However, since data on comparative compliance costs are only beginning to be collected, the study presents a logical first attempt to assess the differential impact of EU Directives. The point is made that these differences partially undermine the workings of the single market, since they result in regulatory variety between countries that is likely to favour domestic competitors.

These initial studies are starting to pay off. In early 2006, the European Commission developed a common approach for assessing administrative costs associated with existing and proposed Community legislation.[17] The Commission has raised its ambition for elaborating a strategy to reduce administrative burdens for businesses operating in the European Union.[18] To ensure large-scale results, it redesigned its pilot project[19] that was a groundbreaker for a large measurement exercise scheduled for 2007. The pilot project's results lay the foundations of the Commission's Action Program for reducing administrative costs, published at the beginning of 2007.[20] The Action Program is intending to launch a large measurement project across the European Union that will identify what legislation is most eligible for administrative costs reduction. As part of this, the Commission proposed that the 2007 Spring European Council fix a reduction target of 25%, to be achieved jointly by the EU and Member

Table 4.1 Transposition ratios 1998–2002

	Germany	France	Portugal	UK
All 87 directives	2.78	0.95	1.86	2.26
17 Common directives	3.15	0.68	1.66	3.72

Source: Ambler, T, Chittenden, F and Obodovski M. (2004) *How Much Regulation is Gold Plate? A Study of UK Elaboration of EU Directives*, The British Chambers of Commerce, London.

[17] European Commission, "Better Regulation for Growth and Jobs", COM (2005)97 final.

[18] The Standard Cost Model Network, www.administrative-burdens.com.

[19] WIFO-CEPS, "Pilot project on administrative burdens", October 2006.

[20] European Commission, op. cit.

States by 2012. This underlines the Commission's commitment to Better Regulation as part of the "Growth and Jobs" strategy.

In September 2004, the OECD's Working Party for Regulatory Management and Reform decided to give highest priority in its 2005–2006 Program of Work to activities on administrative simplification. Therefore, the OECD chose to apply the SCM method in connection to the 'OECD Red Tape Scoreboard' (RTS) and take part in the network. The RTS was approved in the spring of 2005 and it was decided to look at the administrative burdens in the road freight sector and, more specifically, the burdens linked to the events of 'Hiring a new worker' and of 'Operating a vehicle'. In the autumn, an RTS manual, largely based on the SCM methodology, was finalized in order to guide participants when carrying out their measurements. Further, a start-up meeting was held in November 2005 to enhance a common understanding and a consistent approach during the project.[21]

Great interest has been shown in the project. 13 OECD-member countries (USA, Can, NZ, Turkey, NL, D, UK, Fr, DK, It, Be, Nor, Swe) have volunteered to participate in the measurements. Of these, several countries are already experienced in measuring administrative burdens via the SCM methodology due to their measurements at national level.

The OECD, via the RTS, has approached the issue of reducing administrative burdens from a comparative angle. By carrying out benchmarks of selected administrative burdens and analysing the reasons for differences, the RTS project should provide policy advice and best practice examples for simplification to the participating countries.[22]

4.6 Alternative Studies of Compliance Costs

One of the most important critiques of the Standard Cost Model approach to identify and eliminate burdens is that this model does not identify "annoyance factors", i.e. regulations that may have little quantitative impact on businesses, yet are considered a significant irritation.[23]

In different studies, Sandford et al. (1989) argues that psychic or psychological costs and opportunity costs, whilst difficult or impossible to measure satisfactorily, are an important component of compliance costs. Many people experience considerable anxiety and frustration in dealing with their regulatory responsibilities. Sandford points out that some business owners employ a professional adviser primarily to reduce this burden of worry. In this case, the psychic costs become a monetary cost.

[21] The Standard Cost Model Network, www.administrative-burdens.com.

[22] OECD Red Tape Scoreboard (RTS) – 13 countries participating, Lydia Jorgensen.

[23] World Bank, "Group Review of the Dutch Administrative Burden Reduction Program", 2006.

As regards opportunity costs (what it is worth to pay someone to undertake this task and thus take the burden away from the business), again, the Sandford findings indicate that especially smaller businesses perceive their regulatory responsibilities as inconvenient and they would pay somebody else to deal with them. For instance, there is no business interest in collecting sales tax revenues for government. However, a small business owner typically assumes the role of tax collector and absorbs all of the costs and liabilities inherent.[24] Some states compensate small-business owners for their time and expense by allowing them to retain, a proportion, usually a small percentage, of the taxes they collect. While the financial consideration obviously helps small-business owners, most who receive it do not feel that the amount adequately compensates them for their costs.[25]

Furthermore, a distinction has to be made between gross compliance costs (the actual costs incurred) and net compliance costs, net compliance costs being gross compliance costs minus offsetting benefits. Sandford et al. (1981) point out that the regulatory system may have spin-off benefits; for example, stringent record-keeping requirements may force a business to install an efficient financial information system, which may then cut unnecessary expenses. Furthermore, cash flow benefits arise at the expense of the revenue authorities when a business is required to collect tax over a period of time before handing it over to the revenue authorities. Such cash flow benefits arise, for instance, from the PAYE and VAT collection systems in the UK.

In the UK, a series of compliance cost studies have been undertaken at Bath University with the cooperation of Customs and Excise and the Inland Revenue (Sandford, 1973; Sandford et al. 1981, 1989; Inland Revenue 1998). In the Bath University studies, the estimation of compliance costs is based on actual costs (measured costs) incurred by small firms in complying with the tax system. These costs include the value of time spent in compliance by partners, proprietors, qualified accounting staff and other staff as well as fees paid to professional advisers and other costs (such as computing and stationary costs).

Parallel studies on the compliance costs of taxation have been undertaken by the Small Business Research Trust (SBRT 1996, 1998). In the SBRT studies, business owners were asked to estimate their compliance costs as a percentage of their turnover. Thus, the SBRT estimates are based on the beliefs of small business owner/directors, rather than the actual costs, and it could be argued that these estimates may be inflated. More recently, the Manchester Business School (MBS) SME research group has been investigating the tax affairs of the small-medium enterprise economy. Using the MBS Tax Models[26] (Chittenden

---

[24] William J. Dennis, Jr "Administering the Sales Tax", 2002.

[25] Dennis, W.J. Op cit.

[26] The MBS tax models were developed using data from almost 10,000 real businesses to track the effects of taxation on small limited companies (i.e. those employing less than 100 people) and unincorporated businesses (i.e. sole traders and partnerships employing less than 20 people) in Britain as well as quantifying the tax contribution of the small business sector to the UK economy as a whole. The models examine not just the monetary level of taxes (income,

et al. 1996, 1998, 1999a, b; Poutziouris et al. 1999), compliance costs for PAYE-NIC in the small business sector (small limited companies with less than 100 employees and unincorporated businesses with less than 20 employees) were estimated to be £1.12 billion when compliance costs are based on Sandford et al. (1989) indices. This figure represents about 24.2% of the overall projected tax compliance cost burden for the small firms covered by the models, that amount in total to £4.66 billion.

The publication of the Inland Revenue (1998) report of compliance costs for PAYE has made it possible to compare the impact of the SBRT data, the Sandford et al. (1989) data and the latest Inland Revenue results (prepared by the Centre for Fiscal Studies at the University of Bath). This comparison has shown that, when applied to the MBS Tax Models, the Sandford et al. (1989) study compliance figures (when adjusted for inflation) produce results that are much closer to the Inland Revenue (1998) data, than the SBRT (1996, 1998) results. This does not imply that the SBRT data, which presents the views of business owners, is inaccurate. Rather, the SBRT data shows that business owners believe that, as a percentage of their business turnover, the costs of compliance with government regulations are higher than they turn out to be when measured in a structured way.

The difference in the estimation of compliance costs between the two studies may be due to the psychic costs of taxation. These highly subjective costs of compliance concerning stress, worry and anxiety do not easily lend themselves to monetary measurement but are nevertheless real. In the early Bath University studies (Sandford et al., 1981, 1989), these costs have been excluded from the estimated compliance costs. Thus, to the extent that psychic costs are omitted, these studies underestimate compliance costs. On the other hand, it could be argued that the SBRT estimates are based on business owners' beliefs (perceived costs) and might include 'psychic' costs as well.

However, the true position is not very clear. In a study by the University of Bath (Inland Revenue, 1998), compliance costs for PAYE and NICs were measured both in actual terms, what they term 'additive costs', as well as in terms of perceived costs, what they term 'reported costs'. Interestingly, and contrary to expectations, in some size bands, 'additive costs' (actual or measured costs) are lower than 'reported costs' (perceived costs); while in other size bands, the opposite is true. Nevertheless, on balance, perceived compliance costs appear to be higher than actual (measured) compliance costs.

---

corporation, national insurance taxes and uniform business rates) but also the cost to a business of compliance with the tax system: in other words, the estimated cost to a small business of acting as a collector of PAYE and VAT on Government's behalf and of administering their own tax and legal affairs. Taxes deducted from employees earnings i.e. income tax and national insurance contributions are also included as these increase the costs of employing staff. A series of reports under the heading 'Taxing Expansion' have been issued which have focused on the impact that taxation policy has on the growth aspirations of small businesses. Practical cost efficient tax policies to stimulate long-term sustainable small business expansion have been outlined (Chittenden et al., 1996, 1998, 1999a, b; Poutziouris et al., 1999).

Table 4.2 Hours per month spent on government regulations by size of business

Number of employees	Total hours	Hours per person	Responses	Non-response
0	6.5	4.4	102	13
1–2	12.8	6.4	153	14
3–4	16.4	4.1	94	14
5–9	23.8	3.4	130	15
10–19	31.8	2.4	88	14
20–49	41.1	1.4	82	7
50 +	76.7	1.3	23	9
Total	22.6	3.9	672	86

Source: SBRT (2000 vol. 16/No3).

The above studies suggest that compliance costs are important because of their size and, even more importantly, the way in which they are distributed. Apparently, compliance costs are regressive in nature, with the burden falling more heavily on smaller businesses (Sandford et al. 1989; Pope et al. 1991; Sandford and Hasseldine, 1992; Evans et al. 1997). From Dutch surveys, it appears that almost 70% of all administrative burden is on account of small firms (0–9 workers), and almost 15% each on account of medium-sized firms (10–99 workers) and the big firms (100 and more workers). The comparable figures for the share of the value added are respectively 20% (small firms), 30% (medium-sized firms) and 50% (big firms) (Boog et al. 2002). As a consequence, administrative burden as a percentage of value added is for the small firms 9.5%, for the medium-sized firms 1.8% and for the big firms 1.1% only (Wit and Nijsen 2002).

A study by SBRT[27] in the UK confirmed that the burden of red tape falls most heavily on the smallest firms. The survey suggests (see Table 4.2) that on average, small firms with one or two employees spend 5.1 more hours per person per month dealing with government regulations compared to firms employing 50 + .

Nonetheless, a recent study conducted by the British Chambers of Commerce[28] about a sample of Regulatory Impact Assessment (RIA) prepared in 2006-2007 to implement UK legislation (Table 4.3) suggests that RIAs do not

Table 4.3 Quantification of the impact of regulation on small business

COST TO SMEs	NUMBER OF RIAs
Quantified	1
Not quantified but figures stated to be insignificant	64
Not quantified	24
Not discussed	2
Not applicable	9
Total	100

Source: British Chambers of Commerce 2008.

---

27 Survey no. 64 (2000 Quarter 3)

28 T Ambler, F Chittenden and S Iancich , "The British Regulatory System" (British Chambers of Commerce, London, 2008)

take into consideration the extent to which a proposed regulation impacts disproportionately on small business.

In only one RIA was it possible to find a proper quantification of the additional burden of regulation on small businesses while for 64% of the time, no additional burden was claimed. This seems an anomalous result and not in line with the latest research published (see above).

4.7 Summary and Conclusion

In recent years, several OECD countries have used measurements of administrative burdens as part of their national efforts to simplify the regulatory framework. International cooperation is making progress in the area of measuring administrative burdens. However, there is no single model that is appropriate in all countries as it is contingent on the institutional context and the objectives and priorities of the government.

Table 4.4 summarizes some of the most common methodologies available for measuring compliance cost and the relative advantages and drawbacks.

Despite all of this, a number of trends over recent years show the development and direction that the organization of administrative simplification is taking:[29]

Table 4.4 A summary of compliance cost estimation methodologies

	Strengths	Weaknesses
Econometric studies	Powerful means of measuring the impact of regulation.	Substantial amount of data required for the statistical calculation.
Expenditure evaluation	Provides quantifiable data.	Respondent biases. A counterfactual cannot be specified.
Engineering approaches	Direct estimate of the costs.	No consideration of adjustments as result of regulation (e.g. changes in consumer preferences).
General equilibrium models	Sophisticated analysis producing reliable estimates that can be monitored over time.	Substantial amount of data required for the statistical calculation.
Administrative burdens	Focuses on tasks that would not be carried out in the absence of the regulation. Internationally accepted methodology.	Costly to collect data at a national level. The small sample sizes make reliable comparisons over time and between countries impossible. Difficult to isolate "business as usual costs".

[29] World Bank, "Group Review of the Dutch Administrative Burden Reduction Program", 2006.

Table 4.4 (continued)

	Strengths	Weaknesses
Additive costs	Sophisticated analysis producing reliable estimates that can be monitored over time.	Costly and difficult to collect representative data, due to the extent of detail required and need for adequate sample sizes.
Perceived costs	Easier to estimate. Business decisions may be affected by these costs.	Highly variable from business to business. Research questions difficult to formulate without leading the respondent.
Opportunity costs	Help to understand the most burdensome regulations for businesses and variations of these burdens according to different business sizes.	Difficult to express in monetary terms. If obligations reduced, hard to know how the time released would actually be employed.
Psychological costs	Help to understand the most burdensome regulations for businesses and variations of these burdens according to different business sizes.	Difficult to express in monetary terms. Hard to know how feelings of stress or irritation impact on business decisions.

- There is an increasing trend to include the responsibility for administrative simplification within the agency or organization responsible for wider regulatory quality, often including the responsibility for assuring the quality of regulatory impact analysis undertaken by ministries and regulators.
- External committees and taskforces, both permanent and ad hoc, are playing an important role in maintaining the momentum for administrative simplification. These bodies demonstrate the high level of political support given to simplification efforts in many countries and are often able to produce concrete proposals and recommendations within a relatively short period of time.
- Multilevel considerations, both between levels of government within a country and across countries, are becoming increasingly important. This is a consequence of a growing need for administrative simplification and quality regulation in all jurisdictions.

Based on these trends, it seems highly likely that in many countries, administrative simplification and burden reduction programs will continue to become more embedded within the broader regulatory quality system. However, the key challenge will be in identifying and achieving the appropriate balance between simplification and other aspects of improving regulatory quality. Administrative burdens are likely to be a relatively small element of total cost to business of complying with regulation.[30] Firstly, a well-balanced IA system, in which administrative burdens is just one of several factors of concern, would be the appropriate framework in which

[30] NAO, op. cit.

to consolidate the coordination of future policy impact assessments.[31] However, experience from different countries like UK seems to suggest that the preparation of IA may be seen as a tick box exercise which adds no value to the quality of decision making and where the quantification of costs and benefits is rarely carried out with adequate rigor.

Secondly, it is important to understand the effect of regulation on businesses in different sectors and different sizes when estimating the administrative burden cost. This should be done by using, a representative sample for the Price and Quantity measurements in the SCM calculation. Legislation with highly standardized informational requirements may require less interviews/ measurements than others. However, in general the number of interviews per legislative area is limited: leading to very wide confidence intervals.[32] The possibility that a very small number of firms will be sampled for each regulation, and the potential use of a small number of business size categories (e.g. 1–49 employees) without separating out the "0" employee and micro-businesses could reduce the value of the data and make tracking of the changing level of administrative burdens over time a misleading exercise.

Thirdly, to identify the measures that are likely to make a real difference, government should seek to work more directly with businesses and consider any useful qualitative information collected in the measurement exercises. Developing a thorough understanding of business concerns and the commercial realities that they face may be the key to delivering real impacts for business.[33] It follows that consultation with businesses is fundamental to the success of government initiatives to reduce the burden of regulation.[34] In a National Audit Office (NAO) business survey in the UK, however, only 17% of respondents agreed that government consults well before a new regulation, or change to an existing regulation, is introduced. This may reflect departmental approaches to consulting primarily with trade and sector organizations, rather than directly with businesses and the presence of confirmatory bias amongst those conducting the consultation.[35]

The NAO recommends departments to develop strategies that seek the views of the wider business community, particularly those of smaller businesses that are particularly affected by administrative burdens. This should lead government to develop a series of indicators to evaluate the impact of their initiatives to address non-quantified 'irritation factors' and improve the wider business environment. This might include a mix of internal measures and external

---

[31] Ibid.

[32] Manchester Business School: A Summary of UK Standard Cost Model.

[33] NAO, op. cit.

[34] Ibid.

[35] Vibert F., The Itch to Regulate: Confirmation Bias and the EC's New System of Impact Assessment (European Policy Forum, London, 2005).

indicators that capture business perspectives and actions, including segmentation between different sizes, sectors and ages of businesses.[36]

Finally, the introduction of a consistent and regular review process for the costs of compliance is another key challenge government must try to address in the future.[37] One of the limits on attempts to improve control on rule making ex ante is that prior estimates of the potential burden of regulation sometimes differ from the actual burdens experienced in practice. Thus ex post evaluation is essential to ensure that burdens reduction programs have the intended effect. This would allow the performance of regulation to be checked against initial assumptions.

References

Ambler, T., Chittenden, F. and Hwang, C. (2005) *Is EU Regulation Good for Us? A Study of EU Regulations in 2003/4,* The British Chambers of Commerce, London, pp. 44.

Ambler, T., Chittenden, F. and Obodovski, M. (2004) *Are Regulators Raising Their Game? Regulatory Impact Assessments in 2002/3,* the British Chambers of Commerce, London, pp. 18.

Boog, J.J., Jansen, M. and Tom, M.J.F. (2002) *Monitor Administratieve Lasten Bedrijven 2001,* EIM, Zoetermeer, May.

Chittenden, F., Poutziouris, P. and Michaelas, N. (1999a) *The Impact of the 1999 Budget on the Small Business Economy*, National Westminster Bank, London, March.

Chittenden, F., Poutziouris, P. and Michaelas, N. (1999b) "Taxation and Small Firms: Creating Incentives for the Re-Investment of Profits", *Environment and Planning C: Government and Policy*, 17(3).

Chittenden, F., Poutziouris, P., Michaelas, N. and Watts, T. (1998) *The March 1998 Budget and Small Business Taxation*, National Westminster Bank, London.

Chittenden, F., Poutziouris, P. and Watts, T. (1996) *Taxing Expansion: A Model for Fairer Taxes on Small and Medium-Sized Enterprises*, National Westminster Bank, London.

Evans, C., Ritchie, K., Tran-Nam, B. and Walpole, M. (1997) *A Report Into Taxpayer Costs of Compliance*, Australian Taxation Office, Australia.

Froud, J., Boden, R., Ogus, A. and Stubbs, P. (1998) *Controlling the Regulator*, MacMillan Press, London.

Hahn, R.W. (1998) "Government Analysis of the Benefits and Costs of Regulation" *Journal of Economic Perspectives* 12(4): 201–210.

Hahn, R.W. (1999) "Regulatory Reform: Assessing the Governments Numbers" Joint Center: AEI Brookings Joint Center for Regulatory Studies. U.S.

Hahn, R.W. and Hird, J.A. (1991) "The Costs and Benefits of Regulation: Review and Synthesis", *Yale Journal on Regulation*, Winter 8(1): 233–78.

Hahn, R.W. and Litan, R.E. (1998) "An Analysis of the Second Government Draft Report on the Costs and Benefits of Federal Regulations". Joint Center: AEI Brookings Joint Center for Regulatory Studies. U.S.

Hazilla, M. and Kopp, R.J. (1990) "Social Cost of Environmental Quality Regulations: A General Equilibrium Analysis", *Journal of Political Economy*, 98(4).

Inland Revenue. (1998), *The Tax Compliance Costs for Employers of PAYE and National Insurance in 1995–96*, The Centre for Fiscal Studies, University of Bath.

---

[36] NAO, op. cit.

[37] OECD, "Cutting Red Tape: National Strategies for Administrative Simplification", 2006.

Kenneth, J. et al. (1996) "Benefit-Cost Analysis in Environmental Health and Safety Regulation" American Enterprise Institute, The Annapolis Center and Resources for the Future.

Lutter, R. W. (2000) "An Analysis of the EPA's Proposed Lead Hazard Standards for Homes", Joint Center: AEI Brookings Joint Centre for Regulatory Studies. U.S.

Morrison, A.S., Watson, T. and Winston, C. (1998) "Fundamental Flaws of Social Regulation: The Case of Airplane Noise". Joint Center: AEI Brookings Joint Centre for Regulatory Studies. U.S

Moyle, P. (1999) "Pesticides in Ground Water: Will the EPA's New Regulation Decrease Health Risks?". Joint Center: AEI Brookings Joint Centre for Regulatory Studies. U.S.

Pearce, D. (1998) "Cost Benefit Analysis and Environmental Policy", *Oxford Review of Economic Policy,* 14: pp. 84–106.

Pope, J., Fayle, R. and Chen, D.L. (1991) *The Compliance Costs of Public Companies' Income Taxation in Australia 1986/87*, Australia Tax Research Foundation, Sydney.

Poutziouris, P., Chittenden, F. and Michaelas, N., (1999) "Modelling the Impact of Taxation on the Small Business Economy: The NatWest MBS Tax Index for the Self-Employed, Sole-Traders and Partnerships", *Environment and Planning C: Government and Policy*, 17(5), October.

Robinson, J.C. (1995)"The Impact of Environmental and Occupational Health Regulation on Productivity Growth in U.S. Manufacturing", *The Yale Journal of Regulation*, 12: pp. 387–434.

Rutledge, G.L. and Vogan, C. R. (1995) "Pollution Abatement and Control Expenditures, 1993", *Survey of Current Business*, 12(5): pp. 36–46. May

Sandford, C. (1973) 'Hidden costs of Taxation', Institute of Fiscal Studies, Publication, London, No. 6, July.

Sandford, C., Godwin, M. and Hardwick, P. (1989) *Administrative and Compliance Costs of Taxation*, Fiscal Publications, London.

Sandford, C., Godwin, M., Hardwick, P. and Butterworth, I. (1981) *Costs and Benefits of VAT,* Heinemann Educational Books, Oxford.

Sandford, C. and Hasseldine, J. (1992) *The Compliance Costs of Business Taxes in New Zealand*, Institute of Policy studies, Victoria University of Wellington, Wellington.

Small Business Research Trust. (1996) *NatWest Quarterly Survey of Small Businesses in Britain*, Vol. 12, No. 1, SBRT, Milton Keynes.

Small Business Research Trust. (1998) *NatWest SBRT Quarterly Survey of Small Businesses in Britain*, Vol. 14, No. 1, SBRT, Milton Keynes.

Small Business Research Trust. (2000) *Natwest Quarterly Survey of Small Business in Britain*, Vol. 16, No. 3, SBRT, Milton Keynes.

UNICE. (1995) The Union of Industrial and Employer's Confederations of Europe Regulatory Report: Releasing Europe's Potential Targeted Regulatory Reform.

Wit, G. de and Nijsen, A.F.M. (2002) *Administratie tot last van het algemeen,* Economisch Statistische Berichten, Vol. 87, nr. 4353, March 29, p. 248–250

Chapter 5
SCM to Measure Compliance Costs

André Nijsen

Abstract There are three types of compliance costs caused by business regulations, financial costs (taxes, premiums), information compliance costs (administrative burden) and substantive compliance costs (investments etc.). Taxes and premiums are on-budget incomes for government. That is why measuring of financial compliance costs by doing surveys is not that relevant. However, administrative burden and substantive compliance costs are off-budget costs. Besides, administrative burden and substantive compliance costs are hidden costs for businesses too. No bookkeeping system has separate registration for these two types of compliance costs. Therefore, a new instrument was needed to measure these costs of businesses.

One of the most challenging aspects of such a new instrument is to discuss for which target group the results are. Is it the entrepreneurs to help them reduce their own compliance costs? Or, is it the politician or the law maker to facilitate improving the quality of law by avoiding or taking away unnecessary compliance costs? The answer to this question has a big impact on how to measure compliance costs. This chapter tries to answer these questions.

5.1 Introduction

We will start with answering the most relevant questions about the Standard Cost Model (SCM). This instrument is widespread within OECD countries (OECD 2004, OECD 2006). SCM is a useful and potentially low-cost method for determining the costs of businesses of complying with information obligations (more specifically, administrative burdens) imposed on businesses by regulations, ex ante and ex post reform. SCM mostly does not cover all compliance costs, but can be a good proxy – particularly in challenging environments where data is

A. Nijsen (✉)
Adviser Regulatory Reform, Schoonhoven, The Netherlands
e-mail: nijsena@xs4all.nl

A. Nijsen et al. (eds.), *Business Regulation and Public Policy*,
International Studies in Entrepreneurship 20, DOI 10.1007/978-0-387-77678-1_5,

incomplete and where resource capacities are limited – for determining broader compliance costs, like substantive compliance costs (investment costs etc.).

SCM was developed in the mid-1990s of last century in the Netherlands. SCM was named originally, Mistral® a Dutch acronym for Measuring Instrument for Administrative Burden (Burden = Lasten in Dutch). When the Dutch Cabinet decided to implement this instrument, it was renamed Standard Cost Model. Since 2000, SCM has been implemented in other countries, mostly from OECD. Although, a manual was available for the first Dutch implementation of SCM, almost all other countries made, for good reasons, their own manuals and their own adaptations to their own needs.[1]

We will start to discuss the classic implementation of SCM in the field of administrative burden in Section 5.2. Our focus is on the technical description of the model and a sound understanding of the assumptions underlying the SCM. Section 5.2 will be concluded with a SWOT-analysis of the SCM related to other instruments to measure compliance costs. This will be the prelude for Section 5.3 where we discuss a recently developed alternative module of the SCM, SIROCCO (Scanning Instrument Regulatory Other Compliance Costs). SIROCCO and has a focus on substantive compliance costs.

5.2 A Bird's Eye View of the Classic SCM

5.2.1 Introduction

This bird's eye view is written from the perspective of the original Dutch design Mistral® (Nijsen and Vellinga 2002; Nijsen 2003), the forerunner of the Dutch SCM which has been implemented by the Dutch government in 2003. SCM is an instrument to facilitate civil servants to reduce and avoid unnecessary compliance costs. In principle, SCM is suitable to detect all kinds of compliance costs – viz. direct financial costs, substantive costs and information costs – of all kind of actors, viz. businesses, civilians and civil servants. However, most implementations of the SCM are in the field of information obligation compliance costs (the so-called administrative burden) of businesses.

What is the definition of administrative burdens (AB)?

AB are the costs of business to comply with legal information obligations.

5.2.2 How Does SCM Work?

The starting point of every implementation of SCM is an extensive reading of all the articles of a law in order to detect the legal information obligation(s) of

---

[1] Consult the website of the SCM Network to reduce administrative burden for SCM manuals of the different countries.

businesses. This can be a specific existing law (stock) or a planned/new law (flow). An implementation of SCM can cover also the whole stock of existing laws or any wanted selection e.g. a specific legal domain like the fiscal area or all laws affecting a specific sector like transport, or all laws which are relevant for starting businesses, or all laws referring to businesses with employees. It is important to be aware that the texts of laws or regulations seldom are very explicit about information obligations. Many information obligations are hidden behind words like to apply for e.g. permits or licenses or to report or reporting, to register, to declare or to notify, to be supervised etc. This first step is to be concluded by listing up all the relevant information obligations.

The question to be answered in the next step is: What kind of activities a business or an entrepreneur has to carry out in order to comply with these legal information obligations? To answer this question, a connection must be established between the requirements of the law and the activities in the business process. SCM describes the business process in terms of so called standard administrative activities, necessary to produce messages. Examples of standard administrative activities are: getting informed about the information obligation, gathering the necessary data, calculating, checking, consulting, sending the information, archiving etc. There exist several lists of these standard administrative activities, varying from 14 to 18 different activities. However, these lists show much overlap. Messages can be documents, inspections, telephone calls and any other way to transfer information from businesses to government or governments' agencies.

Administrative activities are mostly general in kind. They hardly differ between information obligations of businesses in different sectors and size classes. That is why it appeared to be feasible to construct so-called profiles or blue-prints of standard administrative activities for the different categories of information obligations by consulting experts both from business and from governments. There are about 10 different types of information obligations; for instance, applying for permits or licenses, applying for subsidies, declaring tax income or VAT, to register e.g. the start-up of a business, to notify e.g. of the engagement or dismissal of employees, etc.

Having constructed these blue-prints of standard administrative activities for every relevant information obligation, the time has come to proceed with the next step of SCM, viz. the fieldwork. These blue-prints are the basic elements of the questionnaire to ask businesses/entrepreneurs about the time (minutes) they need to carry out every single standard administrative activity. By multiplying the time with a tariff per hour (labor costs plus overhead), it is possible to calculate the standard compliance cost of every single information obligation. For instance, now we know the compliance costs of one single registration or one single application, or one single notification, or one single permit or licence. This is what we call the Price (P) of an information obligation.

The final step of SCM is to aggregate the compliance costs of the individual information obligations to the macro level. For this purpose, we need the total number of every single information obligation within a specific time period, mostly one year. This number is called the Quantity (Q) of an information obligation. For instance, we need to know the number of licenses in a year, or the number of notifications of a certain kind etc. We don't ask this type of information during the fieldwork. Entrepreneurs don't know this. The most reliable sources to gather data about the number of licences, permits, notifications, declarations etc. are the official registers of government, e.g. the tax authority, or the register of enforcing institutes. Experiences show the gathering of the real data about Q (Quantities) as being one of the most difficult and time consuming elements of the SCM. On the other hand, expert assessments appeared to be good proxies of much data about the quantities.

5.2.3 Technical Description of SCM[2]

This subsection contains a technical description of the way in which the (financial) administrative burden private businesses have to bear is calculated within the framework of Mistral®. Mistral® gives an estimate of how the administrative burden of private businesses varies between policy areas. See the Annexure for a list of symbols used.

5.2.3.1 Decomposition into a Number of Messages

Broadly, we can distinguish two steps in determining the administrative burdens imposed upon private businesses. First, it is determined how many 'messages' are necessary to comply with all information obligations stated in the law. Subsequently, in the next section, the costs per message are determined.

Legislation comprises various policy areas. For each of these policy areas p, the level of administrative burden AB_p can be determined. The total level of administrative burden is the sum of all administrative burdens for all policy areas (there are n_p policy areas):

$$AB = \sum_{p=1}^{n_p} AB_p$$

This is the total level of administrative burden in a country. The level of the administrative burden for a policy area is the cost of all the information obligations set forth in that particular policy area. Assume that there are n_{po} information obligations in policy area p.

The administrative burden of the oth information obligation is denoted by $Cost(Obligation_{po})$.

[2] See Nijsen, André F.M. en Nico Vellinga, Mistral®, A Model to Measure the Administrative Burden of Businesses, Research Report H200110, EIM, Zoetermeer, 2002.

$$AB_p = \sum_{o=1}^{n_{po}} Cost(Obligation_{po})$$

The cost of information obligation o is the sum of the costs of all messages associated with this obligation that have to be sent to the government. It is assumed that there are n_{pom} messages[3] associated with information obligation o. The cost of a single information obligation is:

$$Cost(Obligation_{po}) = \sum_{m=1}^{n_{pom}} Cost(Message_{pom})$$

5.2.3.2 Decomposition of the Costs of a Message

The cost of message m due to information obligation o in policy area p, is:

$$Cost(Message_{pom}) = \sum_{a=1}^{n_{poma}} (InternalCost_{poma} + ExternalCost_{poma})$$

where:

$$InternalCost_{poma} = (1 - \alpha_{poma}) \cdot Frequency_{poma} \cdot InternalTime_{poma} \cdot \frac{InternalTariff_{poma}}{60}$$

and

$$ExternalCost_{poma} = \alpha_{poma} \cdot Frequency_{poma} \cdot ExternalTime_{poma} \cdot \frac{ExternalTariff_{poma}}{60}$$

It is assumed that we have n_{poma} activities associated with message m . Composing a message is the result of a number of administrative activities. These include gathering the requested information, typing a document containing the information, sending the document to the government and finally, making a copy of the document to file it for future reference.

The internal and external cost of message m is the product of the number of times the activity is carried out, multiplied by the time required to carry out the activity and finally, multiplied by the appropriate tariff in terms of money per

[3] Some of the messages are composed of sub-messages. Not every information obligation has the same consequences for all businesses. In that case, we have sub-messages with differing costs expressing these differences. The cost of a sub-message is determined in the same way as the cost of a message in the main text. As a result, the cost of a message with sub-messages is then the sum of the cost of all sub-messages. This element is ignored in the main text to make the description not unnecessarily burdensome.

minute of the person carrying out the activity. The constituent parts of these equations are discussed in the following sub-paragraphs.

Proportion of Outsourcing

Some businesses prefer to outsource part or all of these activities. Small businesses lack, for instance, the qualified personnel to perform certain (administrative) tasks. The personnel working for this business are mainly engaged in the core activity of the business, which can be quite different from an administrative activity. In that case, it is likely to be cheaper to hire an external expert, who can then perform the necessary tasks. We end up with two types of costs, the internal cost for those activities that are carried out within the business and the external cost which constitutes the payments made by private businesses towards other businesses performing the outsourced activities. For each activity, we introduce the proportion of outsourcing α_{poma}. The value of α_{poma} will be close to 1 for policy areas which mainly affect mainly small businesses. Larger businesses will have specialized personal to carry out these activities and the α_{poma} -value for policy areas influencing mainly larger firms will be close to 0. There are also arguments for smaller firms to outsource to a larger extent even if it is more expensive than having someone within their own businesses to carry out this task. It relieves the entrepreneur of the burden of filling out forms for the Internal Revenue Service (IRS). It also relieves him/her of the burden of doing this without making any mistakes that could otherwise lead to legal steps by the IRS.

Frequency[4]

Each activity is carried out $Frequency_{poma}$ times a year and therefore, the number of times the activity is carried out within the firm is one minus the proportion of outsourcing times the frequency. The number of times the activity is carried out by an outside business is the proportion of outsourcing times the frequency.

Internal and External Time

It takes $InternalTime_{poma}$ minutes to carry out this particular activity if it is done within the business itself. An outside business performs the same activity in $ExternaTime_{poma}$ minutes.

---

[4] The frequency can be event driven or calendar driven. Examples of an event-driven information obligations are starting a business, applying for a permit, hiring an employee, notification of a labor accident. Examples of calendar-driven information obligations are a yearly Annual Account, a monthly VAT declaration, etc. In case of a calendar-driven information obligation, we would rather talk of periodicity instead of frequency.

Internal and External Tariff

The internal tariff for the activity when it is executed within the business itself is the amount of money per hour, divided by 60. This tariff is denoted by $InternalTariff_{poma}$. The external tariff is $ExternalTariff_{poma}$ and it is the tariff when the activity is outsourced. The internal tariff is the labor cost including a percentage for overhead costs. The labor cost is composed of the gross wage rate of the person carrying out the activity and a number of surcharges. Surcharges comprise paid holidays, all sorts of emoluments, pension contributions, etc. The percentages used for each of the surcharges are based on official wage and labor cost statistics. When outsourcing is preferred, the going rate for hiring outside help is normally higher than the wage rate if the activity were carried out within the business.

5.2.3.3 An Overview

Figure 5.1 presents a graphic overview of the structure of the SCM/Mistral® process.

5.2.4 Assumptions of SCM

It is important to be aware that SCM does not calculate the administrative burden for an average business. No. SCM allows for calculating the administrative burden of all regulated business caused by one or more information obligations of one specific law, a group of laws or of all relevant laws. This means that a single information obligation is the measuring unit of the SCM and not the business.[5]

The reason for this is as follows: The SCM has been developed in order to facilitate policy makers and law makers to reduce compliance costs as much as possible. Therefore, we need to look at it from a public policy perspective and not from an entrepreneurial view point. In the latter case, the business had to be the measuring unit. The concept ‘information obligation’ fits the public policy perspective. It allows gathering data at the level of every relevant article in a selected law or regulation. This is why the SCM is said to measure compliance costs from a public policy perspective and not from a business perspective. This does not alter the fact that SCM has been developed to reduce or avoid unnecessary compliance costs of businesses. But to facilitate this policy, it is necessary to tackle the problem where it comes from, the public administration. Therefore, the results of SCM must be presented in a format understandable for policy makers and law makers.

---

[5] When data about administrative burden for all information obligations are available, this information can be used as an input for distribution models to calculate administrative burden per business or per branch of industry.

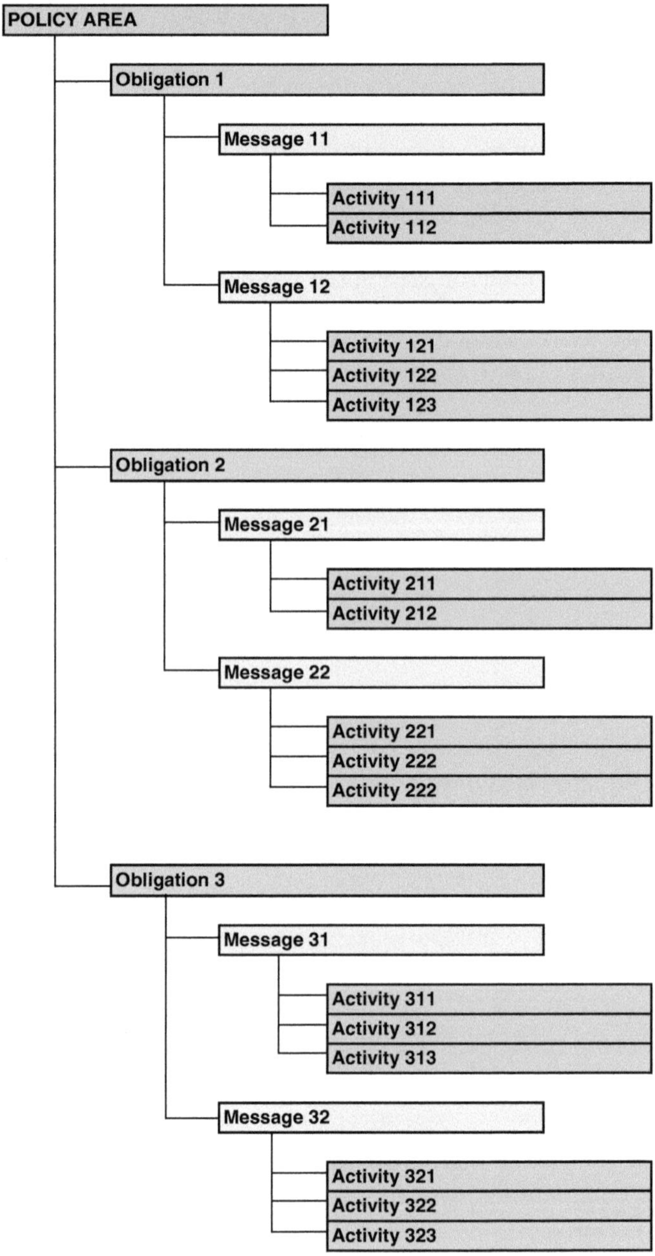

Fig. 5.1 Structure of Mistral® process

Taking the information obligation as the measuring unit has a lot of advantages. The most important one is that SCM does not need to gather data about the business economic impact of complying with the laws. In other words, SCM is not interested in the real, net cost of compliance of businesses, taking account of all the variants of complying. These are what we call the endogenous determinants of compliance costs, which can be influenced by the businesses or entrepreneurs only. SCM is interested in the exogenous determinants of compliance costs of businesses only, which are under the influence and responsibility of parliament and government.

To guarantee a focus on the exogenous compliance costs, it is assumed that all the businesses comply in a 'normally efficient way'. To achieve this, the SCM controls or standardizes the way of compliance by business by:

- selecting the law(s), ex-ante or ex-post, all or just one etc;
- listing all the relevant information obligations of the selected law(s);
- making a blue-print of standard activities for every single information obligation;
- transferring these blue-prints to the questionnaire for the field work with businesses;
- gathering data about the time and cost needed per administrative activity along the lines of this questionnaire.

By doing this, it is guaranteed that every respondent looks from the same perspective at the selected law(s) and will not forget or add activities. Let me remind you that most compliance costs are hidden cost. Entrepreneurs don't register these types of costs in their bookkeeping as a separate item. Most entrepreneurs underestimate the compliance costs substantially (Klein-Blenkers et al. 1980). The blue-print of standard administrative activities helps to prevent the responding entrepreneurs forgetting activities or adding activities which don't originate from legal obligations. The blue-print also prevents perceived compliance costs or annoyance costs from coming in.

Another advantage of taking the information obligation as the measuring unit is the possibility of avoiding big sampling by random selection of businesses. The focus on every single information obligation of one or more selected laws allows for selecting a restricted number of so-called categories of typical firms to gather data about the time necessary to comply with information obligations. The concept 'typical firm' needs some explanation because in business economics, this doesn't exist. The construction of such an artefact is necessary to allow for measuring compliance costs from a public policy perspective. The concept 'typical firm' refers to the legal specifications of the law respectively, the information obligation, or every other relevant category of businesses from the perspective of the manner of compliance with the law. An example of a legal specification of categories of typical firms is the Law Annual Account. The Law Annual Account specifies three different categories of businesses with three different types of information obligations: a small, a medium-sized and a big information obligation. These three categories of businesses are defined by means of the number of employees, net turnover and balance assets. In the case of the Law Annual Account, the number of categories of typical firms is three. Another example of the relevance of different categories of 'typical firms' is complying yourself or by outsourcing; two categories of 'typical firms'.

For every category of typical firms, only 3–5 responding businesses will do because of the relatively small dispersion of results as a consequence of the focus on a 'normally efficient way' of compliance with the information obligation. Let me remind you of the profile or blueprint of standard administrative activities. It is important to realize that SCM is not after finding statistical evidence about the 'real' business' economic administrative burdens of businesses. So SCM is not interested in finding the normal distributions of the administrative burdens of a specific information obligation. In that case, SCM should have to reckon too with the endogenous determinants of administrative burden or, in other words, with inefficient or very efficient ways of complying. No, SCM is interested only in the effect of the exogenous determinants on administrative burdens, e.g. normal efficient compliance. And, what should be understood by 'normal efficient compliance' is mainly determined with the blueprint of administrative activities. There is a lot of empirical evidence that this assumption allows a limited number of responding businesses because of the relatively small dispersion of the results regarding the time businesses need to fulfill specific administrative activities. There is not much variation between the regulated businesses in informing government.

5.2.5 SWOT Analysis of SCM

Literature shows there are more instruments to measure compliance costs (Allers 1994; Nijsen 2003). In Table 5.1 , an overview is presented.

From this table, it appears that none of the available instruments meets the requirement to measure compliance costs from a public policy perspective fully. Therefore, it is necessary to take account of the exogenous determinants of the compliance costs. Only three instruments partially meet this requirement, viz. case studies, survey/face-to-face interviews and simulation models. The newly developed Mistral® model therefore was a combination of these three instruments.

Two variants for measuring administrative burdens were developed which are both relevant for understanding the current implementations of the SCM, viz. a top-down and a bottom-up approach. The top-down approach starts from a business perspective and the bottom-up approach from a public policy perspective. The terms 'top-down' and 'bottom-up' could be misleading in case the perspective is unclear. In this context, the term 'top-down' is used from the perspective of the business sector again. If a quick oversight of all laws is

Table 5.1 Overview of instruments for cost assessment with a focus on measurement of administrative burden from a public policy perspective

Description	Advantages	Disadvantages	Suitable for implementation from a public policy perspective
Documentary (file) research	1. Short time needed. 2. Possibility to compare data from different sources if available. 3. Reliability of factual data.	1. Limited availability. 2. Difficult to assess origin and quality (validation) of data. 3. Format of existing records mostly not tuned to research requirements.	No. Data about exogenous determinants of costs are missing.
Case studies (on the spot)	1. Objective. 2. Reliable.	1. Very time consuming. 2. Validity endangered because respondents react on time measurement. 3. Difficult to guarantee general standards.	Partial. Macro parameters of exogenous determinants are lacking.
Surveys (mail and telephone)	1. Relatively low budget. 2. Suitable for big samples. 3. Suitable to assess averages of the total of administrative burden.	1. Danger of misunderstanding questions. 2. Danger of respondents forgetting non-registered information. 3. Danger of exaggerating by respondents. 4. Non-response endangers representativeness.	No. The data are lacking in details and reliability.
Surveys (face-to-face interviews)	1. High quality (validity). 2. Expert interviewers guarantee quality of answers.	1. Time consuming. 2. Suitable only for small scale surveys. 3. Weak representativeness.	Partial. Macro parameters of exogenous determinants are lacking.
Diary studies	1. Prevents bias in responses on retrospective questions. 2. Relatively low budget.	1. Inaccurate responses because of carelessness and underestimation. 2. Monitoring representativeness necessary.	No. Lack of detailed and reliable data.

Table 5.1 (continued)

Description	Advantages	Disadvantages	Suitable for implementation from a public policy perspective
Simulation models	1. Ex-ante assessments of planned regulation.	1. Applicability to other categories and periods sometimes questionable.	Partial. Micro parameters of exogenous determinants of costs are missing.
	2. Forecasting of assessments for other categories of businesses.	2. Appearance of accuracy.	
	3. Monitoring.	3. Difficult to guarantee general standards.	

Source: Allers (1994) and Nijsen (2003).

desirable, then we are talking of a 'top-down' approach. The opposite case, if detailed information about a specific law is wanted, is called the 'bottom-up' approach. In Table 5.2 , the main characteristics of the two approaches are presented.

The top-down approach starts by examining the costs of the total administration of an enterprise. The second phase is to allocate these costs over the routine business administration and those compulsory administrative procedures resulting from regulations. As a third phase, the costs resulting from compulsory administrative procedures of legislation over the relevant policy areas that businesses have to comply with, have been allocated. This type of information is mostly gathered by means of a questionnaire. A representative sample of businesses is surveyed in order to obtain information about the costs and other relevant data with respect to the individual business (firm size, turnover, profits etc). An important advantage of this approach is that administrative costs and other data become available at the level of the individual business. The large number of businesses and variables involved allow for detailed cross-analysis.

Table 5.2 Overview of approaches and their main characteristics in order to assess administrative burdens

Aspects	Top-down approach: Business perspective	Bottom-up approach: Public policy perspective
Measuring unit	Business	Law/information obligation
Coverage of policy areas	All policy areas	One policy area
Level of aggregation	High	Low
Means	Questionnaire	Expert interviews in combination with group discussions.

Source: Van der Burg and Nijsen (1998).

Experience indicates, however, that this does not necessarily mean that the resulting figures are also accurate. Definitions of administrative procedures are interpreted differently by the entrepreneurs surveyed, who as a result may either underestimate or overestimate the costs involved. Therefore, the outcome of such studies has often given rise to criticism (Van der Burg and Nijsen 1998).

In the bottom-up approach, the relevant regulations are subjected to a detailed examination during with all information obligations and the accompanying administrative activities/procedures are unravelled. The time involved with each activity and the function level at which it is carried out (the necessary qualification) are determined during an intensive multi-stage process of consultation and discussion – both individually and in groups – with experts from businesses, accountants and also employers and enforcing organizations. Instead of focusing on the large variations between individual businesses, the standard situation (normal efficient compliance) and relevant exemptions to this standard from the public policy perspective (qua time needed/costs or qua number of businesses) are determined. These data gathered during the multi-stage process of consultation form the input for Mistral® (Van der Burg and Nijsen 1998). To conclude, in Table 5.3 , the strengths and weaknesses of the top-down and bottom-up approaches are presented.

From Table 5.3, it appears that the top-down approach is very useful to:

- gain an insight into the extent of the total administrative burdens for businesses;
- gain an insight into the policy areas that cause most of the administrative burdens;
- gain an insight into the usefulness of compulsory administrative activities resulting from legislation, as experienced by enterprises;

Table 5.3 Strength and weakness of Top-down* and Bottom-up** approach

Relevant aspects	Top-down	Bottom-up
Representativeness of sample of businesses	+	–
Total scope of policy areas	+	–
Quick overview of administrative burdens by policy area	+	–
Ex-post assessment	+	+
Keys to solutions	–	+
Ex-ante assessment	–	+
Assessment of alternatives	–	+
Accuracy of results (validity and reliability)	–	+
Acceptation of results	–	+

* Questionnaire; ** Structured expert interview (or stopwatch-method in combination with group discussions); + An advantage or strength; – A disadvantage or weakness
Source: Van der Burg and Nijsen (1998).

- obtain a rough estimate of the magnitude of the administrative burdens of a policy area.

The bottom-up approach, being the equivalent of Mistral® or the different SCM derivations, is especially useful:

- to assess the extent of the administrative burdens for businesses in one policy area or for one legislation at a very detailed level and in a fairly accurate way;
- to carry out an ex-ante evaluation of the administrative burdens for businesses of a draft legislation and certain alternatives;
- to find keys that can help to formulate strategies to reduce administrative burdens for businesses in a certain policy area (useful policy instrument);
- when commitment and approval is needed from the various authorities (politicians, representatives of statutory organizations and representatives of employers' organizations) in the field.

To conclude, in order to find the best possible methodology to stimulate the German process of deregulation, in 2005, the Bertelsmann Foundation commissioned an international comparative study to find the best 'bureaucracy index' in the world. Out of 22 bureaucracy indices from all over the world, Mistral® was selected as best on the basis of five selection criteria: Core questions, concepts of the methodology, evaluation of German labor market, evaluation appropriateness for a German bureaucracy index, accuracy of the methodology, political impact, and useable elements of the instrument for a German bureaucracy index (Müller 2005: 79–201). In his study, Müller already indicated the necessity of developing instruments to measure substantive compliance costs too and how this could be done. Related to this, Chapter 18 of this book entails ideas about the development of a RIA coordination system. In the following section of this chapter, the focus will be on the new methodology for measuring substantive compliance cost. Finally, OECD and World Bank (World Bank Group 2007) evaluated the SCM being part of the Dutch reduction policy as leading in the world.

5.3 Alternative Implementations of SCM

5.3.1 Introduction

SCM, especially Mistral®, originally focused on measuring administrative burdens of businesses. However, the first implementation of Mistral® in 1993 included also the enforcing costs of government agencies (Bosch et.al. 1993). The limited scope of the first SCM implementations doesn't have a methodological background. The only reason was a political one. Recently, SCM has been implemented more and more, to measure administrative burdens of civilians and the enforcing costs of government agencies. However, this is out of the scope of this book.

More interesting is the new developed module of the SCM in the field of substantive compliance costs. In 2007, the Dutch Cabinet decided to broaden his reduction policy program 2007–2011 to substantive compliance costs of businesses. Part of this new policy was to develop an instrument to measure substantive compliance costs. This discussion started in 2004-2005, when EIM did a feasibility study about measuring substantive compliance costs (Nijsen et. al. 2005). The following were the main conclusions of this feasibility study:

- It is advisable and feasible to assess substantive compliance costs of all planned or new business regulations (flow).[6]
- It is only advisable and feasible to measure substantive compliance costs of a selected part of existing business regulations (stock).

The main argument for this is that it does not make sense to implement cost reduction policies on regulations which are highly internalized by businesses because skipping these regulations would not lower the costs of businesses. And, it was expected that many substantive obligations will appear to belong to business as usual activities. It should be noted that this is one of the major differences between information obligations and substantive obligations. If well defined, [7] the costs of information obligation would disappear if there was no legislation. No entrepreneur would inform government about his/her compliance behavior or profit or whatever, if there was no information obligation.[8] This subsection will explain what is new about this new SCM module, named SIROCCO (Scanning Instrument Regulations of Other Compliance Costs).

5.3.2 *Substantive Compliance Costs*

Substantive compliance costs are part of business effects of regulations (See Fig. 3.1, Chapter 3). The other types of compliance costs are financial costs (taxes, premiums) and administrative burdens.

What are substantive compliance costs? Substantive compliance costs are all costs to comply with substantive obligations. Substantive obligations are norms, standards, and all other legally obliged codes of conduct to safeguard

---

[6] From June 1 2006 a special SCM module for assessing substantive compliance costs of planned or new regulations is part of the regular Dutch Business Impact Assessment.

[7] The legal obligation to have a bookkeeping system and all third party disclosures (the obligation to inform clients, consumers, patients etc.) are considered to be substantive obligations for reasons of their functionality.

[8] This is the main reason why the Dutch Cabinet decided in 2007 not to take all business regulations to measure substantive compliance costs but only a selection of about 30–35 laws. The base line measurements of information obligations (administrative burden) mostly cover the total of business regulations.

public goals in a direct way. For instance, in order to safeguard safe working conditions in his/her own business, an entrepreneur has to invest in the construction of the building, machines, training, etc. The total costs of these investments are substantive compliance costs. Contrary to reducing administrative burden, reducing substantive costs could endanger public goals in a direct way.

The interesting thing about substantive obligations is that – contrary to information obligations and obligations to pay taxes and premiums – entrepreneurs feel it is quite normal to behave in the way as is stipulated by the law. Most entrepreneurs don't want unsafe working conditions for their workers. Most entrepreneurs don't want their production to bring about environmental pollution. Most entrepreneurs don't want to deliver unsafe products to their consumers or clients. This implies that there can be a lot of business as usual costs in the total of compliance costs.

To facilitate effective reduction policies, it is therefore important to distinguish substantive compliance costs into:

- business as usual costs, costs that would remain if there was no legal obligation;
- Marginal costs, costs that would disappear if there was no legal obligation.

We have called the demarcation line, to separate the total of substantive compliance costs into business as usual costs and marginal costs, the base line. Marginal costs only are relevant for reduction policies. Figure 5.2 presents the results of a pilot survey to measure substantive compliance costs for three separate laws, viz. the Law for Transport of Dangerous Products, the Law to check the Identity of Newly Hired Employees, and the Law Employees Council (Boog and Nijsen 2007).

It is really fascinating to see how different businesses feel about different laws. For instance, the substantive obligations of the Law for Transport of Dangerous Products are totally internalized by the regulated businesses. The reason is that a business code was almost one-to-one transposed into the law. By consequence, the total substantive compliance costs belong to the business as usual costs. Canceling the law would have no effect on the costs of businesses. They would continue the same manner of transportation. The other extreme is the Law for Identification of Newly Hired Employees. The problem is the checking of passports by the employers belonging to potential employees coming from many different countries all over the world in order to prevent illegal labor. Especially employments agencies evaluated the substantive obligations of this law as being highly burdensome. They would stop the prescribed identification proceedings immediately should the law be canceled. This implies that the total substantive compliance costs of this law are marginal costs from the perspective of the employment agencies. It is easy to understand that employment agencies are very much interested in finding alternative solutions for the problem of identification, which are less burdensome for them. In between is the Law Employees Council. The regulated businesses consider almost 70% of total

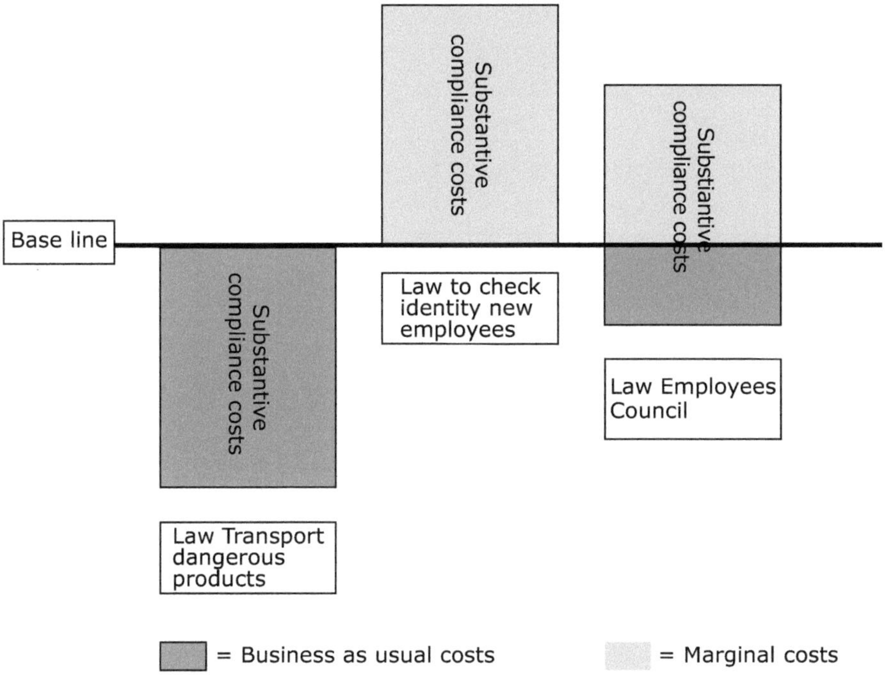

Fig. 5.2 Composition of substantive compliance costs

substantive compliance costs being marginal costs. This implies that the regulated business would drop some prescribed activities but not all of this law. For instance, entrepreneurs would reduce the frequencies of employee consultations, the number of employees involved and the length of time of consultations.

5.3.3 How to Detect Substantive Obligations?

It appears from practice not so easy to detect the difference between the different types of obligations. Figure 5.3 tries to give some assistance.

After the selection of the substantive obligations in a specific law or regulation, the steps to take in SIROCCO are quite identical with the different steps of SCM/Mistral®, viz:

1. Phase of preparation
   - Which categories of regulated businesses are relevant?
   - Which types of obligations?
   - Which types of activities or investments belong to the compliance with the selected substantive obligations (standardization of different ways of efficient compliance per category of typical firms)?

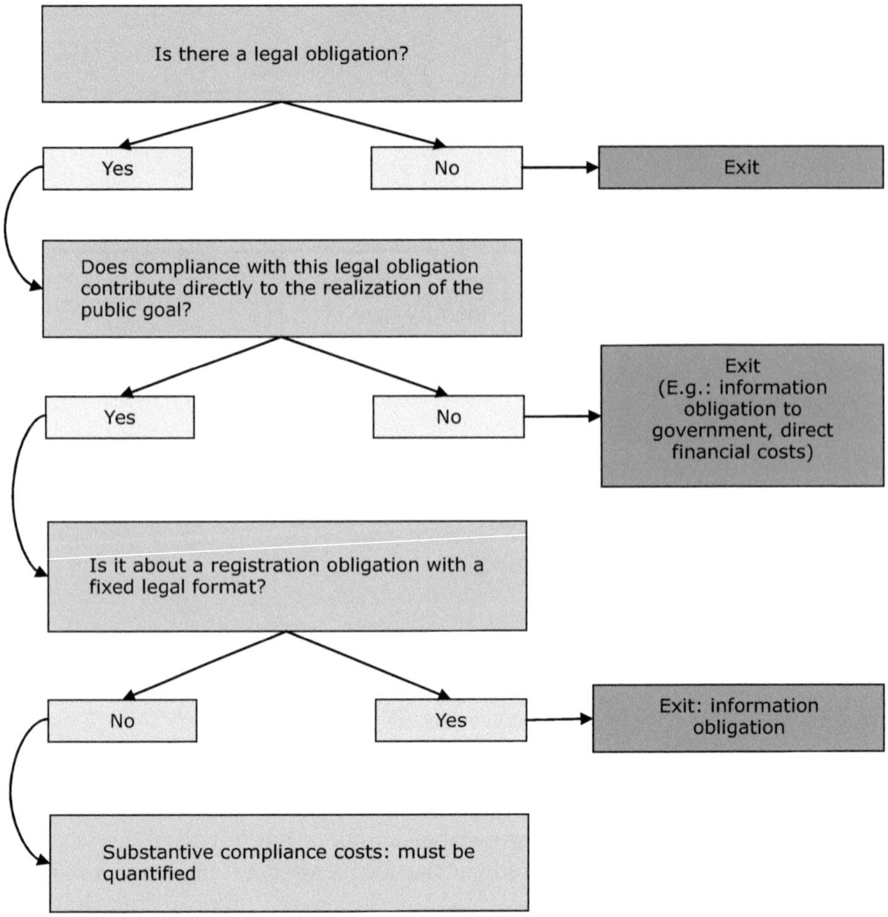

Fig. 5.3 Decision tree to detect substantive obligations for businesses

- Consultation of stakeholders (policy, inspection and businesses) to safeguard support before starting the field work.

2. Phase of field work
   - Selection of respondents per category of typical firm: regulated businesses and suppliers.
   - Gathering of data about Prices (P) and suggestions for reductions with regulated businesses and suppliers.
   - Gathering of data about Quantities (Q) with Inspections, Bureaus of Statistics.
3. Phase of validation and reporting
   - Validation of P parameters by consultation with experts.
   - Drawing up the report.

One of the most striking differences between the measurement of compliance costs of information obligations and of substantive obligations is the wide variation in different ways of complying with substantive obligations. Compliance with information obligations involves filling in documents and transferring the requested information as prescribed by the rules. There is not much variation between the regulated businesses in informing government.

Complying with substantive obligations is quite different. Many regulations don't prescribe how to comply with the substantive obligations. For instance, it is forbidden for businesses to produce noise pollution. To prevent noise pollution, a maximum number of decibels is stipulated in the law. It is easy to understand that a substantive obligation like this has totally different impact depending on the type of industry, e.g. metal manufacturing or banking. But also within a sector, the impact of the obligation to prevent noise pollution may differ between businesses. For example, outdated metal works probably will produce more noise pollution than new metal works with modern machines. Probably, the new metal works would have ordered machines that meet all legal requirements, including regarding the prevention of noise pollution. The legal prescriptions are embedded in the technology of the machines. In order to measure substantive compliance costs adequately, it is relevant to discuss with experts – e.g. inspectors and suppliers of machines – the different modalities of compliance with preventing noise pollution in the relevant part of regulated businesses. For instance, different ways of compliance are earplugs, sheltering noisy machines or investing in new machines that meet the legal requirements. The next step is to assess the Price(P) and Quantity(Q) parameters of these three different ways of complying with (three different categories of typical firms). Consultation with experts is extremely important. Chapter 18 of this book entails an integral discussion about how to measure compliance costs and benefits with the regulated business or norm addressee as a starting point and other measuring instruments.

5.4 Summary and Conclusions

The SCM is a wide spread instrument within the countries of the OECD. Nevertheless, a lot of questions are still to be answered. How does SCM work exactly? What are the most relevant assumptions? What about the suggested lack of representativeness of SCM? What is the meaning of the standardization of a normal efficient way of compliance?

Traditionally, SCM had a focus on administrative burden. More recently, the relevance of substantive compliance costs has been stressed. Businesses are complaining too about unnecessary substantive compliance costs. So, there has been a plea to extend the existing reduction programs to include substantive compliance costs. A new module of SCM has been developed. This new instrument has to meet the requirement to take account of marginal costs of regulated businesses. Marginal costs are the business costs that will disappear if the law should be canceled.

To reduce or avoid unnecessary compliance costs of businesses, politicians and law makers need adequate information. Adequate information has to tell them which laws or regulations are causing unnecessary compliance costs and for which type of regulated businesses in a disproportional way. That is why the SCM and the new module for substantive obligations are looking from a public policy perspective and not from a business perspective. Looking at unnecessary compliance costs is the only way to help entrepreneurs to reduce the endogenous part of compliance costs. It is the responsibility of the entrepreneurs themselves to look after the endogenous part of compliance costs. The best way of doing so is compliance in a 'normally efficient way'. Competition will force entrepreneurs to act in this way.

This discussion of SCM is part of the more comprehensive debate about the construction of a total RIA coordination system at the end of this book.

5.5 Annexure: List of Symbols Used

The following symbols, together with their meaning, are used throughout the previous sub-sections:

α_{poma}	Proportion of outsourcing for activity a , part of message $m$due to information obligation o for policy area p
AB	Total level of the administrative burden for all policy areas in a country
AB_{perc}	Level of the administrative burden for all policy areas as a percentage of the total business expenses
AB_p	Level of the administrative burden for policy area p
$Cost(Message_{pom})$	Cost of message m due to information obligation o for policy area p
$Cost(Obligation_{po})$	Cost of information obligation o for policy area p
$ExternalTariff_{poma}$	External tariff in terms of money per hour for the person-carrying out activity a, part of message m due to information obligation o for policy area p
$ExternalTime_{poma}$	Required time in minutes to perform activity a, part of message m due to information obligation o for policy area p
$Frequency_{poma}$	Frequency of activity a necessary to compose message m due to information obligation o for policy area p
$InternalTariff_{poma}$	Internal tariff in terms of money per hour for the person carrying out activity a, part of message m due to information obligation o for policy area p
$InternalTime_{poma}$	Required time in minutes within the business to perform activity a , part of message m due to information obligation o for policy area p

The indices used:

a activity
m message
o information obligation
p policy area

The various 'number of entities' used:

n_p number of policy areas
n_{po} number of information obligations in policy area
n_{pom} number of messages associated with information obligation in policy area
n_{poma} number of activities in message m associated with information obligation o in policy area p

References

Allers, M.A. (1994), Administrative and Compliance Costs of Taxation and Public Transfers in The Netherlands, Wolters-Noordhof, University Groningen, Groningen (diss.)

Boog, J.J., A.F.M. Nijsen (2007), Pilotonderzoek overige nalevingskosten van bestaande wetgeving; Eindrapportage, (Pilot survey substantive compliance costs of existing laws; Final Report), EIM, Zoetermeer

Bosch, L., A. Kwaak, A.F.M. Nijsen and P.Th. van der Zeijden (1993), Leidt vereenvoudiging van de premieheffing voor de werknemersverzekeringen tot maatschappelijke lastenverlichting? (Simplifying collection of premiums for workers social insurance will it bring social cost reduction?), EIM, Zoetermeer

Burg, B.I. van der, A.F.M. Nijsen (1998), How can administrative burdens of enterprises be assessed? Different methods; advantages and disadvantages, in: Improving the Quality of Legislation in Europe, (ed.) A. Kellerman, G., Azzi, S. Jacobs, R. Deighton-Smith, T.M. C. Asser Institute, Kluwer Law International, The Hague/Boston/London

Klein-Blenkers, F., H.J. Mortsiefer and W. Renske (1980), Die Belastung von Industrieunternehmen durch administrative Leistungen für den Staat – unter besonderer Berücksichtigung kleiner und mittlerer Unternehmen, Verlag Otto Schwartz & Co., Göttingen

Müller, C. (2005), Regulierungsdichte- und Bürokratieindex (ReBiX); Konzept zur Zusammenführung von Verfahren und Methoden zur`Messung und Bewertung von Regulierungsdichte und Bürokratiebelastung für die Wirtschaft, in: S. Empter, F. Frick, R. B. Vehrkamp (eds.), Auf dem Weg zu moderner Regulierung; Eine kritische Bestandsaufnahme, Verlag Bertelsmann Stiftung

Nijsen, A.F.M. (2003), Dansen met de Octopus; Een bestuurskundige visie op informatieverplichtingen van het bedrijfsleven in de sociale rechtstaat (Dancing with the Octopus; Information obligations of enterprises in the social constitutional state from a public administration point of view), Eburon, EIM, Delft, Zoetermeer (diss.)

Nijsen, A.F.M., P. van der Hauw and G. Regter (2005), De kosten van inhoudelijke verplichtingen voor het bedrijfsleven; Definitie en ontwikkeling meetmethode, (Costs of substantive obligations for businesses; Definition and development of methodology), Zoetermeer, Research Report H200501

Nijsen, A.F.M., N. Vellinga (2002), Mistral®, A Model to Measure the Administrative Burden of Businesses, Research Report H200110, EIM, Zoetermeer

OECD (2004), OECD Reviews of Regulatory Reform. Germany. Consolidating Economic and Social Renewal, OECD, Paris.
OECD (2006), Cutting Red Tape. National Strategies for Administrative Simplification, OECD, Paris.
World Bank Group (2007), Review of the Dutch Administrative Burden Reduction Program.

Chapter 6
Tailoring Regulation to the Regulated: The U.S. Regulatory Flexibility Act

William J. Dennis

Abstract Many consider regulatory relief for small business and implementing regulatory objectives a zero-sum game. The U.S. Regulatory Flexibility Act (RFA) of 1980 directly challenges the zero-sum game proposition by requiring regulatory agencies to search for non-zero-sum solutions for regulations having a significant impact on a substantial number of small businesses. This presentation evaluates the Regulatory Flexibility Act, concluding that results have been increasingly positive over time. Yet, the lack of formal measurement, reduced through continuing bureaucratic resistance, and a perceived need for additional legislative modification cloud the generally favorable assessment.

6.1 Prelude

The 1970s was a difficult decade in the United States. Vietnam, the impeachment of President Nixon, energy shortages, stagflation, the increasingly non-competitive "Rust Belt," credit problems, and a regulatory environment that seemingly changed daily, made small business owners a very unhappy group. The mood was therefore predictably dark when 2,000 elected small business owner-delegates from across the country gathered in Washington for the 1980 White House Conference on Small Business.

The Conference was the first such small business gathering since Franklin Roosevelt called one during the Great Depression. That had proven a political disaster (Ziegler, 1979, p. 17). None had been held since. But at the behest of Congress, the Carter White House called another for the purpose of having

---

The author was tangentially involved in development of RFA in the late 1970s and 1980 and has since taken an interest in its implementation from his position in a research foundation whose parent actively supports the Act.

W.J. Dennis (✉)
NFIB Research Foundation, Washington, DC, USA
e-mail: denny.dennis@nfib.org

A. Nijsen et al. (eds.), *Business Regulation and Public Policy*,
International Studies in Entrepreneurship 20, DOI 10.1007/978-0-387-77678-1_6,

small business owners identify and offer solutions to their most pressing problems (U.S. White House Commission on Small Business, 1980). Unspoken, the Conference was also designed as a political safety valve on the eve of what everyone expected would be a very difficult election for incumbents.

From the outset, the regulatory burden was a major focus of Conference discussion. A regulatory mess had arisen in the 1970s. New regulatory agencies, often administering several regulatory programs, appeared recurrently. The rules that these new agencies wrote and enforced, primarily social and environmental, were piled on top of a host of economic regulatory requirements surviving from the 1930s. Small business owners, therefore, confronted a substantial and growing regulatory burden compounded by terrible economic problems and the uncertainty resulting from rapid change.

The Regulatory Flexibility Act (RFA) was just one of the regulatory reform recommendations that emerged from the 1980 White House Conference (U.S. White House Commission on Small Business, 1980). Other regulatory initiatives were more popular. RFA might not even have gained the delegates' attention were it not for prompting by small business-oriented trade associations and Conference "experts." But delegates recognized that the legislative groundwork for RFA had already been laid, passage was politically "doable," and it could happen quickly. Other Conference regulatory recommendations would become entangled in controversial issues of the massive regulatory reform legislation that tortuously, and ultimately unsuccessfully, was moving through the Congress. In fact, the RFA proved the sole regulatory-reform survivor in a regulatory-reform minded Congress (Verkuil, 1982) and, as amended, remains the principle small business-oriented initiative to address the regulatory burden. On September 19, 1980, President Jimmy Carter signed the Regulatory Flexibility Act into law.

The remainder of this discussion is organized as follows: the second section presents the concept of regulatory flexibility and its rationale. The third section outlines the Regulatory Flexibility Act as amended. The fourth examines quantitatively and qualitatively the Act's effectiveness, including the need for modification. The fifth addresses small business owners and entrepreneurs under the Act. The final section discusses lessons learned.

6.2 The Regulatory Flexibility Concept

Regulatory flexibility implies that administrative rules, even laws, are developed to match the regulated when in the public interest to do so. It argues that one set of rules is not always the most efficient and effective means to achieve regulatory objectives. Alternatives applied to portions of the (potentially) regulated can yield socially superior results. In other words, reducing the regulatory burden for small business by applying alternative sets of rules is not necessarily a zero-sum game.

The practical application of regulatory flexibility typically involves "tiering" rules or producing different sets of rules for different collections of businesses. The tiers are normally adjusted to some measure of size. Regulatory flexibility can be employed at various stages of the regulatory process and in many ways. For example, authorities can address the substance of a rule, the paperwork and/or record-keeping requirements that accompany it, or the enforcement procedure and penalties that are inherent. Similarly, authorities can find alternative means of regulation; reduce or totally waive requirements; or phase in rules over longer periods. They can distinguish between those eligible for the tiered rules and those that are not by employee size of business, annual sales, profitability, share of relevant market, or even size of the regulated transaction, e.g., pollutants emitted.

The rationale for regulatory flexibility begins with the disproportionate impact of regulation on small firms. Regulatory compliance, including record-keeping, etc., typically has both a fixed cost and variable cost component. Large firms have more units of output over which to spread fixed costs than small firms, giving the former a relative cost advantage in regulatory compliance. Studies prior to RFA enactment (see Bradford (2004) for a critical evaluation) and subsequently affirm the principle (e.g., Crain, 2005; Crain and Hopkins, 2001; Hopkins, 1995). Bradford summarized the literature concluding that:

1. there are economies of scale in regulatory compliance for many regulations;
2. the economies of scale are due principally to fixed cost, though at times to variable costs as well; and
3. those economies of scale persist over time, i.e., they are not just transitional differences (Bradford, 2004).

The disproportionate impacts argument spills over from direct economic effects into the value of smaller firms. Regulatory flexibility, therefore, is not just about immediate economic differentials, but also about soft costs and longer term and indirect impacts such as the contribution of small firms to competition, innovation, and even the social structure.

Assessment of distributional impacts is unusual if for no other reason than the cost to produce them (Hahn, 2004; Parker, 2003). Yet, when analysis finds that a rule applied to one group yields a net welfare loss and applied to a second group yields a net welfare gain, regulatory flexibility (and common sense) adjusts the proposed rule. In other words, "If the regulator can carve out a class of cases where regulation produces a net loss, it should do so, no matter how that class of cases is described" (Bradford 2004, p. 5). The issue becomes more interesting when a proposed rule yields a social gain if applied to both groups, but yields substantially more social gain if applied to one group than the other.

Brock and Evans examine the incentives created by regulatory "tiering," i.e., using different sets of rules for different groups (Brock and Evans, 1986, 1985). While they generally agree that tiering or regulatory flexibility can be helpful to economic efficiency, they put forward important caveats. The first involves the boundary between exempt, or alternatively regulated, and non-exempt, or non-alternatively regulated groups. Tiering necessarily creates a boundary, a line separating the eligible from the ineligible. If an exemption or other burden reduction measure has value, businesses just below the qualifying point have an incentive to cap growth. Those just over the boundary have an incentive to shrink enough to qualify, e.g., dividing the business in two. Neither is efficient, but both happen (Gates and Leuschner, 2007). The corollary involves less efficient firms in the eligible group(s). If an exemption has value, the most inefficient firms gain a competitive advantage from the exemption vis-à-vis those not exempt. These firms may survive due to the burden reduction while more efficient, non-exempt firms may not. The authors summarize:

> The ideal tiering scheme must balance the social loss from inducing inefficient big businesses contractions and from preserving inefficient small businesses against the social gain from preserving efficient small businesses (Brock and Evans, 1986, p. 180).

There is no inherent reason to confine the number of tiers to just two. Multiple tiers can reduce the economic perversions and inequities of the inevitable "notch" problem of tiering. But the issues of expense, time and data intrude, often turning a desirable abstraction into a practical nightmare.

Brock and Evans raise an additional point. They question the applicability of tiering in industries that have high barriers to price competition, even if the industry is highly deconcentrated (Brock and Evans, 1986, pp. 101–102). They argue that in these industries, incumbent firms have erected artificial barriers to competition keeping businesses in the industry artificially small. Since the purpose of tiering and regulatory flexibility is to promote and enhance competition, policy-maker focus should be directed elsewhere.

The regulatory flexibility concept is not novel nor was it when the Regulatory Flexibility Act was first considered in the late 1970s. Practical examples could easily be found and were frequently cited by witnesses in Congressional testimony supporting RFA (e.g., McKevitt, 1977). The U.S. Regulatory Council, an extension of the White House, identified 43 examples of regulatory flexibility that were operative in 1981 (U.S. Government Accountability Office, 2006). Still, systematic application of the concept as RFA proposed meant replacing what had been heretofore ad hoc practice.

6.3 The Regulatory Flexibility Act of 1980 as Amended

The Regulatory Flexibility Act (RFA) effectively consists of four components: The original Act of 1980; the Small Business Regulatory Enforcement Fairness Act (SBREFA) of 1996 which amends the original Act; Executive Order (E.O.) 13272 of 2003 which focuses on effective implementation; and, a series of court decisions which reinforce judicial review of agency decisions. Together, the four form the essential body of law and practice that is now the Act.

6.3.1 Goals and Objectives of the Act

The Act has had four objectives from the beginning, though not all were formal or explicit. Far from disorienting however, the haze of multiple objectives proved legislatively helpful. It allowed everyone involved to focus on their favorite outcome(s).

The Congressional Findings and Declaration of Purpose of the Act lay out its formal rationale in broad terms (Public Law 96–354). They affirm the value of regulation to protect public safety and welfare while asserting regulatory goals should be achieved with minimal public burden. Uniform laws and regulations impact entities of varying sizes differently. Failure to recognize those differential impacts often creates disproportionate impacts on small business thereby adversely limiting entry and competition, lowering productivity and discouraging innovation. Alternative regulatory approaches which do not conflict with stated objectives of applicable statutes may be available, and should be explored.

Note that the primary purpose of the Act is not to reduce the regulatory burden on smaller businesses per se, though that certainly is a direct result. Rather the primary purpose is to address the disproportionate impact of regulations and its consequences. It is to match regulation with the size of the regulated for reasons of common sense, equity, and the social and economic benefits accruing from a stronger, healthier small business population.

James Morrison, one of the most influential Congressional staff members in development and enactment of RFA, recalls that the primary rationale for the Act was to change the culture of the bureaucracy, i.e. to transform the way the bureaucracy approaches small business (Morrison, 2007). Dr. Morrison relates that the actors intimately involved had no delusions that RFA supporters could craft and enact anything that would yield direct substantive results. They could only hope that by establishing a procedure or process, agency consideration of small business impacts would become ingrained and habitual; over time, habit would change the culture of the bureaucracy as it affected small business.

A third objective, foremost in the minds of most regulatory reform advocates, small business representatives, and small business owners aware of the legislation, was simple burden reduction. This objective was inherently the most controversial and not necessarily shared by those concerned about a zero-sum game. And fourth, an obvious fairness argument was implicit throughout the legislative process. Large firms have the influence and capacity to work the regulatory system; small firms do not.

6.3.2 The "Watchdog"

It is necessary to briefly digress and outline a unique governmental structure that is deeply involved in the Act. The U.S. Small Business Administration (SBA) is an agency of the federal government that administers a large share of its small business support programs. Since 1976, the SBA has had a legally unique, independent unit housed in the agency known as the Office of Advocacy. Advocacy's sole purpose is to represent small business within government. A Chief Counsel for Advocacy who is appointed by the President and is confirmed by the Senate heads it. Supervision of the implementation of the RFA has become a primary responsibility for the Office and the Chief Counsel.

6.3.3 The Process

The Regulatory Flexibility Act creates a process by which the Act's goals are to be achieved. It demands no outcome other than consideration of alternatives when a rule has a "significant impact" on a "substantial number" of small businesses. So long as an agency follows the process, the agency is free to reach any substantive conclusion it deems appropriate. But it must follow the process.

The process is too complex to be detailed here. But in sum, it requires agencies proposing new rules (and periodically reviewing old ones) to determine with evidence if the rule has a "significant impact" on a "substantial number" of small businesses (U.S. Small Business Administration, Office of Advocacy, 2003). If it does/will, the agency must develop and consider alternatives to the regulation. If it rejects the alternatives, it must explain why it did so. If an agency fails to follow the process or does so in a slipshod fashion, an aggrieved party can take the agency to court to obtain relief.

6.4 Effectiveness of the Regulatory Flexibility Act

Regulatory flexibility in 1980 was clearly an innovative and promising approach to many of the regulatory issues small business faced. But does the Act remain a promise for small business or is it yielding results?

The RFA has undergone dramatic change particularly over the last 10-plus years. The early years held promise, but few results. Murray Weidenbaum, one of the nation's foremost authorities on regulation and President Reagan's first Chairman of the Council of Economic Advisors, dismissed the Act claiming "Compliance . . . was minimal" (Weidenbaum, 1997, p. 5). The agencies, according to Weidenbaum, were ignoring RFA's requirements. He blamed the condition on the inability to legally compel the bureaucracy to follow the law. That condition was commonly acknowledged in and out of government. Jere Glover, the Chief Counsel for Advocacy under President Clinton, found himself reduced to the threat of cumbersome legal procedures as virtually his sole enforcement weapon. It was not a long-term solution (Glover, 2007).

Enforcement holes in the original legislation led to overwhelming and bipartisan passage of the Small Business Regulatory Enforcement Fairness Act

(SBREFA) in 1996. SBREFA put teeth in RFA by specifically strengthening judicial review and creating a more rigorous RFA process for two major rule-producers, the Environmental Protection Agency (EPA) and the Occupational Safety and Health Administration (OSHA). Compliance improved. The number of proposed rules for which analyses were conducted more than doubled between 1995 and 1999. One type rose from 22 to 50 and another from 22 to 46 (Francis and Joensen, 2001). Executive Order 13272 further strengthened the regulatory flexibility concept by compelling agencies to develop internal compliance procedures and requiring Advocacy to provide RFA training for rule-makers. These steps, congressional oversight and continual monitoring from the Office of Advocacy have unquestionably increased the effectiveness of the Act over time. Still, sharp complaints often appear focusing on weaknesses in the Act and its application (e.g., Langer, 2007; Phelps, 2001 and See, 2006). And, the Government Accountability Office (GAO) continues to identify many of the same technical issues with the Act that helped undermine it over the years (U.S. Government Accountability Office, 2006).

Though increasingly effective, is the Regulatory Flexibility Act effective? The consensus answer to the question is "yes" and "no." GAO argues that the Act's effectiveness has been mixed (U.S. Government Accountability Office, 2006)[1]. The Office of Advocacy's report on the 25th anniversary of the Act's passage concludes that "... regulatory development and sensitivity to impacts on small entities have improved considerably since the RFA was enacted in 1980. But, (author's italics) *more improvements are needed*" (U.S. Small Business Administration, Office of Advocacy, 2006, p. 46). Thomas M. Sullivan, current Chief Council for Advocacy, recently opined that RFA was doing a "fairly good job" achieving cost savings (Sullivan, 2007a). Another close observer notes that though agencies are doing better finding ways to reduce and find alternatives for regulatory burdens, "...most agencies have not yet fully embraced the RFA and made it part of their agency culture..." (Holman, 2006, pp. 1136–1137). While recognizing problems, former Chief Counsel Glover is more positive. He thinks the Act "has worked remarkably well" (Glover, 2007). However, at a recent congressional hearing, three witnesses representing small business quickly itemized areas where the legislation needed strengthening, e.g., Langer (2007). (Examples appear in Section 6.4.2.4 below.)

6.4.1 Quantifying the Act's Effectiveness

The general absence of numbers creates a significant evaluation problem. In 1998, 18 years after RFA became law, Advocacy began to publish cost savings

[1] The GAO, the investigative arm of the Congress, is one of the most prestigious and authoritative units in the federal government. Numerous GAO reports identify both the promise and problems of RFA. A list of those reports appears in (U.S. Government Accountability Office, 2006).

generated by its formal interventions, i.e., a formal communication with an agency indicating failure to properly produce a required analysis. The data are currently published annually in terms of "first year" savings, i.e., one-time savings, and, where applicable, "annual" savings, i.e., ongoing savings generated each year. Advocacy credits its interventions with saving small businesses $58.4 billion in one-time costs and $19.9 billion in annual (recurring) costs over the last five fiscal years (FY 2002 through FY 2006) in 68 separate actions (author's calculations from Advocacy data contained in annual reports, (U.S. Small Business Administration, Office of Advocacy, 2007, 2006, etc.). These direct, visible savings translate into a little over $5,000 a year for every small employer in the country. Not all small employers benefit, let alone benefit equally or benefit every year. Yet, the overall impact is non-trivial. Occasional issues with data quality appear in the calculations, but the primary problem for present purposes is that they undercount the Act's dollar impact.

Cost-saving estimates occur only when Advocacy has made a formal complaint. Thomas Sullivan and others in the Office of Advocacy point out that informal contacts with agencies during the rule-making process occur far more frequently than formal ones and they have grown substantially more so in recent years (Sullivan, 2007b). No attempt has been made to quantify the impact of such informal communications, but Advocacy thinks the effect of informal communication is large and growing (U.S. Small Business Administration, Office of Advocacy, 2006, p. 5).

6.4.2 *Qualitative Evaluation of the Act's Effectiveness*

Analysts must rely almost exclusively on qualitative data to examine the Act's effectiveness. A growing body of material lends insights, beginning with previously noted assessments of those most intimately involved (Glover, 2007; Langer, 2007; McGibbon, 2007; Sullivan, 2007b; U.S. Government Accountability Office, 2006). But they also are not disinterested parties. The following briefly discusses political support, state replication, training rule-makers and outstanding issues.

6.4.2.1 Political Support as a Measure of Effectiveness

If the regulatory flexibility concept has merit, appropriate implementation should represent a "win-win" for small business and the public. Win-win should enjoy broad political support and encounter relatively little controversy. The same would be true for a change-the-culture objective, though not necessarily for a reduction-in-the-burden goal.

Small business advocates, including small business-oriented trade associations, vigorously support the Act. Some observers assert that the extent of political support for the Act is really a tribute to the political power of small business rather than the merits of the legislation (Pierce, 1998; Sargentich, 1997). Yet, if the Act were not helpful to small business and small business were as powerful as claimed, would it not abandon RFA and exercise its political power to achieve something more worthwhile?

Making the Act effective has been the single highest priority for at least the last two Chief Advocates (one from each major party), both of which have had deep and longstanding ties to the small business community (Glover, 2007; Sullivan, 2007b). The Congress has been highly sympathetic enacting both the original Act and strengthening amendments. In fact, there has not been a single vote cast in subcommittee, committee, or on the floor of either the House or Senate in opposition (Morrison, 2007) and every Administration since Carter has offered varying degrees of support

Public opposition has been minimal, though a different Administration could generate an increase (Sargentich, 1997). Relatively few complaints have been registered that the public interest is undermined by the Act. The major exceptions to the overall pattern have tended toward complaints about favoritism generally shown to smaller firms rather than poor regulatory outcomes (e.g., Pierce, 1998). But even those are not necessarily biting. A lengthy legal analysis written shortly after enactment concluded that RFA was "special interest with a balance" (Verkuil, 1982, p. 271).

6.4.2.2 State Replication

If imitation is the sincerest form of flattery, the actions of American states indicate that the Regulatory Flexibility Act has had a positive effect. From nothing in 2002, 19 of the 50 states by October 2006 implemented regulatory flexibility through statute or executive order (U.S. Small Business Administration, Office of Advocacy, 2007, p. 45). Most others have adopted parts and/or are considering legislation to implement regulatory flexibility in some fashion. Just seven states have not taken steps. The seven are among the least populous, most conservative, and most likely to consider small business impacts in the first place.

States notoriously follow one another. So, successful early adopters proved the key. According to Shawne Carter McGibbon Deputy Chief Counsel for Advocacy, "... success stories from "early adopters" helped convince other states to jump on the bandwagon" (McGibbon, 2007), e.g., U.S. Small Business Administration, Office of Advocacy (2007, pp. 46–47). Regulatory flexibility became a state economic development strategy (McGibbon, 2007).

6.4.2.3 Training Rule-Makers

Training is an input rather than an output for evaluation purposes. But training of regulators appears critical to achieving improved output. For example, reasonable people can differ over one of the Act's critical terms, "a significant impact" on "a substantial number" of small businesses. Even though frequently preparing regulatory analyses, few regulators have had direct experience with small business data or RFA. After halting attempts to train agency rule-makers in their RFA responsibilities, Executive Order 13272 gave training a huge boost in 2003. It required Advocacy to establish a formal training program for agency rule-makers in order to clarify terms and responsibilities under the Act.

Advocacy determined that 66 departments, agencies, and commissions created rules (U.S. Small Business Administration, Office of Advocacy, 2007, p. 4). It has now completed training of personnel from every one of those agencies, many on more than one occasion (Sullivan, 2007b). In fact, after an initial training session, the Internal Revenue Service (IRS), historically one of the most recalcitrant agencies in complying, required all of its regulatory staff to take the training (McGibbon, 2007).

Training does not guarantee compliance. But it seems to have had an effect (McGibbon, 2007). Following training, "most agencies are more willing to share draft documents with Advocacy in an effort to improve their RFA compliance" (U.S. Small Business Administration, Office of Advocacy, 2007, p. 4) and the level of compliance appears elevated.

6.4.2.4 Problems Remain

Problems remain. They indicate continuing struggles to bring agencies into compliance with both the letter and spirit of the law. The Office of Advocacy sent more than 40 formal communications to agencies in FY 2006 on some aspect of their performance relative to RFA (U.S. Small Business Administration, Office of Advocacy, 2007, p. 4). Over 90% were critical.

Advocacy has a small staff working on RFA issues – about 16 professionals. Fourteen are lawyers; two are economists. The number of Advocacy employees working on RFA has remained stable over the years; so has the distribution among lawyers and economists. This distribution indicates the basic issue remains agency compliance rather than analysis, data issues, or the merits of alternatives. Many of the lawyers are senior people whose skills long ago transcended the legal implications of RFA compliance. But as people leave and new ones are hired, success in achieving goals suggests a gradual shift toward economists. That has not occurred.

Small business interests and/or observers suggest additional modifications to the legislation. Some of their proposals appear to have merit; others do not; and, still others appear irrelevant to the present effectiveness issue. For example, the courts ruled that indirect costs are not covered by RFA. But, federal agencies sometimes delegate rule-making responsibility to the states and claim their actions have indirect impacts (Sullivan, 2007a). That is a clear violation of the spirit, if not the letter, of law and requires modification of the Act. Chief Counsel Sullivan has been particularly concerned about codifying E.O. 13272 (Sullivan, 2007b). That idea has considerable merit since a new Administration hostile to regulatory flexibility could repeal the Executive Order before anyone noticed.

A pressing need for data is evident as they are requisite to measure RFA effectiveness, let alone to identify problem areas and slackers (Francis and Joensen, 2001). Some agencies are clearly more compliant than others. But without data, no one can be held accountable. Problem areas cannot be identified. Examples and cases are persuasive, but they do not provide ongoing evidence of progress or lack thereof. The savings estimates noted earlier are no substitute as they address the indirect rather than the direct effectiveness of the Act.

6.4.3 Entrepreneurs and Small Business Owners

The Regulatory Flexibility Act was crafted in an era (late 1970s) when the distinction between entrepreneurs and small business owners was not popularly recognized. The two were usually equated as they often are today. However, the Act's intent was to assist small businesses with their regulatory burdens and if a subset of high-growth or entrepreneurial businesses benefited, so much the better. The terms "entrepreneur" or "entrepreneurial business" were rarely found in congressional debate on RFA and then virtually always as a synonym for small business. Thus, as a general rule, entrepreneurs benefit from the Act to the extent that small business is entrepreneurial.

The de jure equality of the two groups under RFA begs associated issues. For example, are entrepreneurs more likely to be impacted by regulations than non-entrepreneurial small business owners? Are entrepreneurs more cognizant of the regulatory environment and hence more likely to draw attention to regulatory problems that RFA might ameliorate? Do entrepreneurs face different types of regulatory issues than other small business owners? Is RFA enforced to promote the interests of entrepreneurs? These issues remain unanswered.

6.5 Conclusions and Lessons Learned

The American regulatory system is heavily reliant on cost-benefit analysis for evaluating the merit of proposed rules, particularly the largest in terms of cost. Comparative risk assessment is a second tool in the system. The Regulatory Flexibility Act is a small business focused adjunct, though it attains primacy on less costly issues that still have a substantial impact on a significant number of small businesses. That makes the Act effectively the third component of the regulatory suite designed to evaluate regulatory impacts.

The effectiveness of the Regulatory Flexibility Act measured against its four original objectives can only be assessed subjectively. But on balance, the results argue for a favorable judgment. The Act has produced positive outcomes, though they are neither consistent nor earth-shattering. Clearly, the latter half of the Act's tenure has fashioned significantly more results than the former.

Changes in both law and practice helped along the way. Still, many advocates are disappointed. But to what extent is disappointment a function of results and, what of expectations?

The legitimate frustration of RFA advocates has been the repeated failure of agencies to search for disproportionate impacts and regulatory alternatives as the law requires them to do. The law's initial failure to give one authority serious enforcement powers was a grave shortcoming. That problem, now thought to be addressed, was compounded by a still existing failure to establish a data collection system that allows anyone to monitor progress and substantive problems as well as to identify agency scofflaws. Training of rule-makers in RFA began intensively only in the last few years. While successful by all accounts, that assessment is subjective and covers a relatively short time frame. In hindsight, training should have begun immediately upon enactment. A few substantive issues such as inclusion and/or definition of indirect costs remain outstanding.

Often lost in appreciating the viability of RFA is the unwavering political support offered by small business people, small business-oriented organizations, and public officials of both major political parties. That broad support could only occur because the Act demands a process rather than an outcome. Small business would have preferred simple burden reduction legislation. That largely explains any disappointment with the Act. But direct burden reduction legislation was not to be politically, except in the most egregious or obvious situations. That leaves the Regulatory Flexibility Act to provide small business some reduction in the regulatory burden without the liability of a zero-sum game.

References

Bradford, CS (2004) Does Size Matter? An Economic Analysis of Small Business Exemptions from Regulation. J Small Emerging Bus L. 8:1–37

Brock, WA, Evans DS (1985) The Economics of Regulatory Tiering. Rand J Econ. 16:3 398–409

Brock, WA, Evans DS (1986) The Economics of Small Businesses: Their Role and Regulation in the U.S. Economy. Holmes & Meier, New York

Crain, WM (2005) The Impact of Regulatory Costs on Small Firms. Contract SBAHQ-03-M-0522, Office of Advocacy, U.S. Small Business Administration, Washington

Crain, WM, Hopkins TD (2001) The Impact of Regulatory Costs on Small Firms. Contract SBAHQ-00-R-0027, Office of Advocacy, U.S. Small Business Administration, Washington

Francis WJ, Joensen, MA (2001) An Evaluation of Compliance with the Regulatory Flexibility Act by Federal Agencies, Contract SBAHQ-99-C-0011, Office of Advocacy, U.S. Small Business Administration, Washington

Gates, SM, Leuschner, KJ (eds) (2007) In the Name of Entrepreneurship? The Logic and Effects of Special Regulatory Treatment for Small Businesses. Rand Corporation, Santa Monica, CA

Glover, J (2007) Chief Counsel for Advocacy (1994–2000), Office of Advocacy, U.S. Small Business Administration. Currently, Executive Director of the Small Business Technology Coalition. Interview with author.

Hahn, RW (2004) The Economic Analysis of Regulation: A Response to the Critics. Univ Chic Law Rev. 71:1021–1054
Holman, KW (2006) The Regulatory Flexibility Act at 25: Is the Law Achieving Its Goal? Fordham Urban Law J. 33:1119–1137
Hopkins, TD (1995) A Survey of Regulatory Burdens. Contract SBA-8029-OA-93. Office of Advocacy U.S. Small Business Administration, Washington
Langer, A (2007) Senior Manager, Regulatory Affairs, National Federation of Independent Business, Testimony Before the Committee on Small Business, U.S. House of Representatives, December 12
McGibbon, SC (2007) Deputy Chief Counsel, Office of Advocacy, U.S. Small Business Administration. Interview and correspondence with the author.
McKevitt, JD (1977). Washington Counsel, National Federation of Independent Business, Testimony Before the Administrative Practices Subcommittee of the U.S. Senate Judiciary Committee, October 7
Morrison, J (2007) Staff Member, Senate Small Business Committee (1976–1980). Currently, President of the Small Business Exporters' Association. Interview with the author.
Parker, RW (2003) Grading the Government. Univ Chic Law Rev. 70:1345–1486
Pierce, RJ, Jr (1998) Small Is Not Beautiful: The Case Against Special Regulatory Treatment of Small Firms. Adm Law Rev. 50:537–578
Phelps, ED (2001) The Clever Cunning Bureaucrats: Why the Small Business Regulatory Enforcement Act Isn't Working. Pub. Cont. L. J., 31:123–142
Sargentich, TO (1997) The Small Business Regulatory Enforcement Act. Adm Law Rev. 49:23–137
See, MR (2006) Willful Blindness: Federal Agencies' Failure to Comply with the Regulatory Flexibility Act's Periodic Review Requirement – and Current Proposals to Invigorate the Act. Fordham Urban Law J. 33:1199–1255
Skrzycki, C (2008) Top 10 Rules the SBA Doesn't Like, The Washington Post, March 11, p. D2
Sullivan, TM (2007a) Chief Counsel for Advocacy (2001), Testimony Before the Committee on Small Business, U.S. House of Representatives, December 6, www.sba.gov/advo/laws/test07_1206.html
Sullivan, TM (2007b) Chief Counsel for Advocacy (2001), Office of Advocacy, U.S. Small Business Administration, interviews with the author.
U.S. Government Accountability Office (2006) Regulatory Flexibility Act: Congress Should Revisit and Clarify Elements of the Act to Improve Its Effectiveness (GAO-06-998T), Testimony of J. Christopher Mihm before the Subcommittee on Commercial and Administrative Law, Committee on the Judiciary, U.S. House of Representatives. July 20
U.S. Regulatory Council (1981) Tiering Regulations: A Practical Guide. U.S. Regulatory Council, Washington
U.S. Small Business Administration, Office of Advocacy (2003) A Guide for Government Agencies: How to Comply with the Regulatory Flexibility Act. U.S. Small Business Administration, Office of Advocacy, Washington
U.S. Small Business Administration, Office of Advocacy (2006) Report on the Regulatory Flexibility Act, FY 2005. U.S. Small Business Administration, Office of Advocacy, Washington
U.S. Small Business Administration, Office of Advocacy (2007) Report on the Regulatory Flexibility Act, FY 2006. U.S. Small Business Administration, Office of Advocacy, Washington
U.S. White House Commission on Small Business (1980) America's Small Business Economy: Agenda for Action. U.S. White House Commission on Small Business, Washington
Verkuil, PR (1982) A Critical Guide to the Regulatory Flexibility Act. Duke Law J. 1982:213–276
Weidenbaum, M (1997) Regulatory Process Reform: From Ford to Clinton. Regulation 20:1–7
Ziegler, H (1979) The Politics of Small Business. Arno Press, New York

Chapter 7
Tanzania and the Problem of the Missing Middle: A Regulatory Reform Case of the United Republic of Tanzania

Bede Lyimo

Abstract A diagnostic report submitted to the Government of the United Republic of Tanzania in 2004 revealed that 89% of real property and 98% of all businesses operate in the extra-legal economy.[1] Data from the second cycle of the Poverty Reduction Strategy program shows that about 36% of the population live in conditions of income poverty. A National Development Vision 2025 aims at eradication of poverty by 2025[2] which calls for double digit GDP growth over the coming 15 years. This is possible for Tanzania, given its rich natural resources endowment, subject to transformation of the private sector into a dynamic engine of growth through formalization and growth of entrepreneurs that are the drivers of broad-based and shared growth.

Tanzania's dilemma of poverty in the midst of plenty is captured in the concept of the "missing middle", featuring failure of micro firms to graduate into small and medium enterprises that would create a demonstration effect of the benefits of formalization. Tanzania needs efficient mechanisms for contract enforcement to stimulate economic linkages and encourage commercial banking lending. Tanzania needs an efficient labor market, focusing on skills improvement and competence rather than mandatory legislation as the basis for higher returns to labor. Tanzania, and countries with similar problems, need more efficient systems of information management on the business sector and registration of movable and immovable property. Implementation of the program for Business Environment Strengthening for Tanzania addresses these problems. This chapter highlights the hassles and

[1] Institute of Liberty & Democracy (ILD), Lima Peru, 2005. "Property & Business Formalization Program Diagnostic Report for the Government of the United Republic of Tanzania", Report.

[2] The President's Office, Planning Commission, 1999. The Tanzania Development Vision 2025, Dar es Salaam, Government Printer.

B. Lyimo (✉),
The Better Regulation Unit, Dar es Salaam, Tanzania, CRDB Bank Limited, Dar es Salaam, Tanzania
e-mail: bedelyimo@fastmail.fm

A. Nijsen et al. (eds.), *Business Regulation and Public Policy*,
International Studies in Entrepreneurship 20, DOI 10.1007/978-0-387-77678-1_7,

vicissitudes of change management in a regulatory reform process in a developing country environment, and the instruments that are available to handle the challenges involved.

7.1 Introduction

Tanzania is one of 49 Least Developed Countries (LDCs), formally defined by the United Nations system as low income countries with a large proportion of their population living on less than USD 1.00 per day and generally with a GNI of less than USD 1,000 per annum. The economy is characterized by a large informal sector, estimated to accommodate 70% of the economically active population, and approximately 89% of all real property being located in the extra-legal economy. (ILD et al) The general perception is that access to finance is a major constraint against business formalization and growth. Yet, there is emerging an extensive and growing banking sector with substantial resources while lending to the SME sector remains relatively insignificant. This can only be partially explained by dearth of innovative instruments for micro-financing. More fundamental is the fact that impediments in the regulatory framework raises business and financial risks, largely related to difficulties in accessing collateral and recovery of loans, that raises the cost of capital and discourages lending to the Micro Small and Medium sized Enterprises (MSMEs).

This has given rise to a two-tract fundamental problem. First, although there is substantial number of micro-finance institutions targeting micro enterprises, their impact is limited and will remain limited as long as micro enterprises cannot reach the resources of the formal commercial banking sector. Second, the larger commercial financial institutions target middle and large scale enterprises, making smaller firms that transcend the fine line between micro and medium sized firms, bear the brunt of the financial sector's credit shyness which is the genesis of the problem of the missing middle. The essence of this problem is discouragement of emergence of micro firms, and limitation to the few who emerge from growing and graduating into larger enterprises, briefly referred to in the growth literature as "the missing middle". Creating conditions for the emergence and survival of the "missing-middle", in Tanzania and in similar countries, calls for drastic reforms in the regulatory environment.

Apart from the Millennium Development Goals (MDGs) which target reducing poverty by 50% by 2015, Tanzania is also implementing a National Development Vision 2025 whose goal is to eradicate poverty and graduating to a middle income economy with a GDP exceeding the threshold of USD 1,000 per annum by 2025. This vision calls for a relatively high rate of pro-poor growth in the range of 8–10% from henceforth and through the intervening years. This is a tall order, but one that is achievable based on the lessons of economic history on the achievements of the Asian tigers, including

Malaysia and Thailand,[3] during the 1980s and 1990s, and Vietnam in the current decade.

7.1.1 Regulatory Constraints in the Investment Climate

It is in this context that in 1996, Tanzania adapted for implementation an export development strategy (EDS),[4] targeting the tripling of exports in five years, as an instrument for stimulating rapid growth. The EDS was seen as a critical tool for assessing the global market as the source of effective demand levels that can raise output and income generation to achieve and sustain 10% growth, based largely on transformation of the agricultural base, agro-processing and high potential in the services sectors, including tourism and the infrastructure services. The EDS called for prioritization of legal and regulatory reforms as one of four policy pillars that constitute the prerequisite for successful export growth. This prioritization was confirmed by the findings of a series of Paralel reviews of the investment climate undertaken by stakeholders in the public and private sector and consensus on the imperative for change.

From the perspective of the public sector, the Investors Roadmap undertaken with USAID support and published in 1996,[5] identified four levels of problem areas that mitigate against investment in Tanzania – business entry, business operations, reporting requirements and import/export procedures. A sequential review undertaken in 1999 confirmed that ad hoc mitigation measures did not lead to major improvement and more systemic reforms were necessary. From the perspective of the private sector, a review commissioned by the Confederation of Tanzania Industry and undertaken by the Economic and Social Research Foundation, identified a set of 30 legislations that constituted a major impediment in the legal framework and 60 others that were a source of considerable impediment, and called for measures to address the situation. The outcome of consultations based on BEST was essentially designed to address these mitigating constraints with business registration targeting simplified entry conditions, business regulation targeting better reporting requirements and better operations being possible through a more efficient labor market and dispute settlement.

---

[3] Lindaner D.L., Roemer M. (eds), 1994: Asia and Africa Legacies and Opportunities in Development, ICEG and HIID, San Fransisco, Book

[4] The Tanzania Task Force on Export Development, 1996: Tanzania Export Development Strategy and Action Plan (1997–2001), Report. Government of the United Republic of Tanzania, Dar es Salaam.

[5] Coopers & Lybrand, 1996 & 1999. Investors Roadmap of Tanzania, Prepared for the United Republic of Tanzania. Report Dar es Salaam.

7.1.2 Objectives

Reform targeting formalization program identifies two categories of objectives: formalization of businesses through easier entry, operations and exit through simplified registration, streamlined tax regime and simplified labor and social security system; and reforms to allow for growth including dispute settlement, contract formation and enforcement, and business information. In addition, it also identifies the need for a personal identification system (citizens) registry.

Apart from those specific interventions, there is clear realization and appreciation of the need for cross-cutting or cross-sector measures that are necessary to contribute to economic transformation including the harmonization / simplification of administrative procedures and requirements that are imposed on business through regulatory licensing or various reporting requirements. It is envisaged to tackle these impediments through sectoral regulatory licensing reforms. At this juncture, it is useful to look briefly into the various socio-economic structural reform programs that have included components of regulatory reforms and the outcome of their implementation. It is in this context that the necessity of a dedicated program for addressing legal and regulatory impediments in the investment climate can be appreciated.

7.2 Regulatory Reform Initiatives in Tanzania

Over the past 20 years, Tanzania has implemented approximately five major institutional reform programs that have included legislative changes as a major component. These include: The Financial Institutions and Legal Sector Management Upgrading (FILM-UP) initiated in the early 1990s, the Public Sector Reform Program (commenced in 2000); the Local Government Reform Program; the Legal Sector Reform Program (LSRP); the Property and Business Formalization Program and the Program for Business Environment Strengthening for Tanzania, adopted for implementation in 2002.

7.2.1 FILM-UP and Other Reform Programs

During the early 1990s, the Government of the United Republic of Tanzania, with the support of the World Bank, introduced the first phase of regulatory reforms under a project "Financial Institutions and Legal Sector Management Upgrading" (FILM-UP).[6] FILM-UP was the first landmark step that sought to extend reforms under the wider Structural Adjustment Program (SAP) towards

---

[6] FRIGO Consult, 1994. Financial Institutions and Legal Sector Management Upgrading (FILM-UP), Legal Sector Study, Report. Government of the United Republic of Tanzania, Dar es Salaam.

the regulatory framework. SAP had been adopted in 1986, as a long term package of reforms to transform a central command economy into a private sector driven market economy, starting with transformation of monetary and fiscal policies and private sector development based on divestiture of State Owned Enterprises (SOEs).

Among other things, FILM-UP prioritized new legislation in three areas: Creating the legal mandate for privatization of approximately 400 State Owned Enterprises (SOEs); introducing an Investment Promotion Act to stimulate conditions for attracting Foreign Direct Investment; and establishing a legal framework to support the operations of an efficient labor market. FILM-UP also sought to look into the rules and regulations for business by reviewing the insolvency laws. FILM-UP had limited achievements, largely in the area of financial sectors. However, initiatives to reform the labor market legal framework and insolvency laws did not take off in the sense that most draft bills produced under the report, were never submitted to the legislative processes due largely to lack of participation in the process and consequent poor ownership.

Subsequent initiatives in the late 1990s led to implementation of the Public Sector Reform Program (PSRP) and Local Government Reform Program (LGRP), two programs targeting institutional capacity building in the civil service and local government services with minimal attention to regulatory framework reforms. For instance, reforms under the PSRP focused largely on restructuring of government Ministries, Departments and Agencies, commercialization of services that could not be privatized and outsourcing of services that could be more efficiently provided by the private sector. It also focused on retooling and retraining of government institutions in better delivery of core services. The local government reform program also covered the same areas at the local government level. Continuing complaints from the private sector concerning constraints and impediments to competitiveness that continued to prevail in the system galvanized the call for the need for systematic review of the legal and regulatory regime.

The latest program on the regulatory reform agenda is the Legal Sector Reform Program (LSRP) which seeks to transform the legal sector through tackling institutional reforms as well as the underlying legal framework. The demands placed on the legal sector reform program are huge and formidable and there is clear need for LSRP to focus on delivery of criminal justice. Although initiation of LSRP started in the mid-1990s, actual implementation was initiated on a small quick-win ad interim initiative while consultations proceeded on the fundamental reform package whose implementation started in 2006. In the final analysis, the main interventions of LSRP focuses on criminal justice as well as the reform of the institutions which span service delivery in the legal sector.

Two other programs that constitute landmarks on the regulatory reform landmark are the Property and Business Formalization Program (PBFP) (ILD et al) and the Program for Business Environment Strengthening for

Tanzania.[7] Both share the common objective of creating the legal and institutional framework to encourage and promote economic formalization and resolving the problem of the missing middle. The PBFP has contributed tremendously to creating positive publicity on the essence of better regulation and consensus building in the strategic direction of regulatory reforms. The magnitude of the challenge on hand is apparent in evidence which confirms the dormant potential of the private sector hidden in unregistered property evidenced by the fact that about 80% of all property holdings in Dar es Salaam is unregistered property.

7.2.2 The Export Development Strategy

In 1996, the Government of the United Republic of Tanzania received a report for an "Export Development Strategy"[8] articulating strategies for tripling national exports from the then annual average of USD 600 million to an average of USD 18 million within the timeframe of 5 years. The approach was based on building on a rich natural resources endowment base and comparative advantages inherent in six high profile sectors/sub-sectors including tourism, mining, light manufacturing agribusiness, handicrafts, transit trade and fisheries, converting comparative advantages in these sectors to competitive edges and accessing preferential regional and global markets.

The EDS identified four strategic pillars through which government intervention would bring about the transformation underpinning the process of creating the necessary private sector competitive advantages i.e. policy alignment; institutional alignment; infrastructure development; and private sector capacity building. The first strategic pillar on policy alignment called for prioritization of regulatory framework reforms. This pillar provided further rationale for designing a holistic and comprehensive legal and regulatory reform program.

Policy alignment entails interventions to mitigate against constraints in two areas i.e. the legal system and the regulatory framework through action on ten policy priority actions that include, among other things, modernization of commercial law including the company law, bankruptcy legislation, intellectual property legislation, arbitration ordinance; updating laws through review, over-haul, rationalization and modernization of legal system; address administrative inconveniences inherent in duplication and overlap in trade/business licensing regime; revision of import/export or customs procedures; and clarification and development of land policy. In Tanzania, these interventions have

[7] THE UNITED REPUBLIC OF TANZANIA, 2003. Programme for Business Environment Strengthening for Tanzania (BEST) Report, Dar es Salaam.

[8] Tanzania Export Development Strategy and Action Plan (1997–2001): A Dynamic Strategy to Expand and Diversify Exports; Tanzania Task Force on Export Development, Dar es Salaam June 1996.

taken the format of the Program for Business Environment Strengthening for Tanzania (BEST), as a comprehensive package targeting the major impediments in a holistic approach.

7.2.3 Program for Business Environment Strengthening for Tanzania (BEST)

BEST was designed as the vehicle for carrying forward the recommendations of the EDS and for responding to continuing private sector calls for improvements in the business environment as well as government interventions for the development of the private sector as the engine of growth. Two specific initiatives coming from the private sector that influenced the adoption of BEST included the first Investors Road Map 1996 survey, and a study on "Legal, Regulatory and Judicial Reforms" commissioned by the Confederation of Tanzania Industry (CTI) and undertaken by the Economic and Social Research Foundation (ESRF) in 2000.[9]

Four bilateral Development Partners[10] undertook commitment to support the implementation of BEST. Subsequent revision of the program to reflect the event of the World Bank joining the basket of program financiers has deepened its coverage to systematic legal, regulatory reforms and institutional capacity building in nine components comprised of four core areas. This coverage encompasses approximately 70% of the factors that underpin the World Bank's Doing Business indicators. The nine components are: Business Registration, Regulation and Exit; Land Administration Reforms; Labor Law Reforms; Commercial Dispute Resolution; Budget support to Tanzania Investment Centre; BEST Zanzibar Component; Support for Private Sector Advocacy capacity building; and Program Management capacity building.

7.3 Policy Instruments and Institutional Transformation for a Quality Regulatory Framework: Tanzania's Experience

The evolution of regulatory reforms in the industrialized countries in the 1980s took the form of deregulation in the UK and US and regulatory simplification in most European Union countries and targeted the objective of reduction of

[9] The CTI/ESRF study identified 30 laws that were considered as having a major adverse impact on business competitiveness that required major reform and more than 60 others with a less significant impact.

[10] The four Development Partners supporting BEST are: the United Kingdom (Department for International Development – DfID); Danish International Development Agency – DANIDA (Denmark); the Swedish International Development Agency – Sida (Sweden); and the Royal Netherlands Embassy (The Netherlands).

transaction costs. This was achieved through elimination of cumbersome compliance requirements that do not contribute to value addition in production transformation processes but merely seek to meet government reporting requirements and compliance to regulatory regimes necessary for the protection of specific socioeconomic interests such as health, security and environmental considerations. For most firms, transaction costs are the outcome of the time and money it takes to process the compliance requirements. Compliance requirements also create enforcement costs on the part of the Government as well as opportunity costs relating to the lost investments that do not materialize due to excessive impediments that discourage foreign investors or force domestic investors to operate in the informal or Paralegal economy.

Apart from the limited success of FILM-UP, Tanzania also missed a number of opportunities for integrating rigorous regulatory reforms into institutional reform programs designed in the late 1990s and whose implementation started in 2000 such as the PSRP, the LGRP and LSRF, largely because there was no demand coming from the institutions that had the mandate for the sectors in which major regulatory reforms were needed. However, there was apparent demand for these reforms at the political level as evidenced by the initiatives that led to the adoption of the Property and Business Formalization Program.

7.3.1 From Deregulation to Better Regulation

The drive for industry competitiveness in the 1980s crystallized in the concept of competitive advantages as a stimulant for growth and income generation. On one hand, it identifies the government interventions that are necessary to create a platform for competitive advantages. On the other hand, it also delineates factors that underpin the role of the private sector in the continuous striving for higher levels of competitiveness, the drivers that influence those factors such as innovation and technology, as well as creativity and better management practices. Policy reforms, including key elements of the investment climate, are, indeed one of the most effective, low cost initiatives that countries can implement to maximize competitiveness even in situations of limited resources.

Evidence on the efficacy of regulatory reform tools and instruments like the "Swedish Guillotine", the UK's Deregulation Act, and more generic instruments like Regulatory Impact Assessment (RIA) and the Standard Cost Model, within the EU and OECD countries have provided a range of alternatives for the realization of the goal of reducing transaction costs comprising of regulatory and administrative burdens. These developments have produced irreversible evidence of the importance of implementing regulatory reforms to complement achievements in macro-economic stability and infrastructure development, as the prerequisites for the success of other interventions targeting building private sector core competencies for competitiveness such as better education and health facilities, skills development, entrepreneurship, creativity and innovation for competitiveness.

Developing countries now generally accept the power of better regulation as an expedient instrument for minimizing man-made constraints that encumber business competitiveness. However, not all countries are equally ready to go the full length in adopting existing international good practices to inform the process of implementation. This is the challenge, that Sub Saharan Africa, home of 35 out of all 49 LDCs faces, that success of poverty reduction initiatives and measures will depend on success of efforts to improve the investment climate.

For instance, potential micro-level entrepreneurs, who can start a small business with an outlay of US$ 200.00, cannot afford to meet requirements that demand investment of 100% of per capita GDP to cover business entry requirements including dealing with licenses. They will find it impossible to surmount impediments resulting from the long time lag in the process of accessing business location premises, and cannot get fair and expedient justice when their business transactions end in business disputes. Hence Africa's drive to achieve the MDGs as well as national objectives on poverty reduction has to include policy, legal and regulatory reforms as a prerequisite.

7.3.2 Strategic Policy Instruments for Better Regulation

In principle, the initiation of the reform process started with a review of the existing stock of laws and regulations and its inherent problems, and building the rationale for reforms as well as the strategic format of those reforms. This was accomplished in the design of BEST and its modification to include focus on institutional capacity building as an integral component of regulatory reforms. Essentially, this means emphasis on reforming existing regulations to address identified impediments. However, history shows that there has been a tendency for the reasons that led to hardening of regulations over time for impediments to creep back into the regulatory framework. This highlights the need for tackling and improving the existing stock of regulations as well as initiating measures to manage future flow of regulations to ensure that the regime does not descend into an impeding investment climate over time in the future. Essentially, the core instruments for managing the existing stock of regulations are different from those available for managing future stock of regulations. Further, while changing of existing legislation can be accomplished through the application of a specific tool that leads to the repeal or amendment of existing laws, managing the future flow of regulations involves the management of the processes of regulation.

7.3.2.1 Stock of Existing Regulations

This concept seeks to identify and address constraints prevalent in existing and operational legislation and the regulations and administrative measures put in place to facilitate their implementation. A compliance cost review undertaken in 2004 and a diagnostic report on the status of the regulatory sector licensing regime submitted in 2006 identify major problems in existing stock of legislation.

The studies confirmed that the prevailing sectoral policies, the corresponding laws used as instruments for the enforcement of these policies and the regulations and administrative procedures that are put in place to facilitate implementation of these laws, have led to the emergence of a legal regime that imposes unduly high transaction costs for businesses. Other constraints relating to the regulatory framework include high administrative costs and low institutional capacity and infrastructure constraints in public sector institutions responsible for administering the legal and regulatory framework.

A report on the review of the Tanzanian regime published in 2006[11] has identified six major constraining factors that include:

- lack of inter-institutional coordination, increasing duplication and overlap in conformity requirements as well as the problem of multiplicity of compliance instruments and enforcement institutions;
- focus on revenue generation in the adoption and application of regulations;
- rudimentary business classification systems to facilitate systematic business categorization from the perspective of need for regulating;
- regulatory agencies' institutional capacity limitations including little or no use of ICT facilities and infrastructure;
- lack of information on compliance requirements on the part of users; and
- poor enforcement of regulations and low levels of accountability on the part of enforcing agencies.

Three instruments have been applied in resolving constraints in regulatory regimes from the perspective of stock of regulations in the emerging literature. These are the Deregulation Act; the Swedish Guillotine and the Standard Cost Model. In principle, all three seek to address reform of existing legislation in a standard manner with emphasis on variations. The Deregulation Act targets repeal and streamlining of existing primary legislation in an expedited fashion by creating a single parliamentary mandate to review a large number of statutes. The Swedish Guillotine seeks to address largely incognito regulations and/or administrative procedures that tend to crop up at both national and local government levels as public institutions engage in the process of seeking information, generating revenue or enforcing regulations. The guillotine achieves the objective of identifying and eliminating regulations that have become obsolete or irrelevant, duplicative information collection instruments and revenue collection tools that legitimize payment of taxes before income is earned or the imposition of multiple taxes administered by a multiplicity of institutions. Available experience in the application of the Guillotine in Sub-Saharan

[11] Bannock Consulting, 2006. "Consulting Services for the Introduction of a Regulatory Business Licensing System. Report for the Programme for Business Environment Strengthening for Tanzania, Dar es Salaam".

Africa[12] confirms the efficacy of this instrument in identifying and eliminating regulations and administrative requirements that do not serve any useful purpose, by placing the onus of justifying the need or otherwise of each regulation to the regulating agency. Likewise, the Standard Cost model is a useful instrument for determining the magnitude of costs emerging from an overbearing regime and the necessity of reducing the unnecessary burdens in terms of costs. Its application requires the existence of reliable data which therefore reduces its efficacy in a developing country environment.

7.3.2.2 Sustainability of Reform Process (Future Flow of Regulations)

The stock and flow concept in regulatory reforms can be portrayed more clearly through an analogy drawn from the medical field where the stock concept is akin to curative measures to existing ills while the flow concept is closer to preventive medicine which seeks to take a proactive stance to prevent the occurrence of ills. Consequently, the practice in regulatory reforms tends towards phasing of implementation with the curative approach to clear the existing laws of known and unknown constraints taking precedence over measures to address the flow "of new regulations" through ensuring that new constraints do not crop up in the regulatory framework in the course of formulating policy reforms and enacting new laws and regulations. Major instruments available for ensuring good governance and high quality of laws and regulations from current and future reforms include: "Simplification" of administrative procedures; Regulatory Best Practice; and Regulatory Impact Assessment.

The role of computerization in storage, analysis and retrieval of information that is the primary domain of government services to the public sector has created potential for tremendous transformation of government service delivery to the private sector. This is particularly true given that the services called for in the four priority areas depend primarily on efficiency in registration systems that encompass natural persons, business persons and property. Even in the case of efficient dispute resolution, efficient handling of information remains a critical factor to success, as exemplified in the efficacy of computerization of court registries. Efficient registries provide effective mechanisms for managing the regulatory regimes emerging out of reform processes.

Finally, efficient enforcement is an issue with major consequences. For many developing economies, the exigencies of regulation are embedded in a culture of compliance based on enforcement largely through the threat of sanctions, specifically fines, closure of businesses or even imprisonment. There are many cases where goods belonging to traders have been impounded as part of enforcement processes further eroding a very thin capital base for emerging micro entrepreneurs. The end-product of such draconian measures for non-criminal

[12] Musau, B. 2007. Licensing Reform in Kenya, Paper Presented to Workshop on "Licensing Reform and Regulatory Governance for Private Sector Development", Nairobi, Kenya, August 29, 2007.

misdemeanors is the demise of micro and small businesses that discourages innovation and encourages entrepreneurs to set up shop in the Paralegal economy. There is a need for reorientation of compliance towards education for voluntary compliance backed by ethics and codes of conduct administered by business associations. A more systematic approach to compliance enforcement in situations that are not easily amenable to self regulation is that of risk-assessment as a tool for supporting the focus of compliance enforcement to areas of high risk and sampling approaches to implementation.

7.3.2.3 Institutional Capacity Building as an Instrument for Policy Implementation

Institutional development including infrastructure development and capacity building in the public and private sector is such a critical factor that it has become an instrument for efficient reform. The success of even the simplest reform program depends on the extent to which the institutions responsible for reform are oriented towards accepting and implementing change. A conservative institutional framework that tends to resist change and maintain the status quo creates difficulties in adoption of complex changes that may require the introduction of totally new ways of doing business and delivering services to the private sector. Institutional capacity building comprises of human resources development to create requisite skills as well as building the institutional infrastructure, software and working procedures / customs embedded in the vision and mission of a regulatory entity.

Creating new procedures and customs entails human capacity building to create a crop of reformers as well as adoption of national criteria for systematic regulation and entrenchment of tools and instruments of analysis. This type of capacity building is necessary to ensure that regulating agencies are capable of determining the extent to which problems in the investment climate can be resolved solely through regulatory measures and, in that case, the form of regulation that is best suited to address the problem on hand and available alternative measures. In Tanzania's case, decisions have already been made in government to adopt Regulatory Impact Assessment and the underlying concept of Regulatory Best Practice as the national approach to improving the existing regulatory framework and managing the process of change that determines the quality of future laws and regulations.

A fundamental element of institutional reforms that contribute to lower transaction costs involving reducing compliance requirements imposed on the business sector is based on the concept of one-stop-shop center for provision of government services to the people and single point interface in collection of primary information from the people by Government institutions. The public sector's need for information on the citizenry and their socioeconomic undertakings has always been a source of administrative requirements that bring in additional impediments in the form of extra costs and time that have to be spent in responding to government enquiries. Often, different ministries have sent numerous questionnaires to the business sector demanding for information of all types, ranging from business performance to data on employment in spite of the existence of a national statistics bureau whose function is collection, analysis and processing of primary data for use by other government institutions.

The spreading use of ICT through increasing spread of e-government means that it is now possible for government to collect information from the business community only once through a designated institution and for all other public users to share that information. This means that it is possible to have a single interface between the public and the private sector for purposes of collection of data on the national economy and emerging trends, through recognition and designation of unique primary data collector and processing institutions and the linkage between primary collectors with other public users.

Emerging experience shows that enhanced recourse to the concept of "one-stop shop" for government service delivery to members of the public and "one-stop-center" for collection of primary data from the general public for use by government institutions is the essence of a national ICT-based registration system. There is an ongoing process of debate and consultations to determine the extent to which this concept can be used to improve information collection and analysis as an input into policy making and implementation, and how service delivery to the private sector can be streamlined through, for instance, a web-based solution that makes it easier for entrepreneur to process the requirements for business start-up and reporting obligations through the internet.

7.4 Emerging Experience in Tanzania

Reverting to the four priority areas that form the cornerstone of Tanzanian regulatory reforms clearly confirms the superiority of adoption and implementation of ICT-based solutions. Study tours to countries that are successfully implementing ICT-based solutions reveal the following.

7.4.1 Land Registration and Titling

An ICT-based solution on data capturing, processing, storage and retrieval results in an efficient system where paper-based data that is required for efficient service delivery is reduced to minimal documentation that can be stored in a comparatively small space. In this instance, access to both electronic and paper records for, say, a given urban or rural plot for the purposes of registering a transaction can be accomplished within minutes. Compare this with the difficulty of tracing files in a solely paper-based manual system when you have to deal with several hundred thousand files and the live possibility of misplacement of a file either through human error or deliberate initiatives.

The loss of files is known to have undermined efficiency in the timely delivery of services across government departments ranging from institutions responsible for land registration to those responsible for business registration and even the judiciary. Hope for Tanzania to surmount the formidable task of registering titles for landed property for more than 10 million property holders in a total population of 38 million people lies in adoption of an ICT-based solution.

There have been many arguments for and against titling of land in Tanzania. Some have questioned the prudence of a largely rural community in handling titles and the potential loss of property through careless economic transactions such as borrowing and investment in consumption that would lead to forfeiture of land used as collateral. However, available evidence from the great debate of the efficiency of public over private property embedded in communal (through state ownership) versus private property and the forces of the market provide conclusive arguments against the perception of government decisions' superiority over rational individual investment decisions, that include decisions on use of landed property in business transactions. It is estimated that the size of the informal sector is measurable by the value of unregistered landed property estimated at USD 29 billion, which is two and a half times the size of the official economy. (ILD et al) Formal registration and titling of urban landed property and agricultural land is key to the formalization of the Tanzanian economy.

7.4.2 *Business Registration*

What is true for the land registry is equally true for the business registry. The Tanzanian business registry with less than 100,000 companies can be transformed into the nucleus of formalization. The potential for loss of data in a manual registration system is apparent in terms of natural or man-made disasters. It is impossible to create a backup system in a manual database that involves millions of pages. However, the conversion of such a database into electronic format safeguards that data for continued use to underwrite business transactions like registration of mortgages and provision of information to the public on the record and performance of companies and firms. Such information in a rapidly growing and transforming economy is critical for generating the confidence between firms and entrepreneurs that oils deepening forward and backward linkages and growing relationships between small and larger firms, and foreign and local investors.

7.4.3 *Commercial Dispute Resolution*

Perhaps nowhere is loss of data on an ongoing case more painful than in the courts where misplacement or loss of a file can lead to excessive delay in delivery of justice and may culminate in a situation where an undeserving party wins a case. Justice delayed is justice denied. There is ample evidence that delays in fair delivery of justice have often discouraged commercial lending to small and medium enterprises that are the key to a growing economy. The problem of the "missing middle" reflects the lack of access to finance for firms seeking loans ranging from approximately USD 10,000 to approximately 100,000 for the reason that the Micro Finance Institutions do not target this sector while the formal banking sector finds loans in the bracket of USD 50,000 rather small and expensive to administer in situations where forfeiture processes for pledged collateral are cumbersome and difficult to enforce. Enhanced financing risk combined with higher business risks largely contribute to higher costs of capital and a credit squeeze against SMEs even in a situation where the commercial banking system is awash with investment resources.

7.4.4 Labor Market Reforms

Perhaps, this is the most sensitive area of the Tanzanian reforms in view of perceptions held, within society, that is coming from a socialist background and memories of supremacy of the public investment over enterprise private lingers on and the socialist maxim of exploitation may not have given way to the superiority of the motivation of private enterprise and competition in raising productivity and returns to both capital and labor. Yet, there is need to raise awareness of the fundamental working of the labor market and the adverse impact that arbitrary wage increases external to the system can have on monetary policy and inflation through a transmission mechanism that triggers responses in other markets, including the goods market and therefore impact on price level.

A well functioning labor market that sends the right signals to the population in terms of the education levels and skills required for productivity, quality and other competitiveness factors and the linkage between these qualities and returns to labor is the key to Tanzania building the capacity to compete and survive in regional markets and even in its own domestic market. Desire to build competitiveness at the global level is undoubtedly even more demanding and daunting. Labor reforms in the right direction would tend to emphasize the role of productivity in labor, earning higher returns from its share of proceeds earned in the market rather than arbitrary apportionment of perceived returns. There is increasing awareness that successful economies in the 21st century must be knowledge economies where the services sectors, whose competitiveness is based on human capital in the form of skills and technology embedded in human knowledge, are the primary factors for performance. In such a situation, improvement of conditions in the labor market has to start with transformation in the social sectors through better health, education and training for relevant skills rather than mandatory prescription on wages.

Tracking of the impact of policy decisions on the labor market and its impact can only be interpreted in a meaningful way if data confirming the impact on employment in different sectors is available. Whereas data on employment in the public sector and local authorities as well as the formal private sector is available, the only way to come up with realistic data on trends in a large informal sector that accounts for more than 70% of the economy is a series of annual surveys that are bound to be expensive and time consuming. This highlights the importance of a National Registration system that users of information like the authorities responsible for labor policies can draw upon for analytical data on employment and output as an input into the analysis and decisions that would guide the labor market in the right direction.

The message coming from the regulatory reform universe is the need for holistic change process that should encompass the entire spectrum of the regulatory framework. Resistance to change for whatever reasons including relative preference for institutions to continue with systems they are used to, can be a factor of limited awareness of the necessity for change or, in some cases, individual ulterior motives related to rent-seeking behavior. Whatever the reasons for preference to retain the status quo, the message is that one cannot embark on a sustainable system of electronic government if that system is not accompanied with major transformation of the underlying business processes which, in turn, should be underpinned by new regulations and procedures. In turn, new regulations can only emerge from a legal framework that reflects the demands of the time.

The essence of a case study is to draw lessons that can be used by others to avoid problems and address constraints that can make expensive and time consuming mistakes and achieve success much more quickly. It is from this perspective that the next section presents a conclusion and recommendations that can be drawn from the Tanzanian case study.

7.5 Summary, Conclusions and Recommendations

The Tanzanian case study starts with a presentation of evidence on the state of an unduly large informal sector and the different perceptions of the underlying problem. On one hand is the perception that informality is a product of lack of investment capital. On the other hand, there is evidence of availability of substantial volumes of capital and the real problem is lack of access for small enterprises, creating the missing middle in economic agents, linking micro enterprises and medium enterprises and providing the stepping stone for graduation to larger firms. Hence, the real problem is lack of access to finance due to factors that inhibit lending to certain segments in the business community that are prevalent in the legal framework. These factors include lack of collateral due to severe limitations in the operations of registries for natural persons, businesses and property that extend from the underlying legal and regulatory framework to the institutional framework for effective implementation, and poor record management systems based largely on paper records. Further, costly and time consuming measures for contract enforcement, especially for MSMEs, contribute to the problem.

7.5.1 Summary

The phasing of legal and regulatory reforms and the choice implementation instruments adopted in Tanzania reflect a set of public sector interventions against impediments in the investment climate that inhibit business entry and growth as identified through a series of "Investor Road Map" surveys undertaken in Tanzania in 1996, 1999 and 2003.[13] It also reflects private sector advocacy efforts as informed by a review of the judicial, legal and regulatory framework undertaken in 2000.

Tanzania is one of 49 Least Developed Countries (LDCs), countries the majority of whose population subsists on less that US$ 1.00 a day. The economy is characterized by a large informal sector with 70% of the economically active population and 89% of all real property located in the extra-legal economy. Whereas the general perception is that access to finance is the binding constraint against business formalization and growth, the evidence shows that a cumbersome investment climate with high transaction costs is the primary inhibiting factor. For instance, licensing costs for regulated business exceeds 3,000% of GDP and Tanzania is rated lowest in the EAC and SADC regions on the World Bank's Doing Business ranking on the factor of dealing with licenses. Problems in realization of collateral inhibit access to finance for micro, small and medium enterprises and hits particularly hard small enterprises that are not catered for by micro finance institutions and are avoided by the commercial banking sector, creating the problem of "the missing middle" in the continuum of the size of business firms that constitutes the business community.

The main impact of the missing middle is a combination of a growing informal sector and constraints against the growth of the few firms that join the formal economy as micro enterprises from growing and graduating into small and medium enterprises (SMEs). Yet, economic history acknowledges the SME as providing the main force for economic growth in the developing and developed countries, and is the prerequisite for broad based growth in the LDCs. Creating conditions for the survival of firms at the level of the "missing middle" is the challenge that developing countries, and, in particular the LDCs, face. One main area of intervention is that of taking deliberate measures to reduce high transaction costs resulting from cumbersome laws and regulations as well as the need to encourage stronger contractual relationships and economic linkages between larger and smaller firms and between foreign and domestic investors.

Achievement of the MDGs and the Tanzanian national goal of eradicating poverty by 2025 depend on achieving a minimum rate of growth of 8 to 10% within the coming five years and sustaining the same through to 2025. This

[13] Tanzania Investor Road Map: 1996 and 1999

chapter highlights ongoing reforms on four areas: Land administration targeting titling of agricultural land and formalization of urban property; business registration including harmonization of regulatory licensing and registration of natural persons; labor market development including a new legal framework; and improved commercial dispute resolution for fair and rapid justice delivery. It is hoped that this case will inform other LDCs embarking on reforms to shift to the right growth path quickly to generate hope for a better future to the multitude of the poor, wherever they are.

7.5.2 Conclusion

While focusing on mobilization of additional capital from specialized sources and building capacity for the financial sector to adopt innovative financial instruments that can address the problems of access to finance for MSMEs are important and should continue, it is equally critical that simultaneous measures to tackle impediments in the legal and regulatory framework are undertaken. In the Tanzanian case, sector-level initiatives targeting regulatory reforms in the financial sector and in the agricultural sector have been a continuous process for more than a decade and are beginning to bear fruit. There are now more than 35 private sector financial institutions today compared to less than five during the 1990s. However, it is in cross-sectoral programs where past regulatory reform initiatives were less successful and the need for major cross-cutting reforms has become apparent since the second half of the 1990s. The response is the emergence of three cross-cutting programs that seek to address this problem: LSRP; PBFP; and BEST that have emerged since year 2000.

This case study has presented a review of the literature on experience available on how to handle the reforms and address latent problems on resistance to change. Clearly adoption of the instruments for regulatory reforms that are available for reforming existing stock of regulations like, the guillotine and regulatory simplification is critical to achieving a major transformation in the short to medium term. Likewise, adoption of instruments for efficient management of the sectoral policy regimes in the long run is critical in ensuring that regulatory constraints do not creep back into the reformed framework as bureaucrats yearn for a return to well-known yester periods for a variety of reasons, most of which may reflect misconceptions or subliminal and subconscious personal interests rather than national considerations. The most powerful instruments for achieving this include regulatory impact assessment (RIA), simplification measures that include harmonization and consolidation of laws and regulations, institutional transformation and introduction of ICT-based national registration systems. Synonymous with this is the need to introduce voluntary compliance and education to gradually replace sanction-based compliance enforcement wherever this can work.

The concept of a "one-stop-shop" and "single-source" primary data collection centers to address government need for information on its citizens is critical to addressing the problems of multiplicity and duplication syndrome in the legal and institutional framework. Towards this end, adoption of the concept of an interfaced national registration system linking core registration systems for natural persons, businesses and property is paramount.

Today, 20 years after initiating legal and regulatory reforms, the Tanzanian scene has crossed the threshold of resistance. There is today general acceptance of the need for major regulatory reforms and institutional capacity transformation towards information and communication technology based systems. It might appear that there is danger of duplication in view of the number of programs under implementation. However, deliberate cross-sharing of information and mutual cross-representation in coordinating committees across the programs are providing the right solutions and the synergy of higher publicity.

7.5.3 Recommendations

What are the useful lessons to be drawn from the Tanzanian experience to inform others embarking on similar reforms, or even already undertaking reforms, in the most dynamic way forward? The essence of success for a reform program is to ensure cost-effective processes that lead to the desired end-outcome within minimal time and along a least-cost path. The Tanzanian reforms have indeed taken a long-time. It has taken time to ensure that the process is moving in the right direction and it will deliver the desired framework. Challenges remain and challenges will always be there. A holistic approach to reforms, targeting both the legal framework and institutional capacity building is necessary for success. Such a holistic approach has to provide cross sectoral linkages right from program design stage as the means of systematic consensus building towards creating a coordinated system that is built on two concepts: One-stop-shop in business registration and single sources for collection of primary data on the citizenry. Finally, it is important that regulation of businesses is also based on well-established criteria that reflect the necessity of protecting well identified socio-economic interests such as health, environmental and public safety measures.

Background Literature

Consulting Services for the Introduction of a Regulatory Business Licensing System in Tanzania, Final Report commissioned by the Government of the United Republic of Tanzania, Bannock Consulting Ltd, May 2006

Business Environment Strengthening For Tanzania (BEST Program). Enhancing Growth and Reducing Poverty (Program Document), Government of the United Republic of Tanzania, October, 2003

Building a Framework for Conducting Regulatory Impact Analysis (RIA): Tools for Policy makers, OECD, May 2007

Filmup Legal Sector Study: Dissemination of Legal Information and Legal Aid, Frigo Consult, May 1994

Investor Roadmap of Tanzania, Prepared for USAID by Coopers and Lybrand, July 1997 and updated 1999

Legal Sector Reform Program: Medium Term Strategy, Government of the United Republic of Tanzania, December, 2004.

Legal Reform Consultancy to Create an Enabling Regulatory Environment for Investment in Tanzania, Steptoe & Johnson, February 1994

Local Government Reform Program Action Plan and Budget, MRALG, October 1999

Measuring Administrative Costs: UK Guide to the Standard Cost Model, Better Regulation Executive, UK Cabinet Office: September 2005

National Land Policy, Ministry of Lands, Housing and Urban Development, June 1995

Property and Business Formalization Program, Diagnostic Report, Institute of Liberty and Democracy of Lima – Peru, for Government of the United Republic of Tanzania, 2005.

Quick Start Project, Ministry of Justice and Constitutional Affairs, Government of United Republic of Tanzania

Reducing Administrative Burdens: Effective Inspection and Enforcement, Phillip Hampton, for H.M. Treasury, UK, March 2005

Review of the Legal, Regulatory and Judicial Framework regarding Manufacturing and Business Sector in Tanzania, Economic and Social Research Foundation, Nov 1999, commissioned by the Confederation of Tanzania Industries

Regulatory Justice- Making Sanctions More Effective. Final Report, Professor Richard C Macrory, for H.M. Government, Cabinet Office, UK, November, 2006.

Regulatory Impact Analysis in OECD Countries: Challenges for Developing countries; Paper Presented to South Asian 3rd High Level Investment Roundtable, Dhaka, Bangladesh; OECD, June 2005

Regulation – Less is More: Reducing Burdens, Improving Outcomes, Better Regulation Commission, Her Majesty's Government, UK, March 2005

Simplification Plans, A Summary; Her Majesty's Government, UK, December, 2006

Tanzania Development Vision 2025, President's Office, Planning and Privatisation, United Republic of Tanzania, 2000.

Tanzania SME Map – World Bank Group SME Department–September 2001.

Chapter 8
Customized Regulations: How the Dutch Experienced the Reduction of the Burdens Imposed by Regulations

Leo G.M. Stevens

Abstract This chapter stipulates the opposite developments of globalization and Europeanizing on the one hand and, on the other hand, the need for customized regulations. The average citizen and entrepreneur is afraid that the most essential part of the regulation, the flexibility and the content, based on his own responsibility, will be under threat. There is no doubt whatsoever that there are great efficiency benefits to be reaped there. It would be wise to harvest these. Time will learn with what speed and to what extent this change will have to be made. It will be necessary to reduce the burden of regulations, but in doing so to pay attention to not only quantitative but also qualitative objectives. The way in which the pressure of regulations is experienced must also be taken into account. It is possible to choose for another implementation and supervisory culture. We must be willing to take the risk of choosing an approach that aims more strongly to achieve a relationship with the citizen and businesses that is based on trust and that gives them greater responsibility for filling in the method of implementation. In other words, we need to change from a stop and go traffic light system of regulations to the smooth flow of the roundabout.

8.1 Improving the Entrepreneurial Climate

The reduction of regulations and the improvement of the entrepreneurial climate are still mentioned in the same breath. In October 2003, the Netherlands Bureau for Economic Policy Analysis (CPB) published a study with the title 'Four Futures of Europe', in which possible visions of the future were explained in four scenarios. The most significant strategic challenges that are of major importance for our long-term economic perspectives are the aging population, the sustainability of social security and pensions, and the consequences of the emergence of low-wage countries. Western Europe is on the eve of a rise in the

L.G.M. Stevens (✉)
Erasmus University, Rotterdam, The Netherlands
e-mail: lgm.stevens@wxs.nl

A. Nijsen et al. (eds.), *Business Regulation and Public Policy*, 117
International Studies in Entrepreneurship 20, DOI 10.1007/978-0-387-77678-1_8,

rate of aging that will have as consequence that an ever increasing demand will be made on public means in the coming decades. At the same time, the internationalization of our economy and the necessity to make the labor markets more flexible will make it more difficult to accrue these public means. High taxation will slow down economic activity and, in an economy that is increasingly becoming worldwide, this will be accompanied by behavior intended to avoid or escape such taxation. The Netherlands' government has already started considering these consequences. As far as the Netherlands' economy is concerned, it is expected that public means will be scarcer and that it will become more difficult to maintain level of public provisions.

The same trends have also presented the European Union with a challenge. Somewhat pretentious objectives were drawn up at the Lisbon–top 2000, intended to provide guidelines for the policy agenda for the coming years. These objectives involved four items: (1) To become the most dynamic knowledge-economy (productivity agenda); (2) To create more and better jobs (increase participation); (3) To retain and encourage social cohesion (solidarity); (4) To achieve these objectives while still retaining sustainable development (environmental policy). The Lisbon agenda recognizes that there is an important role to be played by entrepreneurs that are able to accept this challenge

Improving the entrepreneurial climate and strengthening entrepreneurship are essential not only to ensure economic growth and the creation of jobs, but also necessary to emphasise the social urgency of vital, innovative entrepreneurship. The trends towards globalization and increasing competition demand flexibility and renewal. Recognizing the importance of entrepreneurship provides the most adequate response. This statement is supported by research showing that in highly developed economies, starting and young enterprises have a positive effect on economic growth. It is therefore very important to ensure that entrepreneurship grows and blossoms in both quality and quantity. Society will benefit because dynamic enterprises will be able to develop successfully and contribute to supporting our economy. However, various measures are needed to achieve these objectives because the motives and goals of the entrepreneurs differ.

Table 8.1 clearly shows that the pressure imposed by regulations is the major obstacle to creating an entrepreneurial climate. It is also apparent that the burden of regulations involved when employing personnel is one of the worst culprits. It is therefore essential that measures should be taken to simplify the complicated salary administration. But, in the meantime, the density of regulation increases and the frequency with which legislation and regulation change is speeding up. Ambiguous regulations also cost entrepreneurs a great deal of time and money. Entrepreneurship can be stimulated by a drastic reduction in the burden of regulations. Labor law, business law, administrative law and fiscal law should be made more serviceable for the social function entrusted to entrepreneurs. It must be possible for the entrepreneur, without hindrance, to choose the most adequate type of legislation. He must be able to adapt his choice without too many problems if developments require him to do so.

Table 8.1 The top ten suggestions made by Dutch entrepreneurs for improving the entrepreneurial climate, The Netherlands

Suggestion	Percentage of SME entrepreneur that found this the most important (%)
Combating administrative burdens	67
Decreased legislation and regulation applying to employees	66
Accessibility to government contracts	35
Facilitating cooperation	35
Facilitating obtaining finance	34
Ensuring that attractive business premises are available	33
Boosting renewal/innovation in businesses	29
Stimulating ICT	24
Stimulating export	18
Other items	6

Source: Rats (2003, p. 7).

Administrative burdens, in particular, must be reduced, and compliance costs, in general, must be limited and contradictory regulations should be eliminated. The removal of thresholds will provide starters with the chance to become entrepreneurs and give existing entrepreneurs more space to be enterprising and grow. This chapter deals with the possibilities to reduce this burden effectively.

8.2 Deterring Regulations

Rules are useful. They offer legal security and form a base for efficient, organized activities. Recognizable rules shape justifiable expectations of a certain type of behavior so that it is not necessary to make new agreements each time. But here again, you can have too much of a good thing. Entrepreneurs – and citizens – are confronted with complicated entanglements of various large scale operations that are accompanied by a progression in the production of regulations that aim to implement these processes and keep them manageable. These operations follow the European-wide trends described previously. The increase in scale of the competitive pressure requires the tax-mix to be adapted, in the same way as the necessity to cover the cost of an aging population and the durability of the environment also requires the familiar, trusted systems and financial relationships to undergo radical changes. These items represent a considerable challenge to the durability of the existing management systems, both as to organization and technology (ICT). The effect has been that the pressure imposed by the regulations has been boosted to such an extent that contra-productive effects are becoming an increasing hazard.

The Dutch Cabinets Balkenende I, II and III (Balkenende was Prime Minister from 2002 to 2006) recognized the risk and have worked hard to reduce the burdens imposed by regulations. They have set out quantitative objectives and expressed the ambition to execute policy to reduce administrative burdens by 25% during the period of the present cabinet – this should result in improving efficiency of businesses by 4 billion euros.

This policy objective does, however, have two dimensions: One quantitative and one qualitative. The cabinet's goal of 25% reduction is of a quantitative (rational) nature. It is based on the old adage 'to measure is to be sure'. In addition, setting this standard has had a sweeping effect. It has underlined the urgency of reducing the burden of regulations. The official noncommittal attitude that used to prevail was swept away in one stroke. Official organizations can be held accountable. To this end, a specific means of calculation has been developed (the Standard Cost Model) to make it possible to calculate how much time and money the entrepreneur spends to comply with the regulations making it obligatory to supply information (IPAL 2003, p. 8). New laws are tested to calculate the administrative burden they represent. The Netherlands has led the way internationally. This model has been embraced by members of the European Union as an instrument to measure administrative burdens. The Standard Cost Model is now being used by 17 members of the EU and by the OESO.

Expressing the burden of regulations as percentages and euros has made a single approach inevitable. When discussing the reduction of the burden of regulations, it is too easy to assume that there are simply too many regulations. But that is not the core of the problem. And also, the effect of such an approach is hindered by the law of diminishing returns. The initial harvest consists of the fruit lowest on the tree that is easiest to pick. And the quantitative target involved and diminishing returns will increase the resistance of those carrying out the work and the supervisors, and there will also be a risk that the task will be strangled by the bureaucracy of the reduction process itself.

The pressure of regulation is a qualitative, emotional perception. The problem is not so much the amount of regulations, but the wrong sort of regulations. Contradictions, the irritating futility or absurdity in regulations can prove a greater burden than a large number of effective, efficient rules that create no trouble. The entrepreneur could not care what type of compliance cost is involved – payment of taxes or premiums, administrative burdens for information transfers or other compliance costs – it is all the same to him. All the theories about administrative costs, the cost of contradictory regulations are for him of little importance. The entrepreneur does not have a theoretical framework into which he fits the burdens imposed on him. He sees the burdens 'just' as a nuisance, inevitable or necessary without trying to trace his emotions to a rational and theoretical source. This fits with his unjustified perception, for example, that an administrative action required to comply with tax law is considered to be more of a burden, measured in time and complexity, than the action required to obtain a subsidy

Scrapping regulations and reducing their number is only part of the problem. It is more important to consider how the regulations are perceived. In spite of the fact that the Dutch government can produce figures to show that the cabinet's objectives are on course and that the objectives set in 2007 will be achieved, entrepreneurs and citizens still have the feeling that the burden of regulations has increased rather than diminished. 'It is like beating your head against a brick wall' is a comment heard all too frequently. In the perception of citizens and in the business world, regulations are becoming ever more far-reaching and score increasingly high on the rigidity scale. That is why the regulation culture needs to change. The question that needs to be posed is whether it is necessary to impose regulations and then 'how?.'

8.3 The Overestimation that Social Changes Can Be Effected by Government

The major cause of the pressure of regulations is the bureaucratic overestimation of the 'shaping' of society and the top-down regulations which ensue from this. This is not purely a Dutch phenomenon, but is also recognizable in most European countries. Regulations are usually too uncompromising and do not match, or insufficiently match, social circumstances. This applies even more to European regulations. Those officials imposing regulations are not able to count on the fundamental certainty that the civilians, businesses and social institutions will recognize the actual purpose of the regulations and then actually comply with them. Being able to be certain of compliance would result in another way of setting standards and monitoring compliance. Open standards could replace regulation complexes that are worked out in detail and greatly improve the functioning of the regulations. Both circumstances, the exaggerated illusion to effect social changes and suspicion as to compliance, often lead to incident regulation. Many officials think that, by issuing new regulations, or tightening existing regulations, they can prevent a repetition of the incidents for which they are held responsible. This is an illusion that increases the pressure exerted by regulation even further. Such regulation-reflexes are to be avoided.

The illusion to effect social changes approach usually results in regulation of means or instruments. It is not the goal that is recorded in legislation, but the means by which that result must be achieved. Regulation of means however often results in an impression of unnecessary burdens more than regulation of targets does. The specific bureaucratic properties of regulation of means are accompanied by the risk that such regulations continuously multiply and split in a way that gives the impression of out of control cell splitting (Westerman 2006). If this propagation process is to be halted, it would be better to replace regulations with more efficient instructions. In this way, the burden of regulations can be reduced: regulations become more durable and more space is created for the entrepreneur's creativity and he is allowed to do business in the most efficient way.[1] Entrepreneurs, in particular often feel entangled in a cocoon of rules and regulations that denies them any freedom of movement.

It is therefore important for us to tackle the cause of regulation production. In the Netherlands, we have managed to get away from the perception that everything dictated from above is effecting social changes and that the policy architects of the social state are able to organize the entire life of society. Such an idea leads only to bureaucracy, to complicated regulations, to extra burdens and to social frustration. Those politicians responsible for policy making must be more modest and show themselves willing to create conditions: citizens, businesses and social institutions should be able to convert their participation into better work and living relationships.

This does not, of course, mean that the usefulness and the necessity of regulations are questioned. A society cannot exist without relationships being regulated and limits being set. Entrepreneurs and civilians do consider regulations to be useful and necessary, but they do not wish to be assaulted by them or to be frustrated in a way that makes no sense. Legislation should be flexible enough to allow the entrepreneur to slip smoothly into the dynamics of social movement. We need to change from the stop and go traffic light regulation system to the smooth flowing roundabout. That also applies to judicial matters. There must be room for adaptations of a personal nature.

The architect of the welfare state has discovered a very effective instrument to achieve his master plan: fiscal policy. Through controlling the flow of money, he is able to stimulate or discourage, make or break. That has – in the Netherlands – resulted in a great many instruments being involved in levying taxes. Taxation plays an important role in social housing, pension schemes, health care, knowledge economy, the environment, European harmonization, improving the international competitive position, strengthening labor participation, cultural policy, doing business in a socially responsible manner etc. Some fiscal measure or other was found for all types of 'good policy objectives'. At the same time, however, these developments call for more official awareness. Each time, it is necessary for these officials to ask themselves whether the fiscal instrument achieved the desired result. Too little account is taken of the feelings of the entrepreneurs and citizens that, in their own circumstances, are usually capable of creating the best possible situation.

8.4 The Burden of European Regulation

Related to Europe, emotions were stronger than rational thinking. In a referendum, the Netherlands voted against a European constitution. This rejection was based mainly on emotional reasons. Thinking rationally, it is, of course, quite obvious that the unification of Europe is a favorable and irreversible

[1] See also: Ministry of Justice, *Ruimte voor zorgplichten (Space for the duty to provide for)*, The Hague, July 2004.

development. In fact, it is really very regrettable that the population of the Netherlands for emotional, but very understandable, reasons sent such a negative signal. But this signal was not only meant for Europe, but also for the Dutch government. At the time at which the referendum took place, the Dutch citizen had had more than enough of all types of current large scale policy changes with their complicated connections. He/she had completely lost track of what was going on and was unable to envisage his/her own position. He/she felt crushed between – often automated – anonymous systems. As this puts a considerable strain on the durability of our governing systems, both organizational and technical, an undesirable feeling of being cramped for space enters the field of enforcement. The burden of regulation and the alienation have now become too great. No one feels comfortable or understood in our own 'polder' country. The addition of a regulating European bureaucracy is then too much of a good thing. Using the welfare theory, it is, certainly at the European level, better to leave the consideration of burdens and benefits to be made by the citizen. Let Europe do whatever needs to be done for Europe and let us regulate those things that can be done at national level. In other words, let us keep man as measure of all things as much as possible.

But, however you look at it, Europe is a reality. The Netherlands may have rejected the European constitution: but it was not a 'no' to the Europe of the citizens. The citizens enjoy the freedom of movement in a Europe without borders. They hope for a peaceful Europe, one offering many opportunities, in which economic well-being goes hand-in-hand with the retention of cultural differences. The 'no' was essentially for bureaucratic Europe: the Europe of meaningless regulations, the distant Europe that is finding it difficult to become a political community because the politicians are held accountable by their own nation and, therefore, may not give anything away to Europe. Frustrations involving national impotence are often blamed on Europe.

In the fiscal policy of the future, national and international systems of regulations and taxation will have to be in tune with each other. Whether we like it or not, we shall have to adapt our tax levies to match the extent of the mobility of basic values of tax levies. Europe – and even the world outside Europe – is a 'level playing field' for mobile basic values such as capital. Only those items that cannot be considered as mobile will be regulated and taxed in the traditional way according to national perceptions. The others will have to fit in the European scale. In the long term, a European corporate tax will be inevitable. I am unable to think of one single reason why we should be unwilling to progress to such a European corporate tax. But before we take the final step, we shall be occupied, for a long time, doing the ground work for the harmonization for corporate taxation and will have to put a great deal of energy into realizing one common agreement about the meaning of the fiscal profit.[2]

---

[2] The IFRS approach will score well among the achievable options. It is clear that standards that have one common interface at international level will also be accepted as useful fiscal alternatives.

8.5 Reinforce the Government Core Tasks

The trends mentioned: globalization and digitalization, individualization with the desired flexibility, the cost of an aging population, environmental problems that go beyond borders, have consequences for the functioning of various federal and central governments within the European Union. They are faced with new challenges. By opening the borders, the difference in administrative culture and political institutions have put under pressure the traditional conceptions of the tasks of the government. The members of the European Union are not allowed to influence competition by providing state support. This means that the margins for government polices to deviate from the norm are becoming ever smaller. Many member states must say goodbye to all sorts of obvious, continuous tax exemptions or special 'artificial' government assignments that are not seen in the same light in other member states and are considered to be part of entrepreneurial activities.

In the Netherlands, there are also other reasons to take another look at the core tasks of the government. There is growing dissatisfaction about the management of the collective sector. The civil service, because of strong emphasis on business economics paradigms, has become a distant organization with no self-esteem, where the only things of importance are products, assignment of costs, measuring performance and settlement. Competition appears to be hollowing out the counter weight provided by the professional requirements of doctors, police, teachers, juvenile carers and scholars. The professional requirements set by legislation, administration and the judicial system are being forced into a tight corner. Citizenship and the responsibility of citizens for public affairs are under threat of being pushed into the background. Democratic participation and public accountability as a characteristic of a democratic constitution is, under the influence of market-oriented thinking, being replaced by customer-oriented business policy (Veenswijk, Hakvoort 1999).

Performance contracts were agreed based on the idea that government services had to be made more measurable. However, insufficient attention was paid to the fact that the performance agreements could result in strategic behavior. As far as administration is concerned, the passion for accountability resulted in excessive attention for measuring and issuing reports. The healthy skills of the carer and the service provided by the civil servant – the immeasurable essence of how the government functions – suffered (Bos 2006, p. 108 ff). The citizen should be able to perceive the government as a correctly operating performer and supervisor. This is much more wide ranging than a service that conforms to market demands. Good communication is an essential condition. That sets limits to systematically dealing with problems. The government may not hide behind anonymous call-centers or computer programs. The citizen must have the opportunity to look the government's representative straight in the eye and be able to rely on the fact that he/she does not function as an automated link in the system, but acts as a social worker and is allowed to do so.

The cabinet itself is now also well aware of the existing administrative crisis. The Balkenende II cabinet recognized the fact that the government has allowed itself to become the ultimate problem solver.[3] The government is expected to supply a solution for all the large and small problems of the increasingly complicated society. At the same time, because of the individualization and multiformity of society, they are expected to supply more customized solutions. More flexible regulation with a selection of choices intended to serve all groups within society led to the increasing density of regulations. This development was, therefore, in many cases counter-productive. The overall picture was lost.

8.6 Fewer Regulations, More Shared Responsibility

'The government is not efficient, reacts too slowly to developments and does not sufficiently involve the citizens in decision forming' this is criticism that is heard very frequently. The Coalition Agreement of February 7, 2007 shows that the political parties that hoisted the current Balkenende Cabinet into power, realize that there are lessons to be learnt. It states that it is necessary to find a new balance between dynamics and certainty. It requires a government that is recognizable, accessible and communicative. And, therefore intensive attention will be paid to the extent of, and experience with, the burden of regulations. During its period in power, the Cabinet Balkenende IV has the intention to decrease the administrative pressure and, once again, set the objective to achieve a 25% reduction of administrative burdens.

The burden of regulations is linked with compliance costs among which are supervisory costs. Reducing the burden of regulations may not be accompanied by neglecting compliance and lowering the quality of supervision. The government may not lose its control by issuing regulations without having the means to ensure adequate compliance. This implies that the government will have to be more modest in its ambition. It is better to delegate tasks that, as to content and administration, can be undertaken by others and do not belong to the government's core business. This demands a discussion as to the core business of the government. And also, arrangements must be made that reduce the burden of regulations, but at the same time ensure the increase in the degree of reliability of compliance. That will require changes in the present, mainly strictly vertical, organized, structure of supervision. It is necessary to develop a supervisory organization that is efficient and effective and meets society's demand for security. Administrators must also be offered a reasonable guarantee that they will receive the administrative information to keep the processes for which they are responsible under control. That will naturally lead to streamlining processes and consequently to standardization.

---

[3] See Action Plan Cabinet 'How to reduce administrative burden', Parliament, year 2003–2004, 29 515, nr. 1.

8.7 Confidence

To be able to achieve the required flexibility, it is necessary for the government to recognize that it is in the interest of the entrepreneur himself to ensure that the rules are faithfully complied with. The average entrepreneur is well aware of this and acts accordingly. When compiling, implementing and checking regulations, the government must base these on the assumption of one common interest: of trust and not distrust. The entrepreneur must be given the space to conform to the regulations in the best possible way and be able to achieve the goal for which they are intended. The supervisory culture must also be tuned to this objective. Any entrepreneur that betrays such trust, may and must be suitably punished.

By setting purposeful standards, without getting bogged down in all sorts of rules, the genuine entrepreneur is provided with more space to carry out his/her business. Open standards allow the entrepreneur to use his/her creativity and freedom, in his/her own particular situation, to do what he/she wishes in the true spirit of the regulation. In practice, open standards have the advantage of efficiency and the opportunity to produce tailor-made work. In this way, regulations can 'breathe freely' with new developments on the markets. There has to be space to experiment and legal standards must be much more generally formulated (Oude Vrielink-van Heften and Dorbeck-Jung 2006, page 11–12). Nowadays, emphasis is too much on prevention. The government has tried too hard, by using regulations, to prevent anything from going wrong. This is an illusion that originates from a 'shaping' of society and hedging-in culture.

Supervisors and entrepreneurs will have to communicate with each other more intensively about the 'why standard' in the 'open plan structure'. The law offers the framework; it will have to be filled in, in consultation with the entrepreneurs. In this way, compliance and guarantee will be increased. The supervisor must, however, stop himself from filling in the details of these standards and not allow himself, in the implementation stage, to be tempted to specify these in a very closely woven network of details and publish them as 'fake' legislation. That will eliminate any chance of the desired flexibility. It goes without saying that sufficient legal certainty must be provided. Entrepreneurs must have clarity as to the framework of the control mechanism (Ambtelijke Commissie Toezicht II 2005, p. 39).

At the present time, we see the check lists and regulations increasing (Van Kempen 2007). Such a phenomenon is patently obvious in the annual reports and in the management of businesses. The American Sarbanes Oxley law (SOx) and the IFRS regulations demand guarantees concerning the internal finance management of the business that are too strict, although there has been no satisfactory agreement reached with businesses about the applicable requirements. Such regulations impose a heavy burden and the accompanying costs can lead to increasing aversion.

The reverse side of open standards is that, in practice, these can lead to more discussions between supervisor and entrepreneur in cases where detailed 'regulations of means' are involved. But, even so, my preference is for open standards. The 'rules are rules' mentality hides the risk that the intrinsic legal value of the law is being hollowed out and that the implementer and supervisor no longer have the possibility to build in any flexibility in their responsibility. They must use their professional judgment in each individual case to transform the word of the law into deeds. Supervisors and implementers must, therefore, continue to retain sufficient policy margin to be able be to make integral considerations within the meaning of the law

The relationship that the government has with entrepreneurs at the present time is characterized too strongly by mistrust. That results in an endless series of regulations and licenses/permits.[4] The exaggerated demand for licences and permits has, in fact, 'solidified suspicion'. It would be more sensible to move onto a different supervisory philosophy. It would be more efficient to make checks based on quick scans and professional risk analyses to obtain a better picture of compliance. This compliance check should be differentiated. The genuine entrepreneur deserves the type of supervision based on trust. The Stevens Commission has recommended that a Supervisory Chamber should be formed to achieve this (Stevens Commission 2006).

8.8 Risk Acceptance

The advice to government is: Do not be afraid to accept the fact that reducing the burden of regulation is a question of mentality, accepting the need to take leave of the 'shaping society' principle and passing on greater social responsibility to citizens, businesses and social institutions. This approach that creates conditions and also creates space is very often more effective than decisive, battened down policy. But, reducing the burden of regulations will be effective only if it is possible to achieve a change in mentality and the government can take the step to change an all-caring welfare state into an active participation state. This change in mentality is necessary in all areas and for all those involved.

At the very moment an incident happens, the entire regulatory machines are set in motion. It is a system that is difficult to halt. Fortunately, the awareness that such regulation reflexes are counter productive is gradually increasing. But changing the mentality regarding regulations is a long and difficult process. We must learn to accept calculated risks and incidents for what they are. The government cannot guarantee a society that is entirely risk free. To do so

---

[4] See also Ben Wientjes (chairman of VNO-NCW employers organization) in: '*Offensief tegen de verstarring gevraagd,*' Het Financieele Dagblad (Economie en Politiek), 25 July 2006, p. 3 ("required – an offensive against fossilisation" In the Dutch Financial Daily Newspaper (Economy and Politics) 25th July 2006, page 3).

would entail issuing regulation upon regulation, check after check and disasters and accidents would still occur and, according to the Pavlov type of reaction, would be followed by even more new regulations and even stricter supervision. The 'pay back' and claim culture has to be kept in check. Too detailed parliamentary checks and the attention of the media both contribute to the creation of administrative burdens.

Legal security and flexibility are uncomfortable neighbors. Open standards are required to ensure flexibility in regulation. Such standards make it possible to take advantage of rapidly developing technology or rapid changes in the environment. The Netherlands tax authorities have recently made a praiseworthy attempt to convert to the supervisory philosophy. In their new policy plan, they present future methodology for compliance, 'horizontal supervision'. In this plan, the focus is on mutual trust between the tax payer and the tax authorities. By introducing their 'framework for horizontal supervision', they hope to achieve two objectives simultaneously: to regain the trust of the tax payer, and at the same time, to become more efficient in performing their maintenance activities. The intention is to state more clearly what responsibility each individual has, what are the possibilities to maintain the law and to register to what extent mutual agreements are complied with. A pilot was started in 2005 involving 20 businesses, the majority of which are listed on the stock exchange. The objective was to come to individual compliance agreements. The aim of this approach is to increase the legal security for the businesses and to avoid tax constructions. Accountants will greet this with applause because they are allergic to (tax) undetermined items on the balance sheet.

It does not matter how constructively such plans are approached, it is essential not to close one's eyes to the risks that accompany them. In addition to the law, there will also be a behavioral covenant that could disturb the equality under the law of the various categories of those liable for taxation, that hollows out the legal interpretation of the law, that weakens the position of the individual taxpayer when confronted by the overwhelming tax authorities and unnecessarily brings the tax advice systems into discredit.

Renewal is being carried out in implementation and supervision in other fields also. The Netherlands Taxonomy Project (NTO) is an important example of an attempt to achieve streamlining the flow of information in a responsible way.

Standardization processes are inevitable in the ever busier and faster world of electronic information. Efficiency requires standardization and harmonization, even though this can also be viewed as a loss of personal style and the added value of multiformity. As time goes on, this will also have to take place on a European scale. But once again, it is important to keep a keen eye on the objective and not to lapse into rigid procedure regulations such as those we experienced when it became compulsory in the Netherlands to submit data electronically. Citizens must not be given the impression that it is being forced upon them. The intention must be to offer practical aids that can be adapted to meet the personal situation and not give the impression that that person feels he/she is obliged to adapt to the system. User-friendly must be seen as a characteristic of the civil service.

The need for reliable information systems is increasing in other areas also. Tax assurance is a new type of sport, in which fiscal advisers see their major task to be that of making the risk of fiscal measures understandable for managers of business. That will lead to splitting the function of the fiscal advisors. The fiscal specialist that advises the supervisory accountant and keeps him up to date about the position of latent and manifest fiscal obligations will be of another type than his colleague that seeks the most favorable fiscal position for his client. Fiscal creativity and security can create a stressful situation and there will be a completely different relationship between the client and the tax supervisor and the client and his tax advisor. Such discussion will arise among accountants working in fiscal circles when they examine the position of the tax advisor compared to that of the tax supervisor, and the question as to whether they may have one common interest will arise.

The tension between flexibility and security is also apparent from developments in the field of the compilation of annual reports. There is growing resistance among the multinational enterprises to the increasing burden of regulations and compliance costs. The American Sarbanes Oxley Act (SOx) and IFRS regulations are named as the major examples of undesirable burdens. There is considerable doubt as to whether it is desirable to give the IFRS regulation- driven and inflexible purpose and the 'fair value' approach a wider range than the stock exchange funds for which the IFRS was primarily developed. For SME entrepreneurs in particular, it is necessary to question whether the disadvantages of the increasing burden of regulations will not be greater than the gain in efficiency of strict, very detailed standardized standards of reporting.

8.9 Summary

The scale advantages offered by internet and those that are the result of globalization and also from 'Europeanizing' can be experienced as a fascinating achievement that is making possible developments of which we could only dream in the past. It is, however, important that this development should continue to feel 'good'. Something that is seen rationally as a spectacular development and also a significant expansion of digital possibilities, can also appear to the individual to be a threat if it is no longer possible to envisage the consequences and all types of authorities start using the digital system and insist that others use them, without first ensuring that such systems are user-friendly. Not everyone feels at home on the electronic highway. Here again, slower traffic needs extra protection. The possibility to be able to have a clear view of the road ahead will be under extra pressure if the traffic rules originate not only in The Hague but also, more and more often, from an anonymous distant Brussels.

The average citizen and entrepreneur is afraid that for him the disadvantages of scale enlargement will be greater than the advantages. That customized regulations will disappear. That the most essential part of the regulation, the flexibility and the content, based on his/her own responsibility, will be under threat. There is also anxiety about the fact that the principle of subsidies will be affected. That things will no longer be dealt with at the level at which this is done best. This also means that Europe must be kept at a distance. This discussion needs to be seen in the light of the XBRL developments and changing supervisory strategies.

There is no doubt whatsoever that there are great efficiency benefits to be reaped there. It would be wise to harvest these. Time will learn with what speed and to what extent this change will have to be made. It will be necessary to reduce the burden of regulations, but in doing so, to pay attention not only to quantitative but also qualitative objectives. The way in which the pressure of regulations is experienced must also be taken into account. It is possible to opt for another implementation and supervisory culture. We must be willing to take the risk of choosing an approach that aims more strongly at achieving a relationship with the citizen and businesses that is based on trust and that gives them greater responsibility for filling in the method of implementation. In other words, we need to change from a stop and go traffic light system of regulations to the smooth flow of the roundabout.

References

Ambtelijke Commissie Toezicht II (2005), Toezicht: naar naleving voor de samenleving. Eindrapport Ambtelijke Commissie Toezicht-II, The Hague, (Official Commission Supervision II Supervision: towards compliance for society. Final report of official Commission Supervision II. The Hague)

Bos, W. (2006), Dit land kan zoveel beter, Uitgeverij Bert Bakker, Amsterdam, (This country can do so much better). Published by Bert Bakker, Amsterdam

IPAL (2003), Interdepartmental Project Direction Administrative Burden , Meten is weten. Handleiding voor het definiëren en meten van administratieve lasten voor het bedrijfsleven, Den Haag, December (Interdepartmental Project Direction Administrative Burden, to measure is to be sure. Instructions for businesses for defining and measuring administrative burdens. The Hague, December)

Kempen van, Arnout, Wantrouwensman van het maatschappelijk verkeer, de Accountant, maart 2007 (The Least-trusted man in social affairs, the Accountant, March 2007)

Oude Vrielink-van Heften, M. & B., Dorbeck-Jung (2006), Kan zelfregulering regeldruk verminderen', Bestuurskunde 2006, jaargang 15, nummer 4, (Is it possible for self-regulation to reduce the pressure of regulation? Public Administration, Volume 15, no.4)

Rats, J.J.M. (2003), "Economisch Beleid & Sectoren (Economic policy and sectors)", MKB-Nederland

Stevens Commission (2006), Het gezicht van toezicht (The face of supervision), March

Veenswijk, M. and J.L.M. Hakvoort (1999), Hoe weerbarstig is de cultuur van de rijksoverheid? Staatscourant , Openbaar bestuur. De grenzen van decentralisatie, opgenomen in de reeks: In statu nascendi, nr. 106, 8 June 1999. (How unmanageable is the Governments culture?)

Westerman, P. (2006/3), De onmogelijkheid van deregulering (The impossibility of deregulation), Nederlands Juristen Blad

Chapter 9
The New Rulemaking

Belaid Rettab

Abstract Laws and regulations have their limitations. In abundance, they might become fu-tile, particularly due to regulatory capture. BIA is called for to reduce costs of doing business in Dubai and to improve the quality of regulations. Corporate social responsibility (CSR) is also viewed to improve the general business environment.

This chapter highlights the impact of regulations on businesses in Dubai and the situation of CSR in the market environment. The chapter calls for CSR (self-regulation) and argues that when fitted in sound public-private partnership framework, could achieve general improvement of the business environment in Dubai.

9.1 Introduction

It has become conventional wisdom that regulations are at best necessary evils to regulate markets and at worst demolition of productivity, employment, and economic growth when they exceed market requirements.

Design of regulations needs to account for regulatory captures – the process through which vested interests bias the incentives of regulators to act in their interest rather than in the interest of the broader public. Regulatory capture results in market failure which is usually used to legitimize direct government interference in economic activities. However, evidence on market failure as a result of central planning reduced significantly support for more state interference.

As a consequence, deregulation starts to become widely adopted, often as part of structural adjustment programs, with the aim of reducing the "regulatory burden" on market economy. It is well established that regulatory governance affects regulatory outcomes, which in turn impacts on business competitiveness and socioeconomic growth.

B. Rettab (✉)
Dubai Chamber of Commerce & Industry, Dubai, UAE
e-mail: Belaid.rettab@dcci.ae

A. Nijsen et al. (eds.), *Business Regulation and Public Policy*,
International Studies in Entrepreneurship 20, DOI 10.1007/978-0-387-77678-1_9,

We posit that regulatory models require radical re-thinking whereby Business Impact Assessment (BIA) is a helpful tool, and it is argued that market-based instrument (e.g., corporate social responsibility (CSR) and business ethics) and self-regulation tend to reduce the scope for capture. In fact, as argued by Arrow (1973), ethical elements enter in some cases into every contract. It is therefore, not adequate to argue that there are enforcement mechanisms such as police and courts; these are themselves services bought and sold.. ...The cost of enforcement becomes bearable only if most transactions take place without attempts at fraud, force, or cheating.

Corporate social responsibility with its strong ethical instruments has become an increasingly common term in the rhetoric surrounding business ethics, and has been widely used by corporations, governments and academics alike. Indeed, one could argue that CSR has also become the mainstream prescription by business and governments for dealing with social and environmental ills. Basically, CSR is a voluntary form of self-regulation (reflexive law) that aims at tackling everything from human rights and labor standards to limiting carbon dioxide emissions that lead to climate change.

The next section discusses problems and benefits of regulations on businesses and stresses the need for BIA to improve quality of regulations. Section 3 discusses the impact of regulations on businesses in Dubai, and reviews the situation of CSR amongst Dubai enterprises. Section 4 argues that when CSR (self-regulation), is perfectly fitted in public-private partnership framework the benefits to the welfare are higher.

9.2 The Problem of Regulation

It has been suggested that in developing countries, where market failures are more pronounced, the case for public regulation is stronger (Stiglitz 1998).

However, regulations may not necessarily correct market distortions and result in welfare improvement due to regulatory capture and incidence of asymmetric information which both bias market incentives and outcomes and result in economic "second best solution".

Effective regulations are supposed to achieve social welfare goals at minimum economic and social costs and internalize external costs. Following Helm (2006), the first causal mechanism is from regulation to transaction cost. If regulations increase costs – either of capital or labor – in effect, it is a tax. Higher costs reduce output, and also lead to a competitive disadvantage in the tradable sector if rivals are less heavily regulated. Conversely, if regulation reduces costs (for example, by protecting sunk costs in utilities, thereby lowering the cost of capital, or ensuring that public goods, which are inputs to firms, are provided), there is a potential competitive advantage. If the net effect is an increase in costs, reducing the performance of factor inputs, this has a negative impact on economic growth.

The efficiency of regulations can be assessed in two ways: (1) The costs of directly administering the regulatory system, which are internalized within government and reflected in the budget appropriations of the regulatory bodies, and (2) the compliance costs of regulation, which are external to the regulatory agency and are charged to producers. The latter costs include cost to comply, avoid and or evade the regulation. See also (Guasch and Hahn 1999). Business Impact Assessment (BIA) proved to be a successful tool in identifying ways for cost reduction but also in reshaping and simplifying administration rules and procedures. In many Middle-East and African countries (MENA), including Dubai-UAE, this tool is still unknown. The UAE could learn a lot from the Dutch experience in this respect. The latter experience has been acknowledged by the World Bank as fruitful.

The quality of regulatory quality can also be assessed in terms of the criteria for good governance. It has been argued that a well-functioning regulatory system is one that balances accountability, transparency, and consistency (Parker 1999, p. 224).

9.3 The Case of Dubai

9.3.1 Impact of Regulations

Evidence on the quality of regulation in developing countries is very limited. But, where research has occurred, evidence suggests that the results of state regulations have been disappointing due to lack of institutions, capacity building, commitment and coordination (Jacobs 2004; Ugaz 2003; Campbell-White and Bhatia 1998; Lanyi 2000 and Schwella 2002).

The extent of compliance with regulations and their impact on businesses were assessed for Dubai as measured by time and cost burden accrued to comply, and effectiveness of the regulation (Rettab and Nijsen 2006). It has been found that more than 50% of the entrepreneurs in the industrial and transportation sectors agreed that it takes a lot of time to comply with regulations. About 50–60% in the trade, industrial and transportation sectors agreed that it costs a lot of money. About 34% of respondents do not agree with some of the regulations or have limited knowledge about the regulations and only 30% of entrepreneurs in the industrial and transportation sectors agreed that regulations are helpful (Table 9.1).

On the one hand, the industrial sector and very small sized businesses appear to be most negatively impacted as regards time and cost involved while complying with regulations. On the other hand, entrepreneurs in the trade sector and smaller businesses seem to be the least negatively impacted. About 30% of the entrepreneurs in the trade sector felt that it takes a lot of time to comply with regulations and about 20% felt that regulations are often found contradictory.

Table 9.1 Impact of regulations by sector, in percentages

Sector	Industry	Trading	Transport	Other services	All sectors
Takes a lot of time	63	30	54	45	49
I don't agree	47	30	15	31	34
Too complicated	27	25	31	31	28
Regulations are contradicting	33	20	23	35	29
Costs a lot of money	60	50	62	35	50
Facilitate a lot	30	15	31	61	30
I have limited knowledge	37	55	31	21	35

Source: Rettab and Nijsen (2006).

Compared to other sectors, entrepreneurs in trade ranked highest for their limited knowledge of regulations. However, according to sizes, very small enterprises have a relatively negative opinion about regulations and very limited knowledge of regulations (Table 9.2).

The survey also investigated the impact of regulations on the general business environment in Dubai. The survey results show that respondents have mixed opinions. Most beneficial regulations were found to be those facilitating easy obtaining of visas, those allowing import, export and re-export at low tariff costs and those allowing free movement of capital.

The majority of the entrepreneurs had the opinion that it is difficult to compete with government organizations and free zone companies operating in the local markets. Price setting and inefficient regulations controlling business licensing[1] were also a major concern of enterprises. As a result, about 65% of the responding entrepreneurs recommended more favorable and transparent regulations aiming at reduction of unfair competition.

Table 9.2 Impact of regulations by size, in percentage

Size	Very small	Small	Medium sized	Large	All size classes
Takes a lot of time	58	53	40	47	49
I don't agree	29	16	43	42	34
Too complicated	29	26	33	21	28
Regulations are contradicting	29	37	23	37	29
Costs a lot of money	50	42	50	58	50
Facilitate a lot	17	42	30	27	30
I have limited knowledge	58	16	40	16	35

Source: Rettab and Nijsen (2006).

[1] Except for Free Zones, the UAE Company law allows not more than 49% foreign ownership in equity of an enterprise.

Administrative burdens in Dubai accrue due to compliance with regulations such as applications for labor visa, authentication and translation of documents, and registration and renewal of vehicle licenses. The general opinion of the majority of entrepreneurs with respect to the above was that compliance costs a lot of money and time. On average, cost of labor visa amounts annually to US$ 37,000 per enterprise, while compliance time amounts to about 148 working days on average per enterprise. For license renewal, the average amount spent annually is about US$ 25,000 per enterprise while the time spent is about 30 working days.

9.3.2 Corporate Social Responsibility in Dubai

Generally speaking, effective CSR may well require good government (e.g., to draft regional and national development plans), and some policy-makers see CSR as a stepping-stone towards legal codification (Blowfield and Frynas 2005; Klein and Harford 2004). World Bank reports, for ex-ample, argued that CSR can be very helpful on the way to improve national legislation in countries that have failed to enforce their laws.

In certain countries and industries, such as MENA countries, there is a lack of market incentives, which undermines the business case of CSR. Businesses are not properly rewarded for their CSR efforts. In addition to that, there are many other flaws in codes of conduct to be found such as issues relating to conflicts of interests within and between countries, absence of assessment and monitoring mechanisms such as BIA case in Europe, and lack of sound enforcement and compliance mechanisms. Furthermore, the risk of turning CSR policies into PR strategies is proving to be a serious threat.

A recent survey of 2,100 company managers from different economic sectors in Dubai reports that critical issues and challenges in the area of CSR are encountered (DERC 2006). The majority of executives place their core values at the heart of their commitment to corporate responsibility on elements such as employee responsibilities (health and safety, training and development), financial transparency, and corporate governance. Less focused areas are found to include environmental responsibilities, anti-discrimination, consumers and community responsibilities. 72% of businesses are "very highly" or "highly" aware of CSR and 93% of businesses responded to be 'very much' or 'much' committed to CSR.

In Dubai, corporate governance issues are prominent among public joint stock companies and government-owned companies with respect to guidelines on disclosure.

Despite the high profile for financial transparency by most companies, more incentives, awareness, mandatory policies and control on financial transparency in the construction sector can further help engage companies on transparency and accountability toward society. The survey (DERC 2006) shows that 98% of companies have independent external auditors, 72% of companies reported regular disclosure of operating results, management remuneration and financial target, and 69% of firms retain auditors and do not change them periodically.

The environment represents a fast-maturing area of alignment. However, the survey findings highlight that few companies actually engage in environmental practices such as conducting environmental impact assessment, consider environmental impacts of the supply chain or install internal measures to prevent environmentally harmful activities. 46% of companies have policies in place to deal with the firm's environmental impact; 53% of companies conduct environmental impact assessments; 82% companies have a health and safety management system; 57% of companies consider the environmental impact of their supplier; and only 24% undertake any form of publicly reporting their CR activities

In consistency with the findings of this survey, we postulate that a major transition in Dubai is underway. Leading companies are progressing in replacing the traditional 'values', 'cultures', and "ways" of practising business with a more strategic and integrated corporate responsibility model. At the core of this transition is the recognition that corporate social responsibility in Dubai has to be taken more seriously and properly operationalized throughout the company.

9.4 The Way Forward

9.4.1 Face the Challenge

Three key issues should be challenged and resolved. First, the debate is hampered by the dogma that CSR is, by definition, voluntary, referring only to activities that go beyond compliance with legal requirements, adopted in response to a variety of market-based drivers.

Second, the problem of voluntary and regulatory approaches which have been too often treated as exclusive to each other, rather than as options within a balanced approach aiming at eradicating irresponsible behavior has to be resolved.

Third, CSR practice needs to be embedded within the legal and regulatory environment, particularly when adherence to legal minima is treated as a baseline for good practice.

9.4.2 Promote Self-regulation

While imperative national regulations have only limited influence beyond national boundaries, new forms of regulations involving business have become the dominant practice. Self-regulation (CSR) by private companies is presently the most rapidly developing field of corporate regulation on the global level. Much of this regulation is being voluntarily opted for not because of encountered enforcement, but due to considerations of self-interest.

There are many reasons why these new forms of regulations have emerged (See also Van Calster and Deketelaere 2001). The following are the main motives for promoting self regulation and the urge to move towards new types of rulemaking in Dubai-UAE:

1. Self-regulation encourages pro-active engagement from industry in the rule making process, and uses the market to encourage ethical behaviors or corporate social responsibility.
2. Self-regulation cuts down on bureaucracy and costs by cooperating closer with business. To give an example: rather than telling companies which technology to use, or to measure the emissions at every single chimney, the introduction of a limited amount of tradable emission certificates for a certain industry has the same result without costly administration and compliance control.
3. Externalities are inspirational for the new rules. Assessing the role of the public sector by considering only those initiatives that provide incentives for business to go "beyond compliance" would fail to take account of the dynamic linkages between voluntary approaches and regulation and the potential for voluntary initiatives of various kinds to crystallize over time into an internalized minimum practised standards.
4. A public-private partnership is a concept, in which government and private sector assume co-responsibility and co-ownership for the delivery of public services. It includes interaction between government and business in which the focus in achieving convergent objectives is on synergy. The objectives of public-private partnership have both social and commercial characteristics and the respective identities and responsibilities of the parties involved remain intact.
5. The greatest deterrent to private participation in a public-private partnership is the regulatory environment and attitude. Private investors will be kept away and will seek a more hospitable place to invest if regulation is unlimited in scope, unclear in operation, and inclined toward micro-management. The regulatory regime must be limited, transparent, fair, and consistent, and government must always keep its promises. Private investors are cautious not only of expropriation but also of many small regulatory actions that together constitute incremental expropriation, taking away the private partner of legitimate recovery of costs and of profit proportional to the risks undertaken.
6. Regulation has to satisfy the demands of both public and private sectors, which can, at times, be conflicting. Public agencies externalize net social benefits as a result of organizational activities, whilst private firms demand adequate returns on their stake. Some essential characteristics of regulatory framework required for public-private partnership formation include a

balance between establishing a system of regulations that ensures accountability of partners and avoiding over regulation that stifles innovations; protection of the legitimate interests of all stakeholders in fostering partnerships; and elimination of unintended consequence of blocking partner participation (ADB 2000).

9.5 Summary and Conclusions

Regulatory capture and incidence of asymmetric information which both bias market incentives and outcomes and result in economic "second best solution" make regulations on their own not able to achieve welfare improvement.

Efficiency of regulations should be, therefore, regularly assessed at three levels, direct costs of administering the regulatory system, compliance costs of regulation charged to businesses, and the regulatory quality in terms of good governance balancing accountability, transparency, and consistency.

The chapter shows that assessment at the above three levels are valid for Dubai where regulations are not that developed yet, the fact which paves the way for an alternative but exceptional course of regulatory design and development.

Currently, inefficient business regulations in Dubai-UAE are of major concern to enterprises which recommend favorable regulations to reduce unfair competition. Furthermore, because imperative national regulations have generally only limited influence beyond national boundaries, new forms of self regulation involving business have become serious alternatives not because of encountered enforcement, but due to considerations of pure self-interest.

Self regulation by businesses is supported by the fact that these voluntary regulations strongly encourage ethical behavior, cut down on bureaucracy, induce market conform incentives and inspirational externalities and enhance co-responsibility and co-ownership for the delivery of public services.

References

Arrow, K. J. (1973). Information and Economic Behavior, Lecture presented to the federation of Swedish Industries, Stockholm, reprinted in Arrow, K. J. (1984), Collected Papers of J. Arrow: The Economics of Information (pp. 136–52). Harvard University Press, Cambridge, MA.

Asian Development Bank (2000). Asia Development Report. Manila: ADB.

Blowfield, M. and Frynas, J. G. (2005). Setting new agendas: critical perspectives on Corporate Social Responsibility in the developing world. International Affairs, 81(3): 499–513.

Campbell-White, O. and Bhatia, A. (1998). Directions in development: Privatization in Africa. World Bank. Washington, DC (1998).

Dubai Ethics Resources Center (2006). Corporate Responsibility Awareness in The United Arab Emirates.

Guasch, J. L. and Hahn, R. W. (1999). The Costs and Benefits of Regulation: Implications for Developing Countries. World Bank Research Observer, 14(1): 137–158.

Helm D. (2006). Regulatory reform, capture, and the regulatory burden. Oxford Review of Economic Policy, 22(2).

Jacobs, S. (2004). Governance of Asia utilities; New regulators struggle in difficult environments. The governance brief, issue 10, ADB Governance and Regional Cooperation Division: Bangkok.

Klein, M. and Harford, T. (2004). Corporate Responsibility-When Will Voluntary Reputation Building Improve Standards? Public Policy for the Private Sector (Note, 274: 3).

Lanyi, A. (2000). The institutional basis of economic reforms. In: Kähkönen, S. and A. Lanyi, Editors. Institutions, incentives and economic reforms in India. Sage Publications, New Delhi and London.

Parker, D. (1999). Regulation of privatised public utilities in the UK: performance and governance, International Journal of Public Sector Management 12(3): 213–235.

Rettab, B. and Nijsen, A. (2006). Impact of Regulations on Dubai Business. Data Management & Business Research, DCCI. ISBN 9948-430-16-6.

Schwella, E. (2002). Regulation and competition in South Africa. Working Paper no. 18. Manchester: Centre on Regulation and Competition, University of Manchester

Stiglitz, J. (1998). Private uses of public interests: incentives and institutions. Journal of Economic Perspectives 12(2): 3–22.

Van Calster, G. and Deketelaere, K. (2001). The use of voluntary agreements in the European community's Environmental Policy. In: Orts, E. and K. Deketelaere, Editors. Environmental contracts comparative approaches to regulatory innovation in the United States and Europe, Kluwer Law International, London.

Ugaz, C. (2003). Consumer participation and pro-poor regulation in Latin America. In: C. Ugaz and C. Waddams Price, Editors, Utility privatization and regulation: A fair deal for consumers, Cheltenham , Edward Elgar.

Chapter 10
Standardization and Compliance Costs: Relevant Developments at EU Level

Frank A.G. den Butter and John Hudson

Abstract This article discusses government regulation and the consequent compliance costs for the private sector from the perspective of transaction cost economics. In many cases, government regulation is shaped as legally binding standards. In order to comply with these standards, private sector firms meet various types of transaction costs, such as the bonding costs that the principal/agent relationship of government regulation brings about. On the other hand, good standards may reduce transaction costs. Therefore, optimal design of government regulation requires the design of standards with the lowest possible transaction costs. Due to network externalities and economics of scale, and in order to guarantee a level playing field, good coordination and unifying standards within the EU can be beneficial. This article provides examples of such standards.

10.1 Introduction

The administrative burden stems from compliance costs imposed on business by government. Compliance costs, in turn, are part of the more broadly defined transaction costs. Compliance costs stem from standards, but as we will argue, standardization may also be used to reduce transaction costs, both in the broad sense of trade transactions and in the more narrow sense of government regulation. Therefore, in order to understand how the administrative burden arises, it is important to understand standardization. In this chapter, we focus on the way (i) standardization impacts upon administrative costs, (ii) how standardization can enhance the efficiency of regulation and (iii) how standardization can be helpful in reducing transaction costs, and consequently reduce compliance costs as part of transaction costs. The chapter proceeds as follows. In Section 10.2, we look at 'the economics of standards'. In Section 10.3, we

F.A.G. den Butter (✉)
Free University Amsterdam, Amsterdam, The Netherlands
e-mail: fbutter@feweb.vu.nl

A. Nijsen et al. (eds.), *Business Regulation and Public Policy*,
International Studies in Entrepreneurship 20, DOI 10.1007/978-0-387-77678-1_10,

look at standardization in the EU and in Section 10.4, specific examples of EU standards. Section 10.5 examines the EU's plans to control the administrative burden and in Section 10.6, we conclude the chapter.

10.2 The Economics of Standards[1]

10.2.1 Standards: A Classification

Figure 10.1 summarizes how various types of standards can be classified according to their role in the economy. This role is encompassed more or less by the following general definition of a standard: "A standard is the specification of the characteristics of goods and services that provides information on the quality of these goods and services and/or enhances their interoperability". The classification of standards is necessarily somewhat fuzzy as the characteristics may differ in different circumstances, which makes a clear separation of roles impossible.

The first distinction made in Figure 10.1 is between public and private standards. This classification refers to the way standards originate. Is the market responsible for their development, or was it a government initiative? The government has the ability to make the standards mandatory through the introduction of legislation. This is in contrast to voluntary standards. A further distinction is that between standards that are related to products and those related to production processes. A problem is that, often, the question whether a product meets a standard can only be answered by an inspection of the production process. This can be very costly, for both business and governments, particularly when the products are not produced domestically. This poses special problems to regulatory standards with respect to imported goods (and

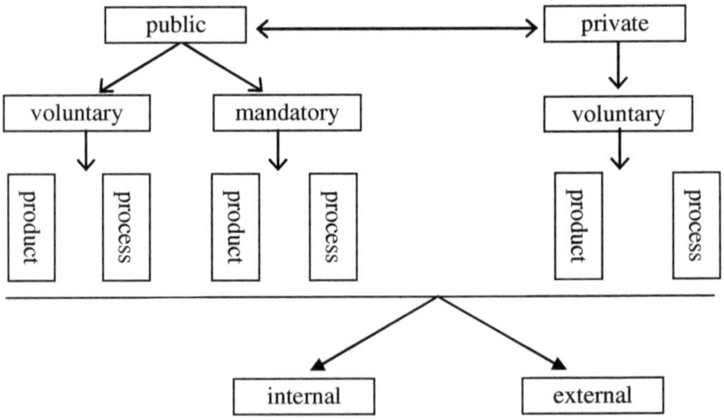

Fig. 10.1 Classification of standards

[1] Parts of this section are based on Den Butter et al. (2007a,b).

services), and may be a reason for international harmonization (e.g. within the EU) of standards. The third categorization of Fig. 10.1 relates to the difference between internal and external standards. Internal standards are subject to the control of companies that set them; external standards are to be considered as given for individual companies. In fact, regulatory standards will always be external standards. Yet they may result in the setting or upgrading of internal standards in a firm, in order to comply with the external regulatory standard.

10.2.2 Reduction of Transaction Costs Through Standards

It has already been mentioned that standards can contribute to the reduction of transaction costs (see Williamson, 1998; North, 1990, 1994) and therefore, more specifically, to the reduction of the administrative burden. It holds both for specialization and coordination of tasks within firms and for transactions at the market level. The more production processes are specialized and split up in various parts, the more coordination is needed and the more important it becomes to reduce transaction costs by means of standardization. On the other hand, a reduction in transaction costs by making better use of standards will promote a further fragmentation of the production process as compliance to these standards becomes less costly. An important reason why standards reduce transaction costs is that standards tend to reduce insecurity and information problems. In the literature, the best known effects of standards are network externalities and a reduction of switching costs (Blind, 2004). Standardization also increases the exportability of products, which facilitates economies of scale.

10.2.2.1 Typology of Transaction Costs

In principle, two types of transaction costs can be distinguished: "Hard" or direct transaction costs and "Soft" or indirect transaction costs. Hard transaction costs relate to costs that are readily perceptible and quantifiable, such as transport charges, import levies and customs authorities' tariffs. Soft transaction costs are much more difficult to observe and measure. One can think of all kinds of costs of making and checking contracts, information costs, costs because of cultural differences and communication failures, tacit knowledge on legal procedures, formation of trust and reputation, network building, costs associated with risks and with rules and regulation in order to reduce risks, security requirements etc. These are of particular relevance for administrative costs.

10.2.2.2 Standards and Market Failure

In general, government intervention, and this includes the area of standards, can only be justified in the presence of market failure. Asymmetric information, which is a form of incomplete information, can be a cause of such market failure. It relates to a situation where the buyer cannot observe the quality or specific characteristics of products. Akerlof (1970) gives the example of the secondhand car salesman. The buyer does not know the quality of car, so that, as a consequence, the bad cars (to speak in Akerlof's terms, the "lemons") are crowding the good cars ("peaches") out of the market. In this case, asymmetric information reduces the supply of good quality products. When asymmetric information results in the inability of consumers to include some relevant aspects of the product in their buying decision, it is possible that only products that score low on these aspects are offered on the market, since they cost less (WTO, 2005). This can be undesirable, and therefore, albeit under conditions, can be a legitimate ground for government intervention.

10.2.2.3 Standards and Trust

Trust is an important mechanism that enables the reduction of transaction costs, especially in the frequent cases of incomplete and/or asymmetric information. In such cases, contracts can never be complete, and trust will always play a role somewhere in the transaction process (Den Butter and Mosch, 2003; Mosch, 2004). Standards may very much contribute to such formation of trust. The reputation and reliability of the quality labels have to be built up slowly, because the formation of a trustworthy reputation will need some time. Explaining the standard and what it stands for to its users on the one hand, as well as adequate supervision, and careful development of a reputation of trust and reliability on the other hand, are needed to make the standard a success. Trust in standards will also contribute to the reduction of compliance costs when it enhances the intrinsic motivation to comply with the standard.

10.2.3 Why Should Governments Bother About Setting Standards for Regulation?

The previous discussion on the relationship between standardization and transaction costs (including compliance costs) suggests that government intervention in standardization can be needed in specific cases. Leaving the development of standards entirely to the market can sometimes result in solutions that are suboptimal from the perspective of social welfare. The existence of market failure is a necessary – though certainly not sufficient – condition for government intervention. Mandatory standards can help with many of the aspects of market failure. Firstly, they result in the removal from the market of all products that do not comply with the minimum standard. Voluntary standards in combination with labeling can provide buyers with sufficient information on quality differences in a situation where both low and high quality products are supplied. Negative labels can be made mandatory by the government for producers of goods that do not comply with a standard. Positive labeling is used by firms to enable the consumer to distinguish (often more expensive) products that comply with high standards. Therefore, standards can reduce, or even take away, the problem of asymmetric information identified by Akerlof, reducing the transaction costs as they enable more and better transactions. This also benefits the reputable firm, particularly ones selling high quality products, who gain from reduced signaling costs and consumer uncertainty.

Apart from internalizing negative externalities, it is especially through reducing information problems that the government can benefit society. This can be done by the introduction of a quality label that provides the user with information on several relevant aspects. Such a multidimensional quality label facilitates the supply of products with various quality levels. This system aims at promoting product differentiation which enhances consumer welfare. Although such a standard does no longer imply a unified set of minimum requirements that all products should comply with, it can still be regarded as a standard. Joining this type of standard can be voluntary or mandatory. It is very likely that producers who have a low score on certain dimensions will not voluntarily join the standard, in the hope that consumers will expect an average quality of the product in the absence of information. This can be undesirable. Therefore, the EU-energy label, for example, is mandatory and must be used by all producers.

The government can also standardize its own services. Such standardization may lead to a considerable reduction of compliance costs when these standards relate to government regulation (e.g. in the case of permits) A special case relates to services provided to multinational organizations. These organizations often have to take all sorts of differences in rules and legislation that exist between different countries into account. This can bring about high transaction costs for them. Especially small countries with legislation that differs substantially from that of other nations will make themselves less attractive to multinationals. Harmonization and less complexity can enhance the ability of a nation to attract foreign investments. An example is harmonization and reducing transaction costs with respect to customs regulation, where many changes already have been made through the WCO (World Customs Organization).

10.2.4 Transaction Costs of Government Regulation

The transaction costs of the implementation of government policy result from the principal/agent (agency) in policy implementation. Here the government acts as principal and the citizens and businesses as agents. In this situation, three types of costs can be distinguished which are all part of the total transaction costs of government regulation. The first type of cost is the costs for the government itself. These are, in the principal/agent terminology, the monitoring costs. Part of these are administration costs, but there are also additional costs which come with the design of the regulatory measures. Therefore, the implementation costs for the government are generally considerably higher than the amounts which appear in the budget (payment of subsidies, receipts of levies). The additional costs include salaries of the civil servants engaged in policy preparation, implementation of regulatory measures and other monitoring activities. Costs also relate to subsidies which are not granted, and allowances for tax exemptions.

The second type of costs is the bonding costs for the citizens and businesses. These consist mainly of compliance costs, which are the focus of this volume. Here, all compliance costs of the laws and legislation by the government should be taken into account. They are the direct financial costs of levies, but also capital investments and all other remaining costs needed to meet the obligations of laws and legislation. These compliance costs also include the costs of informing the government (sheer bonding costs), which can be regarded as the administrative costs in a strict sense. The policy debate on diminishing the administrative burden of government regulation usually focuses on these costs only. Calculating total compliance costs can, however, be rather complicated. For instance, when firms are to meet the requirements of environment legislation or of safety regulations, they have to make all kinds of investments in the production processes and management procedures of the firm. These costs can only be partly counted as transaction costs of government policy, as some of these investment costs would be made anyhow from the firm's own commercial perspective. So, there is a need to separate these kinds of compliance costs into external compliance costs, which are added to the transaction costs, and internal compliance costs, which are not transaction costs originating from government regulation. Of course, such a split between external and internal compliance costs has, to some extent, an arbitrary character and requires a good insight into the management of the firm. Boog and Nijsen (2007) provide an example of how to calculate these various types of compliance costs for specific cases.

The third type of cost is much more difficult to quantify, namely the societal costs of the residual loss. These arise because the reaction of the agents to government regulation will never be in complete agreement with the objectives of the government. The difference is the residual loss. Principal/agent contracts should be designed in such a way that the total agency costs (monitoring costs, bonding costs and residual loss) should be minimized. It implies that agency contracts should not try to reduce residual losses as much as possible, nor should they seek to minimize costs for the government. There should be a good balance between all three types of costs.

The above discussion shows that the principal/agent theory provides an adequate framework for a taxonomy and further categorization of the transaction costs of implementing government regulation. Total transaction costs of government regulation consist of the netted sum of the three components. The expression netted sum indicates that (for e.g.) subsidies granted by the government to private agents are counted as costs by the government, but should be subtracted from the costs incurred by the private agents for obtaining the subsidy and the bonding costs met by these agents to demonstrate to the government that the subsidy is well spent. A similar netting of costs holds in the case of regulatory levies, which are costs for the private agents but are to be subtracted from the administrative costs and other monitoring costs that the government makes when raising the levies. It should, by the way, be noted that in case of regulatory levies, private agents who are subjected to these levies, face higher costs than the sheer amount of the levies. There are additional compliance costs associated with the regulation of the levy, which also have the character of regulatory costs. This aspect is often neglected in decisions about the size of the levies.

Government attempts at minimizing total implementation costs do not come solely from the government. In order to obtain an optimal result, coordination and consultation with stakeholders is needed. This is especially in line with the tradition of compromise and consensus in the Dutch polder model. Such consultation should be institutionalized. It can take place in so-called "matching zones" which are meetings of relevant stakeholders in a specific setting and with a specific agenda in order to come to a low cost compromise. In the principal/agent terminology, these meetings can be seen as the (virtual or actual) meeting place between the principal and the agents, with the purpose, as far as possible, of aligning goals and reducing monitoring and bonding costs. Also important is the choice of participants in these meetings. On the one hand, all interested parties should be represented in the matching zone, but on the other hand, the coordination task should not become too complex. Discussions and consensus formation in these meetings should be restricted to specific regulatory measures and standardization per se and should not be blurred by side issues which can be discussed elsewhere. This problem of forming an optimal composition of participants in the meetings is comparable to that of the optimum scope for administrative entities. In the Netherlands, some (positive) experience with such matching zones was obtained in the field of the implementation and compliance with tax legislation (the Van Lunteren commission). Such stakeholder discussions can also be valuable for the government as they may reveal contradictory legislation from different government departments.

10.3 Standards and Standardization in the EU

10.3.1 The New Approach: In pursuit of the Single Market

In the EU, the choice of standards rather than directives initially stemmed from the difficulties encountered by European institutions in imposing compulsory measures (Brunsson and Jacobsson, 2000). The recourse to standards was therefore a pragmatic response to the absence of any constraining means at the EU's disposal to accompany its regulatory activity and to make the single market an economic reality. Standards facilitate cross border trade and give consumers, and indeed firms, confidence in the quality, safety and specification of goods that comply with those standards. They also reduce search costs which are particularly high for consumers thinking of buying products imported from other countries.

The ‘New Approach’ to standards and regulation in Europe was intended to limit the regulatory function of the Commission and Council to specifying ‘essential requirements’ that producers must meet in terms of safety, health, environmental and consumer protection. Theoretically, at least, these were to be voluntary. Responsibility for developing standards was given to the European Standards Organizations (ESOs). This has led to the proliferation of ‘voluntary standards’ that give products conformity with essential EU directives and thus access to EU markets (Mattli, 2001). However, the need for such access means that in reality, they are not voluntary (Blind, 2004). This lack of clarity raises the possibility that they may be omitted from calculations of the administrative burden.

10.3.2 The EU Standards Architecture: CEN/CENELEC and ETSI

There are three main ESOs: (i) CENELEC, (ii) ETSI, and (iii) CEN. CENELEC prepares ‘voluntary’ electrotechnical standards and ETSI (the European Telecommunications Standards Institute) produces telecommunications standards. CEN, the European Committee for Standardization, focuses on voluntary technical standards which promote free trade, the safety of workers and consumers, the interoperability of networks, environmental protection, the exploitation of research and development programs, and public procurement. It is, for example, responsible for air traffic management standards, automotive fuel standards, common structural rules for the design of buildings, the safety of consumer products, solid biofuels, food, healthcare, the conservation of cultural property, etc. Of the three ESOs, it is mainly CEN who produce standards which impact upon the administrative burden. The Technical Committees (TCs), of which there are currently 275 active ones in CEN alone, play a key role in standard development. The TCs draw on expertise from associated standard bodies which are generally organized by European industry associations (Goerke and Holler, 1998). This too is a cost to business related to regulation, but one which is seldom considered. The standards bodies tend to emphasise consensus, but as final voting is based on a qualified majority, this is more of a subjective than an objective concept. Thus, it is possible that countries have to accept as their national standard something they voted against.

10.4 Examples of European Standards

10.4.1 Examples of European Standards: Packaging and Distribution of Drugs

The Dutch plant of the multinational drugs company Merck, Sharpe & Dohme (MSD) provides an example of how internal and external standards can affect corporate management. MSD Netherlands delivers drugs of the mother company to customers and regions all over the world. The Dutch plant coordinates the logistics, packs the drugs, and makes sure that all rules and legislative requirements have been met. Within MSD, there used to exist an enormous diversity in packages. Thus, MSD developed an internal standard to reduce packing costs, by – for example – using one package for a group of regions. However, standardization of external regulations, which in the case of drugs are set by the EU, national governments and health organizations, is also important for MSD. MSD has to deal with many different prescriptions in various countries with respect to packaging and distribution of drugs. Obviously, increased harmonization would considerably reduce their transaction costs. Harmonization could also be beneficial to public health when the harmonized standards would imply the use of best practices with respect to information on drugs contained in the package. However, up to now, the EU rules for packaging of drugs only provide limited costs advantages to MSD as the individual member states are not fully complying with the EU regulations or have specific local regulations. Nonetheless, the EU is moving in the direction of more uniform regulation in this respect. For example, the European Directorate for the Quality of Medicines and Health Care (EDQM) was set up in 1996 and part of its current mission is to establish and provide official standards for the manufacture and quality control of medicines. Such standards relate to both reducing transaction costs and correcting for market failure.

10.4.2 Examples of European Standards: Food and Product Quality

The EU has an integrated approach to food safety which is designed to ensure effective control systems and compliance with EU standards (Hudson and Hudson, 2008). This covers how farmers produce food, how it is processed, how it is sold and the nature of the information provided on the labeling. The rationale for this lies partly with concerns, partly about health and public safety and partly about facilitating the single market. Underpinning this approach are more than 400 standards developed by CEN in the area of food safety alone as well as others related to general product quality. The European Food Safety Authority (EFSA) was set up in 2002 following a White Paper recommendation of 2000 and partly in response to food health scares such as 'mad cow' disease or BSE (Ugland and Veggeland, 2006). Its role is currently restricted to risk assessment and risk communication to interested parties and the public at large. The EU has recently been considering the role of regulation in protecting consumers and the need to strike a balance between a high level of competitiveness and consumer protection.[2] In part, as always, their concern

[2] More generally, consumer protection is about making sure that all consumer products are safe and that consumer rights are properly protected, that consumers have the information they need to make a judgment and are not misled.

is based on the need to promote trade and competition within the single market. Current legislation allows member states to adopt more stringent regulations – i.e. 'minimum harmonization'. This has resulted in added cost to businesses as they attempt to trade over borders and also increased consumer uncertainty about buying products from other EU countries. Within the context of Section 10.2, these standards correct for market failure and facilitate trust, as do those relating to waste.

10.4.3 Examples of European Standards: Waste Disposal Standards

The WEEE regulations make producers of Electrical and Electronic Equipment (EEE) responsible for these products when they become waste. The aims of the WEEE directive include, e.g., (i) to reduce WEEE disposal to landfill, (ii) provide for a free producer take-back scheme for consumers for end of life equipment, and (iii) to set and achieve targets for recovery, reuse and recycling of different classes of WEEE. At the moment, transposition of the WEEE directive into national law has revealed major differences from one legal system to another. Thus, it is being recommended that the Directive should be revised to increase harmonization (Savage, 2006). Related to WEEE is the RoHS Directive connected with Restrictions of Hazardous Substances in Electrical and Electronic Equipment which, from 2006, put limits on the maximum permitted level of lead, mercury, cadmium, etc. in a product. As is often the case, underpinning this work on RoHS, WEEE and the environment in general is the work of a number of ESO technical committees. For example, CENELEC technical committee TX 111X has developed standard EN 50419: 2006 dealing with the marking of electrical and electronic equipment in accordance with the WEEE directive. All of this puts obligations on firms which they both have to meet and be able to prove they have met.

10.4.4 Examples of European Standards: EU Standards for Financial Transactions in the Capital Markets

According to data from the BIS in 2005, financial transactions in worldwide capital markets amounted to about 1400 trillion dollars. It appears that the direct costs of handling these financial transactions between EU Member States are two to six times as high as in the US. The European Commission aims at reducing the costs of these transactions to a level similar to that in the US (Giovannini, 2001). However, the trading of financial assets involves transaction costs which go far beyond the direct and easily quantifiable trading costs. For example, The London Stock Exchange (LSE, 2002) has calculated that the formation of a European clearing and settlement platform can incur a saving in direct transaction costs of € 1.6 billion. But, estimates of the potential cost savings on indirect costs vary from € 5 billion to € 40 billion per year. The successful completion of a transaction depends to a large extent on the quality of the transaction and speed of communication. However, besides institutional reforms, there is an obvious need for better standardization of the handling of financial asset transactions at the level of the EU. Here, due to differences of the types and sizes of the various stock exchange markets between the EU and the US, a mere copy of the American way of regulation at the EU level seems unwarranted.

Compared to the EU, US asset trade is much more specialized in specific financial products and derivatives, and has large trade turnovers. This specialization (in niche markets) increases the 'asset specificity' of the trade and necessitates specialist knowledge of how to trade these financial products and derivatives. It increases, in principle, the transaction costs but in offering opportunities for professionals to exploit economies of scale in trading large volumes, it may also reduce transaction costs. In the EU, there is also some kind of 'asset specificity' in the financial assets trade but it has a different character than in the US. Here, there are mainly national differences in property rights and regulations that lead to product differentiation. This increases the transaction costs in the EU. Therefore, the EU should develop its own standard on the basis of product harmonization in order to reduce transaction costs. A design for an EU standard which reckons with these differences is given by Den Butter and Corveleijn (2007). This is clearly an example of a standard whose prime purpose is to reduce transaction costs.

10.5 EU Regulation of Standards in the EU

10.5.1 The Adoption of the Dutch Model Throughout the EU

The growth of standards has contributed to the growth of the administrative burden and this has led to growing concern in the EU, as well as in some individual countries. Thus, on March 23, 2005 the European Council requested "the Commission and the Council to consider a common methodology for measuring administrative burdens". The approach proposed by the Commission is based on the Dutch SCM methodology, discussed elsewhere in this volume. It is proposed to use the same core equations, the same relevant cost parameters and the same formulas for expressing the frequency of administrative activities and the same approach in the assessment of the performance of a "normally efficient entity".

The EU has estimated that administrative costs by member states are as in Table 10.1. The EU has calculated that a reduction in the administrative

Table 10.1 Administrative costs by member states as a share of GDP

Austria	4.6%	Ireland	2.4%
Belgium & Luxembourg	2.8%	Italy	4.6%
		Netherlands	3.7%
Czech Republic	3.3%	Poland	5.0%
Germany	1.9%	Portugal	4.6%
Denmark	1.9%	RE*	6.8%
Spain	4.6%	Slovakia	4.6%
Finland	1.5%	Slovenia	4.1%
France	3.7%	Sweden	1.5%
UK	1.5%	EU25	3.5%
Hungary	2.4%		

*RE combines the Baltic member states, Malta and Cyprus.
Source: COM (2006) 691 Final, based on Kox (2005).

burden by 25% would eventually lead to an increase in EU GDP of 1.6% (COM, 2006).

The source of the administrative burden arises from four different levels: (i) international, (ii) EU, (iii) national, (iv) sub-national. The split shown in Table 10.2 suggests that the most important source of burden comes from national governments, although this may be changing as the EU expands its regulatory activities. Specifying where the burden originates can be difficult. Often, a measure originates at, say, EU level to be implemented at national and then sub-national level. Often too, the original impetus would come from an international standards agency such as ISO. At each stage of the chain, there is the potential to add to the original obligation, a process termed 'gold plating'. International law always needs 'transposition'. This is also the case for EU Directives, but not EU Regulations which are directly applicable.

The EU's role is a twofold one; first, in controlling its own administrative burden, and secondly persuading all the member states to follow. At the moment, there is enthusiasm amongst some member states to do this and the Netherlands, Denmark, the Czech Republic and the UK are well down this path. But other states appear less enthusiastic, and without EU pressure, would probably only make limited progress. As such, the EU Commission has set a target for the whole of the EU to reduce administrative costs by 25%. In addition, it is envisaged that targets will also be set in specific policy areas where both the administrative burden is particularly heavy and there is the

Table 10.2 The Distribution of Administrative Costs in Denmark and the Netherlands

Share of administrative costs by origin of legislation	Denmark	Netherlands
Originates directly in international law	28%	43%
International origin but implemented nationally	15%	13%
National Origin	57%	44%

Source: COM (2006) 691 Final, based on Denmark and Netherlands baseline measurement

potential for significant cuts. The EU believes these figures are reasonable and cite results from the four states that have carried out baseline measurements that there is a potential for reductions of this size by focusing on costs originating with both the EU and at the national level. It is also worth emphasizing that three of these four countries have costs below the EU average, as shown in Table 10.1 and one assumes that if a 25% reduction is feasible for these states, then still more could be expected from certain other countries.

10.6 Summary and Conclusions

In the EU, many of the standards and regulations have grown in recent years due to factors such as technical change and rising expectations. Technical change means that products can be produced today which were not previously possible, but the health and safety of products such as mobile phones and GM foods need to be regulated. Rising expectations mean that we have legislation now which we did not have previously simply because we now demand more from products and production processes. But not all the trends are adverse. The development of the computer and the internet will have substantially reduced the compliance costs of e.g. collecting VAT for the government. The growth of EU and international standards will have reduced, and reduced considerably, the administrative costs to firms associated with international trade. Nonetheless, it is probably true that the pressures on the administrative burden will tend upwards in the coming years. This means that if it is a target of government policy to stabilize or even reduce that burden, then finding more efficient ways of doing things, rather than doing fewer things is probably essential, although particular attention needs to be focused on the work of the ESOs to ensure that new standards imposing obligations on business are genuinely necessary.

Standards and associated regulatory activity represent a cost on business, but it is not a cost without benefits for both society and for firms. In terms of society, standards which ensure product quality, particularly related to safety, provide a clear benefit to consumers in correcting for market failure as outlined in Section 10.2. But they also benefit the firm in several ways. First, in addressing the problem of asymmetric information, they provide a guarantee to the consumer that they can buy goods with confidence; this will economize on individual search costs, possibly expand the market and also potentially allow firms to economize on signaling expenditure (Jones and Hudson, 1996). Moreover, firms too benefit from such guarantees. In agriculture, for example, they reduce the spread of infectious diseases amongst livestock. Again, within the context of market failure, other standards and regulatory activity ensure the health and safety of the workforce. This too is an advantage to society, but also to the good employers who do not have to unfairly compete against firms with less rigorous standards. Thus, the design and institutional set-up of government regulation should be such that total transaction costs, i.e. compliance costs for the private sector, implementation and control costs for the regulator and (indirect) costs for society should be minimized. It implies "efficient" regulation and not necessarily deregulation, as insufficient regulation or laxity in execution of regulation may bring about high societal costs in the long run, e.g. because of costly accidents and loss of faith and trust in government. It must also take into account that some regulation and standards can reduce transaction costs for business. Hence, the view that no new regulation can be brought in unless some other burden disappears in many cases is almost certainly wrong and, if followed through, would expose society to unnecessary risk.

Because of this, the next stage in the process of controlling the administrative burden may well be one of measuring not just the 'gross burden' but the net one too. That is measuring both the costs and the benefits. A proper cost/benefit analysis should be a major element in the discussion on the administrative costs of regulation. In case of new regulations or standards, the benefits should exceed the costs, and the regulation should be designed in such a way that, given the warranted scope of regulation, costs should be minimized. Obviously, these costs do not only comprise administrative costs in a narrow sense, but include all kinds of transaction costs mentioned in Section 10.2. Inclusion of these (often soft and difficult to measure) transaction costs in the Dutch SCM methodology seems warranted in order to enhance the quality of that methodology. In addition, it shows that a target of, say, merely reducing administrative costs by 25% can be suboptimal from the perspective of welfare economics. In those cases, where actual deregulation is warranted, i.e. a relaxation of rules and restrictions or of quality standards set to products and production processes, again, a full fledged cost/benefit analysis is in order. Here, the loss of benefits to society of regulation, e.g. of allowing for higher risks or being less strict on internalizing negative externalities, should be smaller than the gains in terms of less transaction costs. However, in as much as the focus is on transaction costs affecting business, it should be on all transaction costs and not just those imposed by government. Hence, if transaction costs are high because of market failure, then government action in reducing the extent of this market failure is as valid an area of concern as reducing the administrative burden per se. Standards impose transaction costs on business, but equally some standards can reduce transaction costs whilst simultaneously benefiting society as a whole. This has been shown in our analysis of the financial and pharmaceutical industries.

References

Akerlof, G.A., 1970, The market for "lemons": quality, uncertainty and the market mechanism, Quarterly Journal of Economics, 84, 488–500.

Blind, K., 2004, The Economics of Standards, Edward Elgar Publishing, Williston.

Boog, J.J. and A.F.M. Nijsen, 2007, Pilotonderzoek overige nalevingskosten van bestaande wetgeving (Pilot research on other compliance costs of existing legislation) EIM, Zoetermeer, 30 March 2007.

Brunsson, N. and B. Jacobsson, 2000, A World of Standards, Oxford University Press, Oxford.
Butter, F.A.G. den and R.H.J. Mosch, 2003, Trade, trust and transaction costs, Tinbergen Institute Discussion Paper TI 2003-082/3.
Butter, F.A.G. den and P. Corveleijn, 2007, Standaardisering van het Europese effectenverkeer (Standards for the European financial assets trade), Economisch Statistische Berichten, 92, 708–711.
Butter, F.A.G. den, S.P.T. Groot, and F. Lazrak, 2007a, Standaards als bron van welvaart (Standards as sources of prosperity), Kwartaalschrift Economie, 4, nr. 2139–165.
Butter, F.A.G. den, S.P.T. Groot, and F. Lazrak, 2007b, The transaction costs perspective on standards as a source of trade and productivity growth, Tinbergen Institute Discussion Paper TI 2007-090-3.
COM 689, 2006, Measuring Administrative Costs and Reducing Administrative Burdens in the European Union, EU Commission, Brussels.
Giovannini, The Group, 2001. Cross-Border Clearing and Settlement Arrangements in the European Union. Brussel. http://ec.europa.eu.
Goerke, L and M.J. Holler, 1998, Strategic standardization in Europe: A public choice perspective, European Journal of Law and Economics, 6, 95–112.
Hudson, C. and J. Hudson (2008) Guaranteeing Quality in the EU: Who Gains Most?, Journal of Regulatory Economics, 33, 283–298.
Jones, P. and J. Hudson, 1996, Standardization and the costs of assessing quality, European Journal of Political Economy, 12, 355–361.
Kox, H.L.M., 2005, Intra-EU differences in regulation-caused administrative burden for companies, CPB Memorandum 136, CPB, The Hague.
London Stock Exchange, 2002, Clearing and Settlement in Europe. Response to the first report of the Giovannini Group.
Mattli, W., 2001, The politics and economics of international institutional standards setting: an introduction, Journal of European Public Policy, 8, 328–344.
Mosch, R.H.J., 2004, The Economic Effects of Trust; Theory and Empirical Evidence, Tinbergen Institute Research Series 340, Thela Thesis, Amsterdam.
North, D.C., 1990, Institutions, Institutional Change and Economic Performance, Cambridge University Press, Cambridge (MA).
North, D.C., 1994, Economic performance through time, American Economic Review, 84, 359–368.
Savage, M., 2006, Implementation of Waste Electric and Electronic Equipment Directive in EU 25, European Commission, Brussels.
Ugland, T. and F. Veggeland, 2006, Experiments in food safety policy integration in the European Union. Journal of Common Market Studies, 44, 607–624.
Williamson, O.E., 1998, Transaction cost economics: how it works; where it is headed, De Economist, 146, 23–58.
World Trade Organization, 2005, World Trade Report 2005, Washington.

Chapter 11
Regulatory Impact Analysis: Integrating Pro-growth Decisions into Public Policy in Developing Countries

Scott Jacobs

Abstract Many countries today have placed regulatory reform programs at the core of their governance and microeconomic strategies. Within those reforms, regulatory impact assessment (RIA) has become a prominent tool by which governments integrate benefits and costs of public policy into a balance that achieves, over time, the country's development priorities. The spread of RIA into less-developed countries is largely due to intense pressures to stimulate growth, particularly pro-poor growth. Although RIA began as a set of analytical methods, RIA has evolved into a framework for public-private cooperation that can greatly improve the relationship between public and private sectors in effective and efficient public policy. Yet business representatives have not, in general, built capacities to assess proposals from governments, nor the capacities to collect relevant and timely information that can support the process of discovering the right solution. The private sector should ensure that it is a constructive partner in the consultation process by supplying timely, relevant, and reliable information through the consultation process.

11.1 Introduction

Many countries today have placed regulatory reform programs at the core of their governance and microeconomic strategies.[1] The objective of a national program of regulatory reform is to achieve – in a progressive, carefully-planned, and rapid manner – a low-cost, low-risk regulatory system[2] that both supports

[1] Much of this paper is based on Scott Jacobs (2006) "Current Trends in Regulatory Impact Analysis: Mainstreaming RIA Into Policy-Making," Jacobs and Associates Reports, 2006.

[2] Scott Jacobs developed the "low-cost, low-risk" criteria for a regulatory system in a report written for the Foreign Investment Advisory Service in 2006. FIAS will publish that report in 2008.

S. Jacobs (✉)
Jacobs and Associates, Washington, DC, USA
e-mail: scottjacobs@regulatoryreform.com

A. Nijsen et al. (eds.), *Business Regulation and Public Policy*, International Studies in Entrepreneurship 20, DOI 10.1007/978-0-387-77678-1_11,

competitiveness and effectively protects public interests. No sustainable regulatory reform program can be unbalanced toward either costs or benefits:

- Most important public policy concerns facing governments – environment quality, consumer rights, definition of property rights, control of new technologies, integration into global markets – are regulatory issues. The success of modern governance depends essentially on the performance of regulation.
- The success of modern economies depends on the continual productivity increases that arise from innovation and competition. Regulatory reform offers an effective strategy for managing the risks of more intense competition while preparing companies to prosper within more open and competitive markets. Improvements to the regulatory framework that reduce the economic cost of inefficient and excessive regulation will support national growth and productivity and ease the strains and risks of the economic structural adjustment needed in most countries.

Regulation must integrate benefits and costs of public policy into a balance that achieves, over time, the country's development priorities. Integration of competing policy priorities is among the most difficult tasks of governance.

Regulatory impact analysis (RIA) is the most common method for integrating multiple non-budget policies into a single decision framework. RIA is one element in the rapid development, since 1980, of the craft of good regulation, one of the distinguishing characteristics of modern public management. In most countries, RIA has evolved from narrow technical methods aimed at cutting costs toward more flexible and sophisticated techniques of problem-solving aimed at fostering a richer and more informed public debate about important public policy issues. The "smart regulation" movement is aimed at improving the performance of the "regulatory state" that is everywhere under pressure to produce more results at lower cost.

Since 1980, RIA has become a global phenomenon in response to widespread pressures for more effective and efficient regulatory governance. In the short period of two decades, RIA has become a prominent tool by which governments learn how to deal effectively with increasingly complex public policy issues in an environment of competitive and open markets (see Fig. 11.1 below). In the mid-1990s, international bodies – the OECD, the WTO, and the European Commission – began to call for empirical methods of decision-making, or explicitly for RIA. Almost all OECD countries have now adopted formal policies mandating the use of RIA in domestic policy-making. In Europe, the U.K. Presidency of the European Union stated in 2005 that "Reducing burdens on business by legislating better, reviewing and simplifying existing EU legislation and using alternatives to regulation will play an important role in strengthening competitiveness."[3] The first strategy in the European Commission's

[3] http://www.eu2005.gov.uk/servlet/Front?pagename=OpenMarket/Xcelerate/ShowPage&c=Page&cid=1114071804875

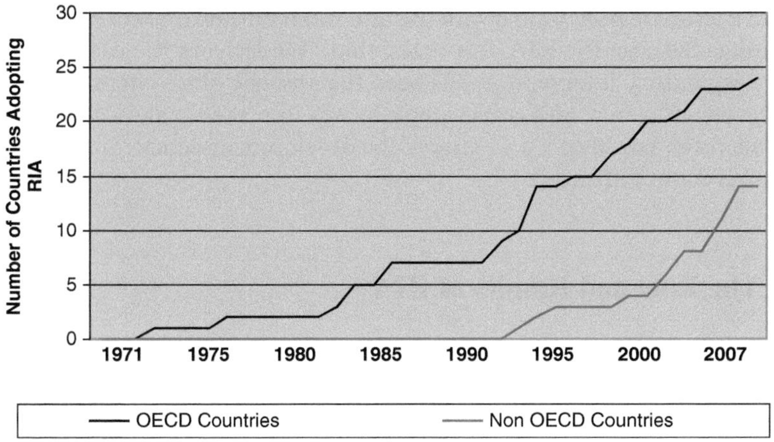

Fig. 11.1 The Rise of RIA, 1970–2007
Copyright: Jacobs and Associates, 2008.

"Better Regulation for Growth and Jobs" was "further promoting the design and application of better regulation tools at the EU level, notably ... impact assessments and simplification...."[4]

Today, RIA, within a larger regulatory reform policy, has become a norm of democratic governance in modern industrialized countries that are integrated into global trade and investment markets. As the techniques of RIA have developed and its relevance to a broader range of problems has become clearer, less-developed countries are also beginning to adopt RIA.

11.2 RIA and Less-Developed Countries

The spread of RIA into less-developed countries is largely due to intense pressures to stimulate growth, particularly pro-poor growth. In South Africa, for example, one reason given for the adoption of RIA was "Unintended regulatory costs and unequal incidence of these costs present a significant financial hurdle to the formalization of small businesses."[5] Similarly, the case for RIA in Uganda included the argument, "RIA is an essential tool to promoting formalization as it is intended to design precise, targeted regulations that

[4] Commission of the European Communities (2005) Better Regulation for Growth and Jobs in the European Union, Communication from the Commission to the Council and the European Parliament, Brussels, 16.3.2005, COM(2005) 97 final.

[5] South Africa Foundation (August 2003) Designing A Regulatory Impact Assessment For South Africa, Johannesburg.

achieve legitimate policy aims with the minimum burden on those affected."[6] In Sri Lanka, the case for RIA was made that "Underlying the cases of unsatisfactory regulatory intervention has been the absence of a systematic approach to integrate efficiency and equity perspectives into the regulation making process. The result has been a widening of the development deficit, an outcome that Sri Lanka cannot afford."[7]

11.3 The Role and Results of RIA

RIA is much more than simply a methodology for collecting and presenting data. RIA has evolved into a structured process, embedded throughout the policy-making machinery, for learning systematically about problems facing a country, and finding the right solutions to those problems. This process of learning through RIA requires a joint process of shared problem-solving among major stakeholders who understand problems from different perspectives and who hold different forms of information about the consequences of various solutions. The implication of "RIA as discovery" about solving problems is that businesses should be involved in RIA in a more much participative and constructive way than simply as a pool of data to be mined by governments.

RIA is, therefore, a framework for public-private cooperation that can greatly improve the relationship between public and private sectors in areas of mutual interest, that is, effective and efficient public policy. RIA can be particularly valuable as a framework for consultation in developing countries, where the relationship between government and businesses is very often one of mutual suspicion, distrust, and lack of capacity for constructive problem-solving, and further weakened by weak checks on the influence of powerful insider interests.

Despite frequent disappointment in the length of time it takes to develop a good national RIA system, there has been substantial progress. A set of RIA tools and methods has been developed and tested that is highly adaptable to varying national conditions and capacities. There is visible convergence in core methods and processes of RIA, but RIA processes and methods are still quickly evolving as, around the world, RIA is being mainstreamed into policy processes.

The results of RIA are also increasingly documented. Available information from various governments and studies indicates a variety of desirable outcomes:

---

[6] Darren Welch, Richard Waddington (November 2005) Introducing Regulatory Impact Assessment in Developing Countries: The Case of Uganda, presented at the International Conference on Reforming the Business Environment: Cairo, Egypt, World Bank.

[7] Malathy Knight-John et al. (April 2005) "Regulatory Impact Assessment: A Tool for Better Regulatory Governance in Sri Lanka?" Public Enterprise Reform, Competition and Regulatory Policy Research Unit, Institute of Policy Studies of Sri Lanka

- RIA, when it is done well, improves the cost-effectiveness of regulatory decisions and reduces the number of low-quality and unnecessary regulations.
- RIA improves the transparency of decisions, and enhances consultation and the participation of affected groups.
- RIA has also improved governmental coherence and intra-ministerial communication.
- Sustained use of RIA, with guidance and training, induced a cultural change among regulators.
- RIA is associated with a universal increase in the use of a range of alternatives to traditional forms of regulation.

Yet neither government nor key stakeholders such as businesses and business associations have built sufficient capacities to use RIA for its highest value. To reach a sustainable level of RIA quality, governments need a clear strategy aimed at the institutionalization of capacities and incentives within the machinery of government. Such a strategy rests on a whole series of good RIA practices: clearer targeting strategies, development of multi-level consultation strategies, more attention to data collection and data quality issues, much more investment in training, more effective quality control through central RIA units and ministerial accountability, better use of scarce scientific resources, and better technical RIA manuals.

Similarly, trade associations and major corporations, who should be key stakeholders in the RIA process, poorly understand their role within a constructive partnership of problem-solving based on RIA. Business representatives have not, in general, built sufficient capacities to assess proposals from governments, nor the capacities to collect relevant and timely information that can support the process of discovering the right solution.

As a result of inadequate preparation by both the public and private sectors, the communication and dialogue aspects of RIA - as opposed to its purely analytical aspect – have been poorly designed or implemented by governments. Yet, the dialogue aspects of RIA process are just as important as the analytical aspects of RIA method to discover how to define problems and to resolve them efficiently.

11.4 The Role of Business Stakeholders in RIA

Regulatory quality depends on a partnership between government and civil society. RIA has developed into a framework through which the many goals of complex societies are integrated, options identified, and trade-offs clearly presented for decision. That requires that impacts on businesses be an important part of the wider RIA scope.

This kind of agenda requires substantial learning on the part of the public sector, as well as on the part of key stakeholders who interact in a new dynamic of public-private problem-solving and accountability. In this context, an important change in the function of RIA can be seen in the past few years as it has become integrated into broader systems of result-oriented policy-making. In this kind of system, the value of RIA is increasingly due to process rather then method. Functionally, RIA is now seen less as an analytical method of arriving at precise answers to quantitative questions, and more as a process of:

- asking the right questions in a structured format to support a wider and more transparent policy debate;
- systematically and consistently examining selected potential impacts arising from government action or non-action;
- communicating the information to decision-makers and stakeholders.[8]

This process of asking, learning, and communicating through a systematic approach is the very core of a government that continually improves its capacities to solve the problems that face its citizens. Essentially, RIA has become one of the methods through which societies speed up learning. Because it is an open and consultative technique, it stimulates social learning, in which various stakeholders involved in the issue gain a clearer sense of the options, and trade-offs, and the consequences of solutions, than in the past. Because it increases opportunities for debate, RIA contributes to the development of a degree of social consensus that allows difficult public policy decisions be made.

For these reasons, consultation with stakeholders is increasingly seen as a key design element of an effective RIA program. This point was clearly made in the 2004–2005 review by the UK's National Audit Office of UK RIAs. The review found that the RIAs that influenced policy were started early in the process, involved good consultation processes, and produced good assessments of the impacts of the policy proposals.[9]

Public consultation is the means by which RIA fosters public debate. In most of the countries using RIA for five years or more, RIA has become a cornerstone of the stakeholder consultation process on regulations. Canada's Treasury Board Secretariat states that "encouraging stakeholder consultation early in the process is perhaps the most important feature of the RIA program."[10]

RIA is pushing consultation to occur sooner, more systematically, and more transparently. For example, the European Commission published in 2002 a consultation communication[11] that lays out minimum standards of

---

[8] This definition of RIA as a process rather than as a document was developed by Jacobs and Associates in 2005.

[9] UK National Audit Office (2005) Evaluation of Regulatory Impact Assessments Compendium Report 2004-05, REPORT BY THE COMPTROLLER AND AUDITOR GENERAL, HC 341 Session 2004-2005, 17 March 2005.

[10] See Treasury Board Secretariat, Website (undated) Number 14: Regulatory Reform through Regulatory Impact Analysis: The Canadian Experience, at http://www.tbs-sct.gc.ca/pubs_pol/dcgpubs/manbetseries/VOL14-1_e.asp

[11] European Commission (2002) Communication from the Commission: Towards a reinforced culture of consultation and dialogue - General principles and minimum standards for consultation of interested parties by the Commission Brussels, COM(2002) 704 final

consultation, and in 2004, it reported that "Efforts to consult widely before proposing legislation reached record levels."[12] The United Kingdom's Cabinet Office reports that "We consult more extensively now than ever before. And, in the vast majority of cases, consultation periods are now at least 12 weeks long, enabling more time for responses and more people to be involved."[13] Ireland's 2005 consultation policy states, "The introduction of RIA in Ireland means that public bodies will, in future, consult more widely and systematically."[14] In the United States, the United Kingdom, and the European Commission, draft RIAs are published on Internet sites for maximum public access. The record is far from perfect: in Sweden, only 48% of RIAs in 2005 reported on how consultation had occurred, up from 35% in 2004.[15] In New Zealand, only final RIAs must be published on the Internet (since 2001).

Consultation with key stakeholders has also become more structured in several countries, a welcome development given the difficulty of eliciting high quality information from the public. These structured approaches include test panels in Denmark, United Kingdom, Germany and the Netherlands, and focus groups (Sweden, Victoria State). The Victoria State RIA Guide (2005) states that preliminary consultation may occur through focus groups and briefing sessions with key stakeholders before deciding that a regulatory proposal is the most appropriate response to an issue. The European Business Test Panel (EBTP), an online survey asking companies representative of the European economy about certain areas of law, could be used in future for RIAs. The UK National Audit Office found in 2005 that "consultation was most effective where departments held ongoing discussions with stakeholders throughout the process, in addition to the formal consultations."

The increased use of consultation has recently given rise, at least in Canada and in the European Commission, to concerns about consultation fatigue. But this concern probably has less to do with the quantity of consultation than with the quality of consultation. Much of the consultation material that is released to the public is still turgid, poorly focused, and difficult to understand. This point was made by the Chair of the UK's Better Regulation Task Force in 2005: "We feel that the problem of consultation fatigue" could be mitigated if consultation exercises were better targeted in the first place and stakeholders could see that their responses had been listened to and had made a difference."[16]

---

[12] Commission of the European Communities (2005) Report from the Commission "Better Lawmaking 2004," Brussels, 21.03.2005, COM(2005) 98 final (12th report)

[13] The UK consultation code is at http://www.cabinetoffice.gov.uk/regulation/consultation/documents/pdf/code.pdf

[14] Ireland Department of the Taoiseach (2005) Reaching Out: Guidelines on Consultation for Public Sector Bodies, Dublin.

[15] The reviewer lamented "It is, for example, inadequate merely to write that 'consultations with the sector have taken place', as unfortunately happens in many cases."

[16] http://www.publications.parliament.uk/pa/ld200506/ldselect/ldeucom/33/33we03.htm

Accountability for responding to consultation is also improving. Regulators in Canada, the United States, the United Kingdom, Ireland (since 2005) and Sweden are required to give feedback on the comments received, explaining to what extent and how they have influenced policy development. For example, the 2004 consultation code in the United Kingdom requires that regulators "clearly explain" how decisions have been reached. Responding to public comments is not yet required in the European Commission.

11.5 Building Better Consultation with Stakeholders as Part of RIA

How do businesses and other key stakeholders actually participate in RIA that integrates public policies with economic realities into a balanced policy? Neither government nor business representatives can do it alone. Consultation is a two-way relationship, in which information is demanded and supplied.

- The public sector is responsible for a clear and predictable process of making information available to the private sector and of listening to what is said.
- The private sector is responsible for ensuring that it is a constructive partner in the consultation process by supplying timely, relevant, and reliable information through the consultation process.

For their part, governments must adopt a consistent, mandatory, and transparent strategy of consultation that applies across the entire public sector. This is particularly important in developing countries, where traditions of public-private dialogue are weak, and where government officials often have little idea of how to carry out an open, evidence-based consultation process. The OECD has noted that "A well-designed and implemented consultation program can contribute to higher-quality regulations by providing a cost-effective source of data on which to base decision-making..."[17]

Any government using RIA systems to improve policy-making should develop a parallel strategy of consultation, based on building capacities in both the public sector and in key stakeholders for constructive and evidence-based dialogue. The mandatory consultation policy should lay out goals, standard methods, and an implementation plan. Such a policy will require investment in new procedures and staff training in how to consult and how to use information from consultations. The policy should consider the following options:

- Consultation Policy in the Public Sector
- Consultation Policy in the Private Sector

---

[17] See OECD (2002) Canada: Maintaining Leadership Through Innovation, Chapter 2, Government Capacity to Ensure High Quality Regulation, Paris.

11.5.1 Consultation Policy in the Public Sector[18]

Each ministry should:

- Adopt a ministerial consultation policy that establishes a minimum standard of consultation ministry-wide.
- Create a standardized format for consultation documents, such as a summary of policy goals, main issues and options, to permit easier access by stakeholders.
- Use simple regulatory impact assessment to make clear the potential consequences for businesses of proposed actions.
- Make consultation accessible to all businesses and stakeholders in the country.

Method of consultation

- Build a unique website for publication and consultation on draft regulations and decisions. Publish open public consultations that are announced at a 'single access point'.
- Create a Business Advisory body as a permanent consultation channel for decisions.
- Develop capacities to implement business focus groups and test panels to discuss draft decisions and regulations.

Timing and response to consultations

- Require consultation early in policy development, before drafting is done, to improve the quality of documents submitted to Ministers.
- Provide sufficient time for response. Staff should allow at least eight weeks for responses to written public consultations.
- Receipt of contributions should be acknowledged.
- Results of open public consultation should be displayed on websites linked to a single access point on the internet.
- Ministerial reactions to stakeholder comments should be summarized in the final policy decision.

For their parts, business associations, key stakeholders in RIA-driven consultations, must build their capacities to collect and communicate information back to the public sector. Consultation is not simply the collection of opinions of what businesses think, but of concrete information and data on business impacts that support specific regulatory approaches that reduce business costs.

---

[18] See Scott Jacobs (2007) Regulatory Reform Strategies: Converging with Europe's Best Regulatory Environments, September, at www.regulatoryreform.com.

11.5.2 Consultation Policy in the Private Sector

To respond to these information needs, business associations should build capacities to:

- Collect information on upcoming government activities (early warning).
- Inform members of trade associations of upcoming issues.
- Identify the specific business impacts in policy decisions.
- Assess the impacts of government actions.
- Collect data from businesses through surveys or focus groups.
- Identify needed reforms or alternative approaches that the government might take at lower cost to business.
- Use empirical evidence and comparative information from other countries to support recommendations.
- Prepare and present position papers, and discuss them with public sector representatives to assist in identifying better policy approaches.
- Monitor results and suggest reforms.

11.6 Summary and Conclusions

The participatory approach to learning about public policy problems and their solutions – in which the public and private sectors work together to exploit their respective information bases – requires a transformation in the relationship among stakeholders in policy making in most countries. It engenders a dynamic in which more and more stakeholders become involved in policy making, and in which public policy officials become more adept at collecting and using information through RIA to find solutions that balance growth, equity, and other public policy goals.

No reform can be successful in moving toward a low-cost, low-risk regulatory system without intensive, transparent, and structured participation from the business sector. Reforms to improved policy processes within the machinery of government must be matched by building capacities in key stakeholders to respond fully to the new information needs of the government. Both partners in the process must agree on basic principles – the form and timing of participation, the kind and quality of information that is relevant to policy, and the responsibilities of both partners in terms of openness and responsiveness. A national regulatory system that is consistent both with the policy priorities of the country and with the realities of doing business within more competitive and open markets requires the skills of all major partners, and these skills are, in most countries, an asset that has been neglected.

References

Commission of the European Communities (2005) Better Regulation for Growth and Jobs in the European Union, Communication from the Commission to the Council and the European Parliament, Brussels, 16.3.2005, COM(2005) 97 final

Department of the Taoiseach (July 2005) Report on the Introduction of Regulatory Impact Analysis, Dublin.
European Commission (2002) Communication from the Commission: Towards a reinforced culture of consultation and dialogue – General principles and minimum standards for consultation of interested parties by the Commission Brussels, COM(2002) 704 final
OECD (2002) *Regulatory Policies in OECD Countries: From Interventionism to Regulatory Governance*, OECD, Paris.
Scott Jacobs (2006) "Current Trends in Regulatory Impact Analysis: Mainstreaming RIA Into Policy-Making," Jacobs and Associates Reports, 2006, at www.regulatoryreform.com.

Background Literature

Andrea Renda (2006) Impact assessment in the EU: the state-of-the-art and the art of the state, Center for European Policy Studies, Brussels.
Canada. External Advisory Committee on Smart Regulation (September 2004) *Smart Regulation: A Regulatory Strategy for Canada*, Ottawa.
European Commission (15 June 2005) *Impact Assessment Guidelines*, SEC(2005) 791, Brussels.
UK Better Regulation TaskForce (March 2005) *Regulation – Less is More. Reducing Burdens, Improving Outcomes*, A BRTF report to the Prime Minister, London.
US Office of the President(1993, 2002) *Regulatory Planning and Review*, Executive Order 12866, as amended by E.O. 13258 (67 Fed. Reg. 9,385 (2002)).

Chapter 12
Why Focus on Enterprises?

Lennart Palm

Abstract The reasons for giving special treatment to enterprises, compared with other stakeholders, are extensive. Companies and entrepreneurship, as such, enjoy no special status. Instead, what counts is the sum total of direct and indirect repercussions of political decisions. This is what dictates their being given special treatment, in terms of the consequences of new and amended business regulations. Business owners are a political minority and will most certainly remain so and few politicians know what everyday life in business is, although many politicians mean well. The politicians' main concern is, of course, the budget but what is self-evident when the state is a stakeholder is deemed by decision-makers to be less obvious where other stakeholders, such as business, are concerned. In a market economy, it is necessary to ensure that companies can compete on equivalent terms. Matters intensively discussed today include, for example, which requirements should be imposed on companies that bid for public contracts. Financial, social and environmental demands are imposed that may go beyond the scope of the actual product or service being procured. Gender equality plans or anti-discrimination clauses may be required, or it may be stipulated how a procured product is to be transported and what fuel the transporter is to use. There is a risk that decision-makers who state their wish for stiffer competition in certain sectors will instead, through their own actions, impair competition in the sectors they are seeking to stimulate.

This is why an early RIA is so important. It should be an analysis that, in an initial phase, is confined to direct effects on companies but is used to assess the effects on society as a whole in the subsequent phase.

L. Palm (✉)
Board of Swedish Industry and Commerce, Stockholm, Sweden
e-mail: lennart.plm@telia.com

A. Nijsen et al. (eds.), *Business Regulation and Public Policy*,
International Studies in Entrepreneurship 20, DOI 10.1007/978-0-387-77678-1_12,

12.1 Introduction

In this chapter, I consider whether, in exploring the implications of proposed new or amended business legislation, there is any justification for treating enterprises as a special case. Might not the impact analysis already performed in many countries today suffice? Should not the procedure for other stakeholders be the same as for companies? And are there any particular reasons why legislators and investigators should, at an early stage of the regulatory process and by advanced means, analyze the effects of regulations on enterprises?

12.2 Enterprises and National Prosperity

Worldwide, business and enterprise are crucially important to the emergence of prosperity. As an economic system, the market economy has proved itself the most dynamic of systems by far. But it must be emphasised that democracy and effective rule of law are preconditions for its long-term efficient functioning. While noting all the boons of the market economy and private enterprise for former developing and ex-Communist countries, we also see the need for well-functioning public institutions if these effects are to endure.

In my home country, Sweden, there are some 630,000[1] companies with an aggregate workforce of 2.9 million people. They form the base for a public sector that employs 1,360,000. The majority of these companies are, as in most countries, small and medium-sized enterprises (SMEs). Companies with fewer than 200 employees make up 99.8% of the total, while the remaining 0.2% with staff numbering 200 or more, employ more than a million. There were approximately 45,000 new business start-ups in 2006.

Conditions for these companies, and how they perform and develop, affect not only the employees concerned but, indirectly, the 1,360,000 public-sector workers and also students, children and pensioners. Profits generated in the business sector have a fundamental influence on the standards citizens can attain in education, healthcare, the environment and elsewhere. Businesses undoubtedly benefit from a well-functioning public sector, but not from a public sector that competes with private enterprise.

12.3 Indirect Effect on Society at Large

What happens if regulations are drawn up in such a way that, in relation to the legislators' aims, they impose not the slightest restriction and burden on individual companies? Effects of various types, and not only on enterprises and their owners, may ensue. Incorrectly designed tax can bring in less government revenue than planned, since companies may be forced to take steps to minimize the damage to themselves. With a tax on ownership, business owners can find

[1] Fokus på Sveriges Ekonomi 2006 ('Focus on Sweden's Economy in 2006'), Ekonomifakta.

alternatives to the company investments concerned. With a corporate tax, they may ponder whether the tax is genuinely competitive; if not, and if the worst comes to the worst, enterprises may consider a full or partial shift in its business. With regulation of working time, firms may consequently feel obliged to cut their opening hours or further rationalize their business. Environmental issues, which are increasingly topical, are another key area in which misguided regulations may result in the elimination of certain firms if, for example, the transitional regulations are unacceptably worded. Overall, effects on individual companies in the form of reduced sales, exports and investments and impaired competitiveness may, in turn, lead to staff cutbacks. The results may then be a tax shortfall for the state, dwindling currency inflows into the country, insufficient competitiveness in relation to foreign countries and reduced competition within the country itself.

12.4 Regulatory Inflation

New regulations affecting enterprises are usually more numerous than those that directly influence private individuals.

An investigation[2] conducted by Fredrik Sterzel, the Professor and former Justice of the Supreme Court, in 1997 on behalf of the Swedish Employers' Confederation, showed that business regulations in Sweden were proliferating twice as fast as other regulations. A growing number of business regulations is, perhaps, hardly surprising in view of all the progress made and new products developed by companies that can affect environmental, social and economic trends alike. But regulatory inflation or 'creep', as such, may prevent compliance from matching the politicians' plans, since it is ever harder for companies to take in all the requirements imposed on them by the legislators.

Tighter requirements may also lower the business start-up rate, especially in sectors subject to extensive regulations. The problem seldom lies in the actual registration of an enterprise; rather, it is a matter of what ensues when the enterprise becomes active in a particular sector. In Sweden, companies have 20,000 pages of business regulations to consider. Far from all of these relate to every company, but the mass of regulations is growing from one year to the next and fines, other penalties and, at worst, imprisonment are the sanctions for non- compliers. Companies in obvious breach of the regulations must, of course, incur sanctions just as individual citizens do. But the massive volume of regulations exacerbates the risks of unintentional breaches, while also inhibiting entrepreneurship, investments and willingness to recruit new staff.

---

[2] Inflation i företagsregler – ett hot mot konkurrenskraften ('Inflation in Business Regulations — a Threat to Competitiveness'), Swedish Employers' Confederation 1997. There is no new investigation available comparing business and "private" legislation but the overall yearly figure is about 2% regulatory inflation.

12.5 Effects on Government Budget: The Legislator's Main Concern

Most proposals for new or amended business regulations arise through a special process that is regulated by laws, ordinances or special written communications. In Sweden, a government commission of inquiry, sometimes with parliamentary representation, is often set up to put forward proposals on how to regulate a sector. Through directives, the government lays down the remit of this commission, which then submits a report containing its proposals to the government. The motives for regulation are often well documented, since the underlying purpose is often to bring about regulation of something that the regulator does not believe can be entrusted to the market itself. There is almost always a requirement that the commission should clarify how its proposals affect public finances, and how it proposes to finance any rise in costs to the state. The latter rise is, of course, a necessity to give politicians and other decision-makers more refined documentation for their decisions. What is self-evident when the state is a stakeholder is deemed by decision-makers to be less obvious where other stakeholders, such as businesses, are concerned. On the contrary, despite the crucial importance of enterprises to national prosperity, the politicians' decision documentation is, with respect to the impact on enterprises, often considerably less well researched than those regarding the state.

Between 2001 and 2007[3] my organization, the Board of Swedish Industry and Commerce for Better Regulation, has examined the quality of regulatory impact analyses (RIAs) that, under ordinances and government communications, Swedish central-government regulators are obliged to present alongside their business-related regulatory proposals. Having examined 200–300 proposals for new or amended business regulations each year, we note that, in brief, the quality of RIAs to date has been extremely low. This applies not least to calculations and/or estimates for the business sector as a whole and for individual enterprises. For example, companies' regulatory costs are stated in only 10% of the proposals. A corresponding figure for costs to the state would never have been accepted by the legislators (Table 12.1).

Sweden is not, however, isolated in this issue. In several EU member states and in the European Commission, the same problems recur. Influencing public finances enjoy the highest priority, while effects on companies are a relatively low priority, although there are exceptions. A survey carried out by Andrea Renda,[4] the Senior Research Fellow at the Centre for European Policy Studies (CEPS) in Brussels, in 2006, states that the first 95 Extended Impact Assessments (ExIAs) completed by Commission DGs provoked widespread disappointment:

[3] Regulation Indicator, 2002–2007, Board of Swedish Industry and Commerce for Better Regulation (NNR).

[4] The European Network for Better Regulation, Brussels, 23 January 2006.

Table 12.1 Quality factors and target fulfilment, 2002–2007 (percentages)

	2007	2006	2005	2004	2003	2002
1. Summary	86	84	93	77	64	49
2. Previous regulations	54	75	86	79	56	55
3. Alternatives described	30	47	53	49	37	26
4. Early consultation	42	42	48	35	36	30
5. Number of companies	40	26	28	25	9	6
6. Costs per company	10	15	17	7	7	4
7. Total costs	17	8	9	5	5	4
8. Competition aspect	35	39	47	43	20	9
9. Gold plating	32	4	7	6	3	5
10. Official review period	89	80	86	75	64	55
11. SimpLex analysis*)	41	42	35	39	51	47
12.Administrative burden:						
Increased	63	53	58	52		
Reduced	12	20	16	16		
Unchanged	25	27	26	32		
EU-based	51	44	44	40		

*) The Simplex ordinance consisted of twelve questions to be put forward and answered by the legislator such as: "What administrative, practical or other measures must SMEs undertake as a result of the proposed legislation? The cost per company and total cost are questions asked in the Simplex ordinance. Total is for a whole branch or likewise and per company is more in depth calculation for a single model company.
Source: NNR

costs were seldom estimated, and business costs were estimated in only 12.6% of the samples.

What, then, causes this trend where impact analyses of business regulations are concerned? First, it may be pointed out that state requirements to carry out RIAs are hardly in short supply. Instead, it is follow-up and quality control that are lacking. In Sweden, RIA requirements are contained in no fewer than three ordinances and in a special government communication for the government offices, but quality control is lacking. Another factor may be that requirements exist but that only portions of companies' costs need to be estimated. Finally, business and company organizations too must assume responsibility for failing to carry out comprehensive and systematic assessment of the quality of RIAs of what are, to enterprises, such important proposals for new and amended business regulations. Failing such documentation, it is more difficult to discuss with decision-makers the need for general measures to improve the quality of the RIAs. From January 1 2008, we have a new ordinance that has a more integrated concept but not a complete one.

12.6 Business Owners a Political Minority

Business owners are and will remain a political minority. They will never win a parliamentary election. When they or other company representatives express their views, they are rightly or wrongly regarded as standing for vested interests, and are, therefore, dismissed all too easily by many legislators.

Neither are companies and business owners over-popular throughout the body politic. Thus, there is scepticism when enterprises and their organizations put forward their opinions on the effects of certain legislative proposals. There is a distinct risk of key indirect effects not being addressed and considered by decision-makers. Their opinions must therefore be voiced through other channels.

It is often asserted that companies and their organizations are a powerful lobby in society. Not infrequently, businesses are said to have resources that other sectors of society lack. This may, admittedly, be true but the fact is that business owners are always a minority when it comes to general elections. They can, of course, become involved in politics like all other citizens, but their entrepreneurship means that they seldom have time to set aside for the political process, which is sluggish by nature, and, in some cases, should be so too.

Few politicians know what everyday life in business is like, although they make company visits and many politicians attempt to stay in touch with the business owners of their constituencies. But the fact that most politicians and legislators naturally focus on members of the public at large, who are not business owners, can never be disregarded. The general public make up the base for a further term of office in the legislative assembly. What the legislator with this focus may find it difficult to understand is the indirect effects that the proposals for new and amended business regulations may have on broad groups of voters. Increased demands may, for example, prompt companies to invest less or even move their production partly or entirely abroad, with less competition and more unemployment as a result.

12.7 Many Politicians Mean Well but Lack Adequate Evaluation Tools

Today, there is broad agreement among politicians that SMEs, in particular, are held back by the regulatory burden they bear. This 'burden', as referred to here, includes the aggregate impact of requirements in individual regulations and regulatory creep. In the period from December 2006 to February 2007, NNR engaged a survey institute[5] and panels of business owners to investigate how the public, opinion-formers and decision-makers see regulatory simplification. In response to the question 'Do you think fewer, simpler regulations would make companies more inclined to recruit new staff?', more than 40% of the decision-makers said that they very much thought so. A slightly smaller number thought this was somewhat true. Asked, 'Do you think the volume of regulations that Swedish companies have to comply with should be reduced?', more than 40% replied that they should be greatly reduced, while slightly over 50%

[5] Regelinsikt ('Regulatory Insight'), survey among the public, decision-makers and opinion-formers, January 2007, Demoskop AB, NNR and the Federation of Swedish Enterprises.

thought they should be reduced in some degree. Only 3% said no. In answer to the question, 'How should the regulations be reduced?', 25% of the decision-makers said it should be done by reducing the provision of information, while 43% want fewer requirements and regulations for SMEs (Figs. 12.1, 12.2 and 12.3).

Systematic efforts to reduce companies' administrative costs that arise owing to state regulations have been initiated in several EU member states. In The Netherlands, it has, up to now, been shown that it is possible to do something

Do you think fewer, simpler regulations would make companies more inclined to recruit staff?

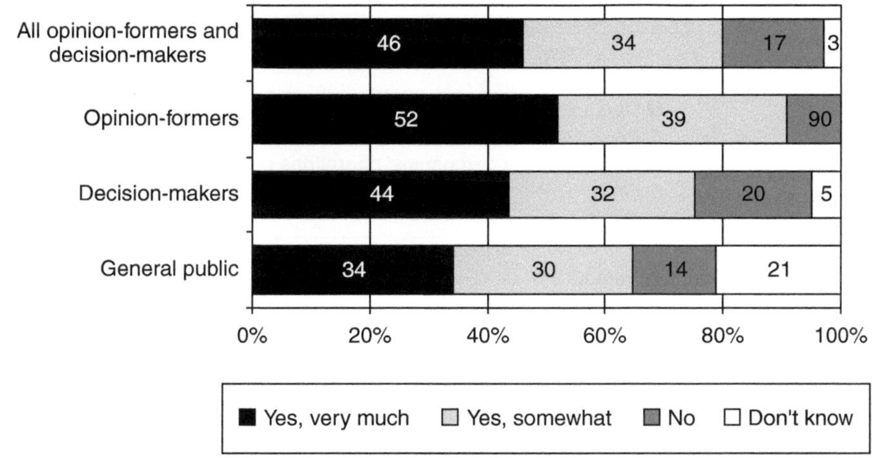

Fig. 12.1 Fewer regulations, higher recruitment rate?
Base: 89 out of 1,000 interviews

Do you think the volume of regulations Swedish companies have to comply with should be reduced?

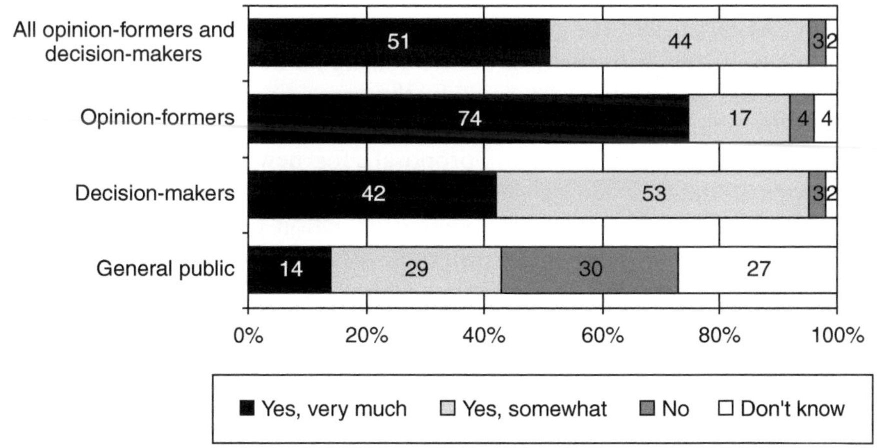

Fig. 12.2 Reduce the volume of regulations?
Base: 89 out of 1,000 interviews

In what manner do you think such a reduction in the regulations should primarily take place?

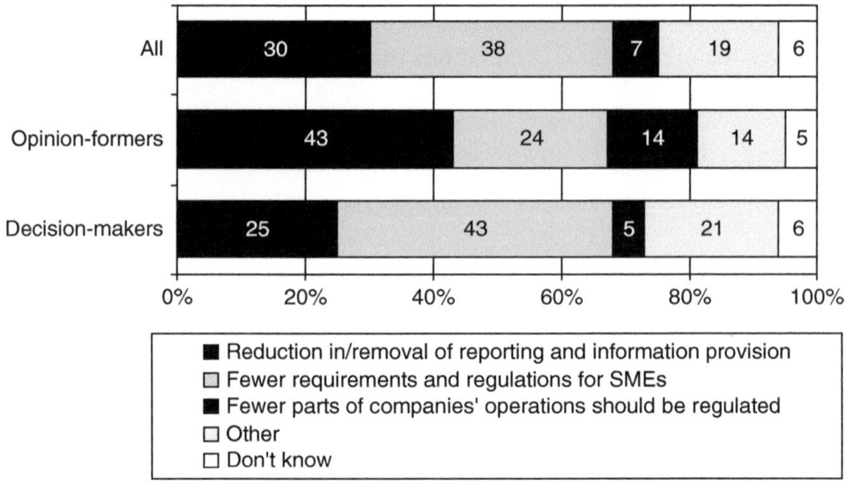

Fig. 12.3 How should the regulations be reduced?
Base: 89 interviews

about administrative costs if the right will exists. However, the road to that destination is beset by obstacles, and great political courage and strength are required to establish measurable targets. The Dutch work has taken over 10 years to achieve, and it was not until the politicians exerted pressure on themselves, creating vigorous organizations both internally and externally, that the work really took off.

In Sweden, there have been a series of government promises of reduced 'red tape' for SMEs. In 1999, the government created the special SimpLex unit in the government offices, with the task of scrutinising all new regulatory proposals from an SME perspective. At roughly the same time, a special ordinance (1998:1820) came into force. This obliged government agencies to carry out special RIAs in conjunction with proposals for new or amended business regulations if these proposals may be deemed to influence conditions for SMEs. In 2003, the government presented its action program for regulatory simplification. The purpose of this program was to develop measures to reduce the administrative burden on enterprises and make implemented and planned measures clearly visible.

At the same time as these programs, communications and declarations, NNR embarked on an assessment of every case submitted to NNR for consultative review by the government, government committees and central-government agencies, with proposals for new or amended business regulations. One of the assessment criteria was whether the proposals entailed a reduced or unchanged administrative burden on companies. Results contained in NNR's Regulation

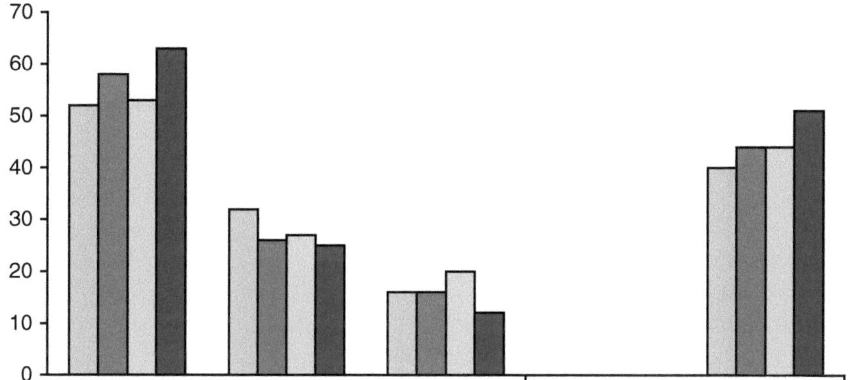

	Increase	Unchanged	Reduced		EU-based
2004	52	32	16		40
2005	58	26	16		44
2006	53	27	20		44
2007	63	25	12		51

Fig. 12.4 Administrative burden and EU-based regulations (percentages)
Source: NNR

Indicator 2007 showed that the administrative burden was exacerbated in more than 60% of the proposals, while it shrank in only 12% (Fig. 12.4).

12.8 Competition Issues

In a market economy, it is necessary to ensure that companies can compete on equivalent terms. The premise must be that a right of free market entry prevails, and that no individual companies are given preferential treatment. When legislators discuss proposals for new business regulations, this dimension must be taken with the utmost seriousness. There is no natural, built-in contradiction between large and small companies. SMEs engage in mutual competition with their fellow SMEs that is just as stiff as with large enterprises, and the latter compete just as hard with their large competitors as with SMEs. Exemptions or special regulations associated with corporate size, number of employees or turnover are certainly conceivable, but the exemptions must then apply to all enterprises in the same category. However, exemptions may be hazardous; they may push development in a direction that is not, in fact, wished by the politicians. If the limits are set too narrowly, the exemptions can be an 'extra' threshold to surmount if a company is considering expansion. On the other hand, tightening legislation in certain areas for all businesses and raising the requirements of written documentation entail risks: both the public sector and private enterprise risk having fewer participants in their procurement procedures when the administrative burden is relatively heavier for SMEs.

Matters intensively discussed today include, for example, which requirements should be imposed on companies that bid for public contracts. Financial, social and environmental demands are imposed that may go beyond the scope of the actual product or service being procured. Gender-equality plans or anti-discrimination clauses may be required, or it may be stipulated how a procured product is to be transported and what fuel the transporter is to use. There is a risk that decision-makers who state their wish for stiffer competition in certain sectors will instead, through their own actions, impair competition in the sectors they are seeking to stimulate.

Companies and entrepreneurship, as such, enjoy no special status. Instead, what counts is the sum total of direct and indirect repercussions of political decisions. This is what dictates their being given special treatment, in terms of the consequences of new and amended business regulations. This is why an early RIA is so important. It should be an analysis that, in the initial phase, is confined to direct effects on companies but is used to assess the effects on society as a whole in the subsequent phase.

In many EU countries, extensive work along Dutch lines has been initiated to reduce administrative costs incurred by companies as a result of state regulations. Governments have primarily concentrated on reducing administrative costs, and this is because this portion of the impact on businesses is the least politically sensitive. With an attitude like this, governments need no great substantial changes in the regulations. Thanks to the Standard Cost Model, it is also possible to measure how well governments are succeeding in their objectives of reducing the burdens. Nevertheless, it is important to bear in mind that companies' administrative expenses due to regulations usually make up a small portion of the total costs imposed on businesses by the regulations.

12.9 Early Analysis with Extensive Consultations

In my opinion, the reasons for giving special treatment to enterprises, compared with other stakeholders, are extensive. But if the effects of this 'special treatment' are to be good, RIAs must be carried out at an early stage of the regulatory process. A preliminary analysis should, of course, be carried out to provide a reasonable indication of how the proposal will affect companies. If the analysis shows that a more complete analysis should be done, this must be of a more comprehensive nature. Surveys[6] carried out by the Board of Swedish Industry and Commerce for Better Regulation and other bodies show that administrative costs usually make up only a minor portion of total regulatory

[6] The Total Costs of Regulations to Businesses in Sweden, 1 December 2006, NNR.

expenses. It is therefore important for material and financial costs to be included in the RIA.

Material costs arise because of requirements that enterprises invest in facilities or staff, adapt products or adjust costs to implement such measures as rehabilitation or measures associated with the work environment. Financial costs arise as a result of requirements to pay taxes and contributions.

To obtain an analysis with substantially acceptable content, frequent consultations with stakeholders must be held. Posting proposals on websites for the purpose of obtaining feedback from individual enterprises may be a good idea, but this is not how the regulator can obtain the close contact with stakeholders that is required to yield more substantial information. In many cases, it may also be necessary for the regulator to liaise closely with the Competition Authority, since both individual companies and their sector organizations may sometimes put their own interests before competition. This may have adverse implications for new companies seeking to enter the market.

Summing up, I consider that there are compelling reasons for treating proposals for business regulations as a special case, in terms of investigating their consequences. Finding out, at an early stage of the regulatory process, what their impact will be is essential groundwork. Only then can their effects on other sectors of society be clarified.

12.10 Summary

In this chapter, I consider whether, in exploring the implications of proposed new or amended business legislation, there is any justification for treating enterprises as a special case. Worldwide, business and enterprise are crucially important to the emergence of prosperity.

In my home country, Sweden, there are some 630,000 companies with an aggregate workforce of 2.9 million people. They form the base for a public sector that employs 1,360,000. The majority of these companies are, as in most countries, small and medium-sized enterprises (SMEs). Companies with fewer than 200 employees make up 99.8% of the total, while the remaining 0.2% , with staff numbering 200 or more, employs more than a million. There were approximately 45,000 new business start-ups in 2006.

Conditions for these companies, and how they perform and develop, affect not only the employees concerned but, indirectly, the 1,360,000 public-sector workers and also students, children and pensioners.

What happens if regulations are drawn up in such a way that, in relation to the legislators' aims, they impose not the slightest restriction and burden on individual companies? Overall, effects on individual companies in the form of reduced sales, exports and investments and impaired competitiveness may, in turn, lead to staff cutbacks. The results may then be a tax shortfall for the state, dwindling currency inflows into the country, insufficient competitiveness in relation to foreign countries and reduced competition within the country itself. New regulations affecting enterprises are usually more numerous than those that directly influence private individuals. But regulatory inflation or 'creep', as such, may prevent compliance from matching the politicians' plans, since it is ever harder for companies to take in all the requirements imposed on them by the legislators.

But the massive volume of regulations exacerbate the risks of unintentional breaches, while also inhibiting entrepreneurship, investments and willingness to recruit new staff.

Most proposals for new or amended business regulations arise through a special process that is regulated by laws, ordinances or special written communications. What is self-evident when the state is a stakeholder is deemed by decision-makers to be less obvious where other stakeholders, such as businesses, are concerned. On the contrary, despite the crucial importance of enterprises to national prosperity, the politicians' decision documentation is, with respect to the impact on enterprises, often considerably less well researched than those regarding the state.

Sweden is not, however, isolated in this issue. In several EU member states and in the European Commission, the same problems recur. Influencing public finances enjoy the highest priority, while effects on companies are a relatively low priority, although there are exceptions.

What, then, causes this trend where impact analyses of business regulations are concerned? First, it may be pointed out that state requirements to carry out RIAs are hardly in short supply. Instead, it is follow-up and quality control that are lacking.

Business owners are and will remain a political minority. Neither are companies and business owners over-popular throughout the body politic. Thus, there is scepticism when enterprises and their organizations put forward their opinions on the effects of certain legislative proposals. There is a distinct risk of key indirect effects not being addressed and considered by decision-makers. Their opinions must therefore be voiced through other channels.

Few politicians know what everyday life in business is like, although they make company visits and many politicians attempt to stay in touch with the business owners of their constituencies.

In a market economy, it is necessary to ensure that companies can compete on equivalent terms. There is a risk that decision-makers who state their wish for stiffer competition in certain sectors will instead, through their own actions, impair competition in the sectors they are seeking to stimulate.

Companies and entrepreneurship, as such, enjoy no special status. Instead, what counts is the sum total of direct and indirect repercussions of political decisions. This is what dictates their being given special treatment, in terms of the consequences of new and amended business regulations. This is why an early RIA is so important. It should be an analysis that, in an initial phase, is confined to direct effects on companies but is used to assess the effects on society as a whole in the subsequent phase.

References

European Network for Better Regulation, Brussels, 23 January 2006.
'Fokus på Sveriges Ekonomi' ('Focus on the Swedish Economy in 2006'), Ekonomifakta: Inflation i företagsregler – ett hot mot konkurrenskraften ('Inflation in Business Regulations — a Threat to Competitiveness').
Regelinsikt ('Regulatory Insight'), survey among the public, decision-makers and opinion-formers, January 2007, Demoskop AB, NNR and the Federation of Swedish Enterprises.
Regulation Indicator 2002–2007, Board of Swedish Industry and Commerce for Better Regulation (NNR).
Swedish Employers' Confederation, 1997.
The Total Costs of Regulations to Businesses in Sweden, 1 December 2006, NNR.

Chapter 13
Compliance Costs and the Policy Process

Peter van Hoesel

Abstract In this chapter, the public policy process is viewed as a continuous source of compliance costs. Explanations are sought for the phenomenon that a substantial part of these costs could have been evaded or prevented and for the fact that it is a very arduous task to expel unnecessary (or unwanted) compliance costs afterwards. Main drivers behind unnecessary compliance costs are described per stage in the policy process. The key factor for improving policies and reducing compliance costs is adequate information.

13.1 Introduction

Every time when a social or economic problem is transformed into a public policy problem, new compliance costs for businesses and citizens in the end will be inevitable. In the past 60 years, compliance costs caused by public policies gradually have grown to the present high level because of the adoption of many new policy problems. Moreover, after the adoption of a policy problem, the policy itself gradually has been refined into a complex system, in order to get optimal policy solutions for all involved interest groups,[1] gradually adding extra compliance costs.

The following questions will be answered. How do compliance costs arise in the different stages of the policy process? Which specific risks for causing unnecessary compliance costs can be detected in each stage of the policy process, or in other words, what are the main drivers behind unnecessary compliance costs? And what can be undertaken to minimize the level of compliance costs? The answers to these questions are sought by breaking down the

[1] See L.A. Geelhoed, 'Wetgeving en bestuur in de semi-soevereine staat' in: Vervlechting en verschuivin-gen van wetgevingscomplexen aan het begin van de 21e eeuw, Publicaties van de Staatsrechtkring, nr. 12, Tjeenk Willink, Zwolle, 1996.

P. van Hoesel (✉)
Erasmus University Rotterdam, Rotterdam, The Netherlands; Panteia, Zoetermeer, The Netherlands
e-mail: p.van.hoesel@panteia.nl

A. Nijsen et al. (eds.), *Business Regulation and Public Policy*,
International Studies in Entrepreneurship 20, DOI 10.1007/978-0-387-77678-1_13,

policy process into six stages, showing the specific risks for the creation of compliance costs per policy stage, illustrating these risks with characteristic examples and proposing measures or methods for reducing those risks.

Elsewhere in this book, the concept 'compliance costs' is explained comprehensively. In the present chapter, the concept is used in its broadest meaning. It contains all information costs, costs of advice, investments costs and exploitation costs for businesses (and citizens) that are or will be caused by a public policy. In the many examples that are given, these costs are not described specifically, because the drivers behind unnecessary compliance costs will have their negative effects on all types of compliance costs. So, in most cases, the general concept 'compliance costs' is used without specification. In some appropriate cases, the smaller concept 'administrative burdens' is used.

The following section of this chapter is devoted to the breakdown of the policy process into a policy cycle of six stages with an overview of the main drivers of unnecessary compliance costs. The sections 13.3 to 13.8 are subsequently devoted to the six stages of the policy cycle. In the last section, a conclusion is drawn and some general recommendations are given.

13.2 The Policy Process as a Continuous Source of Compliance Costs

The policy process is a long chain of steps, activities and events. As will be described in the next sections of this chapter, any step in the policy process may contribute to the creation of compliance costs, for businesses as well as for citizens.

For the purpose of this chapter, the policy process is divided into six policy stages, or in other words into a 'policy cycle',[2] because during each stage in the policy cycle, specific drivers of compliance costs have to be taken into account.

The first stage, agenda setting, concerns the recognition of problems in society that need attention from policy makers, on the basis of a hopefully sound analysis of these problems. The main driver of compliance costs during this stage is insufficient problem analysis, such as: a quick-and-dirty analysis is used, there is no analysis available at all, a sound analysis is used selectively or wrongly, a sound analysis is deliberately or unintentionally neglected.

The second stage, goal setting, concerns the improvements governing bodies want to strive for on behalf of their citizens. The main driver of compliance costs during the stage is the setting of inadequate goals, such as incompatible goals, vague goals, complex goals.

The third stage, designing policy measures, concerns the choice for the appropriate means needed for accomplishing the policy goals. The main driver of compliance costs during this stage is insufficient ex ante evaluation, such as a

---

[2] The model of a 'policy cycle' with several subsequent stages has been heavily criticized; on the other hand, this practical model appears to be used by many scientists and other authors in the area of public administration, as Peter Hupe points out in his book 'Overheid als politiek; over de grondslagen van beleid', Van Gorcum, Assen, 2007.

quick and dirty ex ante evaluation, no ex ante evaluation at all, selective uses of an ex ante evaluation, wrong assumptions in the minds of policy makers.

The fourth stage, decision-making, concerns the final decisions politicians have to make on the basis of the outputs from the foregoing stages. The main driver of compliance costs during this stage is a hampered decision, such as a partial decision, a decision on the basis of wrong amendments, a decision inconsistent with other policies, a decision without time horizon for the policy.

The fifth stage, implementation, concerns the introduction of the new (or adjusted) policy and subsequently an optimal execution of the policy. The main driver of compliance costs during this stage is an inadequate approach, such as bad communication, little preparation, a complex cooperation structure, lack of room for adjustment, insufficient process evaluation.

The sixth stage, evaluation, concerns the learning process that is being followed for the feedback to policy makers, in order to be able to adjust the policy. The main driver of compliance costs during this stage is insufficient learning, such as lack of availability of a monitor system, insufficient ex post evaluation, neglect of evaluation results.

Figure 13.1 gives an overview of this policy cycle together with the main drivers of compliance costs.

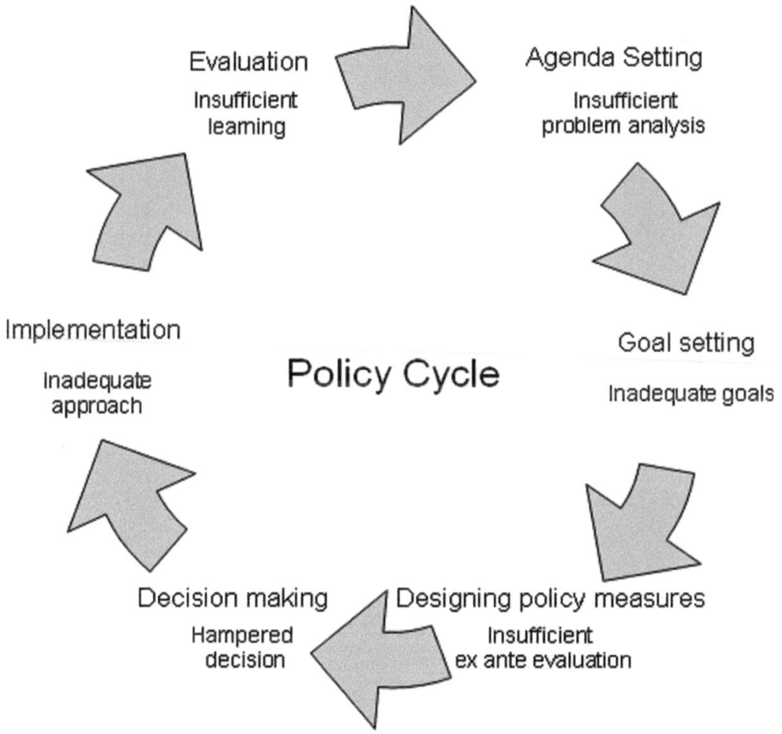

Fig. 13.1 Drivers of compliance costs in the policy cycle

During the policy process, many people are involved, differing from stage to stage. In each stage, main actors in that stage need adequate information to enable them to carry out their tasks properly. When the information supply is organized effectively, the information costs during the policy process will be lower than in situations where, time and again, ad hoc information needs have to be fulfilled.

More importantly, when the information supply falls short or the available information is used improperly, the risks of unnecessary compliance costs will be high. The common problem in all policy stages is the following: When only one step in the policy process appears to be wrong, the quality of the policy will be affected. One wrong step even may result in a policy failure. So, when at any moment during the police process the information supply or the use of available information falls short, the rest of the policy cycle may become a lost case. Information supply and use during the policy process turns out to be a key factor for the level of compliance costs.

In the following sections, we'll explore how this key factor is working and how improvements can be made.

13.3 The Stage of Agenda Setting

When policymakers create policy measures on the basis of an insufficient problem analysis, such measures simply can't be of much help to society, resulting in a bad cost/benefit ratio of the policy. Also, compliance costs will share in this bad ratio, so a substantial part of these costs will be unnecessary. In some cases, society even is confronted with 'empty policies',[3] only creating unnecessary compliance costs for businesses and citizens. So, a sound analysis of the problem is a must, including an evaluation of already existing policies. However, in many cases, the problem analysis appears to be insufficient, which is not recognized in the stage of agenda setting but later on, as can be reconstructed from ex post policy evaluations.[4] The question is why such an insufficiency happens so often.

The first explanation is that political parties, individual politicians, lobby organizations, journalists and other stakeholders, all have their specific perceptions of problems. Policy problems to a certain extent are constructs in the minds of stakeholders.[5] Looking for instance at the problem of a low level of

[3] M.S. de Vries uses the concept of 'empty policy' in his article 'Problemen op de agenda' in: Prof. dr. A. Hoogerwerf & prof. dr. M. Herweijer, 'Overheidsbeleid', Kluwer, Alphen a/d/ Rijn, 2003.

[4] For instance, evaluation reports of the Dutch National Audit Office time and again show a lack of analysis in the beginning of the policy process.

[5] See Thomas A. Birkland, 'Agenda setting in Public Policy', in: Frank Fischer, Gerald J. Miller & Mara S. Sidney, 'Handbook of Public Policy Analysis', CRC Press, Boca Raton, 2007.

innovation in many businesses, lobby organizations of entrepreneurs point out that the financial world is quite unresponsive, while banks and private equity funds indicate that the quality of most business plans is too low. Policy research shows, however, that lack of money is not the main problem, but lack of knowledge. So, policy measures addressing the finance problem will be far less effective than policy measures addressing the knowledge problem. Compliance costs simply can be lowered by giving less attention to the finance problem.

To give another example, looking at the problem of unemployment, employers may think that most unemployed people are unfit for jobs; in the view of left wing political parties, they may be seen as victims of capitalism while right wing parties may consider their problems as their own faults, while employment offices may see them as troublesome clients. On the other hand, policy researchers know that most unemployed people are able to find a suitable job provided they find an entrance to the world of employers. So, a policy researcher will come to the conclusion that the most effective policy measure would be to invest a lot in creating far more opportunities for contacts in the labor market, while other measures like extra training, protection against dismissal and a high level of social security will be less effective. Compliance costs can be lowered by putting less effort or rather no effort in ineffective labor market policies.

A sound analysis of a policy researcher, however, often is not seen or believed by abovementioned stakeholders, or only a part of the analysis that is compatible with their views will be selected. After all, their own views are solidly anchored in their minds. Quick and dirty but attractive analyses will be adopted easily, while unattractive quick and dirty analyses easily can be put aside with the argument that they are too dirty. A phenomenon related to this selective attitude of stakeholders is that non-interventions seldom are taken into account. Stakeholders appear to be so possessed by their own views and so ambitious to solve the perceived problems, that they don't want to consider the possibility of a non-intervention, while this may be the best option for society and obviously the best option from the viewpoint of preventing compliance costs. Solutions for this 'attitude-problem' can only be weak, like pointing out repeatedly how important good problem analyses are and ensuring that at least one good analysis is available. In the end, it all depends on the willingness of politicians to accept such analyses. Maybe, it will help a bit when they become aware of the negative effects of their unwillingness on compliance costs.

A second explanation is that social problems are changing due to changes in society, so a problem analysis that was made in the past may become invalid after a while. As a consequence, good policies from the past decade may become quite ineffective in the present or next decade. Not only because the problems themselves are changing, but also because stakeholders develop adaptive behavior mechanisms with respect to policies, which may result in counter-effective consequences.

For instance, when employment figures are stagnating because of a considerable growth of self-employment, laws that try to regulate relations between employers and employees may need a revision. When the quality of the environment with respect to certain emissions is improved strongly, it would be advisable to move the subsidy budget to other environmental issues. When citizens gradually learn to avoid certain tax measures, the finance minister has to adjust his/her policy.

So, you need to reconsider old policies from time to time in order to keep them effective or, even better from the point of view of compliance costs, to end policies that have become obsolete. An optimal situation would be, when policy measures and policy programs all would have an automatic expiration date, so that prolongation of a policy would require an explicit new decision. The long term, not to say structural, character of most current policies is a major source of unnecessary costs, for the government, for the business sector and for other stakeholders. Of course, this will require a system of recurrent policy analyses.

A third explanation is that the available knowledge about problems in society is always limited. Even when information seems to be available abundantly, it is not easy to select the appropriate part that is usable for a problem analysis. And even when you make a careful selection, to a certain extent, you will be confronted with a lack of knowledge. In many cases, the information stems from the past, so you have to make an update at least. In other cases, you may be confronted with a so-called 'ill-structured' problem,[6] which, by definition, is a problem we don't understand well. It makes no sense to develop full-scale policies for problems that aren't understood well; only small-scale policy experiments will make sense in such cases.

This third difficulty seems to make the job of an analyst a bit hopeless, but it would be a wrong conclusion to decide to skip the analysis at all. Even a good problem analysis can't give all the answers, but it will help reduce the number of policy failures substantially, by showing obvious mistakes in problem perceptions and by reducing the number of directions where adequate solutions may be found. The only feasible solution to this third difficulty is an adequate knowledge management system, which, nowadays, is easier to develop than some decades ago.

13.4 The Stage of Setting Policy Goals

At first sight, setting policy goals doesn't seem a difficult job for politicians, so mostly they are not aware of the risks of easily made choices. There may be three types of risks during the stage of setting policy goals that could yield less adequate or even inadequate policy goals, with negative consequences for compliance costs.

---

[6] See for the concept of 'ill-structured problems' William N. Dunn, Public Policy Analysis, Prentice Hall, Englewood Cliffs, 2004.

Policy goals have to be compatible with the policy problem, which can only be established by an explicit link to the involved problem analysis. When this link is not established, the fit between problem and goal may be weak, resulting in less compatible or even incompatible goals and, as a consequence, creating unnecessary compliance costs.

When, for instance, traffic safety is a problem in a local community, it will be insufficient to state the policy in terms of reducing the number of accidents, when the perception of the safety level in the community appears to be an important issue. Only addressing accident numbers may result in heavier traffic measures than the community, including the business sector, would like.

When unemployment in a region is a problem and the policy goal is to create extra jobs, this will be insufficient when the unemployed workforce is largely unskilled. In such a situation, a policy program aiming at job creation easily will cause a lot of futile efforts in the business sector. A better policy goal would be to improve the educational level of the workforce.

When the economy in a region is shrinking and the policy goal is to raise the innovation level of the industry, this may be insufficient when the labor force in the region is also shrinking. An innovation program may end in much effort and little outcome for the business sector, when the problem of the shrinking labor force isn't accounted for.

The risk of incompatible policy goals can only be diminished by extending the problem analysis (from the foregoing policy stage) to a further analysis of the proposed policy goals in relation to the policy problem.

Policy goals have to serve as targets for policy measures that will be taken. This implies the risk of insufficiency with respect to the five SMART criteria.[7] When a policy goal doesn't meet such criteria, the results of the policy will be quite uncertain, in spite of many efforts of involved parties. When stakeholders or target groups aren't committed to the policy goals, their efforts will be low and the effects of the policy will even be lower, so a substantial part of the compliance costs will be needless. When goals are confusing, extra compliance costs are needed to solve the confusion.

For instance, when authorities in cooperation with businesses try to reduce the number of burglaries without stating the percentage of reduction of that number and the time they need to reach that percentage, a lot of money may be spent for only a small result. When business owners are asked to clean up the garbage within a distance of 100 meters around their shops or their restaurants, this is likely to be an unrealistic and unacceptable goal that only will cause frustration.

You have even more vague goals, like for instance making businesses more innovative, creating regional employment opportunities, reducing unsafe areas,

---

[7] The SMART criteria are based on the concept 'Management by Objectives', introduced in 1954 by Peter Drucker in his book 'The Practice of Management'. It took several decades before this concept also permeated to the public sector. SMART stands for: Specific, Measurable, Achievable, Realistic, Time-related.

less segregation in poor residential areas. This type of vague goals needs a lot of concretization in order to facilitate effective compliance.

Only stating policy goals in terms of outputs of government agencies will not do; policy goals must also be formulated in terms of outcomes[8] for society, more specifically for enterprises and citizens. So, it is not enough to count the number of clients that is being served, you also need the success ratio. And it is not enough to count the number of criminals that have been arrested, you also need data about the level of criminality in a community.

On the other hand, only stating a policy goal in terms of outcomes is insufficient either. For instance, when the government wants to reduce energy consumption, it will be insufficient to formulate this goal in terms of a general reduction percentage, you will also need specific goals for different business sectors and you will likely need some sub-goals like the amounts of money needed for necessary investments or the assistance energy firms have to offer to different business sectors.

The risk of 'un-SMART' goals can be reduced to a great extent by sufficient interaction with businesses, citizens and professionals about the goal setting.

Last but not least, there is the danger of dividing the population into (many) different interest groups.[9] Different interest groups require more complex regulations for reaching the involved policy goals. This complexity will contribute strongly to compliance costs.

Different subsidy instruments for different business sectors are, of course, more complex than one instrument for all sectors.

Tax reductions for many different purposes make the tax system complex and not transparent. Income policies in the Netherlands have developed many interest groups in the past decades, like 'young disabled people' or 'mothers in social security'. The Dutch income tax law maybe would win the prize of the most extreme example of policy refining, because it renders a different tax rate for every individual citizen. For business owners, the income tax system turns out to be even more complex than for other citizens.

An extra complication will arise, when the demarcation between different interest groups is difficult or vague. When agencies have to look for target groups like poor households, people with an unhealthy lifestyle, businesses working with moonlighters, businesses with a high level of R&D, they will have to put a lot of effort in finding those groups, which also will ask for much effort in the business sector.

---

[8] Amongst others, the importance of the distinction between 'outputs' and 'outcomes' is being pointed out by Evert Vedung, 'Public Policy Making and Program Evaluation', Transaction Publishers, New Brunswick/London, 1997.

[9] L.A. Geelhoed pays attention to this phenomenon, which he calls 'extension of the policy balance', in the article 'Wetgeving en bestuur in de semi-soevereine rechtstaat', in: 'Vervlechting en verschuiving van wetscomplexen aan het begin van de 21e eeuw', Publicaties van de Staatsrechtkring, 12, Tjeenk Willink, Zwolle 1996.

The phenomenon of refining policies for many interest groups does also create a group of stakeholders that will profit from complex policies. For instance, tax consultants earn their money unravelling the complex tax system or looking for holes in the system, while business owners have to pay these expensive consultants, powerless as they are against the bureaucracy that goes with a complex tax system. Because of the need for consultants, complex regulations will bring along huge administrative burdens for the business sector. This is not only true for the area of tax policy, but for all policy areas. Tax consultants are not likely to plead for a simpler tax system, because they don't want to see their income as well as their professional status reduced. Professionals earning their money in other policy areas will show the same attitude. Also, government agencies will fiercely defend their position, when there is a pressure for reducing the complexity of their tasks. Understandably, they don't like to lose jobs and their professional status. Meanwhile, politicians rather are inclined to create new exceptions than to diminish the number of interest groups, stimulated as they are by various lobbyists.

As a consequence, simplifying laws is a major assignment for a government because of an enormous resistance to change in the 'iron triangle':[10] political parties, lobby organizations and professionals who owe their jobs to high complexity. An easy solution for this problem is not available, only long and enduring efforts from a strong government may tackle this problem. Meanwhile, it is always advisable to look for unnecessary divisions in the goal setting in new policies. Adequate policy analyses will help detect such divisions.

13.5 The Stage of Designing Policy Measures

The stage of designing policy measures likely is the most dangerous stage for the creation of unnecessary compliance costs. The many serious pitfalls during this stage can only be evaded by thorough ex ante evaluation. Do we have evidence-based policies? [11] Have the assumptions[12] about the expected effects been made correctly? How is compensation offered for the 'collateral damage' that can be expected from the measures? Are the policy instruments acceptable and practicable for businesses? When we don't have the proper answers to these questions, we may expect a lot of problems as soon as the policy measures are being implemented, creating huge compliance costs for the business sector.

---

[10] Werner Jann & Kai Wegrich use for this tripartite coalition the telling name 'Eisernen Dreieck', i.e. Iron Triangle. Die Zeit, Hamburg, 17-11-2005.

[11] In his article 'Over beleidsonderzoek en sociologie in de toekomst' Frans Leeuw points out that policy research more and more has to fulfill the standards of the Campbell Collaboration. In: Godfried Engbersen en Jos de Haan, 'Balans en toekomst van de sociologie', Pallas Publications/Amsterdam University Press, 2006.

[12] See A. Hoogerwerf, 'Beleid berust op veronderstellingen', in: Acta Politica, 4, 1984.

However, evidence-based policies are difficult to develop because of the natural impatience of politicians. A proper ex ante evaluation yielding real evidence, like a field experiment or a simulation study, needs much time and painstaking effort. It is understandable that politicians don't want to wait for the results of such studies, because they are expected to show decisiveness within quite a short time. Therefore, they rather risk the costs and frustrations of a failing policy than wait for the results of an ex ante evaluation. Maybe politicians are insufficiently aware of the fact that the costs of policy failures have to be paid for not only by the taxpayer, but also by the business sector in the form of unnecessary compliance costs.

So, it would be better for politicians to compromise at least on quicker types of ex ante evaluation, like an inventory of policies in other regions or a feasibility study in cooperation with the business sector. Such studies will help to reduce the failure percentage considerably. In cases of complex policy programs, it is always advisable to choose a more sophisticated type of ex ante evaluation and to accept the delay.

Let us look at some examples showing the negative effects of insufficient ex ante evaluation.

Labor cost subsidies for employers are one of many policy instruments for getting long-term unemployed people at work. The reasoning is, that long-term unemployed people are less productive, so you have to lower their labor costs to compensate for this. Such a compensating measure may lower the threshold to jobs. This argumentation is not entirely wrong, but is far from complete. The mere existence of such a measure affirms the bad image of long-term unemployed people, so it will be rather a warning signal than a stimulating measure. Ex ante evaluation would show, that employers aren't waiting for labor cost subsidies, but are waiting for applicants who are able to meet the job demands. They are even willing to try long-term unemployed people, when they can test them without costs of dismissal. But they rarely see applicants that are long-term unemployed, because long-term unemployment makes people afraid for the labor market. So, it would be more effective to concentrate on helping the long-term unemployed to overcome their fears and to give employers a 'no risk' guarantee. Maybe a labor cost subsidy also will help a bit, but without other measures, it will not suffice. It would be better to skip the labor cost subsidy anyway, because it creates only a little extra value while, on the other hand, it causes an extra administrative burden for employers.

Many environmental policy instruments are based on a price stimulus. That will work to a certain extent, but will also create of lot of administrative burdens because you don't get a subsidy or a tax reduction without proving your good conduct by informing the government agencies. Ex ante evaluation would show, that policy measures dealing with the sources of pollution are much easier for businesses and citizens, because these measures don't cause compliance costs, except for industries closely related to these sources. For instance, it is easier when soot filters or low noise tires are already installed in cars by the factory than when you have to make an extra effort to get these things in your car. A simple ban on the production of certain chemical products is easier than to discourage their use by a heavy taxation.

A new railway or motorway can be desirable from the point of view of traffic flows, but ex ante evaluation will also indicate a lot of collateral damage: buildings that have to be removed, businesses that have to move to another location, depreciation of real estate, lower quality of life for people living at short distance, etc. By digging tunnels, this kind of damage will be avoided to a great extent. On the other hand, tunnels are quite expensive. In the Netherlands, this has led to a standstill of many plans for new traffic infrastructure. This standstill also leads to extra costs for the business sector because of traffic congestions.

Detailed 'how to act' rules with respect to working conditions will create a lot of compliance costs. Ex ante evaluation would show that these costs could be reduced largely by giving different business sectors the opportunity to fill in those details themselves, while the law is formulated in terms of general or sector goal settings instead of detailed prescriptions. Moreover, the effectiveness of this approach should be higher because each sector will try to choose methods that will bring along an optimal cost-benefit ratio, which is also beneficial for achieving the policy goals.

These examples show the need for thorough ex ante evaluation. Ex ante evaluation is extremely important for the quality of a policy, so the best advice would be to take no policy decisions anymore without adequate ex ante evaluation.

13.6 The Stage of Decision-Making

During the stage of decision-making, the quality of the policy can be affected by a hampered decision, such as a decision on the basis of wrong amendments, a partial decision, a decision that is inconsistent or not transparent in relation to other policies, a decision without time horizon. Such a hampered decision will always have a negative effect on compliance costs.

In parliament, in provincial councils or in municipal councils, there is the ever existing danger of wrong amendments, undermining the effectiveness and efficiency of proposed policy measures. The pressures of lobby organizations are high, so most politicians feel tempted to give in a little bit, which may be devastating for the quality of the policy or, at least, will have a negative effect on the compliance costs for businesses.

When the parliament wants certain exceptions in the tax legislation for a category of entrepreneurs or, even worse, for several categories of entrepreneurs, an elegant proposal for a simpler tax system can easily become a mess. A lobby organization prompting for such exceptions apparently doesn't have in mind the disadvantages of a complex system, while on other occasions, this organization complains heavily about the high level of administrative burdens.

When a municipal council decides for softer traffic safety measures (for instance lower speed ramps) than was advised by traffic experts, because the neighbourhood is complaining about possible damage to their houses, the effectiveness of such a measure will be only a small fraction of what was originally intended. The original policy goal won't be achieved, because the speed of cars will hardly be influenced. People living in the district including businesses will only suffer from the inconveniences caused by the reconstruction of the roads.

When a regional authority wants to attract more business in the region by creating some benefits for companies who are willing to move to that region, this policy could be hampered severely when the regional council wants to apply a set of strictly formulated criteria for the admittance of new companies. Of course, this also leads to an extra administrative burden for the applying companies.

The main problem with amendments is lack of ex ante evaluation. So, the only good solution for getting good amendments is delay of the decision until the effects of the amendments have been made clear.

Another type of problem will arise, when in a policy proposal important issues are neglected, which possibly leads to a partial decision causing extra compliance costs.

A nice proposal for a new shopping mall in the city center may be rejected by the city council, when inhabitants point out that the proposal doesn't account for the extra traffic that will be attracted. It is also thinkable that the proposal will be accepted after a promise from the mayor that the traffic problem will be solved in due time. Such a partial decision will easily lead to extra expenses for businesses, when they want to get an optimal traffic solution.

A proposal for an innovation in the educational system may be rejected, when it appears that extra training for teachers wasn't accounted for. When the proposal nevertheless is accepted, the innovation can easily lead to fewer skills with graduates, causing extra training costs in the business sector.

When the parliament, reacting to incidents, instantly wants to have more and closer supervision of the food quality in restaurants, the already high level of administrative burdens for restaurants will grow further, while this may be only a partial solution for the prevention of such incidents.

It is better to reject a bad proposal than trying to fix it with ad hoc amendments, because there is no time to analyze the merits of these amendments properly.

Finally, every policy decision enlarges the problem of growing complexity because of the ever-growing number of rules that are created by decision-makers, leading to more and more inconsistencies and intransparencies. The existence of several layers in public administration, municipalities, provinces or states, countries, and supranational bodies like the EU, is an important source of complexity.

The number of new rules exceeds by far the number of abolished rules. For instance, in Germany more than 27,000 norms rule the daily life of the business sector and this number grows by 500 yearly.[13] Due to the complexity of public administration, you come across several conflicting regulations. An inventory

[13] These numbers are mentioned by Werner Jann & Kai Wegrich, 'Gefangen in eisernen Dreieck', Die Zeit, Hamburg, 17-11-2005.

of the ministry of Economic Affairs in the Netherlands, for example, brought up nearly 800 conflicting rules.[14] For entrepreneurs, it is a mission impossible to comply with regulations that are each other's opposite.

The mere number of regulations is a huge barrier for entrepreneurs to become aware of all obligations they have to comply with or all possible benefits they would like to share. Which entrepreneur is able to mention more than three subsidy schemes out of a total number of many hundreds? Which entrepreneur knows all relevant rules on working conditions or on the environment? Which entrepreneur is aware of all relevant details of the social security system?

The overruling power of a higher-level body now and then causes a disturbing situation. For instance, economic policy of the EU forbids countries to take certain locally necessary environmental measures, while on the other hand, these countries can't fulfill the demands of their own environmental policies or even the demands of the EU policies with respect to the environment. All kinds of costs for businesses in order to meet the demands of the existing rules wouldn't be necessary when those new measures could be taken.

A proposal for a free economic zone will not be consistent with market regulations of the EU, while it would be great for stimulating innovation. Innovative businesses have to meet many regulations, so the compliance costs of these businesses will be higher than average. A free zone would be a simple solution for this phenomenon.

A province overruling a spatial plan of a city will block the economic policy of the city for many years, which of course has several repercussions for entrepreneurs, like disinvestments, delays and extra costs.

There is no easy solution for the problem of growing complexity. To make a beginning, a relatively simple solution would be to provide every decision with a time horizon, which enables the automatic disappearance of old policies, unless they are prolonged or refreshed. A structural solution would be a systematic search in all policy areas for obsolete policies, unnecessary complex policies and inconsistent policies, followed by the removal of these policies or, at least, the removal of their damaging sections.

13.7 The Stage of Implementation

The implementation of policy measures is the next dangerous stage in the policy process.[15] Will the policy be executed as meant by policy makers? Are government agencies and other involved organizations prepared for the changes they have to make? Is the private sector well informed? Are entrepreneurs reacting as

---

[14] The number of 800 is based on the EIM report 'Meldpunt Tegenstrijdige Regelgeving', Zoetermeer, 2003.

[15] Already in 1973 Presmann & Wildavsky wrote a book with the revealing title 'Implementation: How Great Expectations in Washington Are Dashed in Oakland', Berkeley, University of California Press.

policymakers hoped they would? Is there room for adjustment, when the execution is faced with setbacks? The realization of new policy decisions goes with a series of implementation steps. When the implementation is suboptimal, we may expect a lot of unnecessary compliance costs for the business sector.

The first main step in the stage of implementation is communication: to citizens, to trade organizations, to business owners, to government agencies, to private organizations that will be involved with the implementation. Bad communication leads to confusion, delay and extra compliance costs.

For instance, a business manager needs to know of new prescriptions about the use of certain chemical substances before he will implement those prescriptions. Also, he will be helped with information about alternative solutions, when the new prescriptions demand for a substantial investment. Maybe there is an accompanying subsidy scheme that has to be explained. Of course, government agencies involved with the implementation of such prescriptions have to be informed in an early stage, to enable them to give the correct answers to business managers. When the information is insufficient, this will lead to extra efforts for businesses.

Before a renovation program for a village center starts, arrangements have to be made with entrepreneurs having a business in this center, so they will be able to continue their business during the reconstruction. An early warning enables entrepreneurs to take anticipatory measures with lower costs.

When certain changes in the tax system have to be introduced, it is wise to inform tax consultants at an early stage before introducing the changes. The consultants will then be able to behave as allies of the government during the introduction period, meanwhile reducing the adaptation costs for businesses.

When communication fails, the effects of the new policy will, at least, be delayed, but also extra costs for the implementation will have to be made, not only by government agencies but also for businesses. So, an adequate communication scheme will pay off for both parties. Communication research will help a lot to get such schemes. Citizens are supposed to know the law, so a governmental body can easily administer penalties for violations even when the communication was bad, but this will result in unnecessary costs for citizens including the business sector and it will also evoke many complaints about the attitude of the authorities. Communication by punishment is a bad solution from the point of view of reducing compliance costs.

The second main step is the adaptation to a new policy by government agencies and other organizations involved with the implementation: via instructions and training, via changes in their working process and via new contracts with the government. In many circumstances, necessary changes in ICT appear to be a major bottleneck. In some cases, a complete change of the whole organizational structure will be needed. When the implementing organizations don't get enough time for adaptation, the implementation will be hazardous, with many failures as a consequence and cause unnecessary burdens for citizens and businesses.

A tax office that is not sufficiently prepared for a new allowance system compensating medical expenses of millions of people with a low income will create a lot of problems, as appeared recently in the Netherlands.

A labor office has to take some time to implement new software needed for the execution of new policy measures with respect to the activation of unemployed youngsters. When they, meanwhile, have to work with old software their efficiency will be low, causing extra costs for businesses that are supposed to create trainee posts for these youngsters.

An extra problem during this second step will arise, when a cooperation structure between different agencies and/or private organizations has to be established.

Problems with criminal youth that have to be tackled via a cooperation of local authorities, the police, child protection agencies, youth welfare institutions, schools, labor offices, employers' organizations, will require a lot of adjustments with these organizations, not to say a revolution. Inefficiencies during the adjustment period will bring along extra costs, also for the involved businesses.

A revitalization program for depressed areas will only be successful when there is enough synergy between governmental agencies, local authorities, public works departments, housing agencies, owners of real estate, construction firms, neighborhood councils, social agencies, economic agencies and more. You can imagine the trouble they will have trying to learn how to cooperate successfully with so many partners. The adaptation costs for all involved organizations will be high.

Adaptation costs for businesses can be lowered by taking enough time for the adaptation of the new policy by government agencies or other organizations that are involved with the implementation. The costs of a too short adaptation period may become much higher than the costs of a later introduction.

The third main step of implementation is the first stage of execution of the policy, the 'try-out' stage, during which several faults in the operational process may occur and also unexpected reactions from target groups may be observed. The length of this stage depends of the complexity of the policy. All involved parties, including politicians, have to be prepared for necessary adjustments during this step.

Examples of failures in the operational process are: a mailing is wrongly addressed because of a failure in the software, a labor office sends unemployed people to employers in wrong sectors, certain questions in a form are not understood by entrepreneurs, the application of a set of criteria for a license or a subsidy leads to misunderstandings and therefore to wrong decisions.

Examples of unexpected reactions from target groups are: a high level of abuse of a tax regulation, far less use of a public service than was expected, far more use of a public service exhausting the budget rapidly, business owners preferring to move their business to better regions instead of accepting severe regional measures, criminality spreading swiftly to areas other than those where extra measures have been announced, illegal dumping of garbage after the introduction of a new tariff system.

When adjustments aren't made as soon as possible, all stakeholders will have to make unnecessary costs. Swift adjustments can be made when the policy leaves room to agencies for adjusting the policy to a certain extent or when the responsible politicians respond rapidly to reported problems. Process evaluations will help a lot to detect all kinds of problems in this first execution stage.

13.8 The Stage of Evaluation

Finally, there is the stage of evaluation. Do we have an adequate monitoring system? Does the public sector learn from evaluation studies? Are the effects of the policy on the policy goals satisfactory? What are the real costs for the business sector?

When there is no learning cycle, the benefit/cost ratio of the policy will be suboptimal, creating a lot of unnecessary costs for businesses as well as for other stakeholders.

Partly due to the influence of National Audit Offices, policy evaluation or program evaluation[16] nowadays is a normal phenomenon. Nevertheless, policy evaluation yet falls short in too many cases and the effects of policy evaluations mostly are quite unsatisfactory. So, the provision of the necessary feedback to policy makers is yet insufficient. In an ideal situation, you would have a nice policy circle, but mostly we see only a fanciful line that, by coincidence, crosses the paths of politicians. As described above, politicians are more influenced by other stakeholders than by policy analysts. While in situations where they would be willing to be influenced by a policy evaluation, in many cases, a proper evaluation is not available.

Meanwhile, several promising developments can be observed.

In many policy areas, monitors have been developed generating a constant stream of relevant policy information. For example, the Dutch Police Monitor delivers yearly information about all types of criminal acts, also on the small scale level of a village and a city district. This kind of information is nowadays used in every municipality for setting local priorities in the tasks of the police force, resulting, for instance, in a more effective cooperation with the business sector. In Rotterdam, the city council has decided to follow developments in city districts in detail in order to improve the quality of life, especially in depressed areas. This also leads to better relations between business owners and bureaucratic bodies of Rotterdam.

The Dutch government also monitors the reduction of administrative burdens, on behalf of the detection of successes or failures from reduction measures

---

[16] See among others the handbook from Joseph S. Wholey, Harry P. Hatry & Kathryn E. Newcomer, 'Handbook of Practical Program Evaluation', Jossey-Bass, 2004.

that have been taken. However, the business sector yet doesn't notice a decrease of administrative burdens. On one hand, the validity of the measurements of these costs is not always satisfactory, so the results can be quite misleading. On the other hand, as mentioned above, it is a hell of a job to change policies in the desired direction. Also, organizations lobbying for the business sector mostly counteract big changes, because of the protection of vested interests of their members.

Parliaments now and then organize their own investigations. For example, a decade ago the Dutch Parliament investigated the causes of the high number of people who were disabled for labor, resulting in major reforms of the social security system and in a complete transformation of the organizational structure of the government agencies in this domain. These reforms may not have diminished compliance costs for businesses, but the effect on reintegration of disabled people has been positive, so the cost/benefit ratio has improved.

Recently, educational policy was being evaluated by the Dutch parliament, showing twenty years of wrong policy making. Hopefully, this will lead to adjustments in the educational system, which, amongst others, will reduce the costs for businesses with respect to the cooperation with the educational system.

Public managers more and more want to have high quality policy research instead of quick-and-dirty analyses. Their only problem is that most budgets for policy research are insufficient for the higher expenses that will be required. Meanwhile, the Internet helps civil servants a lot in their search for information that can be used in their work. Their only problem is to select the appropriate information out of a superfluous overload of information.

Quality assurance systems nowadays are a normal phenomenon in the public sector. This is not always a guarantee for an adequate feedback, because such a system can also be used in misguided ways or even for misleading purposes. Furthermore, we have to acknowledge that such systems will add to the administrative burden; think, for instance, of measurements of client satisfaction. On the other hand, if such a measurement really contributes to a better service, there also will be an important gain. For example, when permits can be provided by the city administration within a few days instead of a few months, this is a great gain for the business sector.

However, when we look at reports of good evaluation studies, in many cases, the effects of policy programs are unsatisfactory to a lesser or greater extent. The main reason is that the policy process works out far from optimal, as described above. Also, the impact of good evaluation studies suffers from this phenomenon. Even evident results are sometimes completely neglected because of opposite interests or simply because of lack of interest.

The only power that is able to overcome this problem is the power of governing bodies. When they decide to take sound policy analyses seriously and accept the consequences of the conclusions from evaluation studies, real progress can be made in getting better policies, less unnecessary costs caused by the execution of policies and last, but not least, less unnecessary compliance costs.

13.9 Conclusion and Recommendations

In all policy areas, every step in the public policy process involves the risk of causing unnecessary compliance costs for businesses as well as for citizens. Compliance costs for the business sector can be reduced enormously, when the quality of the steps in the policy process will be raised to levels that will create successful policies. It is of utmost importance to create lean and mean policies in order to reduce compliance costs, not only when new policies are being developed but also through a continuous evaluation of existing policies.

The key factor for improving policies and reducing compliance costs is adequate information. The information supply is gradually improving, but not yet at a satisfactory level. The use of available information is unsatisfactory. Especially the improvement of the use of information by politicians and other stakeholders is difficult. It demands strong and enduring efforts from civil servants, politicians and lobby organizations. But it is the only way to go, if we want to take the issue of reduction of compliance costs seriously. It is important to note that a better use of information is also beneficial for the quality of public policy.

Three relatively simple measures would help to get the improvement process going:

- Governing bodies should be allowed to take measures only with an automatic expiration date. So, bad or obsolete policy measures can be stopped easily at the expiration date. A disadvantage may be that a good policy measure also can be stopped easily by a next government because of opportunistic political reasons, but from the point of view of reducing compliance costs, even this wouldn't be bad.
- Take no decisions anymore on new policies or on major changes in old policies without a proper ex ante evaluation. The costs of these evaluations are only a fraction of the costs of wrong policies. It is quite remarkable that ex post evaluations are far more common than ex ante evaluations, while the benefits from ex ante evaluations probably are much higher than the benefits from ex post evaluations.
- Ask the private sector which subsidy schemes, tax facilities or other facilities they would like to exchange for a general tax reduction. Interviews with many entrepreneurs indicate that they are willing to give up most policies that were specifically designed to help the business sector. This will save huge amounts of compliance costs. Of course, also the costs of the involved government agencies will be reduced substantially.

Three relatively heavy measures would bring more substantial improvements:

- Follow a zero-base-budgeting approach for all current policies in order to get a set of possibly obsolete policies, make an extra evaluation of these policies to be sure and, when it is clear that they can be abolished, end these policies as soon as possible. Support the discovery of obsolete policies with appropriate rewards for the involved employees. A lot of compliance costs will be saved together with a lot of tax payers' money.

- Select per governing body at least three policy programs that seem to be susceptible for simplification. Give per policy program an assignment to independent experts to re-engineer the program, of course with sufficient interaction with the involved parties. Repeat this approach after a decade. This will likely turn out to be the most difficult but also the most promising approach for the reduction of compliance costs and public expenses as well.
- Ask the private sector which regulations can be simplified by giving businesses more responsibility for good conduct and ask them how this can be arranged. Change these regulations according to their answers. Employers' organizations strongly favor such a change in the public policy culture. By this approach, compliance costs with respect to the involved policies can be reduced to a fraction of the present costs.

However, in the present political culture, such a program of policy simplification may not be feasible. Probably, we first need a cultural change from 'protective, dividing and commanding' politics into 'stimulating, synergizing and challenging' politics. The steadily growing entrepreneurial attitude among citizens may help to accomplish this change of culture.

For politicians, a nice side effect of a program of policy simplification would be that they would gain back respect and trust from their citizens. In the past decade, politics gradually has lost much respect and trust. Politicians and political parties who dare to go for simplification, first will be discouraged by the abovementioned iron triangle, but eventually will receive the benefits from their courage.

References

Birkland, T.A. 'Agenda Setting in Public Policy', in: F. Fischer, G.J. Miller & M.S. Sidney, 'Handbook of Public Policy Analysis', CRC Press, Boca Raton, 2007

Drucker, P. 'The Practice of Management', Harper & Row, New York, 1954

Dunn, W.N. 'Public Policy Analysis', Prentice Hall, Englewood Cliffs, 2004

Geelhoed, L.A. 'Wetgeving en bestuur in de semi-soevereine staat' in: Vervlechting en verschuivingen van wetgevingscomplexen aan het begin van de 21e eeuw, Publicaties van de Staatsrechtkring, nr. 12, Tjeenk Willink, Zwolle, 1996

Hoogerwerf, A. 'Beleid berust op veronderstellingen', in: Acta Politica, 4, 1984

Hupe, P. 'Overheid als politiek; over de grondslagen van beleid', Van Gorcum, Assen, 2007

Jann, W. & K. Wegrich 'Gefangen in eisernen Dreieck', Die Zeit, Hamburg, 17-11-2005

Leeuw, F.L. 'Over beleidsonderzoek en sociologie in de toekomst', in: G. Engbersen en J. de Haan, 'Balans en toekomst van de sociologie', Pallas Publications/Amsterdam University Press, 2006.

Presmann, J.L. & A.Wildavsky 'Implementation: How Great Expectations in Washington Are Dashed in Oakland', Berkeley, University of California Press, 1973

Vedung, E. 'Public Policy Making and Program Evaluation', Transaction Publishers, New Brunswick/London, 1997

Vendrig, J.P. 'Meldpunt Tegenstrijdige Regelgeving', EIM, Zoetermeer, 2003

Vries, M.S. de 'Problemen op de agenda' in: Prof. dr. A. Hoogerwerf & Prof. dr. M. Herweijer, 'Overheidsbeleid', Kluwer, Alphen a/d/ Rijn, 2003

Wholey, J.S., H.P. Hatry & K.E. Newcomer, 'Handbook of Practical Program Evaluation', Jossey-Bass, 2004

Chapter 14
How to Build Regulatory Reform and Regulatory Systems

Frank Frick

Abstract Regulation matters! It organizes markets and societies and is therefore a cornerstone of freedom and welfare. But regulation may also cause problems, unnecessary burdens, unintended side-effects and costs. The aim of this chapter is to give evidence that – and how – regulatory systems can be built to become more effective than most of them are today. With a heuristic approach, this chapter is looking for successful measures and trying to identify patterns.

Based on three principles, (i) a robust, responsible and flexible architecture, (ii) the necessary perspective of the beholder (here: business) and (iii) a target-oriented strategy, a regulatory system should be built on evidence-based solutions, acceptance within the businesses by consultation, the monitoring and steering of the regulatory process, independent scrutiny and legitimacy and a political program to make the cross cutting issue powerful.

14.1 Why Is There a New Global Interest in Building or Reforming Regulatory Systems?

The rule of law is one of modern society's cornerstones. Yet businesses, citizens and even administration claim to be overwhelmed by too much red tape. However, to argue against a popular half-truth, regulation does not always lead to a loss of freedom. Regulation does not need to entail high costs for the individual and for companies. And less regulation is not always better regulation, i.e. when state-controlled markets are liberalized. Statutory rights and obligations protect citizens and businesses against arbitrary acts in both the public and private sectors, thus laying the foundation for freedom, prosperity and fair competition.

F. Frick (✉)
Bertelsmann Stiftung, Gütersloh, Germany
e-mail: Frank.Frick@Bertelsmann.de

A. Nijsen et al. (eds.), *Business Regulation and Public Policy*,
International Studies in Entrepreneurship 20, DOI 10.1007/978-0-387-77678-1_14,

14.1.1 What We Already Know About Good Regulations

Whether and how well a society attains these goals, however, is not determined by the mere presence or the sheer quantity of regulations. Other factors are equally important:

- How transparent and comprehensible the regulations are to citizens and businesses.
- Whether and how well laws, rules and regulations serve their intended purposes.
- What undesirable side effects and, especially, what costs they entail.
- How the costs of establishing and monitoring compliance with regulations compare to their benefits.
- How the regulations are implemented.

More and more, society is becoming aware that regulations, while necessary, also impose high costs on individuals, businesses and the public sector alike. Regulations that are unclear, poorly designed or simply unnecessary can prevent achievement of the intended social and economic goals by imposing needless, irritating, costly burdens. Therefore, governments all over the world initiate programs on "cutting red tape" or "better regulation". Most of them agree on some basic principles on regulations.

Regulations ought to be . . .

- Comprehensible and understandable for all regulatees, thus easy to comply
- Low in burdens
- Cost-efficient and cost-effective
- Responsive, empowering and flexible
- Enforceable
- Non-discriminatory and consistent
- Result-oriented.

Of course, these prescriptive regulatory goals are not suitable for a kind of regulatory quick check, as empirical research on regulation shows, but they do give an impression of what modern, better or smart mean in a regulatory sense. The contribution of these goals is that they help focus our actions. They also point out that regulations often pursue contradictory goals which have to be somehow resolved in the policy process – by well informed policy-makers.

14.1.2 The Discourse on Better Regulation and Deregulation

In the past, public sector reform has often been associated with the vague goal of deregulation and with the modern state's retreat in the face of financial pressures and increasingly complex requirements. For most people, regulatory reform is undoubtedly still associated with the notion of deregulation and is seen by many as an ideologically biased and politically controversial concept.

Luckily, in recent years, a new and surprisingly vital debate on regulatory reform has commenced on a global scale among scholars, policymakers and practitioners. The current debate on "better regulation" adds a new aspect to international regulatory reform: Not only does better regulation aim at less regulation per se, but also at finding more effective ways of designing and enforcing regulations, without creating unnecessary burdens. The better-regulation approach emphasizes feasible methods and instruments that can deliver clear evidence in order to create more effective policy making processes. In my opinion, there are three factors to explain the global debate on regulatory reform:

- In globalized markets, sound regulation matters in terms of attracting entrepreneurs and capital and is therefore fostering economic growth.
- There is an increasing interest of stakeholder to be involved in the early stages in policy making and also in designing regulations.
- Awareness among civil servants and politicians that success of regulation lies in the perception of the beholder is on the rise. So more and more, perspectives change and additional questions are asked. What is important for the regulatee? How can we manage compliance?

14.1.3 Debating Regulatory Governance

Radaelli and De Franceso mention in their recent study on "Regulatory Quality in Europe"[1] that international organizations have focused on the impact of the regulatory reform movement. Both the OECD and the World Bank have prioritized regulation in their programs for good governance. By doing so, they acknowledged the potential of regulatory reform in terms of governance, participation of stakeholders, and more balanced state–society relations. What started out as a movement to open up economic sectors to competition has now become a debate about models of governance, accountability, and the role of public interests in regulatory choice.

With the goal of the Lisbon Agenda to make the EU the most competitive knowledge-based society, regulatory reform has become a priority for EU-member states and European institutions.[2] The European Union therefore tries to modernize the stock of legislation (by simplifying existing legislation and reducing administrative burdens), and uses impact assessment and consultation in the policy process.

Many recent studies and reviews on international competitiveness show efficient regulations and regulatory reform are essential for OECD-countries trying to enhance competitiveness and modernize their administrative

---

[1] Radelli, Claudio M.; De Francesco, Fabrizio: Regulatory quality in Europe. Concepts, measures and policy processes. Manchester, New York, 2007.

[2] Commission of the European Communities 2008, COM(2008) 32 final.

structures, while for the developing world, it is the key for accessing world markets and securing public and economic order.

Therefore, regulatory reform is not an issue found exclusively in the industrialized world. One could say that the debate on regulatory reform subdivides into two interrelated streams: OECD member states, which are concerned with the question of how to reform the present regulatory environment, and developing countries, which tend to concentrate on how to design new, effective regulatory governance structures. A number of other nations, such as China and Russia, are somewhere in between.

14.1.4 The Focus of Regulatory Reform: The Political Program, the Cross-Cutting Approach and Managing Cultural Change

Looking at the development of regulatory reform, three aspects stand out: Firstly, there is the shift from sector-oriented reform to horizontal, cross-sectoral reform by identifying institutional models and tools that are applicable across sectors, e.g. independent regulatory bodies and the use of market-friendly alternatives to the former "command-and-control"-regulation.

Secondly, priority is given to regulatory management, the attempt to move beyond individual reforms. Mainly located in the core executive, these efforts strive to manage the effects of regulation, are setting goals, deliver high-quality regulations focusing on transparency and accountability. Simply put, regulatory management tries to create cultural change.

Thirdly, the emergence of "better regulation" as a concept, as a political, normative program. The switch from deregulation to the regulation of the policy process is changing the coordinates of politics. This paradigm shift is perhaps the most important point because it links the administrative and scientific approach to the political sphere. And it means: high quality regulation does not necessarily mean low levels of regulation!

14.2 What Are the Challenges for Future Regulatory Regimes?

Regulatory systems nowadays have to cope with five main requirements:

- Evidence-based solutions for any kind of regulatory problem
- Acceptance within the businesses and the citizenship
- Monitoring and management of the regulatory process
- Independent scrutiny and legitimacy
- A political programming to make the cross cutting issue powerful and understandable.

14.2.1 *Evidence-Based Solutions for any Kind of Regulatory Problem*

It is a popular cliché that we live in an "Information Age." We widely assume that this mounting torrent of data is a force for positive change. However, it is equally plausible that the ever-increasing ability to gather and analyze information can become an impediment rather than an aid to good policy making. How can we best leverage information and analysis so that they facilitate rather than frustrate the regulatory reform agenda? How do we incorporate the many voices of a democratic society into the regulatory process, while still moving forward efficiently? How can we include data and analysis in our decision-making and, if we do, how do we decide what the "best available information" is? What sorts of tools can help us to accomplish these tasks?

There is a lack of evidence on impact or dynamics of regulation. There is a lack of transparency on the costs of regulation. Measuring the administrative burden and policy/compliance costs is widely seen as a big step forward – but certainly not the full story. What are the real benefits? Which trade-offs exist? Are there indicators for regulatory quality? To what extent can data be quantified and who should be charged with doing so? How should priorities be set? And how is it possible to account for unquantifiable factors, e.g. those related to social and environmental impact?

We have to look at evidence-based policymaking through a variety of lenses. We have to examine how different players, including parliamentary actors and external organizations, can help to facilitate the use of evidence in the regulatory process. Applying a more technical lens, we also have to investigate how tools such as cost-benefit analysis, impact assessment and e-lawmaking can contribute to the better regulation agenda.

The UK Better Regulation Executive has developed online training to give Government officials an overview of the new Impact Assessment process (launched in April 2008) and the SCM methodology. This comes on top of the development of the Administrative Burdens Calculator – both a tool for officials to model the impact of new proposals and the public interface with the results of the administrative burden measurement exercise carried out in 2005.

Impact assessment (IA) in the EU is a process aimed at structuring and supporting the development of policies, especially to consider the effects of policy proposals in their economic, social and environmental dimensions and to simplify and improve the regulatory environment. Based on an independent evaluation of the impact assessment system as it has evolved and been implemented since 2002, the commission will launch the revised guidelines in June 2008.

14.2.2 *Acceptance Within the Businesses and the Citizenship*

Frequently, there are insufficient explanations of the reasons for a specific regulation. Regulatory reform is designed to improve the delivery of public sector regulation and its enforcement. Yet what is the best way to achieve this? Public administrators are certainly experts in their field, but what about more technical questions of economics and overall social trends? To improve regulation-related processes, all constituents and stakeholders must be involved. But is this common sense? The following are Examples of stakeholders' involvements:

- The economist is concerned about efficiency.
- The civil servant is concerned with following the appropriate procedures and rules.
- The politician is concerned with the response of media and voters.
- The businessman (or woman) is concerned with minimizing costs and enhancing competitiveness.
- The citizen is concerned with protection and security.

Yet stakeholder involvement is hardly common practice, and those processes that do consider stakeholders face numerous problems. What is the best way to share experience and gather information from all stakeholders in order to create optimal, democratic, decision-making processes? The UK and the EU expand their consultation procedures, use it to gather information on how to deal with a problem and share the evidence to build up awareness of a problem and acceptance of a solution. Building on best practices at Member State level (Belgium, The Netherlands and the United Kingdom), the EU offers online consultation and provides the opportunity to contribute directly to improving the quality of legislation.[3]

14.2.3 Monitoring and Management of the Regulatory Process

There are complex interactions and side-effects arising from regulations. "Steering" rather than "rowing" characterizes successful public administration. But, how do we apply this principle to regulatory reform? The challenges are numerous – among others, a large number of individual actors in diverse ministries and at many levels of government, and the sheer resistance to change encountered in many bureaucracies. "Steering" cannot reasonably consist of actively managing every aspect of the regulatory process. With this in mind, how can we effectively target our efforts to create self-sustaining regulatory institutions while, at the same time, safeguarding the public interest, and change practices within existing institutions to better reflect best practices?

Specifically, we have to explore how reform structures can be designed and what kind of support can help to achieve results. We have to know which strategies facilitate effective work in a media-oriented environment. We have to explore ways to operate effectively in a system with multiple levels of

---

[3] see: www.berr.gov.uk/consultations, www.kafka.be or www.ec.europa.eu/enterprise/regulation/better_regulation/consultations_en.htm

governance (EU-Nation-Region-Municipality). And – last but not least – there is the need to identify and develop a competent cadre of professionals to assist in leading the effort. How to promote and steer regulatory reform? The success of regulatory reform does not only depend on having sufficient tools. Just as important – perhaps more so – is how reform processes are constructed and monitored, especially given the cross-cutting nature of regulatory reform. Typically, a central coordinating unit exists to motivate individual agencies and departments to participate and to ensure that the enforcement is integrated. One example is the Better Regulation Executive (BRE) in the UK, in the beginning located in cabinet office and now in BERR.[4] The BRE leads the regulatory reform agenda across government. Working with and through others, BRE's aims are to work with departments to improve the design and communication of new regulations, and to cooperate with regulators to simplify existing regulations. Also, BRE works with regulators (including local authorities) and departments to change attitudes and approaches to regulation to become more risk-based. The question is how to do this effectively. The coordinating unit can challenge and enable, but it cannot do the job itself – something its partners are well aware of.

Obviously, the regulatory oversight like BRE in GB, Regulatory Reform Group (formerly IPAL) in the Netherlands, the US Office of Information and Regulatory Affairs (OMB-OIRA) or the European Commission's Impact Assessment Board (IAB) vary considerably. Especially the scope of activities covered by oversight bodies, including guidance, the degree of quantification measures and the processes to ensure high quality analysis differ. These mechanisms to analyze or to steer have a remarkable influence on regulatory decisions.[5]

Similarly important is the question which indicators are chosen and monitored to measure the success of regulatory reform. We need criteria, indicators, to measure whether regulation is good. Therefore we need at least three different sets of indicators:

- Indicators of the design of better regulation, measuring the input
- Indicators of activity and output, e.g. concerning consultations, impact assessments, use of alternative instruments
- Outcome indicators, e.g. compliance rates, impact on competitiveness and innovation.

While outcome measurements are often difficult, indicators for the quality of the process are very important.

The coordinating unit must also generate sufficient political backing. How can policymakers be encouraged to support reform? And how to make it even

[4] BERR: The Department for Business, Enterprise & Regulatory Reform. www.berr.gov.uk

[5] It would be interesting to draw a comparison between different approaches to regulatory monitoring, the approaches to centralised oversight and quality control., and the strength and weaknesses of different systems.

more complex? There is a loss of political steering capabilities due to emerging complexity in transnational business, spreading technologies and societal subsystems and networks. The state and public service find themselves in the position of not being the sole regulator. Their role has changed over the years – from autocratic command-and-control regulators to a new role of the regulatory guardian, mediator of the public interest, and partner in regulatory partnership. But the state and the public service will have to deal with this challenge and include this new steering reality in their regulatory framework. This means that the state does not lose its influence but will have to make more use of business and civil society potentials and cooperation in regulation by a certain empowerment. Business and civil society, on the other hand, have to take up this task and signal their willingness to cooperate in new partnerships.

14.2.4 Independent Scrutiny and Legitimacy

How to challenge regulatory reform? In Europe we see a growing number of independent watchdogs for better regulation issues. National parliaments and administrative agencies draft pass and enforce laws – so why shouldn't they also be responsible for ensuring the quality of their work? In practice, improving quality by improving processes is a challenging task. Individual incentives rarely focus on the common good. In today's media society, moreover, the political process is geared towards implementing new programs quickly, not on evaluating and optimizing existing programs. As British, German and Dutch reform efforts have shown, when it comes to better regulation, an independent watchdog agency can prove useful. Not surprisingly then, the European Union is thinking along these same lines by introducing the "High Level Group of Independent Stakeholders on Administrative Burdens" – although with a very limited scope on monitoring the reduction of costs of information obligations only within existing legislation.

But how much independence should an oversight body have? In Sweden, there is only the privately financed watchdog today. The business organization established this watchdog to advice the government – and government is interested in supporting and improving this process.

How can such an institution be financed without compromising its independence? How should it stand vis-à-vis policymakers, government agencies and the media if it is to build trust without being too lenient? Recently, the British government launched a strategic change from the 'Better Regulation Commission' to the 'Risk and Regulation Advisory Council' (RRAC) with a much smaller scope and responsibility. There is the argument that there are enough resources to steer, monitor and scrutinize regulatory reform by the National Audit Office (NAO) and the Better Regulation Executive (BRE). But for the public it might not be the same thing whether a government institution or an independent watchdog is scrutinizing.

14.2.5 Political Programming to Make the Cross-Cutting Issue Powerful and Understandable

We have to bear in mind that legislation is the primary responsibility of parliaments. For the engagement of parliamentarians, this means there is a demand for a good procedural structure. Therefore, we should give parliament several tools to investigate and scrutinize in any area of regulation. We have to increase the responsibility of politicians and their willingness to listen to the public, to economy, to expertise. Better Regulation can't be realized without political support and political entrepreneurship! In terms of governance, this also requires personal responsibility within the government for coordination and pushing the issue forward. Sometimes, it will also be necessary to have the courage to stand up for your own convictions because from the departmental perspective better regulation often causes unpopular decisions.

14.3 Cornerstones of a Sound Regulatory Architecture

For designing or redesigning regulatory regimes, the primary focus is of utmost importance. Success is in the eye of the beholder. Therefore, be aware that for enterprises, the quality of regulation consists of a target oriented rule, a minimal amount of burden, good enforcement and clear communication, i.e. can any instrument to reduce administrative burden achieve success if the regulatory framework is ineffective or execution is not customer-oriented? Will businesses really feel the impact of our efforts just by changing laws and not changing service procedures? Can an efficient and effective public administration strengthen public trust without transparency? And, last but not least, what about policy? How can we improve regulatory quality when we have to implement what are essentially bad programs?

Therefore, we should integrate:

- Substantively effective regulation
- High regulatory quality
- Customer-oriented implementation
- Stringent political and administrative process.

Tangible effects will only be achieved with an enhanced concept (Table 14.1).

What should robust governance architecture for steering regulatory reform programs look like? The more complex the regulatory problem is, the more important it becomes to follow these three principles:

Table 14.1 Four Dimensions of Better Regulation

Content Good policy	Regulatory quality Better regulation	Implementation commitment Good administration	Process/ Structure Good governance
• Has the strategic goal been defined? • Have measureable outcomes been defined?	• Have the best measures been selected? • Have costs to the government, citizens, and businesses been minimized?	• Is implementation customer-oriented?	• Are politicians supportive of the regulation? • Has ex-post-evaluation been conducted? • Has support from important actors been obtained?

- First, it is important that the architecture of the regulatory system is robust, responsive and flexible; leadership should be clear about the targets and principles and also about which effects are managed.
- Second, equally important is that the citizens' and business perspectives are consistently taken into account and that the leadership communicates with the public and manages expectations. Especially in the beginning, it is important that changes are immediately perceptible to the public and transparency is maintained regarding the main figures of progress.
- Third: It is important to think about regulatory choice and the tools used to accomplish our goals. However, nobody should just rely on tools, it is necessary to develop a holistic better regulation strategy.

Based on these principles, five building blocks emerge for constructing a sound regulatory framework:

- Vision and a political program
- Evidence-based policy making
- Consultation
- Steering Better Regulation
- Ensure scrutiny by an independent watchdog.

14.3.1 Vision and Political Program

Regulatory systems are based on constitutional rights, historical decisions and cultural aspects defining behavior. To change these systems carefully means to establish a new social contract regarding sharing responsibility and burden between the three sectors state, market, private. This explains the emphasis on risk in the Anglo-Saxon debate, because the attitude regarding risk is an important element of regulatory culture.

To change the culture for Better Regulation, a change in the culture of policy making is needed. Strong support and commitment by the head of government is essential – otherwise, better regulation initiatives might get stuck in line with ministries' interests. If "better regulation" is a key factor of the political agenda, it can be promoted in the public and people can get involved without raising expectations to unsustainable levels.

After engaging politics, the civil servants, the stakeholders and civil society have to be convinced to put pressure on the political process. Especially in federal states, the responsible institutions for law-making and enforcement should work together to get the best results.

14.3.2 Evidence-Based Policy Making

Impact assessments have proven to gather knowledge and to add evidence. There is a need to know what choices there are and what effects, side-effects and costs might occur. Regulators should be forced to reflect and to document their reflections.

One danger might actually be to have too much choice. The problem is often to restrain oneself on the main effects. Another problem is the selection of target-oriented measures. There is, sometimes, too little knowledge on the trade-offs between self-regulation, other modes of regulation, law and government regulation. Regulators tend to stick to the measures they are used to. There is also very little evidence about third party regulation, where standards etc. are applied without government interest/involvement.

14.3.3 Consultation

By early consultations, legislation can be optimized. Stakeholder involvement and consultation is necessary to gather information and opinion to ensure regulatory quality. But the most important factor is to ensure acceptance.

Participatory democracy enhances participatory rights of citizens alongside of elections. It raises incentive to participate, e.g. by public hearings, by the obligation of agencies to answer and to give reasonable foundation for the decision finally found. Fortunately, e-government and e-participation lower the costs considerably, Internet-fostered accessibility of administrative information enhances the availability of regulative guidance and interpretation papers. For consultation, a 'Code of Practice' on timing, duration, clarity on scope, responsiveness, accessibility, capacity and monitoring is helpful. A lot of governments and regulators have recognized that they can enhance democratic legitimacy by broadening participation.

14.3.4 Steering Better Regulation

Political programs on better regulation have to be implemented. A robust governance architecture for steering regulatory reform initiates a cycle of better regulation and improves compliance.

To ensure sustainability of regulatory reform institutionalization, structures and processes have to follow a strategy that defines outcome first, then looks for tools. Quantifiable targets are important. They keep the topic on the political agenda. Transparency in measurements and publishing results enhances credibility. Sharing performance data is the first step to involve people. Simplifications and reductions should be noticeable and felt by businesses and the public.

14.3.5 Ensure Scrutiny by an Independent Watchdog

Continuous improvement is a question of trust. A watchdog is helpful as an engine for better regulation within the reform system. Furthermore, it helps to scrutinize/challenge the work of the government, listens to concerns, provides appeal mechanisms and helps to communicate the success stories.

Watchdogs should be independent, maybe mandated by parliament to underline their independence. They should be well-funded and have access to all information and figures necessary to scrutinize governmental programs. And most important, they should be an obligatory part of the regulatory process. Only then, politicians will listen to the recommendations of a watchdog.

14.4 Summary and Conclusion

It is increasingly evident that regulatory reform and streamlined regulatory architectures are key elements not only to enhance national competitiveness but also for efforts geared toward supra-nationalization (e.g. Europeanization) and the creation of common markets (e.g. the Single European Market, NAFTA or Mercosur), as well as the harmonization of regulatory standards resulting from such efforts. Therefore, future efforts in redesigning regulatory architecture have to consider aspects and actors on different international and national levels. In a global economy, regulation is a complex process of decision making and a question of multilevel governance. Today's international organizations do not have the power and the coordination mechanisms to find solutions for future problems in regulation – at least, not yet. But the debate on the weakness of UN, World Bank, IMF, and the Doha process may be a starting point for creating the necessary institutional setting for a global regulatory regime that can facilitate health, welfare and peace.

Better regulation is a cornerstone of competitiveness and welfare. If we are not successful, the stock of regulation will increase still further while quality of regulation and enforcement practice will worsen,

- Costs and burdens for businesses, citizens and administration will rise
- The faith of regulated parties in the rule of law will erode and
- The compliance level will drop.

Key factors of successful regulatory reform are the political will and measurable goals, well-functioning institutions, evidence, acceptance and trust.

Regulatory reform is a multi-faceted task that requires cooperation between all political levels and all stakeholder groups. Clearly, a public debate about the overall principles of better regulation is needed. And it is a question of leadership, strong institutions and managerial capacity. Simply put, good regulatory management requires cultural change.

References

Jacobzone, S., C. Choi, and C. Miguet: Indicators of Regulatory Management Systems – OECD Working Paper, September 2007.

Radelli, C. M., De Francesco, Fabrizio: Regulatory quality in Europe. Concepts, Measures and Policy Processes. Manchester, New York, 2007.

Chapter 15
Institutions for Better Regulation: The Example of the Netherlands, 2002–2007

Robin Linschoten, Jeroen Nijland, and Jaap Sleifer

Abstract This chapter describes the institutions for cutting administrative burdens in the Netherlands. Based on an evaluation of the World Bank, the following criteria are discerned: Measurement, reduction targets, coordinating minister, and incorporation in the regulatory process. The chapter examines how the institutions helped to change the policy culture. Moreover, it is argued that the institutions can be effectively applied in other countries and for a broader scope of better regulation including administrative burdens for citizens and compliance costs.

15.1 Introduction

In the first episode of "Yes Minister", a BBC series from the 1980s, the new minister of administrative affairs aims to introduce open government. In this episode, the permanent secretary reminds the new minister of his remarks on red tape when he was still a member of the opposition. "Is the minister aware that planning procedures make building a bungalow in the 20th century slower than building a cathedral in the 12th century?" Even though the episode did not elaborate on cutting red tape, it is not so difficult to imagine an episode where honest attempts to cut red tape end up in various bureaucratic manipulations.

How can a minister avoid the (unintended) distortions that so often arise in the bureaucratic machinery? This chapter looks at the experiences in the Netherlands from 2002 to 2007. During these years, the Netherlands had two programs for reducing administrative burdens: one for businesses and one for citizens. For the prevailing cabinet Balkenende II, the reduction of administrative burdens was on the top of the political agenda. There were two

R. Linschoten (✉)
Dutch Advisory Board on Administrative Burden (Actal), The Hague, The Netherlands
e-mail: info@actal.nl

A. Nijsen et al. (eds.), *Business Regulation and Public Policy*, International Studies in Entrepreneurship 20, DOI 10.1007/978-0-387-77678-1_15,

coordinating ministers. The minister of finance, Gerrit Zalm, led the approach for businesses. The ministers of the interior, Tom de Graaf and his successors Alexander Pechtold and during the cabinet Balkenende III Atzo Nicolaï, led the approach for citizens. The emphasis of this chapter will be on the program for businesses.

Reports of World Bank (2007) and OECD (2007) have heralded the Dutch approach for reducing administrative burdens for companies as world leader.[1] Based on the review by World Bank, there are four criteria for success: (a) measurement; (b) reduction targets for each ministry; (c) strong coordinating minister; (d) incorporation in the regulatory process. This chapter discusses these criteria for success in more detail. Another question that will be addressed is the culture change. Was there a significant change of culture among regulators? In the final parts of this chapter, it will be discussed how the Dutch example can be copied to other countries and to the broader domain of impact assessment in general.

15.2 Four Criteria for Success

The first criterion for success is measurement, especially the zero base measurement. In the Netherlands, the zero base measurement calculated all the administrative burdens that originated from the existing regulations in 2002 (base year). Its importance, according to World Bank, is that it provides decision makers with a counterfactual: What are the burdens by continuation of existing policies? Moreover, the zero base measurement shows precisely how much a ministry contributes to the overall administrative burdens. Or even more specific, how much a particular law contributes to administrative burdens.

For the purpose of this chapter, it makes no sense to address all the details of the methodology for calculating the administrative burdens, i.e. the standard cost model. The standard cost model is a simple and straightforward set of definitions for bookkeeping. It departs from the information and reporting obligations for firms and citizens that originate from legislation. For each of these obligations, the administrative burdens are estimated by a very simple formula:

$$AB = Q^*P$$

Where AB stands for “Administrative Burden”, Q stands for quantity and P stands for price. Quantities are the product of the number of firms that are involved and the frequency that these firms have to fulfill the specific obligation. Prices are determined in panels with policy advisers and representatives of businesses and are based on the time that is needed to complete obligations and also related costs (e.g. proofs of an accountant).

[1] World Bank Group, Review of the Dutch Administrative Burden Reduction Program (Washington 2007); OECD, Cutting red tape: Administrative simplification in the Netherlands (Paris 2007).

Besides the zero base measurement that maps out all the existing obligations for 2002, the World Bank criterion of measurement also includes the Dutch requirement to account for all the effects on administrative burdens when existing regulations are changed or abolished and when new regulations are imposed. Obviously, all these accounts have to follow the methodology of the standard cost model. What new information obligations are added – what existing information obligations are abolished or altered – how many companies does it concern – what are the overall effects on administrative burdens?

From a policy perspective, one of the great merits of the standard cost model is that it offers transparency in some of the societal effects (administrative burdens) of regulation. All state-imposed burdens on companies are directly linked to specific regulations and, therefore, to the specific (responsible) ministries. This makes it a useful management tool, as it allows steering of the overall burdens of each ministry. For this purpose, it is very important that the zero base measurement covers all relevant regulations.

The second criterion is the reduction target for each ministry. In the Netherlands, the overall reduction target was set at 25% of all the administrative burdens according to the zero base measurement. Alternatively, it could have been a target of either 20% or 30% , as the percentage was set politically and lacks a scientific basis. Still, based on the experiences from 2002 to 2007, it seems clear that the 25% target has been very effective. The percentage required serious efforts to reconsider existing regulations, and also proved to be a realistic and attainable goal.

Targets were set for each ministry – and ministries were the responsible actors for meeting these targets. Doing so, the not in my backyard (NIMBY) mechanism could effectively be avoided. All the ministries developed strategies to reduce their part of the administrative burdens. Looking at the intended measures of the ministries, decreasing administrative burdens were ex ante calculated and fixed in a yearly ceiling of administrative burdens. To prevent functional autonomy of the reduction targets, i.e. the situation where the reduction target gets confused with the ultimate objective to relieve actual burdens for businesses, the Netherlands carefully involved stakeholders (in so-called Mixed Committees) when the zero base measurement was carried out. Furthermore, it was promoted to involve stakeholders during the drafting of new legislation.

Based on an evaluation of the progress in 2006, it can be concluded that most ministries will meet their target in 2007. The table below shows the total administrative burden for businesses per ministry in 2002 according to the zero base measurement – and also the projected reduction in 2007 (Table 15.1).

Rather than evaluating the accomplishments of the individual ministries, we would like to stress that the table shows that all ministries substantially reduced their administrative burdens. For achieving this purpose, all ministries established a coordinating unit consisting of 1 to 5 officials, to make sure that the program for cutting the department's administrative burdens was carried out effectively. The units of the different departments frequently met in the

Table 15.1 Overview of the burdens in 2002 and the reductions in 2007 per ministry

	Total administrative burdens for businesses 2002	Net projected reduction in 2007
Finance	4325	915 (21%)
Social Affairs & Employment	2533	680 (27%)
Health, Welfare & Sport	3181	755 (24%)
Justice	2500	903 (36%)
Housing, Spatial Planning & Environment	1714	519 (30%)
Transport, Public Works & Water Management	917	264 (29%)
Economic Affairs	672	60 (9%)
Agriculture, Nature & Food Quality	430	158 (37%)
Education, Culture & Science	18	5 (28%)
Interior & Kingdom Relations	17	– 9 (–53%)
Total	16307	4251 (26%)

Source: IPAL, Dit willen we even kwijt (Oktober 2006)

COAL-network, which stimulated the border-crossing nature of the Dutch approach. The COAL-network was headed by IPAL, i.e. the officials of the then coordinating minister, Gerrit Zalm.[2]

Besides the first criterion (measurement) and the second criterion (reduction target), the third criterion for success is a strong coordinating minister. The coordinating minister functions as a warrant that cutting red tape withstands the pressure caused by other policy objectives. In other words, the ministers of the departments have several policy objectives, so that reducing administrative burdens is easily crowded out by other policy objectives, unless there is an effective safeguard. In the Netherlands, the counterbalance was provided by the minister of finance. Being the coordinating minister for the reduction of administrative burdens for companies, he had to make sure that all ministries actually met their reduction targets.

The effectiveness of the counterbalance very much depends on the strength (or power) of the coordinating minister. With Gerrit Zalm, the Netherlands was blessed with an experienced and widely recognized statesman, who was also very dedicated to the issue. Moreover, in his position as the minister of finance, linking the reduction of administrative burdens to the budget cycle, he had an instrument to sanction underperforming ministries. Doing so, he ensured that cutting administrative burdens remained a top priority during the cabinet Balkenende II. The official duties were carried out by IPAL, including safeguarding proper measurement, monitoring and preparations for the council of ministers.

[2] COAL stands for "coordinatoren administratieve lasten", which is the Dutch equivalent for coordinators of administrative burdens; IPAL – now the Regulatory Reform Group – stands for "interdepartementale projectdirectie administratieve lasten".

The fourth criterion for success is the incorporation in the regulatory process and the role of the independent watchdog, Actal.[3] Besides reducing the stock of regulation, it is necessary to contain the flow of (new) regulation. Therefore, the reduction target of 25% was defined as a net target, i.e. the target takes into account all increases and decreases of the administrative burdens due to regulatory changes.[4]

Ministries are obliged to include a quantitative and qualitative assessment of the effects on the administrative burdens for all new regulations. The assessments are reviewed by the independent advisory board on administrative burden (Actal). The review by Actal perfectly fits into the procedures that are involved during the regulatory process. There are several reviews of other agencies that also take place when new regulations are prepared, including environmental effects, economic impact analysis, quality of regulation, privacy, etc. By incorporating the assessment of the administrative burdens into the regulatory process, it has become a matter of good governance.

15.3 The Proof of the Pudding

Based on the experience in the Netherlands, it appears that the four criteria for success are all necessary ingredients for achieving the goals of the better regulation agenda. Only when all these criteria are met, the institutional infrastructure generates the appropriate incentives for cutting red tape. This can be illustrated best by a historical comparison of the cutting administrative burdens for companies program before 2000 and after 2002. For reasons of comprehensiveness, the program for citizens is also included in our comparison.

Table 15.2 summarizes the key characteristics of three Dutch programs on reducing administrative burdens. It distinguishes the heralded program for cutting administrative burdens for businesses as it existed from 2002 to 2007; the historical program for reducing administrative burdens for businesses as it existed before 2000; and the program for reducing administrative burdens for citizens that started in 2005.

For the Netherlands, the year 2000 marks the point of transition towards a systematic approach for reducing administrative burdens for businesses. For this transition, the Dutch government is indebted to some earlier reports on cutting red tape during the 1980s and 1990s and some early attempts within a

[3] Actal stands for "Adviescollege toetsing administratieve lasten", i.e. Dutch Advisory Board on Administrative Burden.

[4] The net target relates to the fixed yearly ceiling of administrative burdens for ministries. When administrative burdens from new regulations exceed the ceiling, ministries have to compensate for the new burdens so that the ceiling is not overstepped.

Table 15.2 Key characteristics of the Dutch programs for reducing administrative burdens

	Businesses		Citizens
Criterion	Since 2002	Before 2000	Since 2005
Measurement	Zero base measurement	No zero base measurement	Partial zero base measurement
Targets	Net targets for each ministry	Gross overall target	Net targets for each ministry
Coordinating minister	Ministry of Finance	[Ministry of Economic Affairs]	Ministry of the Interior
Incorporation in regulatory process	Ex ante measurement for new regulation	No ex ante measurement for new regulation	Ex ante measurement for new regulation

Sources: see text

broader deregulation agenda (minister of economic affairs, Wijers).[5] In 2000, there was already a second reduction target on administrative burdens for businesses. It all began with a reduction target of 10% under Prime Minister Kok. When his government reported meeting the reduction target, an additional 15% was demanded by Parliament.

In retrospect, the early reduction targets showed two major shortcomings. Firstly, the targets were not attributed to specific ministries. As a result, individual ministries were tempted to avoid participation (not in my backyard behavior). Secondly, the targets were defined as gross targets. As a result, the reductions of administrative burdens from existing regulations were partly offset by new administrative burdens from new regulations. When the program for cutting administrative burdens for companies started in 2000, it largely followed the advice of the reports of the commission, Slechte. The program included a coordinating minister, a coordinating unit, and an independent watchdog, Actal. The minister of economic affairs, who had put the issue on the political agenda in the first place, became the coordinating minister.

The need for a net reduction target immediately became clear. At that time, studies of EIM measured the actual reduction of administrative burdens, accounting for the reductions as well as the increases from new regulations.[6] It appeared that government policy on administrative burdens was less successful than expected. Such findings led to the conclusion that it was also important to make a zero base measurement and to require ex-ante measurement according to the standard cost model for each new regulation.

Some of the changes went simultaneously. From 2002 onwards, the coordination shifted towards the ministry of finance. This is a relatively strong position with adequate carrots and sticks because of the linkage to the budget cycle.

---

[5] Commissie tot verlichting van administratieve verplichtingen voor het bedrijfsleven (Grapperhaus), Heerendiensten (The Hague 1985); Commissie Administratieve Lasten (Slechte), Regels zonder overlast; minder, eenvoudiger, sneller (The Hague 1999).

[6] EIM, Monitor administratieve lasten bedrijven (several years).

During the same year, the zero base measurement was completed and a new (net) target of 25% was set. In other words, from that moment on, the program for cutting administrative burdens for companies fulfilled all the criteria that were distinguished by World Bank in 2007.

When the ministry of the interior started the program for cutting administrative burdens for citizens in 2005, the lessons learned from the experiences with reducing administrative burdens for businesses were carefully studied. A very similar infrastructure as the one that was already there for businesses was also developed for citizens. This includes a partial zero base measurement, a coordinating unit at the ministry of the interior (PAL), net reduction targets for each ministry, coordinating units at each ministry, a regular meeting of these coordinating units in ICRAL (that is headed by PAL).[7] For new regulations, ex ante measurement was required and had to pass Actal. Despite the discontinuity of the coordinating minister – since the start of the program for citizens in 2005, there were three different ministers – the program managed to deliver.

Looking at the criteria of World Bank, the main difference seems that the zero base measurement has only mapped out parts of the information obligations for citizens. However, it should be noted that the program for citizens learned its lessons in 2005. At that time, the program for businesses was struggling with its communication. Even though the approach proved to be effective within the ministries, the emphasis in the press was much more on the still existent bureaucratic futilities rather than the problems that were solved. Headlines mentioned that entrepreneurs did not notice any of the "calculated" relief. To some extent, there emerged a gap between public perception of administrative burdens and the political perception of the whole operation.

Before discussing how this context influenced the outline of the administrative burdens for citizens' program, it is stressed that most of the discrepancy between public opinion and government calculations relates to methodology. Firstly, for public opinion, administrative burdens relate to all sorts of paperwork and obligations, regardless of source, origin and nature. For the program, there were clear definitions – relating to the competences of the coordinating ministry – that were much narrower than what influences public opinion. Secondly, in the Dutch bookkeeping procedures, the reductions were booked in when new laws were published, which is earlier than implementation. Thirdly, the objective of cutting administrative burdens implied new (and easier) legislation. From the perspective of an entrepreneur, some of these new legislations might reduce the yearly burdens; however, it also brought about one-off costs.

For the reduction program for citizens, the communication issues were translated into an emphasis on noticeable effects. Some of the amendments

[7] PAL stands for "Programma Administratieve Lasten" (Program Administrative Burdens) and ICRAL stands for Interdepartementale Coördinatoren Reductie Administratieve Lasten (Interde-partemental Coordinators for Reducing Administrative Burden).

were good; especially the development of target groups (e.g. disabled persons, elderly) for whom administrative burdens are very high because they are confronted with cumulating requirements from different regulations. Other amendments were probably less fortunate; such as the decision to make a partial base line measurement (including only the burdens from the 20% regulations with the most information obligations). Whereas the communication of a systematic approach clearly called for broadening the program on cutting red tape, the program for cutting administrative burdens for citizens narrowed it down.

Still, the administrative burdens for citizens program managed to realize a substantial reduction, even though political commitment on reducing administrative burdens for citizens seems to be much weaker than for companies. On the one hand, the program for businesses benefits from the advocacy of business organizations. On the other hand, higher political commitment to the program for businesses relates to the strong position of the (Dutch) minister of finance. To quote an operative of the Nixon administration: "When you've got 'em by the balls, their hearts and minds will follow". The counterbalance of the coordinating minister (e.g. the linkage to the budget cycle) is rather crucial.

15.4 Culture Change

According to common wisdom, institutions, habits and cultures are sticky and therefore difficult to alter. A main accomplishment of the Dutch "infrastructure" for regulatory reform is that it has proven its value for breaking through the pre-eminent inertia of the regulatory process. Before 2000, hardly any new proposal took into consideration the effects on administrative burdens. Since that date, the number of new regulations that include a consideration of the effects on administrative burdens boosted. The graph below shows the number of hits in new regulations on a query for "administrative burdens".

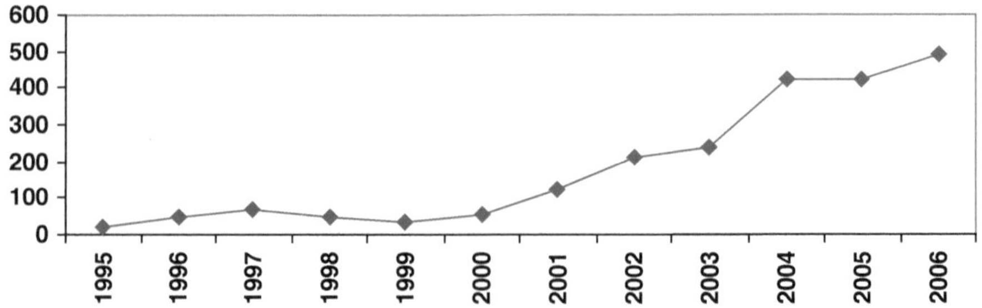

Fig. 15.1 Hits on "administrative burdens" in new regulations, 1995–2006
Source: Robin Linschoten, Hans Kamps, Jaap Sleifer, "Cultuuromslag in de wetgeving" in: *Regelmaat 2008/2*

Based on the experiences of the independent watchdog, Actal, that are partly documented in their annual reports, it is clear that while the number of new regulations with an explicit account of the effects on administrative burdens increased, the quality of these accounts also improved. As a result, the opinions of Actal on new proposals have grown more and more positive.

Besides the macro-figures that arise from monitoring, there are survey studies from 2005 and 2007 that provide insightful information of the individual civil servants who make new regulations.[8] These survey studies help reveal the decisive characteristics for the support of civil servants for the better regulation agenda. Moreover, these survey studies also help determine how the institutional infrastructure should be designed for the maximum compliance of civil servants on the reduction of administrative burdens.

The aim of the survey studies is to determine the degree of internalization for each ministry. Internalization is defined as the culture change of civil servants towards better regulation issues. It is measured as an average of their scores for knowledge, attitude and behavior on administrative burdens. According to this research, civil servants who complied to the better regulation agenda best were the ones who had regular contacts with businesses (or citizens) that are addressed by the regulations and civil servants who had several dossiers that had to pass the Actal test. Also, a regular contact with enforcement agencies contributes to this culture change.

The contributing function of Actal towards the mindset of civil servants is explicitly confirmed by some of the top level civil servants, who believe that the role of the Actal-test is a conditio sine qua non for an enduring and serious consideration of the effects of new regulations for administrative burdens. Their remarks relate to the function of Actal in the institutional infrastructure. Other parts of the institutional infrastructure that prove to be important at the level of ministries are the early consideration of the effects of administrative burdens (i.e. during the first research on policy options), regular events to bring administrative burdens under the attention (conferences, mailings), and a centralized coordination to meet the reduction target.

15.5 A Reproducible Experiment?

Presently, several countries face the same challenges as in the Netherlands. The methodology of the standard cost model and the zero base measurements has been adopted in numerous countries. Also, the criteria of a (net) reduction target, ex ante measurement and a coordinating ministry are widely recognized. Especially, Germany has adopted a very similar administrative burdens

[8] IOO, Verinnerlijking administratieve lasten (Leiden 2005); see also the English translation by the Working Party on Regulatory Management and Reform of the OECD, Internalisation of Administrative Burdens (Paris 2006) Room document 12; IOO, Verinnerlijking administratieve lasten (Leiden 2007).

program. Also, in countries like Denmark, Sweden and the United Kingdom, there are several great similarities. Obviously, some elements of the success criteria need to be adjusted to the national differences. For instance, until early 2007, the prime minister coordinated the reduction program in the United Kingdom. In the UK constellation, this was as effective as coordination by the minister of finance in the Netherlands.

Recently also, the European Union has started a program to cut administrative burdens for businesses. In our view, adjusting the Dutch recipe for cutting administrative burdens to the European institutions poses a great challenge. Where countries function basically along the old concepts of "divisions of powers", Europe has developed a system of "institutional balance" based on overlapping jurisdictions.[9] Still, step by step, all the ingredients are introduced; a zero base measurement, a coordinating commissioner (Verheugen), a reduction target of 25% , an independent watchdog (High Level Group of Independent Stakeholders on Administrative Burdens), etc.

Within the Netherlands, the first reproduction of the success has been the broadening of administrative burdens for citizens. Since June 2006, most of the ingredients have been applied to the education sector also, i.e. a zero-base measurement, reduction targets, incorporation in the regulatory process including a scrutiny by Actal. The present challenge is to reproduce the success of administrative burdens to the broader domain of all compliance costs. Two independent studies by the bureaus, EIM and Regioplan, already proved that it is possible to measure compliance costs.[10] In our view, this implies that it is technically possible to make a zero base measurement, introduce ex ante measurement and impose reduction targets.

According to Actal, broadening the program to compliance costs is necessary, though may prove more difficult in practice as there is still the criterion of a strong coordinating minister. Presently, the cabinet Balkenende IV (since 2007) has shifted some of the pre-existing responsibilities.[11] Although the safeguard through linkage to the budget cycle still exists and the role of the minister of finance is still warranted, the main coordination tasks of the reduction program are taken care of by two secretaries of state. Moreover, in the view of Actal, the broadening to all compliance costs is picked up with great caution, meaning that there will be only partial zero base measurements in this area. Also, the structure of ex ante measurement and independent scrutiny of these measurements is not the same as it was for administrative burdens for businesses.

---

[9] Alberto Alesina and Roberto Perotti, "The European Union: A Politically Incorrect View" in: Journal of Economic Perspectives (Volume 18, Number 4) pp. 27–48.

[10] EIM, Pilotonderzoek overige nalevingskosten van bestaande wetgeving (Zoetermeer 2007); Regioplan beleidsonderzoek, Overige nalevingskosten gemeten. Proefmeting reductiepotentieel-methode (Amsterdam 2007).

[11] Tweede Kamer 2006–2007, 29515, nr. 202.

If the new cabinet would have implemented the same infrastructure as the previous cabinet had for administrative burdens, Actal would plainly conclude that the program would work. Now the cabinet has not made an exact copy, according to Actal, it depends much more on the political rigour towards the issue, the (political) influence of the coordinating state secretaries, and the commitment of the civil servants. That could be vulnerability or a risk. However, it may also hold some new opportunities. Actal finds it too early to make up the balance sheet yet.

Obviously, the cabinet and the coordinating unit are confident that the broadening to compliance costs will work well. They emphasize that main pillars of the infrastructure for compliance costs are very similar as for administrative burdens. It is their view that the modifications are minor and desirable because of some specific requirements of dealing with compliance costs and because of preventing fatigue at the ministries.

15.6 Summary and Conclusions

The Dutch example for cutting red tape is a showcase for setting up the appropriate institutions for better regulation. Looking at the Dutch experience, the following criteria appear to be decisive elements of the "institutional infrastructure".

1. The Standard Cost Model (SCM) and the zero base measurement. This provided the Netherlands with a bookkeeping system for the administrative burdens.
2. Net targets for each ministry of reducing administrative burdens by 25%. Firstly, it is important to have a target for *each* ministry to avoid the "not in my backyard" mechanism. Secondly, the 25% target works effectively as an incentive.
3. A strong coordinating minister, who functions as a counterbalance so that the issue is not crowded out by other policy objectives. In the Netherlands, the reduction of administrative burdens is linked to the budget cycle.
4. Incorporation in the regulatory process where it is required that new regulations are scrutinized by the independent watchdog Actal. For starters, the *net* result makes it necessary to account for plusses and minuses – and also for the flow of new regulations.

Besides the benefits for businesses (and the economy), a major result of the program on administrative burdens is the culture change i.e. the shift in the mindset of civil servants who consider taking into account the effects on administrative burdens more and more as a matter of good governance.

The Dutch institutional infrastructure for better regulation has delivered valuable results. Moreover, it appears that its recipe can be copied by other countries and can be applied for a broader scope than administrative burdens for businesses (e.g. administrative burdens for citizens, compliance costs).

References

Alberto Alesina and Roberto Perotti (2004), "The European Union: A Politically Incorrect View" in: Journal of Economic Perspectives (Volume 18, Number 4) pp. 27–48

Commissie Administratieve Lasten (Slechte) (1999), Regels zonder overlast; minder eenvoudiger, sneller, The Hague

Commissie tot verlichting van administratieve verplichtingen voor het bedrijfsleven (Grapperhaus) (1985), Heerendiensten, The Hague

EIM, Monitor administratieve lasten (several years), Zoetermeer

EIM (2007), Pilotonderzoek overage nalevingskosten van bestaande wetgeving, Zoetermeer

IOO (2005), Verinnerlijking administratieve lasten, Leiden [see also the English translation by the Working Party on Regulatory Management and Reform of the OECD, Internalisation of Administrative Burdens (Paris 2006) Room document 12

IOO (2007), Verinnerlijking administratieve lasten, Leiden

IPAL (2006), Dit willen we even kwijt, The Hague

Linschoten Robin, Hans Kamps, Jaap Sleifer (2008), "Cultuuromslag in de wetgeving" in Regelmaat 2008/2

OECD (2007), Cutting red tape: administrative simplification in the Netherlands, Paris

Regioplan beleidsonderzoek (2007), Overige nalevingskosten gemeten. Proefmeting reductiepotentieelmethode, Amsterdam

Tweede Kamer (2006–2007), 29515, nr. 202

World Bank Group (2007), Review of the Dutch Administrative Burden Reduction Program, Washington

Chapter 16
We Need to Dig a New Suez Canal: How Can ICT Help Changing Compliance Costs in the Next 20 Years?

Arre Zuurmond and Frank Robben

Abstract In this chapter, we explore the paper-based functional hierarchy (Mintzbergs' machine bureaucracy) as one of the important origins of the administrative burden. In such a functional hierarchy, the knowledge of the professionals on the one hand and the information of the clients on the other are two important resources. Both resources need to be managed for the organization to be effective and efficient.

In the functional hierarchy the professional knowledge and the information of clients both are organized in stovepipes. Both resources have a low level of integration, intra-organizational as well as inter-organizational. We witness two trends. First, ICTs ('classical ICT' and internet technology) create an inter-organizational information infrastructure that is becoming interoperable. Second, professional knowledge is becoming modularized, with organizations starting to share their professionals and their knowledge in focusing on core competencies, outsourcing all other activities (and the relevant knowledge) and creating shared service centers.

This results in a radical transformation of organizations. This transformed organizational infrastructure can deliver integrated services, by pooling different modules into one service delivery value chain and reusing all relevant information that is readily available in the interoperable, inter-organizational information infrastructure. This transformation of the organization results in potentially high levels of reduction of the administrative burden, without reducing the number and the level of norms and regulations.

16.1 Introduction

The administrative burden can be explained by the number and detail of the rules that are applied to any business in a country. Since more and more rules are implemented, the administrative burden grows. Although it is correct to see the

A. Zuurmond (✉)
Delft University, Delft, The Netherlands; Zenc, The Hague, The Netherlands
e-mail: arre.zuurmond@zenc.nl

A. Nijsen et al. (eds.), *Business Regulation and Public Policy*,
International Studies in Entrepreneurship 20, DOI 10.1007/978-0-387-77678-1_16,

rules as the source of administrative burden, it is in many cases not possible to reduce the number (or the details) of rules, which would be the easiest and most logical way to reduce the administrative burden. In this chapter, we accept the number of rules as given, and develop another strategy to reduce the level of administrative burden. In this strategy, the organizational structure is the source of the administrative burden and transformation of the organization, using the new possibilities of ICT will help reduce the levels of administrative burden.

16.2 Paper-Based Functional Hierarchy as the Origin of Administrative Burden

16.2.1 Introduction

The history of western organizational structure starts with traditional, feudal organizations. Relations were based on tradition, acquired through heredity (Weber 1972). With the process of modernisation, the rationalization of organizational structures started. In Adam Smith's Wealth of Nations, we can see an early example of this rationalization. According to Smith, the economic surplus accrues, using a rationalized organizational structure with high levels of division of labor: 'This great increase (... in efficiency... (az)), in consequence of the division of labor, (..) is owing to three different circumstances; first, to the increase of dexterity in every particular workman; secondly, to the saving of the time which is commonly lost in passing from one species of work to another; and lastly, to the invention of a great number of machines which facilitate and abridge labor, and enable one man to do the work of many (Smith 1776).'

Frederick Taylor developed this line of thinking further, introducing the concept of scientific management. In his view, organizations needed to be structured in a functional hierarchy, with highly specialized workers each performing a small, well-defined task. Scientific norms define the design of the work process and the structure of the organization. In Taylors' view, workers, management and society at large would gain (Taylor 1911: Introduction).

Max Weber also created a mechanistic, centralistic view on organizational structures. To him, power, authority, effectiveness and obedience were important norms for organizations. In his ideal type of the rational legal bureaucracy, we find hierarchization, centralization, formalization, specialization and standardization. These five elements constitute the structure of the organization, leading to the most effective and efficient organizations ever seen in the world (Weber 1972: 128).

All three writers on organization follow a more or less identical line of reasoning: Economy and our western, capitalist culture of modernization dictate the need for efficient organizations. Mechanistic, hierarchical, functional structures perform best to meet this need. Functional hierarchies are part of the larger modernization and globalization scheme.

All three writers depict a formal, mechanistic type of organization that is very powerful because of its functional division of labor. As Weber puts it, these organizations have two important resources: The knowledge of the profession ('vocational knowledge', 'business rules', or 'Fachwissen'), and the information in the files ('Dienstwissen'). Every functional department works with trained professionals that carry with them their specific vocational knowledge. This knowledge is stove-piped knowledge, tuned to the specific needs of only the function at issue. In the process of rationalization, every organization and every department within the organization is specialized into a separate knowledge domain, creating many islands of knowledge. It is the task of management to integrate these islands of knowledge.

Each of these knowledge domains gathers its own information. Applying the professional knowledge ('business rules') to this information results in actions or decisions with regard to the client of the organization. The client provides the information; the professional applies his vocational knowledge and returns the service, based on the confrontation of his professional knowledge to the client information. Both the information provided by the client, as well as the decision taken (mostly in a paper document) are filed in the filing cabinet of the professional.

16.2.2 Paper as the Technology to Create, Use, Communicate and Store Information

In the time of Weber, Taylor and certainly the time of Adam Smith, paper was the technology that was used to store and transmit information. Paper forms needed to be filled in to request a certain delivery. Decisions of the organization were also put on paper and sent to the client as well as stored (in copy) by the professional. To read this information, professionals were needed. They would typically read the filled forms, apply their knowledge and then start to produce a new paper (the decision).

Communication between departments is based on paper: forms would be sent from one department to the other. Management would typically check the information and the forms, before the form was sent to the next department. In a typical organization we will find different departments, each taking care of a subset of tasks based on specific, professional knowledge, creating their own files and forms. Below an example of this type of organization is depicted (see Fig. 16.1).

16.2.3 Source of Administrative Burden

With this functional hierarchy, with its paper ridden communication, we can understand the original source of the administrative burden: every organization, and within every organization in many cases, every department creates its own paper forms and starts to ask the client of the organization for information fitted to its specific needs. The client has to fill in every separate form. With the growth of rules and regulations, more organizations have been created, each taking care of one specialized task. The more detailed and intricate the

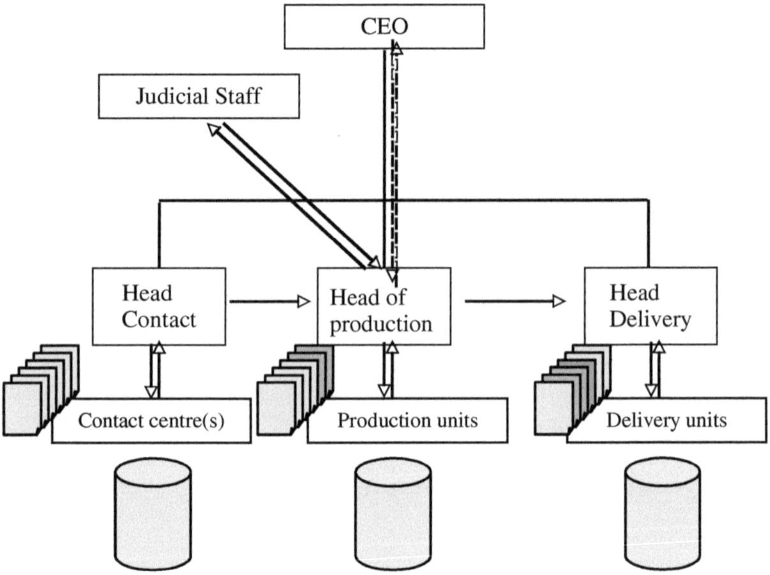

Fig. 16.1 Paper-based organization

regulation, the more information is needed and the more specific departments are created. The client is seen as the source of the information, and thus, all information has to be delivered by the client.

From the perspective of the client, we see a different picture: the client has to go to many offices, and in every office, all sorts of information has to be delivered. Much of the information to be delivered at one counter has to be delivered at other counters as well. Thus, the client experiences high levels of administrative burden, and since the number of regulations and the details of these regulations has exploded, and thus the number of public organizations that have contacts with organizations has exploded as well, the level of administrative burden has risen to unprecedented heights.

16.3 Changes in the Organization of Information and the Organization of Knowledge

16.3.1 Introduction

In the previous sections, we have depicted the origins of the administrative burden. Administrative burden is caused by the fact that organizational knowledge is organized in a functional hierarchy, which leads to the stove-piped application of this knowledge. Every department not only has its own knowledge domain, but also organizes the information needed to apply this knowledge, separately. In the days of Weber and Taylor, the environment of the functional hierarchy was stable, simple and not interdependent. But in modern times, this organizational environment changes (dynamic, complex and interdependent), and society at large has many more demands. When such an environment exists, the use of a functional hierarchy with separate information gathering, using paper forms, per separate department, leads to a high level of administrative burden.

Two strategies are being developed to cope with the changing environment of organizations. First, information technology is introduced, to be able to create, process and transmit information more easily across borders of departments and organizations. Second, another way of organizing is developed, more along the lines of core competencies, where all non-core competencies are outsourced or organized in shared services. In this section, we will describe both strategies, starting with the developments within the domain of ICTs.

16.3.2 The Potential of ICT: Classical ICTs and Internet

16.3.2.1 Introduction

Now that we have described the origins of the administrative burden, we can start to look at Information and Communication Technologies (ICTs) and internet. Information and communication technology, starting with the punch cards as developed by IBM, and later with computers (ENIAC) and more recently, the internet, can be seen as social artefacts, or social constructs. E.g., the internet has been developed by the American Ministry of Defense, in an attempt to create communication protocols that were less vulnerable for enemy attacks. The promise is that new ICTs can help reduce the administrative burden. How can we understand these technologies?

We discern two different ICTs: the classical ICTs, as applied by organizations starting in the 1960s, mainly in the back office. Next, we discern internet, as a technology that developed outside the organizations, but starts to connect to organizations and their classical ICTs. In the last years, it has become more difficult to discern the two technologies, since they are converging.

16.3.2.2 Classical ICTs

A first step is to categorize the ICTs. ICTs can be categorized in many different ways, e.g. by the sort of technology used (hardware, software, communication technology), the generation (e.g. fourth generation programming software), or the topology (network, stand alone, etc.). Since this chapter focuses on the relation between organizational structure and the use of ICTs, we will use Venkatraman's approach to business IT-alignment (Henderson and

Venkatraman, 1992). In this approach, ICTs have to be in line with the organizational strategy and design. Four ICT-layers[1] are relevant:

- Functionality: What information systems are in use and what are the tasks these systems are performing (operational systems, financial systems, office automation software, etc.).
- Data: Every piece of functionality ('information system') creates, reads, uses or deletes data. To manage this data handling, organizations need information management, based on an organizational information model.
- IT-infrastructure: To operate the functionality and to work with data, organizations need hardware (computers, servers) and communication technology (networks, routers, etc.).
- IT-staff: Depending on the introduced information systems, the level of sophistication of the data management, and the size and complexity of the IT-infrastructure, an organization has a larger or smaller IT department with more or with less specific IT functions (e.g. data-manager, network-manager, helpdesk, etc.).

A second element of the categorization is the stage, the level of sophistication of every layer of ICT as we have discerned. Here, we use the insights of Richard Nolan, which were later amended to accommodate for recent developments. In a seminal article in the Harvard Business Review, Richard Nolan introduced his stages of EDP-growth (Nolan 1973, 1974, 1979). According to Nolan, the growth of the scope and use of ICTs took place in six stages. The first three and the last three stages each combined into an S-curve.

In the first S-curve, growth of ICT was rapid, but every department within the organization developed its ICT separate from the other departments. Every functional department developed its own Information System. This is called 'island automation' (nowadays described as stove-piped ICT), since the ICT cannot be connected, not on the level of functionality, nor with regard to the data. Mostly, the technical infrastructure is also based on different technical standards, which, in turn, means that the knowledge and expertise of the IT staff can necessarily only be fragmented.

The second S-curve is reached only if the organization changes the scope of its ICT. The scope now is the whole of the organization. The organization introduces an information strategy and information policy, in line with the business strategy. A functional architecture and a data model are developed, which determine the technical infrastructure. Standardization of functionality, data and technical infrastructure is introduced, enabling the IT department to deliver a higher quality of products, with declining TCO (total cost of ownership).

In the mid-1990s, the Nolan model was amended by introducing three additional S-curves, thus acknowledging that organizations start to cooperate with regard to their ICTs (Cavaye a.o. 1998). The scope of ICTs has started

[1] The terms 'layers' and 'architectures' are equivalents

to become inter-organizational and this will lead to even higher levels of use of ICTs by all organizations involved. This cooperation can be on all four architectures. The cooperation is started mostly within the scope of one certain sector.

More recently, we have witnessed an even broader scope: national ICT strategies (e.g., the E-envoy), which try to create standards and stimulate the development of e-government throughout all governmental sectors. Finally, in certain areas, we find an even broader scope: international cooperation with regard to shared ICT components, leading to international exchange of information. An early example of this might be the introduction of the ISBN numbers, which make every book with an ISBN traceable, but also the 10-digit ISDN system for phone numbers, the European standard for banking numbers, or the technical standards for reading smart cards or digital signatures are examples of this international cooperation. In all these cases, we see high volumes of information shared at the international level, and strong connectivity at that level: the ICTs involved have standards that have an international scope, thus facilitating still higher levels of use of ICTs. This results in the following model (see Fig. 16.2).

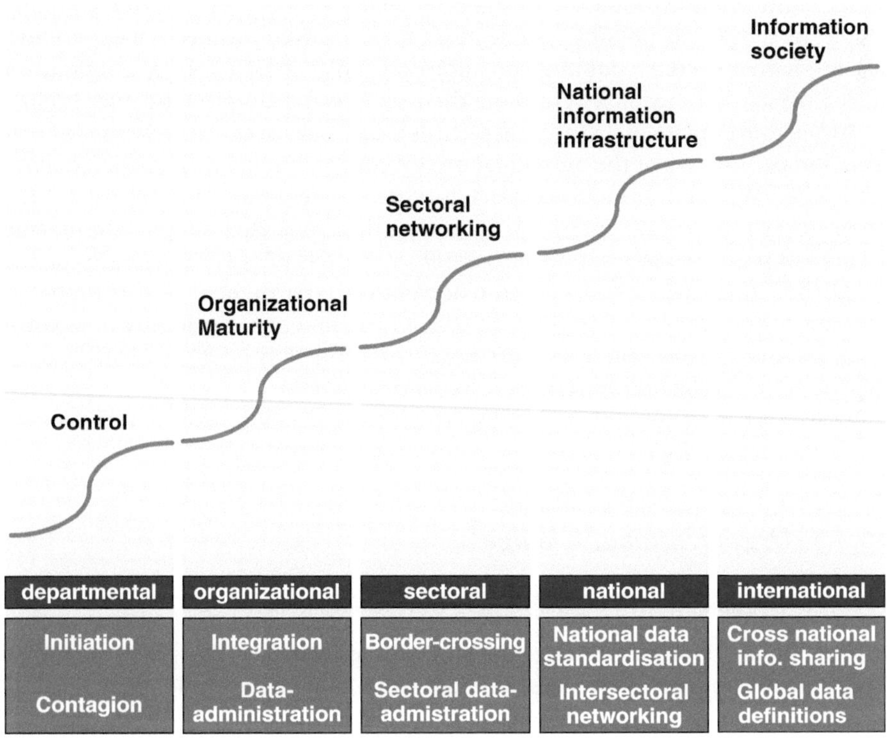

Fig. 16.2 Stages in ICT architecture

Combining the business ICT alignment model of Venkatraman and the Nolan + model, we now are able to conceptualise and categorize internal ICTs into two dimensions: the four architectural ICT layers and the five stages of EDP growth.

16.3.2.3 Internet

Much can be said about internet. In this chapter, we focus on organizational use of the internet. The use of internet by organizations follows a certain growth path. An interesting approach can be found in the five 'maturity plateaus', which Accenture uses to describe the development of internet use by governments.

The first experiences with internet are very simple ('Online presence'). The organization starts to use a website, where some information is published online. Few services are made available through the internet and only provided by early adopters.

On the second plateau ('Basic capability'), internet presence is higher. A central internet plan is created and a legislative framework developed for the use of internet. Some solutions around internet security and certification are introduced, giving way to quick-win transaction capabilities on the internet (e-commerce is starting).

At the third plateau ('Service availability'), the way services are offered on the internet is changed. We witness the creation of basic portals ('shopping malls') and organizations try to make as many services as possible available online, as quickly as possible. Some more sophisticated transaction capabilities are implemented (e.g. banking on internet). Also, cross-agency cooperation starts, where these agencies combine their services leading to customer focus.

At the fourth plateau ('Mature service delivery'), services are no longer offered from the perspective of the individual organizations, but are now clustered along life events. We see transactional portals where citizens can find service clusters ('one stop shops' on the internet). To realize these one stop shops, inter-agency relationships and collaboration across different levels of government are started.

At the fifth plateau ('Service transformation'), permanent improvement of customer service delivery is the vision. E-Government is no longer a separate initiative but part of wider service transformation that is implemented across the whole of public administration (Accenture 2003).

These five plateaus can be combined with the development of ICTs, into a single model (see Fig. 16.3).

16.3.3 Organizational Change[2]

16.3.3.1 Organizations Focus on Their Core Competencies

In the old days, organizations developed their strategy by analyzing their environment for developments and deciding how they could best react to

---

[2] This section is based on research performed together with Marco Meesters (Zuurmond and Meesters, 2007).

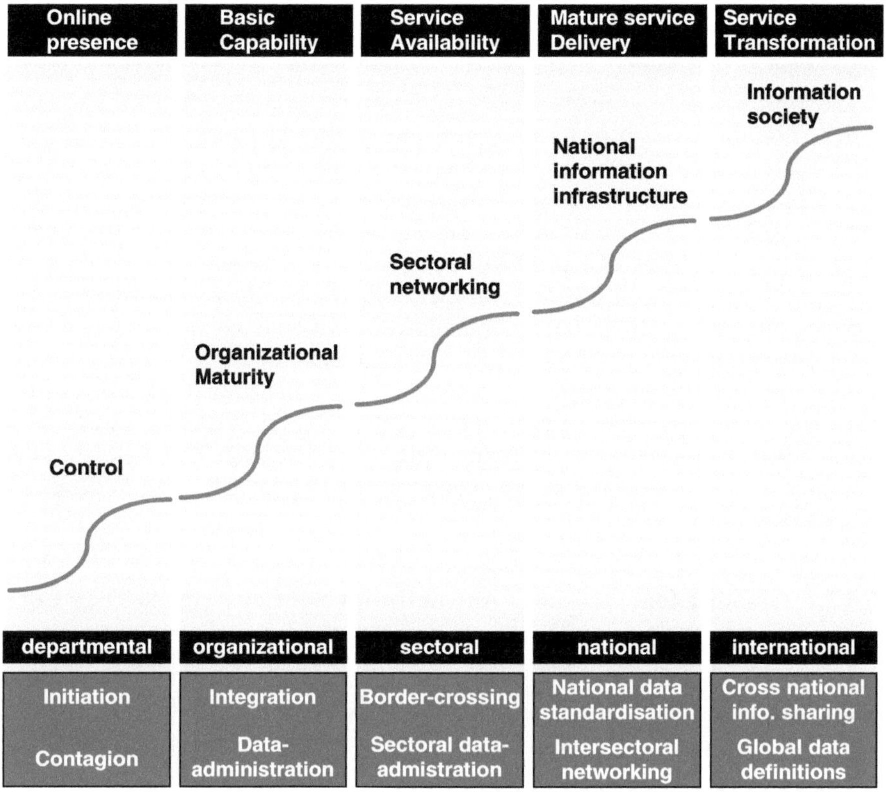

Fig. 16.3 Stages of ICT architecture and Maturity level

these developments. Based on an analysis of its competitors and buyer and supplier power, an organization was able to decide on its desired position in the market and on the actions necessary to achieve this position. In the 1990s, this practice changed. Organizations started to acknowledge that they were unique and that this uniqueness needed to be central in the process of strategy formulation. To operationalize the uniqueness of an organization, the term "core competencies" was introduced.

Core competencies are those combinations of production skills and technologies that distinguish organizations from other organizations. "Core competencies are the collective learning in the organization, especially how to coordinate diverse production skills and integrate multiple streams of technology" (Prahalad & Hamel, 1990). Because of the specific combination of competencies available in an organization, this organization can outperform its competitors in producing certain products. According to Prahalad and Hamel, core competencies have to pass three tests. "First, a core competence provides potential access to a wide variety of markets. [...] Second, a core competence should make a significant contribution to the perceived customer benefits of the end product. [...] Finally, a core competence should be difficult for competitors to imitate".

The notion of core competencies provides an essential insight for the strategy formulation of an organization. Organizations should strive to make optimal use of their core competencies. This has two implications. First, organizations should produce as much different products or services as possible using their core competencies. Since core competencies may be used for diverse products or services, organizations can produce a portfolio of products and services. By enlarging the portfolio of products and services they produce, organizations can optimize the use of their core competencies. Second, organizations should search for possibilities for selling their core products. Focusing on core competencies means that organizations mostly produce half-products that have to be processed further by other organizations. Organizations should produce those half-products that are useful for many other organizations. This way, they can maximize the take-off of their core products, and therefore the use of their core competencies.

16.3.3.2 Organizations Outsource Any Activities Not Connected to Their Core Competencies

Organizations that focus on their core competencies, stop performing activities that do not make use of their core competencies. Since these activities are often essential for producing products and services that have value for the customers, the organization outsources these activities to other organizations. Organizations outsource more and more activities to other organizations that are specialized in performing these activities. Organizations specialize in certain activities, leading to vertical disintegration at the level of the production chain (Sturgeon 2000; Wynstra 2006).

Outsourcing "represents the fundamental decision to reject the internalization of an activity" (Gilley and Rasheed, 2000). Outsourcing leads to an increased importance of the suppliers of an organization. To optimize the result of outsourcing, organizations take a number of steps (Monczka 2004). First, organizations need to develop a purchasing strategy in which they decide what the requirements for the activities are. Second, they need to find the best suppliers for the activities they need. Third, they need to establish appropriate strategic alliances with these suppliers. Fourth, they need to integrate these suppliers into their business processes. Fifth, they need to manage and develop their relationship with these suppliers. Finally, they need to manage the costs across the supply chain.

Outsourcing may lead to increased quality of the performance in functional areas. Organizations that outsource their non-core activities are able to achieve cost- and quality advantages. The supplier of the outsourced activity is able to perform the activity with higher quality and with lesser costs than the organization itself. The supplier has core competencies that enable him to provide higher quality. Moreover, since the supplier focuses on this activity, it is possible to follow the newest technological developments. Moreover, the buyer can focus on his own core competencies, which enables the organization “to increase managerial attention and resource allocation to those tasks that it does best and to rely on management teams in other organizations to oversee tasks at which the outsourcing firm is at a relative disadvantage” (Gilley and Rasheed, 2000).

16.3.3.3 Organizations Create Shared Service Centers for Common Processes

Next to outsourcing non-core activities, organizations start analyzing their business process and the business processes of other organizations. Especially, government organizations realize that parts of these business processes are common for various organizations. These may be called common business processes. Common business processes are business processes that (1) are executed in various organizations and (2) have similar goals and outputs (OECD 2005). These business processes offer opportunities, by organizing them centrally, to increase efficiency and quality. The OECD report identifies a number of possibilities to achieve this. Organizations can create knowledge centers, may create referential models or may implement shared information systems. However, the most far-reaching (and therefore probably resulting in the most fundamental improvements) is the centralization of the common business process in one organizational entity. When there is no organizational entity in the value chain with the necessary competencies, a new organizational entity, a shared service center, needs to be created.

Korsten identifies a shared service center as “a result-oriented inter-organizational cooperation, optionally concentrated in one organizational entity, that has the tasks of offering services in the area of a certain supportive function or in the area of policy development or execution to individual partner-organizations, based on a contract” (Korsten 2005). Essential differences with traditional staff departments are (1) that a shared service center has integral responsibility for the products (or services) that it delivers, (2) that beforehand agreement is reached on the characteristics of these products and services (e.g. the quality and the price) and (3) that the shared service center offers its services to a number of different partner-organizations, in the value chain or in other value chains.

It is a common misconception that shared service centers may only be possible for back office processes and for supportive processes. Every organization has some universal supportive functions like human resource management or ICT maintenance. Research (OECD 2005; Strikwerda 2006) shows that common business processes may also be found in front office processes or primary processes. Think for example of shared front offices for municipal service delivery or of a shared service center for the collection of administrative fines (Centraal Justitiëel Incasso Bureau in the Netherlands).

Opheij and Willems (2004) identify a number of advantages of shared service centers:

- Efficiencies of scale.
- The potential to share costs and investments between cooperating (the creating) organizations.
- Employees are forced to be sharp and business-like because they work for customers.
- Working for customers enhances motivation of employees.
- Customers of SSCs need not worry about the "how", only about the characteristics of the end-product they wish.
- Cooperation leads to added value for the end-customer (society).

The following are some of the disadvantages that Opheij and Willems identify:

- The risk of increasing bureaucracy and overhead, for example because of contract negotiations.
- The risk of goal displacement: the SSC earns more by selling more of its products, not by producing higher quality.
- The risk of long decision-making processes, since all participating organizations need to be involved.
- The loss of autonomy for customers of the SSC.

16.3.3.4 The Modular Organization

Analyzed from a value chain perspective, the trends mentioned above, the focus on core competencies, the outsourcing of non-core activities to specialized organizations and the creation of shared service centers, lead to the creation of networks. These networks consist of relatively small, specialized organizations that focus on a small number of activities that each depend on their specific core competence. Together, these organizations form value chains, in which they produce products or services. Cooperation between the organizations is essential for the production of these products and services. Organizations operate in various value chains: their activities may be used for the production of various services or products.

Several academics identify this trend as modularization. Modularization is a concept that came from engineering information systems and was introduced in organization theory in the automobile industry. "Modularity is a general systems concept: it is a continuum describing the degree to which a system's components can be separated and recombined, and it refers both to the tightness of coupling between components and the degree to which the 'rules' of the systems architecture enable (or prohibit) the mixing and matching of components" (Schilling 2000; quoted in Brüggemeier et al., 2006). When applied to production processes of networks of organizations, modularity means that business processes are divided into process modules. These process modules together form the total business process. However, different modules may be executed by different organizations.

Brüggemeier et al. (2006) identify three elements in modularization: "[1] The module as unit that may be limited, distinguished and combined, [2] the connections between these modules and [3] the directions that enable the combination of different modules" (p. 66). The modules are parts of the total business process. These parts need to be recognizable as a unit. There must be clear limits on what the process module does and what it does not do. When process modules are clearly defined, changes within separate process modules may be made, without this meaning that the whole system has to change. There also have to be connections between different process modules. By definition, process modules only execute a part of a business process, so by themselves, they don't deliver services for society. At the same time, process modules may be used for various service delivery processes. The combination of process modules into specific service delivery processes is called "orchestration". To enable making different combinations of process modules, at a system level, there have to be rules or directions on the interfaces of process modules. These rules are laid down in an "architecture".

Each process module may be appointed to the organization that is best capable of executing the module. This may be an existing organization in the value chain or a newly created organizational entity (shared service center). The decision which organization executes which process module has to be made on the chain-level. The resulting organization structure is that of the "modular organization" (Strikwerda 2006). The modular organization is made up of organizational modules. An organizational module is "an isolated set of activities that knows a certain degree of alternative use within the architecture of products, services and creation processes, of which the output can be contracted and the performance can be judged financially" (Strikwerda 2006). Organizational modules may be derivates of the traditional organizations, or may be newly created shared service centers. In this modular organization, we see "[organizational] modules that cooperate in constantly changing configurations to increase the performance of an organization, in term of higher efficiency and more differentiation in products and services" (Strikwerda 2006).

Strikwerda summarizes the advantages of the modular organization (Strikwerda 2006):

- A higher level of efficiency, because an end is made to 'averaging' in the traditional value chain.
- More differentiation in products and services, while reducing costs at the same time.
- Realizing innovation and efficiency under uncertain circumstances.
- Exploitation of knowledge according to the 'multiplier-model'.
- Optimizing organizations contribution to the value chain or the production network.
- Easily adaptable organizational boundaries and activities.
- Realizing big changes in small steps.
- Managing complexity without simplification.

16.4 Technology and Organizational Transformation

In the previous sections, we have shown two strategies. The first strategy focused on how information is organized, using ICTs to organize the information in a different way than in the era of paper. This showed us that ICTs and internet create an information infrastructure that develops in layers (functionality, data, infrastructure, ICT organization) and in five stages. Thus, the organization of information is changing.

Second, we showed the strategy of organizing the professional and his/her knowledge. Here, we have depicted the development towards modularization, where professional knowledge was organized around core competencies, and all other elements were either outsourced or brought into shared service centers.

In this paragraph, we concentrate on what happens if we combine both strategies: how do organizations transform if they organize their knowledge into modular departments, using outsourcing and shared services for all activities that are not part of their core competencies, while they, at the same time, organize the information of their clients into an inter-organizational information infrastructure.

Here, we can use the insights of Joan Woodward and Lawrence and Lorsch. Joan Woodward studied the relation between organizational structure and technology (Woodward 1965). She discovered that the structure varied from non-hierarchical, through hierarchical, back to non-hierarchical, depending on the amount and intensity with which the organization uses technology.

A simple informal structure with a lot of horizontal communication evolves, when organizations produce customized units (a ship, a house, a handmade car, etc.). Here, the Taylorist or Weberian division of labor has not been introduced. We will find an intense, personal contact, and because information flows in a natural informal way, there are low levels of administrative burden.

A strict, vertical, mechanistic bureaucracy evolves when organizations produce 'batches' of a certain product, e.g. 100,000 cars of a specific type, bricks, etc. The organization uses technology to produce these large numbers of goods and has implemented a high level of division of labor to maximize on efficiency. A lot of paper work goes around in this organization: the technostructure (that part of the staff that dictates how the operational work is designed and that checks whether or not all tasks have been performed conform specifications) develops the forms that have to be filled in time and time again, and every worker has to fill in forms for different sort of activities (e.g. number of hours worked, piece rates, damage reports, etc.) (Mintzberg 1979). In this situation, the administrative burden enhances: different forms have to be filled in, and in some cases, different departments within the organization use their own forms to be filled in by clients, to operate their specific function.

A process organization evolves when the use of technology is maximal. The organization produces goods not by amount, but by quantities (liters, volume, etc, like milk, petrol, sugar). Here, we find an informal, non-hierarchical organizational structure again. But this organization is very different from the first. In this case, highly specialized professionals run the factory, all machines are connected (pipes) and they manage the continuous flow of production. The professionals share their professional backgrounds (e.g. chemistry), the machines 'contain' their knowledge and production protocols are a part of the shared, consolidated knowledge infrastructure. Thus, horizontal and informal communication becomes more important again, rather than hierarchical positions and vertical communication. In terms of structure, we find a more or less organic structure (informal, horizontal communication) with a high level of central control that is affected by the technology introduced. This type of organization is information intensive, but still has lower levels of administrative burden, since the quality of service is high and, through the interconnectedness, the reuse of information within the organization is maximal.

Lawrence and Lorsch (1967) find that organizational performance is determined by the ability to cope with the organizational environment. The degree of differentiation into sub-systems is dependent on the environment. Each organizational sub-system adapts to that part of the environment most relevant to the sub-system in question. If the organizational environment is complex, dynamic and highly interdependent, the organization decentralizes its decision making power, introduces boundary spanners and other coordination mechanisms. From a structural point of view, this organization looks more like a professional bureaucracy (informal, organic structure with decentralization and little central control), where organizations with a non-complex, steady and non-interdependent environment create structures that look like Mintzbergs' machine bureaucracy.

As contingency theory depicts, the environments of organizations become more complex, dynamic and interdependent, and thus organizations change from machine bureaucracies to professional bureaucracies. With this change, the administrative burden enlarges: the professional bureaucracy is less well integrated and the information is not easily shared amongst the professionals of the different departments (see Fig. 16.4).

Essential for the functioning of a modular organization is that the activities of the organizational entities are attuned. The output of one organizational entity has to be processed by the next organizational entity, so the second organizational entity should be able to use the output of the first. In other words, activities of the organizational entities should be interoperable. "Interoperability means the ability of information and communication technology (ICT) systems and of the business processes they support to exchange data and to enable the sharing of information and knowledge." (European Commission 2004; in Kubicek & Cimander, 2005).

To achieve this interoperability, a common infrastructure is necessary. The infrastructure consists of a number of rules that all organizational units abide by and that ensures that organizational entities' activities are attuned. The strategy of the organization of information, in layers and stages, as depicted in earlier sections, shows us how organizational entities (modules) can tap into

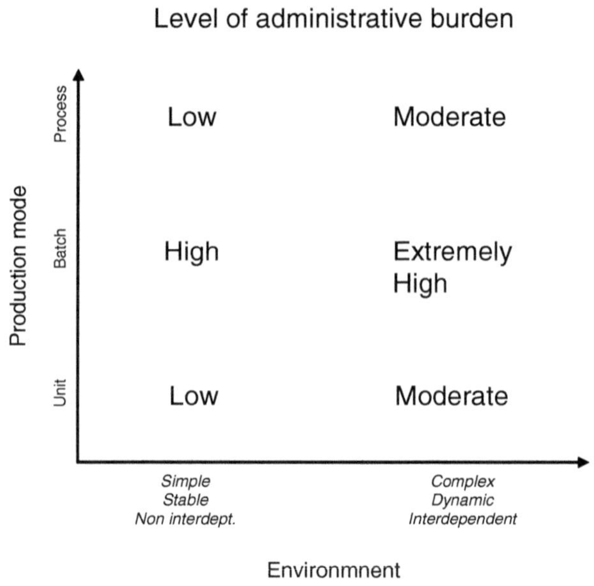

Fig. 16.4 Complexity of organizations and administrative burden

the inter-organizational information infrastructure, to make maximum use of already available information and to provide other modules with information that is created by the entity itself. Thus, a strategy of high quality of information is combined with high levels of efficiency in the reuse of this information.

The combination of both strategies, creating an inter-organizational information infrastructure and a modularized organizational structure, enables organizations to work in different value chains at the same time. They can integrate services into one common front office, enabling clients to use a one stop shop for every life event. They can also develop common business processes, or shared services for back office processes or secondary processes. In all different situations, they can recombine information that is already delivered by clients, and they can present information that they create to other organizations, in order to reduce the number of contacts the clients have with the organizations, as well as to reduce the amount of information that has to be delivered.

At each level, a limited set of rules has to be agreed upon to ensure interoperability. The infrastructure ensures interoperability between the organizations and thereby enables organizational modules to cooperate in constantly changing combinations, depending on what societal issues need to be resolved. Zuurmond (1994; 2003) calls this organization the "infrastructural organization", or as a variation on Weber's bureaucracy, the "infocracy". This, in turn, creates the possibility for organizations to reduce the level of administrative burden, even if the number of norms, rules, regulations and the corresponding number of organizational units that operate to realize those norms and to implement the subsequent rules and regulations.

Thus, basically there are two strategies to cope with administrative burden. Either, in strategy one, it is attempted to reduce the number of rules and norms an entity has to comply with. The second strategy accepts the fact that there are more and more rules and norms, given the changes in the organizational environment (more dynamic, complex and interdependent). Here, organizational change using inter-organizational information infrastructures are introduced. Then another configuration comes into existence, combining a high number and a high level of norms, with a changing environment, in a transformed organization (see Fig. 16.5).

Norms					
Number of societal norms	Low			High	
Level of norms to comply to	Low			High	
Number laws and regulations	Low	Strategy one		High	
Details laws and regulations	Low			High	
Number implementing agencies	Low			High	
Professionalism of agencies	Low			High	
Environment					
Complexity	Simple			Complex	
Dynamics	Stable			Dynamic	
Dependency	Not dependent			Interdependent	
Organization					
Production mode	Unit	Batch	Process	Chain	Network
Modularity	Low			High	
Outsourcing	None	Strategy two		All non core competencies	
Shared services	None			Maximum	
Technology					
Internet	**Online availability**	**Basic capability**	**Service availability**	**Mature service delivery**	**Service trans-formation**
Functionality	**Islands of automation**	Intraorg. integration	Sectoral inter operability	**National inter operability**	**Global service orientation**
Information	**No modelling**	Strategy two modeling	Sectoral information **models**	**National Data Standards Authentic registrations**	**International Data Standards**
Technological infrastructure	**No inter-operability**	**Enterprise architectures**	**SOA**	**SOA**	**SOA**
ICT-departments					

Fig. 16.5 Strategies to cope with administrative burden

16.5 Summary and Conclusions

In this chapter, we have developed another strategy to reduce the level of administrative burden. The first strategy was to reduce the number of norms, rules, regulations and to reduce the corresponding number of public agencies that are created to implement all those rules. The second strategy accepts that the number of norms, as well as the fact that the quality level rises for every norm that society creates. It also accepts that public administration creates more and more organization, with more and more departments with higher quality professionals that, through regulations, seek to realize compliance with all these increases in number and levels of rules.

This alternative strategy focuses on the realization of an inter-organizational infrastructure on the one hand, and an organizational change on the other hand. In combination, this results in an organizational transformation. The result is a network of interconnected, modular organizations that can integrate services in their front offices, that can deploy common business processes and that can join back offices and share services. Using an interoperable information infrastructure, they can share all relevant information. This creates the possibility to reduce the administrative burden, even in a society that is characterized by a complex, dynamic and interdependent environment on the one hand and a society that has high demands, in terms of norms and regulations, on the other hand.

References

Accenture, (2003), E-government leadership: Engaging the customer (www.accenture.com/xdoc/en/newsroom/epresskit/egovernment/egovepress.pdf)

Brüggemeier, M., A. Dovifat, and K. Lenk (2006), "Open Choice": Improving public sector performance with process reorganization methodology, Berlin.

Cavaye, A.L.M., P. Mantelaers, W. Vd Berg, and A. Zuurmond (1998), 'Towards guidelines for the development and management of Transnational Information Systems', *Australian Journal of Information Systems*, 5(2), May, pp. 13–21.

European Commission, European Interoperability Framework for Pan-European eGovernment Services, Luxemburg: Office for Official Publications of the European Communities, 2004.

Gilley, K.M. and A. Rasheed (2000), Making more by doing less: an analysis of outsourcing and its effects on firm performance, in: *Journal of management*, Vol. 26, no. 4, 763–790.

Henderson, J., and N. Venkatraman (1992), "Strategic Alignment: A model for organizational transformation through information technology," in T. Kochan & M. Unseem, eds, *Transforming Organizations*, Oxford University Press, NY.

Korsten, A.F.A. (2005), Shared Service Centers, een concept voor samenwerking tussen gemeenten, FAMO-jaarcongres.

Kubicek, H., and R. Cimander (2005), Interoperability in eGovernment, a survey of information needs of different EU stakeholders, in: *European Review of Political Technologies*, December 2005.

Lawrence, P., and J. Lorsch (1967), "Differentiation and Integration in Complex Organizations" Administrative Science Quarterly 12, 1–30.

Mintzberg, H. (1979), *The Structuring of Organizations.* Englewood Cliffs, N.J..

Monczka, R.M. (2004), Purchasing Excellence: Best practices from abroad and application in The Netherlands.

Nolan, R.L. (1973), Managing the computer resource: a stage hypothesis. in: *Communications of the ACM.* Vol. 16, pp. 399–405.

Nolan, R.L., and C.F. Gibson (1974), Managing the four stages of EDP growth. in: *Harvard Business Review.* Vol. 51, pp. 76–88.

Nolan, R.L. (1979), Managing the crisis in data processing. in: *Harvard Business Review.* Vol. 57, pp. 115–126.

OECD (2005), e-government for better government, Paris.

Opheij, W. and F. Willems (2004), Shared Service Centers: balanceren tussen pracht en macht, in: *Holland Management Review*, nr. 95.

Prahalad, C.K., and G. Hamel (1990), The core competence of the corporation, in: *Harvard Business Review*, may–june.

Schilling, M. (2000), Toward a general modular systems theory and its application to interfirm product modularity. *Academy of Management Review* 25: 312–334..

Smith, A. (1776), *An Inquiry into the Nature and Causes of the Wealth of Nations,* in two volumes, W. Straham and T. Cadell, In the Strand, London, MDCCLXXVI first facsimile published in 1966 by Augustus M.Kelley Publishers, New York, New York, second facsimile printed by Sentry Press, New York, NY.

Strikwerda, H. (2006), Na het shared service center: de modulaire organisatie, in: *Holland Management Review*, jrg. 23, nr. 106, maart-apr, pp. 45–50.

Sturgeon, T.J. (2000), How do we define value chains and production networks?, Background paper prepared for the Bellagio Value Chains workshop, Bellagio, Italy.

Taylor, F.W. (1911), Principles of Scientific Management, Harper & Row, New York.

Weber, M. (1972), Wirtschaft und Gesellschaft. Tübingen.

Woodward, J. (1965), *Industrial Organization: Theory and Practice.* Oxford.

Wynstra, F. (2006), Inkoop, Leveranciers en innovatie: van VOC tot Space Shuttle. Rotterdam.

Zuurmond, A. (1994), De Infocratie, een theoretische en empirische heroriëntatie op Weber's ideaaltype in het informatietijdperk, (The infocracy, a theoretical and empirical reorientation on Max Weber's ideal type in the information age), Uitgeverij Phaedrus, proefschrift Rotterdam.

Zuurmond, A. (2003), De Verwaarloosde staat: pleidooi voor een Copernicaanse wending in het Openbaar Bestuur, Leiden.

Zuurmond, A., and M. Meesters (2007), ICT en de moderne Politieorganisatie, in: Rosenthal, U., E.R. Muller, C.J.F.J. Fijnaut (red.) *Politie, studies naar haar werking en organisatie*, Samson, Alphen aan de Rijn.

Chapter 17
Macroeconomic Policies, Bureaucracy and Deregulation: The Choice of the Exchange Rate Regime

Ansgar Belke

Abstract This chapter examines the contemporaneous relationship between the exchange rate regime and structural economic reforms over a period of 30 years. Using panel data techniques, we look at both a broad ("world sample") and an OECD country sample. We investigate empirically whether structural reforms are complements or substitutes for monetary commitment in the attempt to improve macroeconomic performance. Our results suggest that, on average, an exchange rate rule positively correlates with the overall structural reforms and trade liberalization in particular. We do not find a significant and robust impact of exchange rate commitment on labor and product market reform, on the other hand. The results are similar for both the wider, more heterogeneous world sample and the panel of OECD economies. They contradict the hypothesis that exchange rate commitments may have slowed down the pace of structural reform, but neither provide robust evidence that losing the possibility of an exchange rate adjustment promotes labor and product market reforms.

17.1 Introduction

This chapter investigates which policies and institutions serve best to improve the quality of enterprise regulatory climate. How to define regulation? Regulations can be divided into two main categories: Social and economic regulation. Social regulation concerns the protection of public interest such as health and safety, while economic regulation concerns markets decisions such as pricing, competition, market entry, or exit (Baldwin, Scott and Hood, 1998; Meier, 1985, p. 3; and Ogus, 1994, pp. 4 f.). The OECD has added a third category, namely administrative regulations which are defined as: "paperwork and administrative formalities through which governments collect information and intervene in individual economic decisions (. . .) enabling governments to

A. Belke (✉)
University of Duisburg-Essen, and IZA, Bonn, Germany
e-mail: Ansgar.belke@uni-due.de

A. Nijsen et al. (eds.), *Business Regulation and Public Policy*,
International Studies in Entrepreneurship 20, DOI 10.1007/978-0-387-77678-1_17,

exercise and implement regulatory objectives, including monitoring compliance with such regulations" (OECD, 2003, p. 14 see also World Bank, 2006).

However, administrative regulations should not be regarded as independent regulations as such, but as part of either social or economic regulations. Any instruments of lowering the degree of deregulation or, equivalently, supply-side reforms, will fail if they are not well embedded in a suitable political institutional environment. This view is all the more valid if one takes into account that the discussion about the necessity of reforms to lower the degree of deregulation, and that of bureaucracy in particular, in continental European countries like Germany is highly politicized and deeply embedded in the traditional and controversial debate about the pros and cons of supply side economics. Opponents to significant deregulation even put the former on the same level with Reagonomics and Thatcherism and, instead, appeal to the Dutch consensus model of lowering bureaucracy as a sub-species of regulation.

This chapter investigates an often overlooked aspect in this context and asks *what is the relevance of the choice of a specific exchange rate regime* – for instance, sticking to flexible rates or entering a monetary union – in open economies *as a kind of implicit and maybe non-intended political macroeconomic support of reduction policies.* The remaining parts of this contribution will consist of a mixture of new insights and a review and summary of existing literature – especially own empirical work on the topic (Belke, Herz and Vogel, 2006 and 2006a).

In the following, we present an empirical analysis of the relationship between monetary commitment in the form of an exchange rate peg and structural economic reforms. We investigate whether empirically the implementation of structural reforms and an exchange rate commitment constitute either alternative or complementary policy choices. Theoretical arguments exist for both relations.

What do we add to the literature and what results do we obtain? Given some quite contrasting case-study results surveyed in Belke, Herz and Vogel (2006), we conduct an econometric analysis for a large sample of countries which goes beyond the EMU focus in van Poeck and Borghijs (2001), Bertola and Boeri (2001), Duval and Elmeskov (2005) and IMF (2004), which are rare examples of empirical investigations in this field.[1] We define market-oriented structural

[1] Van Poeck and Borghijs (2001) argue that the prospect of qualifying for EMU should provide as big an incentive for labor-market reform as EMU membership itself. They conclude that EMU countries did not reform more than other countries and, unlike elsewhere, their progress on reform seemed unrelated to the initial level of unemployment. For a period from the early 1990s up to 1999, Bertola and Boeri (2001), they only focus cash transfers to people of working age (unemployment benefits) and on job protection. They arrive at exactly opposite conclusions: reforms accelerated more in the euro area than outside.

The IMF (2004) looks at the impact of a range of factors including macroeconomic conditions, political institutions, reform design and variables aimed to capture attitudes towards structural reform on different policy areas across OECD countries from the reforms as economic liberalization according to the definition of the Economic Freedom of the World (EFW) index and the sub-indices money and banking system, government size, labor market, credit and business regulation, and impediments to international trade, respectively (Gwartney and Lawson, 2003; Gwartney et al., 2006). We thus investigate a wider range of economic reforms than Duval and Elmeskov (2005). The latter study, which in terms of empirical strategy and theoretical motivation is closest to ours, limits itself to different aspects of labor market reforms and investigates changes in unemployment benefit systems, labor taxation, employment protection legislation, product market regulation and retirement schemes.

The remainder of the chapter is structured as follows: Section 17.2 discusses the main theoretical links between monetary autonomy and structural reforms. Panel estimates are presented in Section 17.3. The regressions include a set of additional variables and a number of robustness checks. Section 17.4 summarizes the main results and concludes.

17.2 Theory: Conflicting Views on the Relationship Between Monetary Rules and Structural Reforms

The discussion on monetary policy autonomy and structural reforms is characterized by a wide spectrum of conflicting views. We start with a sketch of the literature on monetary policy autonomy and reforms and refer to a prominent example of loss of monetary autonomy: the irrevocable fixing of exchange rates under European Monetary Union (EMU). In the run-up to EMU, a number of studies tried to assess the incentive effects of alternative monetary policy strategies on labor market reforms.[2]

According to the proponents of a liberal view, EMU as a classical variant of a rule-based monetary policy should have a disciplinary impact on national labor markets. EMU enhances the credibility of monetary policy and thereby lowers inflation expectations. Negative employment effects as a result of (too) high wage claims can no longer be accommodated by discretionary monetary policy. Insofar as the single currency increases transparency, the costs of structural rigidities, as reflected by relative prices, become more evident. Lower trading costs and higher transparency jointly tend to foster competition in goods markets, which, in turn, reduces the available product market rents. With shrinking rents, the incentive to resist reforms should also decline.

---

mid-1970s up to the late 1990s. It finds that EU membership leads to faster moves towards liberalization of product markets. However, it does not clarify whether this represents an effect of EMU and/or policies to prepare for EMU. See also Duval and Elmeskov (2005), p. 10.

[2] For a survey see Duval and Elmeskov (2005) and Hochreiter and Tavlas (2005).

Taken together, if changes in monetary policy and the nominal exchange rate are not available, and if labor is immobile as is the case in most parts of the Euro area, there is no other option except undertaking reforms in order to facilitate the market-based adjustment to shocks. Hence, a credible currency peg has often been interpreted as a version of Mrs. Thatcher's There-Is-No-Alternative (TINA) strategy.[3]

However, there are also important arguments against a positive impact of monetary rules on economic reform. First, based on OECD macro model simulations, it was often argued with respect to EMU that the so-called up-front costs of structural reforms may be larger within a currency union. Removing restrictions in financial markets tends to stimulate demand more than labor market reforms and hence allows an easier and quicker "crowding-in" of the positive supply side effects of reforms (Bean, 1998; Duval and Elmeskov, 2005: 10–12; Saint-Paul and Bentolila, 2000). The prior in this case would be that rule-based monetary policy regimes like European Monetary Union lead to more reforms in the financial market than in the labor market.

Secondly, Calmfors (1997) and Sibert and Sutherland (1997) argue that monetary policy with its mainly short-run real effects is not likely to diminish structural unemployment significantly. Hence, rule-based monetary policy does not necessarily imply more reform pressure. In the same line, empirical analysis indicates that the capability of exchange rates to absorb asymmetric shocks to labor and goods markets is rather low. Hence, flexibility of exchange rates does not seem to be a good substitute for reforms and the degree of reforms is not necessarily higher under fixed exchange rates (Belke and Gros, 1999).

Thirdly, the limited evidence of price convergence for instance among core-EMS countries does not point to any significant impact of exchange rate stabilization on product market competition. There are still product market rents to be captured and there is still resistance to reforms (Haffner et al., 2000). During the discussions about the pros and cons of EMU at the end of the 1990s, it was also argued that market-oriented reforms could achieve a 'double dividend' if monetary policy was discretionary (autonomous). As a first effect, reforms reduce –like a rule-based monetary policy – the costs of structural unemployment. They also lessen equilibrium inflation since they diminish the credibility problem of discretionary monetary policy. This second effect is absent in the case of rule-based monetary policy since it does not suffer from a credibility problem by definition. The usual result of this literature is that for individual member countries, a fixed exchange rate rule like EMU implies a lower degree of reforms than an autonomous monetary policy, where reforms reduce both unemployment and the inflation bias. In contrast, a rule-based monetary policy inside EMU limits the benefits of reforms to a positive impact

[3] See Bean (1998), Calmfors (1998: 28); Duval and Elmeskov (2005: 5) and Saint-Paul and Bentolila (2000).

on employment. Expressed more generally, the degree of reforms is therefore higher in the case of autonomous policy (discretion) and lower in the case of commitment (Calmfors, 1997, 1998; Gruener and Hefeker, 1996).

Finally, fixed exchange rate pegs as a special case of a monetary rule eliminate the exchange rate risk, which should enhance capital inflows. Having access to more foreign capital might reduce the incentive to reform financial markets. In this sense, fixed exchange rates tend to lower the degree of reforms as well.

Hence, our central question relates to the correlation between reform intensity and the degree of autonomy of monetary policy, which in turn might be determined to a large degree by the exchange rate regime (Duval and Elmeskov, 2005: 9 and 23 ff.). In this respect, our approach strictly follows Duval and Elmeskov (2005: 25) who measure the loss of monetary autonomy by the degree of commitment to a fixed exchange rate.

Economic openness is generally related to the share of exports and imports in GDP. A stronger exposure of firms to international competition is often assumed to increase the pressure and the incentives for market-oriented reforms. In open economies, output and employment tend to be highly responsive to price competitiveness so that there are stronger incentives to reform (Katzenstein, 1985; and Nickell, 2005: 2–3). However, empirical evidence is not especially supportive of the view that open economies are more likely to liberalize. Although Pitlik and Wirth (2003) report a positive impact of economic openness on market-oriented reforms, Herz and Vogel (2005) and Pitlik (2004) do not find robust significant coefficients of economic openness for their overall reform indicator. Only in the case of trade policy do they find a positive effect of economic openness on liberalization. Our theoretical discussion seems to indicate a possible solution to this empirical puzzle. The key insight borrowed, for instance, from the political economy literature on openness, size of governments and reform efforts (Rodrik, 1996, and other papers by this author) is that more open economies are more likely to implement rule-based exchange rate stabilization and, hence, generally implement less reforms.

17.3 Empirical Analysis

17.3.1 Hypotheses

In the following, we investigate whether a significant positive correlation between exchange rate flexibility and market liberalization exists if the usual impact factors like the macroeconomic environment or political and institutional impediments to economic reforms are controlled. Hence, we test for a significant coefficient of our measure of exchange rate flexibility in regressions using reform indices as the dependent variable and check for robustness of the results. In accordance with Section 17.2, the following hypotheses are expected to hold:

1. If the view of excessive reforms under monetary policy autonomy which also implies that exchange rate rules and reforms are substitutes is correct, the degree of reforms will be higher under more flexible exchange rates, net of other factors.
2. However, if the view of exchange rate fixing as a structural whip and, hence, of complementarity between exchange rate rules and reforms is valid, one should expect the contrary, namely a negative correlation of exchange rate flexibility with the degree of reforms, net of other factors.
3. If third factors like the initial need for reforms, the so-called problem pressure, dominate the relationship, the exchange rate regime should turn out to be less significant.

Note that (1) to (3) should be valid not only for labor market reforms but also for complementary structural reforms in the goods and the financial markets.

17.3.2 Data and Definitions

We estimate and test the conjectured correlation of the exchange rate regime with the degree of market-oriented reforms based on a panel of 123 countries and two different subsets of countries. The first sub-sample covers 105 countries with more than one million inhabitants. Excluding the 18 smallest states might help to remove the noise due to their specific economic and political structure. The second subset comprises 23 OECD economies, which represent a relatively homogenous group of countries. Our samples cover the period 1970–2000 in order to exploit all available data. In line with our theoretical model, our empirical analysis focuses on the pattern of the correlation between the exchange rate regime and the contemporaneous degree of market-oriented reforms.

As dependent variable, we use the extent of economic liberalization as measured by the Economic Freedom of the World (EFW) index: the index of overall liberalization and the sub-indices for international trade, money and banking system, government and labor market, credit and business regulation (Gwartney and Lawson, 2003; Gwartney et al., 2006). Additionally, we consider the regulation of labor markets, which is itself a sub-index of the more comprehensive regulation measure. These indices range from one to ten, with a high value corresponding to a high level of economic freedom. We use data from the 2006 report, which is the most recent data vintage. The EFW index and the sub-indices are available in five-year intervals over the period 1970–2000.

Among the explaining variables, our discussion focuses on the measure of exchange rate flexibility. In Section 17.2, we argued that we prefer to measure the loss of monetary autonomy by the participation in fixed exchange rate agreements. This approach allows exploiting a wider cross-country/time-series data-set of structural reforms than would otherwise be possible. As a result, we feel justified to apply an econometric analysis of reform determinants which includes the degree of exchange rate flexibility as one of the explanatory variables.

However, one obvious drawback of our analysis is that it does not cover some of the idiosyncratic characteristics of currency unions compared with other fixed exchange rate arrangements. Obviously, the argument that a credible exchange rate rule fosters liberalization, as emphasized in Section 17.2, is even more compelling in the case of a currency union like EMU than in the case of a reversible fixed exchange rate regime. We therefore use the Reinhart and Rogoff (2002) index of de facto exchange rate arrangements to account for the wide spectrum of exchange rate regimes. Reinhart and Rogoff (2002) distinguish between exchange rate pegs (1), limited flexibility (2), managed floating (3), and freely floating (4). Thus, the higher the index value the higher is the de facto flexibility of exchange rates. For our purpose and due to the time structure of the EFW data, we average the Reinhart and Rogoff (2002) index values over five-year intervals.

Table 17.1 contains some summary statistics on the indicators of economic reform and the exchange rate regime as our key variables. It quantifies the share

Table 17.1 Summary statistics (percentages) on economic reforms and exchange rate policy 1970–2000

		Change of reform and exchange rate indicator		
Sample	Indicator	$=0$	>0	<0
All 123 countries	Overall reform index	0.00	0.68	0.32
	Government sector reform	0.00	0.52	0.48
	Monetary sector reform	0.01	0.55	0.44
	Trade policy reform	0.01	0.64	0.35
	Regulatory reform	0.03	0.56	0.41
	Labor market reform	0.08	0.44	0.48
	Exchange rate regime	0.53	0.27	0.20
105 countries	Overall reform index	0.00	0.67	0.33
(more than 1 mio. inhabitants)	Government sector reform	0.00	0.53	0.47
	Monetary sector reform	0.01	0.56	0.43
	Trade policy reform	0.01	0.64	0.36
	Regulatory reform	0.02	0.56	0.41
	Labor market reform	0.08	0.44	0.48
	Exchange rate regime	0.51	0.28	0.21
23 OECD countries	Overall reform index	0.00	0.75	0.25
	Government sector reform	0.00	0.45	0.55
	Monetary sector reform	0.00	0.59	0.41
	Trade policy reform	0.00	0.69	0.31
	Regulatory reform	0.02	0.63	0.35
	Labor market reform	0.10	0.42	0.48
	Exchange rate regime	0.55	0.26	0.20

of reform and no-reform events across our different country samples. Equivalently, the table also indicates the percentage shares of shifts and persistence in exchange rate policy, respectively. The numbers show a fairly high amount of changes in either direction, whereby in most cases, increases clearly dominate decreases in economic freedom. Exchange rate policy appears much more persistent, on the other hand. In about half the cases, countries keep their exchange rate regimes over a horizon of five years. In cases, where the exchange rate regime was changed, the numbers indicate a slight dominance of more flexibility over stronger exchange rate pegs.

The additional control variables which we consider include inflation, economic growth, openness and the log of real per-capita GDP as proxies of the pressure to reform. Data are available from the World Development Indicators database (World Bank, 2002). Economic openness is defined as exports plus imports relative to GDP. To account for the potential endogeneity and in accordance with other contributions (Herz and Vogel, 2005; Pitlik, 2004; Pitlik and Wirth, 2003; Lora, 2000), we take these variables in first lags. Since we introduce the four proxies of reform pressure in lagged form, we are controlling for endogeneity, but at the same time, we are also testing for Granger-causality. Hence, the results gained in the empirical analysis can also be read in this framework.

A final set of controls accounts for political and institutional barriers to policy reforms. Here, we include POLCON5 and the number of government changes. POLCON5 (Henisz, 2002) measures the effective political restrictions on executive behavior. It accounts for the veto powers of the executive, two legislative chambers, the sub-national entities and an independent judiciary. The index ranges from zero to one, with higher values indicating stronger political constraints on the government. Given the time structure of our dependent variable, we take average values of POLCON5 for the respective five-year interval. GOVCHANGES counts the number of government changes that entail a significant programmatic reorientation. The data are taken from Beck et al. (2001). The credibility and reliability of economic policy is assumed to decrease with the number of government changes. Frequent changes shorten the administration's time horizon and lead to a stronger discounting of positive future payoffs from reforms.

17.3.3 Empirical Model and Results

17.3.3.1 Empirical Model

To investigate the empirical relationship between reforms on the one side and the exchange rate regime and political as well as institutional characteristics on the other, we estimate the equation

$$\Delta EFW_{it} = \alpha_0 + \alpha_1 EFW_{i,t-1} + \alpha_2 EXR_{it} + \alpha_3' X_{i,t-1} + \alpha_4' Y_{it} + \lambda_t + \varepsilon_{it}$$

where ΔEFW represents the change in economic freedom as our index of reforms. EXR is our measure for exchange rate flexibility, X is the vector of macroeconomic variables (growth, inflation, openness, per-capita GDP), Y captures the political and institutional determinants of reforms, and *i* is a country index. Lagged EFW accounts for the prevailing status of economic freedom or, put differently, the prevailing reform gap. Most importantly, we expect $\alpha_2>0$ to hold, if a high degree of exchange rate flexibility leads to more reforms (see Section 17.2). However, if the hypothesis of more reforms under a regime of fixed exchange rates is valid, one should expect the contrary, namely $\alpha_2<0$. To account for unobserved heterogeneity across time, we add time-specific effects (λ_t).

Although individual specific effects are a key advantage of panel data analysis, we do not include them to capture the impact of unobserved variables that may otherwise bias the other coefficient estimates. We exclude individual country dummies, because the short time-series dimension of the panel (six observations at maximum) would render any country-dummy estimate very imprecise and consume many degrees of freedom. Furthermore, country-specific effects drop out under the GMM first-difference estimator. Instead, we argue that the distinction and separate estimation of our world sample, a large-country and an OECD country sample and the introduction of structural and macroeconomic variables in the regression equation should capture some structural country heterogeneity.

The lagged dependent variable figures among the regressors in our empirical model. This leads OLS estimates of the coefficients to be biased (Baltagi, 2005; Hsiao, 2003). We therefore estimate our dynamic equation with the *GMM difference estimator* proposed by Arellano and Bond (1991) and report the one-step estimates in Tables 17.2, 17.3, and 17.4 (1-step GMM DIFF). The GMM estimator uses lagged values of the explanatory variables as instruments and thus accounts for potential endogeneity of the regressors. Thus, the GMM estimation includes, for instance, lagged values of our measure of exchange rate flexibility as instrument for the contemporaneous realization of exchange rate flexibility to achieve consistent estimates even if the variable is endogenous or not strictly exogenous, at least. It hence mitigates the issue of reverse causality among reforms and exchange rate flexibility appearing in our context.[4]

To check the robustness of the results, we also apply the *GMM system estimator* developed by Arellano and Bover (1995) and Blundell and Bond

[4] There is an additional argument speaking against reverse causality. In what way should a supranational variable like exchange rate flexibility be influenced by a national variable as the change in the EFW index at all? As far as at least two parties are necessary to agree upon a peg, this appears to be a good argument in favour of, at least, partial exogeneity of exchange rate policy.

Table 17.2 Panel estimates for overall liberalization (t-values in parentheses, significance levels: 10%*, 5%**, 1%***)

	World sample		Population > 1.000.000		OECD	
	GMM-DIFF	GMM-SYS	GMM-DIFF	GMM-SYS	GMM-DIFF	GMM-SYS
EXR flexibility	−0.32** (−2.66)	−0.18** (−2.13)	−0.28** (−2.40)	−0.17** (−1.98)	−0.17* (−1.93)	0.02 (0.54)
EFW (t−1)	−0.47*** (−4.18)	−0.22** (−2.33)	−0.48*** (−4.27)	−0.22** (−2.20)	−0.46*** (−3.34)	−0.42** (−2.54)
Inflation (t−1)	0.04 (1.17)	0.06 (1.20)	0.04 (1.18)	0.06 (1.35)	0.53 (0.69)	0.06 (0.07)
Growth (t−1)	0.99 (0.88)	0.18 (0.15)	1.54 (1.27)	0.46 (0.34)	1.58 (0.39)	−2.60 (−0.55)
Openness (t−1)	0.73* (1.78)	−0.17 (−0.89)	0.75* (1.81)	−0.13 (−0.46)	−1.90*** (−2.79)	0.09 (0.79)
LnRGDPpc (t−1)	−0.62*** (−2.71)	0.08 (1.13)	−0.74*** (−2.99)	0.09 (1.12)	−0.98 (−1.56)	−0.01 (−0.03)
POLCONV	0.79*** (3.41)	0.72*** (3.42)	0.83*** (3.42)	0.72*** (2.94)	0.41 (0.64)	1.26** (2.36)
GOVCHANGES	−0.16*** (−4.08)	−0.13*** (−2.94)	−0.18*** (−4.83)	−0.15*** (−3.71)	−0.11 (−1.55)	−0.04 (−0.65)
Constant	0.04 (0.48)	0.90* (1.90)	0.04 (0.40)	0.85* (1.73)	0.08 (0.96)	1.97 (0.80)
Time effects	28.2***	17.4***	32.7***	21.3***	30.3***	17.6***
AR (1)	−3.46***	−4.27***	−3.21***	−4.01***	−3.31***	−2.87***
AR (2)	−1.29	−0.76	−1.56	−1.04	−0.94	−0.95
Sargan test (p-value)	0.02**	0.15	0.02**	0.13	0.02**	0.72
Observations	326	420	304	392	89	112

Table 17.3 Panel estimates for trade liberalization (t-values in parentheses, significance levels: 10%*, 5%**, 1%***)

	World sample		Population > 1.000.000		OECD	
	GMM-DIFF	GMM-SYS	GMM-DIFF	GMM-SYS	GMM-DIFF	GMM-SYS
EXR flexibility	−0.42** (−2.35)	−0.34*** (−3.15)	−0.43** (−2.36)	−0.40*** (−3.58)	−0.32** (−2.15)	−0.10* (−1.86)
T (t−1)	−0.60*** (−6.60)	−0.58*** (−6.82)	−0.59*** (−6.05)	−0.55*** (−6.31)	−0.67*** (−4.07)	−0.37* (−1.80)
Inflation (t−1)	−0.02 (−0.49)	−0.05 (−1.05)	−0.02 (−0.49)	−0.05 (−1.16)	−1.36 (−1.39)	−1.23 (−1.15)
Growth (t−1)	−3.60 (−1.54)	−4.30** (−2.08)	−4.45* (−1.77)	−5.11** (−2.25)	1.65 (0.31)	−6.77 (−1.01)
Openness (t−1)	−1.78*** (−2.77)	−0.13 (−0.41)	−2.08*** (−3.05)	−0.18 (−0.43)	−1.48 (−1.44)	0.22 (1.03)
LnRGDPpc (t−1)	0.11 (0.28)	0.24** (2.18)	0.28 (0.64)	0.29*** (2.58)	−1.28 (−1.06)	−0.34 (−0.65)
POLCONV	0.83** (2.21)	1.01*** (3.48)	0.89** (2.20)	0.77*** (2.68)	1.85 (1.18)	1.28 (1.07)
GOVCHANGES	−0.10 (−1.23)	−0.03 (−0.39)	−0.12 (−1.45)	−0.06 (−0.80)	−0.11* (−1.83)	−0.03 (−0.64)
Constant	−0.02 (−0.18)	2.17*** (2.74)	−0.05 (0.36)	1.91** (2.30)	0.11 (0.63)	5.85 (1.12)
Time effects	20.6***	22.2***	18.7***	22.3***	9.42*	24.8***
AR (1)	−3.77***	−3.60***	−3.68***	−3.55***	−2.18**	−2.45**
AR (2)	0.70	0.19	0.54	0.15	−0.89	−0.50
Sargan test (p-value)	0.01***	0.45	0.01***	0.35	0.14	0.96
Observations	334	426	311	397	89	112

Table 17.4 Panel estimates for money and banking sector reform (t-values in parentheses, significance levels: 10%*, 5%**, 1%***)

	World sample		Population > 1.000.000		OECD	
	GMM-DIFF	GMM-SYS	GMM-DIFF	GMM-SYS	GMM-DIFF	GMM-SYS
EXR flexibility	−0.46* (−1.79)	−0.25* (−1.67)	−0.26 (−1.09)	−0.14 (−0.94)	−0.30 (−1.01)	−0.25 (−1.53)
M (t−1)	−0.26*** (−2.61)	−0.20*** (−2.70)	−0.36*** (−3.61)	−0.19*** (−2.49)	−0.20 (−1.41)	−0.01 (−0.04)
Inflation (t−1)	0.14*** (2.62)	0.15*** (3.41)	0.15*** (2.61)	0.16*** (2.82)	3.35 (1.02)	10.8 (1.28)
Growth (t−1)	15.1*** (4.64)	9.91*** (3.92)	15.9*** (4.60)	9.77*** (3.25)	−0.27 (−0.02)	11.0 (0.88)
Openness (t−1)	2.75** (2.49)	0.14 (0.46)	3.69*** (2.88)	0.37 (0.78)	−4.02* (−1.74)	−0.47 (−1.47)
LnRGDPpc (t−1)	−2.76*** (−4.64)	−0.12 (−0.78)	−2.88*** (−4.18)	−0.11 (−0.64)	1.68 (0.91)	−1.24 (−1.17)
POLCONV	1.21 (1.61)	1.56*** (3.12)	1.19 (1.61)	1.37*** (2.81)	0.41 (0.23)	11.6 (1.56)
GOVCHANGES	−0.52*** (−3.99)	−0.37*** (−3.13)	−0.54*** (−4.15)	−0.35*** (−2.76)	−0.18 (−0.79)	0.01 (0.05)
Constant	0.32* (1.66)	2.36** (2.24)	0.22 (1.08)	1.99* (1.76)	−0.11 (−0.32)	2.93 (0.75)
Time effects	25.8***	13.4***	28.4***	11.9**	14.1***	9.16*
AR (1)	−5.54***	−5.11***	−5.14***	−4.85***	−3.17***	−2.58***
AR (2)	−1.29	−1.61	−1.28	−1.55	1.57	1.10
Sargan test (p-value)	0.02**	0.30	0.01***	0.18	0.04**	0.65
Observations	365	460	337	425	89	112

(1998). GMM system uses the regression equation in levels and in first differences and thus exploits the information in both levels and differences of the variables. It uses past lagged differences and levels of the regressors as instruments, respectively. The Sargan test indicates the validity of the instrument choice. If the null hypothesis is statistically not rejected, the instruments pass the test; they are valid by this criterion. GMM system yields substantial efficiency gains over the GMM difference estimator in panels with a short time dimension and for α_1 close to zero (see Baltagi, 2005). Tables 17.2, 17.3, and 17.4 report the two-step estimates of GMM system with the Windmeijer (2000) extension that corrects for the downward bias in two-step standard errors.

Arellano and Bond (1991) found the one-step Sargan test to over-reject in the presence of heteroscedasticity. Inference on the model specification should thus prefer the two-step Sargan results (2-step GMM SYS). AR(1) and AR(2) are the empirical realizations of the test statistics of first and second order residual autocorrelation. Significance means that the null hypothesis of no autocorrelation is rejected – as is often the case for AR(1) but never for AR(2).[5]

17.3.3.2 Results

This section presents the regression results for our broad country sample and for the sample of high-income OECD economies, respectively. We report the regression results for overall liberalization, and liberalization in the sub-areas of international trade, money and banking system, government, market regulation, and labor market regulation as dependent variables. Tables 17.2, 17.3, and 17.4 display the GMM estimates for each of the indicators of economic liberalization. A robust result, which is strongly significant in the large majority of the regressions, is the negative impact of the initial level of economic freedom on the extent of subsequent market-oriented reforms. The higher the initial level of economic freedom, the lower is the scope and the need for further liberalization. The negative coefficient values also imply a conditional convergence in economic policy (Duval and Elmeskov, 2005: 23 ff.). Labor market regulation is a notable exception.

The GMM-DIFF results in the Tables are 1-step whereas those for GMM-SYS are 2-step. This fits with the observation that the Sargan results are worse for GMM-DIFF. According to our remarks in the last paragraph of Section 17.3.3.1, this means that the 1-step Sargan results should not be dramatized. In the case of 1-step GMM-DIFF, we used 1-step because the standard errors are not biased as is the case with AR(2). However, in the case of GMM-SYS, there is a (Windmeijer) correction of the 2-step bias available which we applied.

[5] It is important to note that the absence of AR(2) is the necessary condition for unbiased and efficient estimation with GMM-DIFF and GMM-SYS, but not of AR(1). First order residual autocorrelation in the starting equation is no problem since both estimators work with first differences. Hence, the significance of AR(1) does not limit the validity of our results.

Hence, we tabulate 2-step GMM-SYS in our tables.[6] AR(1) and AR(2) are untouched by these considerations and only the absence of AR(2) is important. The main interest of this chapter of the book lies in a thorough empirical investigation of the correlation of the exchange rate system with market-oriented reforms, however.

In Table 17.2 we find a robust negative impact of higher exchange rate flexibility on overall liberalization, as measured by the chain-linked EFW index, in our worldwide sample. This result indicates complementarity between exchange rate rules and reforms. In the OECD sub-sample, this relationship loses the robust significance found in the larger samples, however.

For trade liberalization (Table 17.3), we obtain a robust and negatively significant correlation between exchange rate flexibility and economic reform for both the worldwide and the OECD country sample. The result is compatible with the idea that the exchange rate peg can be a complementary measure to facilitate cross-border exchanges and to reap the gains from international trade. Furthermore, the GMM system estimates in Table 17.4 provide some evidence in favour of complementarity of exchange rate commitment and money and banking sector reform (merely) at the world level.

However, the exchange rate variable is across the board insignificant in our regressions for government-sector reform, labor market, credit and business regulation, and its sub-index labor market reform (as reported in Belke, Herz and Vogel, 2006). Hence, the estimates provide no empirical evidence for any relationship between the adoption of an exchange rate rule and the extent of structural reforms in these important fields of economic policy. This is compatible with our view that the up-front costs of reforms in the areas of product and labor markets are higher than in other areas and that insider-outsider forces are at work in these areas which might hamper significant reform progress. Our results again confirm that it is easier to overcome reform resistance in areas which cannot be controlled by labor market insiders as, for instance, trade and money and banking. None of our estimates provides evidence in favour of hypothesis (1) and the idea that exchange rate rules and structural reforms might be substitutes.

How can we reconcile the negative coefficient values for the overall index on the one hand, and the insignificance of the exchange rate indicator for the sub-indices government size and market (i.e., labor, credit and business) regulation on the other hand? One candidate explanation is that the observed complementarity between fixed exchange rates and market-oriented reforms is entirely driven by the positive correlation between the exchange rate commitment and the liberalization of trade and to a certain extent – at the world level – also by

[6] In the case of the 1-step estimators, heteroscedasticity tends to strengthen the bias towards the significance of the Sargan test. Hence, one could readily interpret our results as evidence of heteroscedasticity. However, both estimators (GMM-DIFF and GMM-SYS) use heteroscedasticity-robust standard errors. This should make the estimated coefficients quite robust.

the complementarity between the exchange rate commitment and money and banking sector reform. The positive correlation between the exchange rate commitment and trade liberalization coincides with the view of the exchange rate peg as an instrument to facilitate international trade and to reap the full benefits of economic integration. Indeed, the complementarity between trade and exchange rate commitment was a prominent argument in the context and in favour of European Monetary Union (Emerson et al., 1992). The complementarity between the exchange rate commitment and money and banking sector reform can be related to the positive impact of the exchange rate commitment on price stability and the credibility of monetary policy. Low inflation is itself an important component of the reform sub-indicator. A sound banking system should strengthen the credibility and lower the risk of exchange rate crises. Given that the latter argument applies especially for developing countries, it is not particularly surprising to see the nexus between exchange rate regime and financial system to vanish for the group of high-income OECD economies.

A second point to keep in mind is that, contrary to the overall indicator, the indices for trade, money and banking, government size, market regulation and labor market reform are not chain-linked. Missing data in the construction of these indicators may therefore distort their values. The latter will then distort the results and diminish the accuracy with which the extent of reforms is measured.

Taken together, the finding of no positive correlation between exchange rate flexibility and structural reforms contradicts the hypothesis that the exchange rate commitment and reforms are substitutes. Instead, the robust negative correlation between exchange rate flexibility and trade liberalization as well as the negative relationship between exchange rate flexibility and both overall reform and money and banking sector reform at the world level point to a complementarity of the exchange rate commitment and structural reforms in several areas of economic policy. The exchange rate indicator is insignificant for government sector reform, market regulation, and labor market regulation, indicating that the exchange rate regime plays no particular role in these areas of structural reform. Note however that the non-chain-linked nature of our sub-indicator data may bias our results in the direction of finding no significant relationship.

Concerning the other control variables, we find a significant negative impact of the initial level of economic freedom on subsequent reforms, except for labor market regulation and for banking and government sector reform in the OECD. For the world sample, we furthermore find a positive impact of political constraints on overall reform and trade liberalization and a negative impact of government instability on overall liberalization, government size and money and banking sector reform. The macroeconomic control variables play only a limited role in our regressions. High inflation and economic growth both have a ro-bust and positive impact on money and banking sector reform in the world sample, but not in the high-income OECD economies. Within the world sample, a ten percentage point higher inflation is associated with an additional improvement in the reform index of about 0.02 percentage points. In contrast, economic growth does not seem to throughout promote a further liberalization of international trade. The negative impact of initial per-capita income on overall liberalization and public sector reform as well as the positive impact on money and banking sector reform and the reduction of trade and market regulation in the world sample are not robust across the estimators. Also, the positive impact of growth on overall reform and the negative impact of openness on trade liberalization are not robust. GMM, in differences, gives a significant negative coefficient for openness on trade liberalization, a negatively significant coefficient for openness, inflation and initial income levels on regulatory reform, and a negative impact on openness on money and banking sector reform for OECD countries. However, the GMM system estimator does not confirm their significance.

In another contribution (Belke, Herz and Vogel, 2006), we focus more specifically on labor market reforms and a limited sample of OECD countries. The structural reforms are again proxied by the Economic Freedom of the World index whereas the monetary policy constraint is measured by a monetary commitment index. In that paper, we also find no evidence for the Calmfors hypothesis, which claims a positive relationship between exchange rate flexibility and structural reforms. The result is entirely compatible with our findings in this section. For further robustness checks of the estimation results presented in this chapter, see Belke, Herz and Vogel (2006).

17.4 Summary and Conclusions

In this chapter of the book, we have investigated the relationship between the exchange rate regime and the degree of structural reforms using panel data techniques. We looked at a broad sample of countries (the "world sample") and a sample of OECD economies. As dependent variable, we have used the degree of market-oriented reforms. As independent variables, we have introduced an indicator of exchange rate flexibility and a number of control variables such as economic performance to account for reform pressures and for the institutional impediments to reform.

Taken together, our results do not back the hypothesis that exchange rate rules and structural reforms might be substitutes. Some of our estimates are, in contrast, compatible with a complementary relationship between the exchange rate commitment and structural reforms. Our results may even imply a causal linkage from an exchange rate rule to the degree of overall reforms. Thus, limiting monetary autonomy via an exchange rate rule on average facilitates and strengthens liberalization in certain fields. However, the positive correlation is not replicated for labor and product market reforms. It is especially in these areas, however, that we would expect the exchange rate commitment to induce the strongest pressure and the largest incentives for painful, but in the long run, beneficial structural change.

Our analysis thus leaves us with three results. First, it appears to be true that a look at the aggregated level of reform effort and its macroeconomic determinants is worth it. The main efficiency issues are neither better addressed through a disaggregated approach nor are the interactions of rigidities and, for instance, labor market and goods market performance, too complex to be able to stand up against a too high level of regulation and, more specifically, of bureaucracy and in favour of regulatory reform. Second, it provides no evidence for monetary commitment and structural reforms being substitutes or alternative policy choices. Third, one should not exaggerate the complementarity of exchange rate rules and the degree of structural reforms in view of the large status-quo bias and the path-dependence of the political process. The results provide no empirical justification to favour monetary autonomy in open economies on the ground of its allegedly positive impact on structural reforms, however. Monetary rules are the only option to support sound supply-side reform policies in an efficient way. Urging, for instance, the European Central Bank to go for discretionary monetary policy in the wake of structural weaknesses in some countries of the euro area like, above all, Italy, would certainly lead to bad prospects for better regulation and a higher degree of international competitiveness of the euro area as a whole – the danger of a liraization of the euro might in this case no longer be excluded (Belke and Gros, 2007; and Leiner-Killinger et al. 2007). In our view, this insight maybe constitutes the most robust empirical result of the analysis.

What prospects for further deregulation in Europe then? Not at least due to the economic rise of the BRIC countries (Brazil, India and China), the competitive pressures on Europe have increased significantly since the time of the Mandelkern report (2001) and the Commission's first coherent action plan (European Commission, 2002), where the reference points for deregulation were the three pillars of the early Lisbon strategy (competitiveness, social cohesion, and sustainable development) and the White Paper on governance. It did not come as a surprise that, with the Barroso Commission, there has been a redefinition of better regulation as a regulatory reform. This recasting exercise has aligned better regulation with the 'growth and jobs' priorities of Lisbon and may as a result possibly succeed in containing the proliferation of objectives by drawing political attention to specific goals, such as the reduction of administrative burdens (Radaelli, 2007).

Acknowledgment I am grateful for valuable comments from Gulcin Ozkan, University of York, Christoph Müller, University of Hohenheim, John Hudson, University of Bath, Gerrit B. Koester, Deutsche Bundes-bank, and other participants in the conferences "Bürokratieabbau in Europa", November 11th, 2007, in Magdeburg, Schloss Wendgräben, Germany, organized by the Konrad-Adenauer-Stiftung, in the Conference on "The Travails of the Eurozone", Money, Macro & Finance Research Group and University Association for Contemporary European Studies, March 24th, 2006, in Edinburgh, and in the 2008 Annual

Meeting of the European Public Choice Society (EPCS), Jena. This chapter is based on my talk "Bürokratieabbau in Europa – Ein Reformvergleich in den EU-Mitgliedstaaten" given at the first conference, on my speech about "Monetary Policy as a Driver of Structural Reforms" (Session: "Structural Reform and the Euro", delivered on the second occasion) and "Macroeconomic Policies, Bureaucracy and Deregulation – The Choice of the Exchange Rate Regime" (Session: "Money II", delivered on the third occasion). The usual caveats apply.

References

Arellano, M. and Bond, S. (1991). Some Tests of Specification for Panel Data: Monte Carlo Evidence and an Application to Employment Equations. *Review of Economic Studies* 58: 277–297.

Arellano, M. and Bover, O. (1995). Another Look at the Instrumental Variables Estimation of Error-Component Models. *Journal of Econometrics* 68: 29–51.

Baldwin, R., Scott, C. and Hood, C. (1998). "Introduction" in Baldwin, R., Scott, C., and Hood, C. (eds.), *A Reader on Regulation*. Oxford: Oxford University Press.

Baltagi, B. (2005). *Econometric Analysis of Panel Data*. Chichester: John Wiley and sons.

Bean, C. (1998). The Interaction of Aggregate-demand Policies and Labor-market Reform. *Swedish Economic Policy Review* 5(2): 353–382.

Beck, T., Clarke, G., Groff, A., Keefer, P. and Walsh, P. (2001). New Tools in Comparative Political Economy: The Database of Political Institutions. *World Bank Economic Review* 15(1): 165–176.

Belke, A. and Gros, D. (1999). Estimating the Costs and Benefits of EMU: The Impact of External Shocks on Labor Markets. *Weltwirtschaftliches Archiv* 135: 1–48.

Belke, A. and Gros, D. (2007): Instability of the Eurozone? On Monetary Policy, House Prices and Labor Market Reforms, IZA Discussion Paper No. 2547, Institute for the Study of Labor, Bonn.

Belke, A., Herz, B. and Vogel, L. (2006). Reforms, Exchange Rates and Monetary Commitment: A Panel Analysis for OECD Countries. *Open Economies Review* 18: 369–388.

Belke, A., Herz, B. and Vogel, L. (2006a). Beyond Trade – Is Reform Effort Affected by the Exchange Rate Regime? A Panel Analysis for the World versus OECD Countries. *Économie Internationale* 107: 29–58.

Bertola, G. and Boeri, T. (2001). *EMU Labor Markets Two Years on: Microeconomic Tensions and Institutional Evolution*. Paper presented at the Workshop "The Functioning of EMU: Challenges of the Early Years" organized by the Directorate General for Economic and Financial Affairs, European Commission, Brussels, 21–22 March 2001, April 27th 2001 version.

Blundell, R. and Bond, S. (1998). Initial Conditions and Moment Restrictions in Dynamic Panel Data Models. *Journal of Econometrics* 87: 115–143.

Calmfors, L. (1997). Unemployment, Labor-Market Reform and EMU. IIES Seminar *Paper* 639. Institute for International Economic Studies, Stockholm.

Calmfors, L. (1998). Macroeconomic Policy, Wage Setting and Employment – What Difference Does the EMU Make?. *Oxford Economic Policy Review* 14: 125–151.

Duval, R. and Elmeskov, J. (2005). The Effects of EMU on Structural Reforms in Labor and Product Markets. *OECD Economics Department Working Papers* 438.

Emerson, M., Gros, D., Halianer, A., Pisani-Ferry, T. and Reichenbach, W. (1992). One Market, One Money. Oxford University Press, Oxford.

European Commission (2002). *Action Plan: Simplifying and Improving the Regulatory Environment*, Communication from the Commission, COM(2002) 278 final, Brussels, 5 June.

Gruener, H.S. and Hefeker, C. (1996). Militant Labor and Inflation Aversion – The Impact of EMU on Labor Union Interaction. University Bonn, *SFB 303 Discussion Paper A-539*.

Gwartney, J. and Lawson, R. (2003). The Concept and Measurement of Economic Freedom. *European Journal of Political Economy* 19(3): 405–430.

Gwartney, J., Lawson, R., Park, W. and Skipton, C. (2006). Economic Freedom of the World: 2006 Annual Report.Fraser Institute, Vancouver.
Haffner, R.C.G., Nickell, S., Nicoletti, G., Scarpetta, S., Zoega, G. (2000). *European Integration, Liberalisation and Labor Market Performance*: Report for the Fondazione Rodolfo DeBenedetti.
Henisz, W. (2002). The Institutional Environment for Infrastructure Investment. *Industrial and Corporate Change* 11(2): 355–389.
Herz, B. and Vogel, L. (2005). *Determinants of Market-Oriented Policy Reforms: An Empirical Analysis*. Mimeo.
Hochreiter, E. and Tavlas, G.S. (2005). The Two Roads to the Euro: The Monetary Experiences of Austria and Greece. In S. Schadler (Ed.), *Euro Adoption in Central and Eastern Europe – Opportunities and Challenges*. Washington, DC: International Monetary Fund.
Hsiao, C. (2003). *Analysis of Panel Data*. Cambridge: Cambridge University Press.
IMF (2004). *Fostering Structural Reforms in Industrial Countries*. Chapter III in World Economic Outlook. Advancing Structural Reforms, International Monetary Fund, Washington, DC
Katzenstein, P. (1985). *Small States in World Markets*. Ithaca: Cornell University Press.
Leiner-Killinger, N., Lopěz Pérez, V., Stiegert, R. and Vitale, G. (2007). *Structural Reforms in EMU and the Role of Monetary Policy*. ECB Occasional Paper Series 66. European Central Bank. Frankfurt/Main. July.
Lora, E. (2000). What Makes Reforms Likely? Timing and Sequencing of Structural Reforms in Latin America. *Inter-American Development Bank Working Paper* 424. Washington.
Mandelkern (Group on Better Regulation) (2001). Final Report, Brussels, 13 November.
Meier, K. J. (1985). *Regulation. Politics, Bureaucracy, and Economics*. New York. St. Martin's Press.
Nickell, S. (2005). Comments on Duval, R., Elmeskov, J. "The Effects of EMU on Structural Reforms in Labor and Product Markets,". Mimeo. Paper prepared for the Conference on "What Effects is EMU Having on the Euro Area and its Member Countries?" organized by the European Central Bank in Frankfurt. June.
OECD (2003). *From Red Tape to Smart Tape. Administrative Simplification in OECD Countries*. Paris: OECD.
Ogus, A. (1994). *Regulation. Legal Form and Economic Theory*. Oxford: Clarendon Press.
Pitlik, H. and Wirth, S. (2003). Do Crises Promote the Extent of Economic Liberalization?. *European Journal of Political Economy* 19(3): 565–581.
Pitlik, H. (2004). Are Less Constrained Governments Really More Successful in Executing Market-Oriented Policy Changes?. Diskussionsbeiträge aus dem Institut für Volkswirtschaftslehre der Universität Hohenheim 255/2005. University Hohenheim, Stuttgart.
Radaelli, C.M. (2007). Whither Better Regulation for the Lisbon Agenda?. *Journal of European Public Policy* 14(2): 190–207.
Reinhart, C.M. and Rogoff, K.S. (2002). The Modern History of Exchange Rate Regime Arrangements: A Reinterpretation. *NBER Working Paper* 8963, National Bureau of Economic Research. Cambridge, Mass.
Rodrik, D. (1996). Understanding Economic Policy Reform. *Journal of Economic Literature* 34(1): 9–41.
Saint-Paul, G. and Bentolila, S. (2000). Will EMU Increase Eurosclerosis?, International Macroeconomics and Labor Economics, *CEPR Discussion Paper* 2423, April, London.
Sibert, A.C. and Sutherland, A. (1997). Monetary Regimes and Labor Market Reform. *CEPR Discussion Paper* 1731, November. London.
van Poeck, A., Borghijs, A. (2001). *EMU and Labor Market Reform: Needs, Incentives and Realisations*. Oxford: Blackwell Publishers.
Windmeijer, F. (2000). A Finite Sample Correction for the Variance of Linear Two-Step GMM Estimators. *IFS Working Paper* W00/ 19.
World Bank (2002). *World Development Indicators*. Washington, DC: World Bank Publications.
World Bank (2006). *Doing Business in 2007 – How to Reform*. Washington: The World Bank.

Chapter 18
Development of an RIA Coordination System with a Focus on SME and Start-Ups

Christoph Müller and André Nijsen

Abstract Measuring compliance costs of businesses like administrative burden is hot stuff, from scientific view point as well from policy praxis. Also, the number of persons involved has increased considerably from a small inner circle of scientist and ministerial experts to rather big numbers of politicians, public officers and private consultants, specialized in public advisory. Almost by consequence, the debate about concepts, definitions and methodology starts again, every time new participants are joining the debate.

In the debates, there are mostly two key questions. First, are there arguments to introduce the public goals of regulations in the measurements or could the measurement be restricted to the costs of the regulated parties (businesses, citizens etc.) only? Second, which methodology is most appropriate to measure benefits and costs of regulations?

This chapter tries to bring more transparency in order to stimulate a more impartial discussion about the topic deregulation and its consequences. Important elements of this transparency are an adequate categorization of the separate cost and benefit effects, a systematic evaluation of these cost and benefit effects, and finally, an evaluation of the available techniques/methodologies. Such transparency could be the guidance for all who are involved in the law making process and the measurement of compliance effects.

18.1 Introduction

The measurement of regulation-dependent, administrative burdens in businesses has developed into a theme intensively discussed on both the scientific and the practical side. Priority is methodically given to two questions here. First, to what extent should and can the public goals of the

C. Müller (✉)
University of Sankt Gallen, St. Gallen, Switzerland
e-mail: christoph.mueller@unisg.ch

A. Nijsen et al. (eds.), *Business Regulation and Public Policy*, International Studies in Entrepreneurship 20, DOI 10.1007/978-0-387-77678-1_18,

regulation be considered, in addition to the directly resulting compliance costs for the norm addressees, i.e. the 'recipient' of the regulation, who must primarily bear the costs? Second, with which of the available measuring methods can the individual cost and benefit effects best be measured? A third question is added to these two questions, which gains in importance when viewed against the background of the significance of SME for the economic performances of a country as well as that of start-ups for the future economic growth of a country. Which special features must be considered in the design and use of measuring methods in respect of SME and start-ups?

The basic methodology is characterized by the study of literature, practical experience in the execution of measurement projects, and by the normative development of the systematic cost and benefit effects, the individual trial steps and the decision tree for use of the method.

This chapter therefore sets itself the overriding goal of reorganizing the existing complex structure in terms of a coordinate system and thus creating transparency. Transparency is capable of ensuring a proper discussion and the success of deregulation efforts.

The measuring methods presented in the last few years and the current discussion topics will be considered for this purpose. The creators of legislation processes and their measurement partners will thus be provided with decision and systematization proposals.

The challenge from an economic viewpoint is shown in the following table, which shows a measurement of the competitiveness of selected countries on the basis of their regulatory framework, impediments caused by bureaucracy and, in general, the regulation of the economy based on data from the World Competitiveness Report of IMD Lausanne. The goal must therefore be to reduce burdens for businesses arising from regulations and bureaucracy (Table 18.1).

The progression of this chapter is divided into five central steps:

1. First of all, the methods, the requirements made on them, and the actors found in the regulation market are presented briefly.
2. The cost and benefit effects coming into question are then systematized in a partially new schema.
3. On the basis of these, the trial steps to be used for determining the norm addressees and the cost–benefit effects are derived.
4. A usage-related assessment of the measuring methods available is then performed with the help of criteria-controlled questions.
5. Finally, ideas are presented for the implementation of measurements and Les-sons Learned. After the presentation, the creators / persons involved in the regulation process should be provided with directions, which will enable them to introduce the questions and trial steps that will lead to their goal and to use the appropriate methods, depending on the purpose of the analysis.

Table 18.1 Competitiveness in relation to regulatory framework, bureaucracy and regulation of the economy

Regulatory framework		Bureaucracy		Regulation of the economy	
Denmark	6.9	Denmark	6.1	Denmark	4
Ireland	5.7	Switzerland	4.8	Austria	8
Switzerland	5.6	Sweden	4.4	USA	11
Austria	5.6	Austria	4.2	Ireland	12
USA	5.5	Norway	4.1	Sweden	16
Norway	5.3	Ireland	4.1	Switzerland	17
Netherlands	4.8	Netherlands	3.8	Netherlands	19
Japan	4.6	USA	3.4	UK	20
Sweden	4.5	Japan	3.1	France	22
UK	4.1	France	2.8	Norway	27
Germany	3.9	UK	2.5	Germany	30
France	3.3	Germany	2.2	Japan	41
Legend:		Legend:		Legend:	
1 = impedes competitiveness of companies		1 = impedes commercial activities		Summary of 22 criteria for "Regulation of the economy". Ranking within a selection of 60 countries and regions.	
10 = promotes competitiveness of companies		10 = does not impede commercial activities			

Source: Fueglistaller, Schliesser, and Federer, 2007, p. 12, according to IMD World Competitiveness Online 2005 and IMD World Competitiveness Yearbook 2004, cited in Brunetti, A., Scheidegger, E., Grundlinien des Aktionsprogramms für vereinfachte Regulierung, in: Die Volkswirtschaft, 2/2006.

18.2 Methods, Requirements and Actors in the Regulation Market

18.2.1 Overview of RIA[1]

18.2.1.1 Introduction

Compliance costs and reduction policies have become one of the central themes of economic policy in Europe. Overall, the individual actors are now confronted with a wealth of options and methods for promoting this reduction.[2]

All in all, four basic or classic types of measuring methods (Regulatory Impact Assessments) are differentiated:

- Cost–benefit analysis
- Cost-effectiveness analysis

[1] For a more extensive description of the methods available see Chapter 4

[2] Cf. Empter, S., Frick, F., and Verhkamp, R. (Hrsg., 2005) with publication of the three expert reports triggering this discussion by Sturm, R. / Müller, M.; Jann, W. / Wegrich, K. / Veit, S. and Müller, C., as well as the conclusions of Ernst, T., Hellmann, T., Prager, J.

- Risk-(risk) analysis
- Cost analysis.

The primary goal of regulatory impact assessments (RIAs) is to make explicit the intended and unintended effects of law making for civilians and businesses. The RIA instruments enable politicians to achieve a better understanding of these types of effects in order to stimulate the probability of an optimal allocation of social capital. The implementation of RIAs is not a guarantee for lesser lawmaking than would be the case without the existence of RIA instrumentation. RIAs can improve the effectiveness and efficiencies of policies. In addition, lawmaking will have to foster economic growth and competition or restrict these as little as possible, taking accounts of the social boundary conditions of the achievement of the related public goals. As soon as the economic goals conflict with other policy goals, we will need some kind of mechanism to optimize the net social benefit of a law. RIAs can support such trade-offs. [Kip Viscusi, 1997: 175–208]

Most types of different RIAs include the public goal involved in their considerations. Cost/benefit analyses in particular include the public goal involved by comparing the benefits of the public goal of the law and the costs caused by the same law. The significance of the public goal to be achieved is an explicit part of cost/benefit analyses (Mishan, 1988). Related to cost-effectiveness analyses, the main point of the analysis is the cost/benefit ratio per achieved profit unit, e.g. the lower number of traffic victims. The main purpose is to select the most beneficial policy measure from a social perspective, by comparing a number of possible policy measures. The public goal as such is not questioned. Risk-(risk)-analyses are focusing on one aspect of the public goal involved only. This aspect is the risk of an unwanted happening, which should be kept as low as possible. Contrary to cost/benefit analyses and cost-effectiveness analyses, cost assessments are not part of the analyses. The central element of the analyses is the probability calculus of the expected success of the policy measure. The difference between risk-analyses and risk-risk-analyses is the number of risks involved in the assessment. Finally, cost assessments abstract from the benefits and focus on the costs of a specific policy measure. Such a one-sided approach will produce limited information, of course. Cost assessments allow for balancing the degree of allowance of a specific policy measure and the degree of stringency. The more complex and encompassing a policy measure is, the more the costs will increase. The basic assumption is that the costs will increase gradually with increasing complexity of a policy measure, but explosively from a certain point. Cost assessments can be helpful for finding out where the culmination point of the costs will appear with the highest probability. The cost-effectiveness analysis and the risk-analysis are not relevant for our context, viz. asking for more awareness for the costs of the norm addressees, the regulated businesses. The two types of RIAs remain the cost/benefit analysis and the cost assessment (Hopkins, 1997). The Dutch Standard Cost Model (SCM) is the most well known exponent of the compliance costs instrumentation

(Nijsen and Vellinga, 2002). Recently, the SCM has broadened its focus from compliance costs of information obligations (administrative burden) to compliance costs of substantive obligations (Nijsen et al., 2005a, b and 2006).

18.2.1.2 Alternatives

The influence on innovation and competitiveness can be determined by means of surveys of SME or experiments with businesses on their decision behavior, for example. This makes it possible to find out whether a regulation causes defined threshold values or catalysts, from which business decisions are influenced in the long term. However, little experience exists apart from surveys. The macro- and socioeconomic effects of compliance can, in turn, be calculated by means of economic simulation models, for example. If such measurements are to be used, resource can be made to initial Swedish experiences with the measurement of the overall costs of regulations for businesses [cf. the report by Hedström on a measurement project with six SME by the Swedish Chamber of Industry and Commerce (Hedström, 2007)]. The SME compatibility test of the Swiss Federation also falls into this category (cf. method under www.seco.admin.ch as well as the cited short reports on the tests). Interviews are conducted in 10–12 specifically selected SME, with the goal of determining primary and secondary cost effects (e.g. information obligations, costs for investment funds, influence on competitiveness) as well as impending problems during execution. Ten individual steps are required. The test is designed to provide information on how the state should act. However, it omits any fundamental systematic of cost and benefit effects, does not aim at any form of representativeness and only determines 'Mega trends'. Experiments/laboratory tests could be used to find out whether there are defined threshold values or catalysts in the framework of a regulation, from which a business decision is in principle made differently. The decision not to make an investment, relocation abroad or moving into illicit employment can be seen as examples here.

In relation to the method of Regulatory Impact Assessments, the Better Regulation Guide and Regulatory Impact Assessment come from Great Britain. From Switzerland comes the regulation density indicator, the regulatory impact assessment, the SME compatibility tests of the Federation and individual cantons as well as (new), the 128 methodically determined individual measures, which particularly apply to the 50 laws which most burden the economy. A new addition is the previously mentioned measuring instrument for substantive obligations.

18.2.1.3 Evaluation

The use of these RIA methods in practice shows that in many cases, it is sufficient to concentrate on the essential laws. The 20%–80% to 5%–95% rule regularly proves true, as in Brandenburg, Denmark, Great Britain and the Netherlands, because only a small number of laws are responsible for the majority of duties and compliance costs of information obligations. And these, in turn, only represent approximately 30% of the overall compliance costs according to British experiences – the other 70% are in many cases not yet measured at all. A further problem which must be resolved for the measurements consists in handling the degree of complexity of the regulations and their quantification. Thus, the Federal Statistical Office of Germany uses four criteria for classification into 'simple – average – complex': number of data requests, effort required for data determination, familiarity with the duty to furnish information, procedural method. These classifications can easily be incorporated into the calculations with the Standard Cost Models. Following this brief overview of the methods and important empirical findings, the requirements on the measuring methods and the actors involved will be examined in more detail.

18.2.2 Methodological Requirements

18.2.2.1 Use-Related Assessment

For use-related assessment of the methods, in addition to questions of application, procedure and the limits of the methods, for example, general requirements must also be fulfilled. These are explained below. The questions are dealt with in Annexure I. An appropriate method should be:

1. *Practicable*: A method must be usable without prolonged training or familiarization and must not admit any freedom of interpretation which will impede understanding of the results.
2. *Easily understandable*: For use of a method, only variables which are generally accepted and easily understandable should be used. In addition, it must be possible to obtain or calculate the figures easily, and the systematics of the method must be quickly understandable.
3. *Accepted by reference groups*: All reference groups involved in a method such as government/administration, economy/SME, politics, parties, public and media must be able to accept the method.
4. *SME and start-up reference*: A method must take account the characteristics of SME (approx. 99% of all companies), especially as far as dealing with regulations/administrative burdens is concerned. The fixed cost effect, according to which SMEs are disproportionately affected by administrative burdens because of their small number of staff, is important here. Entrepreneurs are also directly involved as a rule. Entrepreneurial freedom must be retained or increased, without having to set aside constitutional principles as a result. It is, therefore, not a matter of giving SME special treatment, but rather reducing the resulting costs and ensuring better planning ability in respect of regulations. It must also be ensured that regulations do not impede or prevent the foundation of (innovative) start-ups. An example of this is provided by the results of the World Bank on the time and effort required for the foundation of a GmbH company (Table 18.2).

Table 18.2 Time and effort (expenditure) for founding a company

Number of procedures (necessary interactions between companies and external authorities)		Number of days until all procedures are completed		Amount of costs for founding a company (in % of BSP per head)	
Sweden	3	USA	5	Denmark	0.0
Denmark	3	Denmark	5	USA	0.5
Norway	4	France	8	UK	0.7
Ireland	4	Netherlands	11	Sweden	0.7
USA	5	Norway	13	France	1.2
Switzerland	6	Sweden	16	Norway	2.7
UK	6	UK	18	Germany	4.7
Netherlands	7	Switzerland	20	Ireland	5.3
France	7	Ireland	24	Austria	5.7
Austria	9	Germany	24	Switzerland	8.7
Germany	9	Austria	29	Japan	10.7
Japan	11	Japan	31	Netherlands	13.0

Source: Fueglistaller, Schliesser, and Federer, 2007, p. 8, according to World Bank, Doing Business in 2006, www.doingbusiness.org and Federal Council, Vereinfachung des unternehmerischen Alltags, Bern, 2006, p. 22)

5. *Methodical base*: This can be assumed, if the method has already been proven in use in other countries. This particularly applies to the initial phase of measurements. In later phases, new methodical territory can also be entered. The respective method must be a fundamental system and permit general conclusions.
6. *Efficient use*: A method must keep the time and effort which it triggers as low as possible. This relates to its use in the government/administration or by external parties, the inclusion of SME and review by a neutral body.
7. *Selective*: Only the regulations/administrative burdens which will in all probability have a large influence on businesses must be recorded and addressed.
8. *Pragmatic*: Achieving 100% accuracy of the measurements should not be the goal. Rather, the solution must be oriented to an 80:20 solution, i.e. the aim should be a high but not perfect accuracy of the measurements. This will also make it possible to examine several regulation alternatives, in order to reach a solution relatively quickly.
9. *Verifiable and transparent*: It must be possible for the government/administration or specialized external parties to implement the method. In connection with these measurements, a simple verification must be performed by a neutral body, i.e. one that is independent of the measurement. Methodology and results must be made completely accessible to the public.
10. *Reliable and valid*: The requirements for scientific test procedures must be fulfilled. On the one hand, the application should come to the same result,

irrespective of the persons/institutions performing it, and on the other hand, the relevant values should also actually be measured.

11. *Integration into the regulation process*: The method must not be seen as a detached instrument, but must be integrated into the regulation process. It is closely linked to the political strategy and concrete policy of the government as well as the form of the institutions executing it. This applies to the procedure from initiation through enactment, execution through to review of the laws.
12. *Internationally adaptable and comparable*: It must be possible for a method to be adapted to conventional international methods, so that comparisons are also possible. This also allows the use of international experts, so that a transfer of expertise can take place.
13. *Easily enforceable*: The measurement of the effects of regulations can meet with resistance from interest groups. A method must therefore be easily enforceable and not trigger any political debate on principles. It is therefore important to, first of all, discuss facts and financial consequences for businesses and not to trigger a discussion of the political goals of government supporters or antagonists. This is the concern of parliament and government.
14. *No influence by special interest politics*: The method must be immune to interventions or infiltration by lobbyists, who could manipulate the purpose of the measurements. This can be assumed if the group of interviewees is too small, or if only those who will profit from or who oppose a regulation are included.
15. *Linking to OECD and the World Bank recommendations*: The requirements made on the methods must ultimately be consistent with the results of the current OECD World Bank evaluation of the successful Dutch model, mentioned at the outset. This has been categorized as the leading model in the world (World Bank Group 2007).

18.2.2.2 New Ventures and Regulations

With regard to the requirements on measuring methods, the special features of SME and start-ups have been highlighted.

These specificities can be further differentiated on the basis of the international comparison figures presented at the outset. The individual factors of the Global Entrepreneurship Monitor reports provide indications for differentiation into young and established businesses. These factors are also collected annually for over 40 countries. Of the 13 individual factors of the GEM reports, the following factors with regulation reference are particularly relevant for young businesses (GEM Report 2006):

- Protection of intellectual property
- Policy 2: Regulation and taxes
- Market Openness 2: Market entry barriers
- Market Openness 1: Market changes.

Legal protection for intellectual property, free enterprise, low-hindrance regulations and low market entry barriers are basic prerequisites for the development of founding companies. In relation to these three factors, the countries to the fore of the GEM ranking should be particularly highlighted as positive examples: USA, Singapore, United Arab Emirates, Iceland, Belgium, Finland and Australia. For established companies, it is more important to defend their market positions, to be able to erect high market entry barriers against newcomers and to impose high compliance costs on young companies by setting high regulation standards. An example of this is the pharmaceutical industry, because large companies with well-established processes and relationships with the concerned authorities particularly profit from the highly regulated production processes and the complex approval processes for new drugs (despite the burdens). The GEM Report therefore comes to the conclusion, in relation to industrial countries, that countries with better (poorer) structural conditions tend to present a higher (lower) founding quota (p.27).

A concrete example of the continuous reduction of impeding regulations for SME and start-ups is Switzerland.[3] Improving the structural conditions has been a subject of economic policy for ten years. Individual measures packages have been continually defined and implemented since 1998, the year of the first scientific studies by the Ministry of Economic Affairs. The 16 measures implemented up to 2005 cover the areas of quality and coherence of regulation and regulation processes, authorizations in international exchange and within the domestic market, as well as process coordination between federation and cantons. The 25 measures underway by 2007 are aimed at reducing the administrative burdens for businesses from different legal domains. The current 87 measures comprise five main topics from the areas of simplification of regulations/reduction of administrative burdens, as well as improvement of processes between state and businesses: E-simplification, authorization reduction, regulation simplification, assessment of regulation consequences (SME-test, SME-forum), SME coordination organ. The development of practical Internet portals for start-ups and SME at both Federation and canton level is also at the center of the endeavours. The SME Admin website should be mentioned in this regard. It enables company registration via the Internet in dialog with commercial registers and national insurance.

18.2.3 The Actors on the Market of Regulation

For a classification of the various participants in the regulation market, it is helpful to keep the five conceivable starting points for the measurement of

[3] See Fueglistaller, Schiesser, and Federer, 2007, p. 17, according to the Federal Council, 2006, p. 6

Table 18.3 Regulation processes

Actors, products, effects	Regulation Processes				
	Input	Policy making	Output	Impact	Outcome
Participants, products, norm addressees	Citizens, businesses, associations, interest groups, parties, legislative, executive	Involved institutions as well as process of legislative procedure	Regulation, laws, ordinances, administrative regulations affecting the norm addressees specified for regulation input	Intermediate goals, (foresighted) behavior of actors	Intended or unintended achievement of goals, social effect

regulations in mind in the background. These are geared towards the regulation processes Input, Policy Making, Output, Impact, and Outcome (Table 18.3).

In the present context, the political processes (decision tree with targeted use of methods), the regulation output (concrete regulation) and the regulation outcome (cost/benefit effects) play a particularly important role.

The starting point for any discussion on compliance costs e.g. administrative burdens is the cost–benefit effects of the regulation. The beneficiaries and the burdened parties cannot come from the same groups, therefore, depending on the standpoint, the benefit or cost argument is given special emphasis. The burdened company initially sees the costs arising for it, but not the benefits occurring on the side of the state or the consumers. On the other hand, the regulating government does not see the burdened company but, above all, the beneficiary group from which it hopes to subsequently obtain votes. It is, therefore, important to specify the norm addressee of a regulation, i.e. for which group/ actors the regulation is created and who will have to comply with and who must bear the associated costs.

It is also interesting to see that citizens can and do play two roles. A role as free citizen or constituent, and a role as subject (norm addressee). As free citizen, he can say, "I consider it important for businesses to set up their production processes to be as environmentally-friendly as possible." If parliament and the state set up corresponding regulations (with substantive obligations and information obligations for companies), there will undoubtedly be additional costs for companies. If these additional costs are then expressed in the prices of the products and services, the free citizen, in principle, can have the option of purchasing a comparable cheaper product from another production country, which does not have or which has fewer environmentally-friendly regulations. The question now arises as to what extent the roles of free citizen and subject can be politically separated? In the result, it appears that free citizens can present their political preferences free of charge, without paying a price for this as consumers. This brief debate shows how important it is to always consider who the norm addressees of a regulation are, and what effects this regulation has for these norm addressees.

A differentiation according to norm addressees or cost units is therefore necessary. This is understood to include all institutions or groups on whom a regulation has measurable financial effects. It is thus understood to include all institutions or persons at whom a regulation is quintessentially aimed or who are affected by it and who must bear its financial effects, which in turn can be measured by means of the labor costs required, the time expenditure, the investment costs and the frequency. The norm addressees can be commercial organizational units (businesses according to the industrial sector classification of the European Union or UN) non-profit organizations, citizens and administrative units. The businesses must generally be differentiated into large companies and small and medium-sized enterprises (SME), due to the fixed cost effect. It must also be emphasized that cost and benefit effects can also arise for other organizations than those actually addressed. Collateral effects (collateral damages and collateral benefits) then occur.

The result of these considerations is that the norm addressees of a regulation must, first of all, be precisely identified, before the cost and benefit effects can be determined and allocated in detail. The norm addressees are then the starting point for the cost and benefit measurements during the subsequent procedure. The norm addresses are thus made the focus of the analysis, which was too seldom the case previously, because the process was usually seen from the perspective of the regulation or the regulator and consequently, the body of laws as an end in itself. The following questions must now be asked and answered adequately:

- Who is the norm addressee of the regulation, i.e. at which norm addressees is the regulation actually aimed, who has to comply with the rule?
- Which norm addressees are affected by the actual compliance costs of the regulation?
- Which norm addressees are affected by the actual benefits of the regulation?
- Which interests do the norm addressees pursue?
- Do collateral benefits or damages also result for businesses/citizens other than the norm addressees?

After this short discussion of the available methods as well as the actors and norm addressees of the regulation, the conceivable cost and benefit effects will be analyzed in more detail in the next section.

18.3 Systematizing Costs–Benefits Effects

18.3.1 Introduction

There are already a large number of proposals in literature with regard to systematizing the arising cost and benefit effects of regulations, although these generally only discuss the cost side and, to some extent, differ from each other. A standard systematization for cost and benefit effects will therefore be proposed at this point. A differentiation is made between primary (direct) and secondary (indirect) business effects of regulations. The direct cost effects can be differentiated into regulation costs (substantive obligations) and information costs (administrative burden). The direct financial costs, the costs of information transfer to third parties – both of which are to some extent omitted in international literature or are assigned to information costs,[4] – and the costs in the production or service process are categorized as compliance costs. The secondary cost effects include both categories of influence on competition (including unintended collateral damages) and the economic effects. The following figure illustrates this classification, before the provision of more detailed information:

18.3.2 Cost Effects

Figure 18.1 shows the most important types of cost effects of the regulation of businesses. The main categories are:

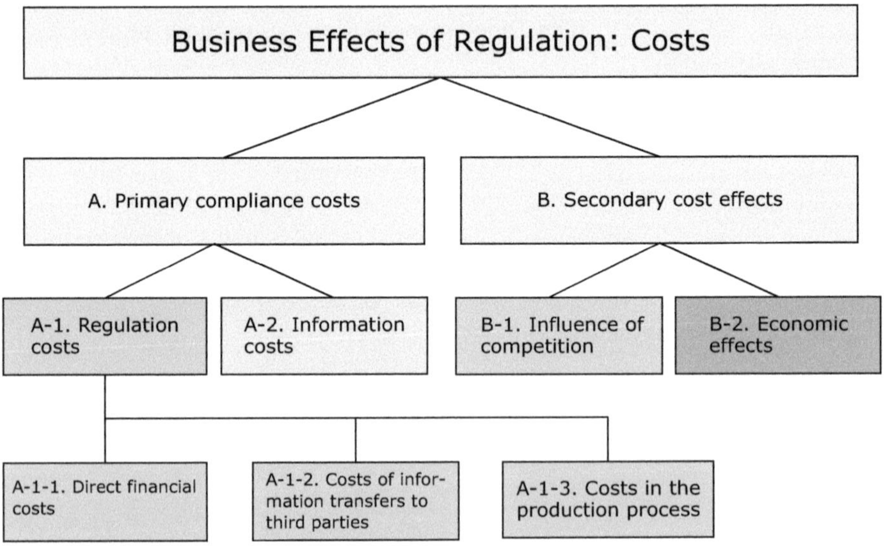

Fig. 18.1 Business effects of regulation: Costs

[4] Recently Dutch Government decided to categorize third party disclosure being substantive obligations and the compliance costs of it as substantive costs and no longer as administrative burdens.

A. Primary compliance costs, and
B. Secondary cost effects.

A: Primary compliance cost effects, which can be determined at the level of the norm addressee only, here an individual company:

- A-1: Regulation costs or substantive obligation costs which result in a coordination of behavior or a distribution of resources. The regulator uses these to achieve his intended political goals; therefore, any discussion of them cannot be neutral. For this reason, measurement is also disproportionately more difficult than for the information cost effects following under B.
  - A-1-1: Direct financial cost effects: Direct tax payments and state-administered duties.
  - A-1-2: Costs of information transfer to third parties such as customers, patients etc., which also result in a coordination of behavior, such as the package insert for drugs. Public or private parties who are commissioned by the authorities with monitoring the behavior of norm addressees – e.g. tax advisers, certification bodies, TÜV – are not considered third parties. These are assigned to the authorities in this context.
  - A-1-3: Costs in the production and service process, such as e.g. the required installation of a particle filter.
- A-2: Information cost effects or costs of information obligations which, from the regulator's viewpoint, fulfill a decision function for political and administrative actors, as well as a control function. In practice, this means the provision of information by businesses for the state, so that it can act or control. It should be noted that, in addition to the state, private organizations such as associations or organizations used/legitimized by the state, such as chambers of industry and commerce, impose information obligations on businesses. Sometimes, a reduction in information obligations by the state is immediately replaced on the private side, as in the case of the abolishment of certain statistical obligations by the Baden-Württemberg state and their immediate reintroduction by trade associations. These information costs result from compliance with the legal duties to furnish information – so-called administrative burden, such as the time for procuring, reading, understanding, complying with and examining regulation texts on particle filters; the costs are normally divided between internal (employees) and external (consultants); new processes may also need to be introduced/defined.

B: *Secondary cost effects*, which can be determined for businesses as norm addressees but also for businesses in general:

- B-1: Influence of competition & innovation: Financially ascertainable effect of the regulation on quotation prices and the resulting consequences for the competitive situation and for the future innovation potential. If . a business in one country is burdened with a regulation that is only nationally applicable, but its foreign competitors are not, then its competitive situation will deteriorate, simply on account of this regulation. The problem with regard to measurement is the hypothetical determination of change in a static model versus the actual dynamic change and reaction of customers and competitors in reality. Therefore, it is useful to develop a questionnaire with the main possible effects, which can be derived from the regulation content. During face to face – interviews, these effects have to be checked and the amount of investment or the amount of competition disadvantage towards competitors without regulation has to be evaluated.

- B-2: Economic effects: These include the aggregated effects of a regulation at the level of the economy, which can be measured with the help of economic indicators. These also include, in a broad sense, the so-called irritation costs, where the sum of regulations results in irritation amongst entrepreneurs, and then economically significant effects due to the shifting of production on account of employment law or production technology; 'over-regulation' from the entrepreneur's viewpoint. In this way, costs which are initially entrepreneurial become economic costs. Irritation costs are, in general, the effect of regulations hindering the entrepreneur at the highest degree in his activities. Therefore, in face to face interviews, entrepreneurs could be asked about specific regulations which are responsible for irritations. Comparing all answers of a sample of entrepreneurs, it should be possible to select, in a pragmatic way, the most irritating regulations.
- B-2a: There are two special kinds of economic effects. First, the opportunity costs resulting from delays. Usually, companies wish to execute their investment or constructing decisions without delays. Therefore, it is an important factor of service quality to enable the government to take quick, consistent and reliable decisions. Otherwise, the results are opportunity costs since the companies have to wait and cannot proceed with productive activities and the production of goods and services. A useful method for measuring these costs is the French 'Net Present Value' – method with the comparison of a project situation with and without delay.[5] Second, the quality of service and the enforcement practices performed by the administration. This leads to enforcement costs which are the result of low or high quality of enforcement routines in relation to best practice solutions. There are two possibilities to measure these enforcement costs: First with a questionnaire and face to face interviews with companies and government about the costs and proposals for improvements; second, with a test of enforcement of a standard procedure according to the regulation.

18.3.3 Benefit Effects

The current discussion is primarily and also, in detail, aimed at the arising cost effects. The benefit effects of regulations are, on the other hand, considered in

[5] See DGME – Mesures et réduction des charges administratives, 2007

more general terms, and not closely linked to the cost effects. For this reason, a communication gap also results between those persons who place special emphasis on the cost effects and those who place special emphasis on the benefit effects. This problem will be countered with a structured analysis of the benefit effects. In the case of the arising benefit effects, a differentiation can likewise be made between primary and secondary benefit effects. In the following systematization, the argumentation is from the perspective of the norm addressees.

A: *Primary compliance benefit effects*: These produce a directly measurable benefit for the norm addressee. This includes:

- A-1 Direct regulation benefit effects:
  - A-1-1: Direct payments, such as transfers paid by public bodies, which produce benefit effects for the norm addressees. Subsidy payments can be cited here as an example. These benefit effects, which appear as a cost item from the state's perspective, can be directly recorded without problem.
- A-2: Compliance benefit effects:
  - A-2-1: Targeted benefit: The targeted benefit is the benefit which was actually intended with the regulation. This is the case, for example, with a business that is able to reduce non-productive time due to illness, because the business complies with regulations in the area of occupational health and safety. In this case, there is both a cost and a benefit effect for one and the same norm addressee.

B: *Secondary benefit effects*, which result in benefit effects for businesses not being the norm addressees:

- B-1: Producer and investment benefits. Producer benefits include the turnover/revenue that a business obtains with a product/service, which are triggered by a regulation and result in a corresponding producer benefit effect. For example, a manufacturer of particle filters will achieve a correspondingly quantifiable benefit effect as a result of a defined, precisely specified regulation, which leads to the installation of this particle filter by other companies. This can also constitute a type of hidden subsidy. Investment benefits arise for businesses that are commissioned with execution of the norm addressees' investment decisions, e.g. the creation of new machines, products etc..
- B-2: Provider benefit effects arise for businesses/persons who perform work directly for another business, the norm addressee, in order to fulfill its information obligations or substantive obligations, and who would not be called in without these legal obligations. Examples of these are staff who are only employed to fulfill administrative costs; consultants such as tax consultants or engineers, who must be brought in for the interpretation and fulfilment of the regulation, federal employees, who would have no further function without regulation tasks. These benefit effects can be viewed in the sense of a collateral benefit for these example groups, as the regulation is not directly addressed to them, but they nevertheless profit from it. On the other

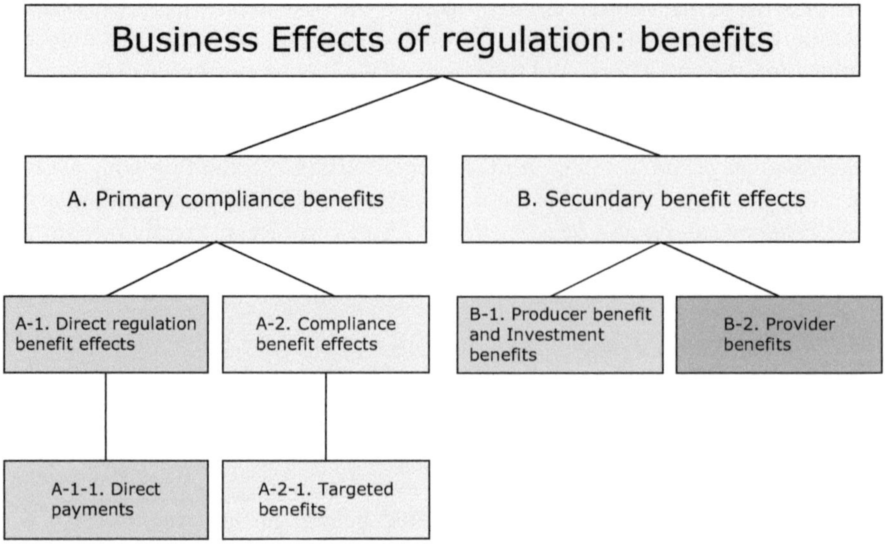

Fig. 18.2 Business effects of regulation: benefits

hand, the businesses that must employ these example groups must bear the aforementioned cost effects. Good, on the one hand, and bad on the other.

Figure 18.2 summarizes these compliance benefit effects.

18.4 Trials to Search for Norm Addressees and Cost–Benefit Effects

18.4.1 Introduction

To enable systematic recording of the specified cost and benefit effects, the execution of defined trial steps is recommended for ex ante or ex-post assessment of the regulation consequences. The classic starting point of such a decision tree is a cost–benefit consideration at social level ('top down'). The background of such a consideration consists in the fact that discussions on deregulation are quickly elevated to this level by its opponents, in order to show its inalienability. For example, an official in a German ministry has said that laws are made for equity, the environment, specific sections of the population, and not to save businesses costs. This makes it apparent that in professions other than commercial professions, no thinking in terms of cost categories or in respect of the secondary effects of regulations appears to take place. These arguments can only be taken up and discussed if the benefit dimension is incorporated in a tangibly accessible manner. However, this has, as a rule, previously taken place in general terms on an aggregated level, making the discussion virtually uncontestable and universally accepted. Thus, topics such as labor market regulations and consumer protection are systematically withdrawn from any critical discussion in Germany, because they are seen and defended as purely positive and worthy of protection by those responsible (labor market politicians, bargaining parties and consumer protection agencies).

Nevertheless, a pure discussion of only the information obligation costs/administrative costs has the considerable – proven – advantage that, once detached from political wishful thinking, the cost effects of regulations for the norm addressees can be concretely identified. This has repeatedly emerged as a sweeping argument for such a procedure in Dutch and German discussions. However, the benefit side of a regulation remains hidden, and will therefore be taken up here.

18.4.2 Changing the Procedure

It is therefore proposed to change the procedure of these cost–benefit considerations. In the developed systematic the cost–benefit consideration is applied 'bottom-up', i.e. from the viewpoint of the individual norm addressee. In the same way that some of the cost effects can be concretely measured with the help of the Standard Cost Model, the benefit effects can also be concretely recorded. Thus the norm addressee, in this case, the individual business, is the starting point of the cost–benefit measurement. In aggregate terms, this consequently also results in a cost–benefit measurement on a social level. The argumentation for this is as follows. If the measured cost effects (substantive compliance costs or administrative burden) are higher than the benefit effects for the norm addressee, the regulation should not be further pursued, unless there are high benefit effects on a social level. This procedure takes a new approach to dealing pragmatically yet to some extent precisely with the specified problems. It allows a methodical answer to be given to a political problem, which should lead to a rational and objectively traceable decision. The rationale is a profit-profit aim: low compliance costs will lead to a higher degree of compliance and consequently to a better achievement of the public goals. The compliance of norm addressees is the best guarantee for achieving public goals. Without compliance, no realistic public goal!!

All in all, four variants/outcomes of this cost–benefit trial are thus conceivable:

- Variant a: The cost effects for the norm addressee are higher than the benefit effects for the norm addressee and there are no higher benefit effects on a social level: The regulation should not be further pursued.
- Variant b: As Variant a, but there are high benefit effects (collateral benefits) on a social level; a more detailed examination must then be carried out, in order to keep the arising compliance cost effects as low as possible.
- Variant c: The benefit effects for the norm addressee are higher than the cost effects for the norm addressee; a more detailed examination of the cost effects must then be carried out in order to keep the arising compliance cost effects as low as possible.

- Variant d: As Variant c, but there are high cost effects (collateral damages) on a social level; the regulation should be abandoned in this form.

18.4.3 The Six Trial Steps: Usage-Related Assessment

Within the framework of this trial, following the presentation of the conceivable variants of the trial outcome, individual trial steps with corresponding questions must be answered. It is restrictively assumed that these refer only to new laws and ordinances with companies as norm addressees:[6]

- *Trial question 1*: Which businesses are norm addressees of the regulation? Which businesses are the norm addressees, who must ultimately comply with the regulation?
  - To which branches do the affected businesses belong, are these all branches, or just a precisely definable section?
  - How many businesses are actually affected?
  - What is the distribution based on the size of the affected businesses: what is the proportion of SME to large companies?
- *Trial question 2a*: Which type of direct obligation (primary effects) must the norm addressee of the regulation comply with?
  - Direct financial payments and/or
  - Transfer of information to third parties, modifications in the production process and/or
  - Duties to furnish the authority with information?
- *Trial question 2b*: Which type of indirect effects (secondary effects) on competition and economic effects can be identified?
  - Competitive effects
  - Economic effects
- *Trial question 3*: Which primary and secondary cost effects result for the norm addressees and how high are they? How high are the costs arising for the identified norm addressees? It is important to note that only a rough cost estimate (Quick Scan) can occur at this point.
  - Cost effect of the compliance costs with the three subdivisions?
  - Estimated amount of these costs (compliance costs)?.
  - Cost effect of the costs of information obligations?
  - Estimated amount of these costs (administrative burdens)?
  - Cost effect in relation to the competitive position?
  - Estimated amount of these costs?
  - Cost effect on economic level?
  - Estimated amount of these costs?

[6] Naturally similar questions can also be put if the norm addressees are state or citizens.

This trial is thus based on the identified cost effects. In the next step, the analysis on the individual business level will be followed by an analysis in relation to the determined economic costs. Possible answers are:

- The total costs are low, e.g. less than 3% of the added value, consequently a green light can be given and the regulation can be further pursued.
- The total costs are high, e.g. more than 3% of the added value: The result is, on the one hand, a detailed cost measurement and, on the other, a brief to seek reduction and optimization possibilities as well as conceivable alternatives.

- *Trial question 4*: Which primary and secondary benefits can be determined and at which level?
  - Which type of benefit effects for the norm addressees: Primary benefit effects: Direct payments? Compliance benefits: Targeted benefits? Secondary benefit effects: Producer benefits or Provider benefits?
  - How great are the individual benefit effects arising for the norm addressee(s)?
  - Which other benefit effects occur for non-norm addressees and/or the environment in general?
  - How great are the other benefit effects per non-norm addressee?
- *Trial question 5*: Are the costs passed on? On the basis of the cost analysis performed above, it must be ascertained to what extent a passing-on of the costs, for example to consumers, is likely, and at which level this passing on will take place. It is therefore necessary to ascertain:
  - Are costs passed on to consumers – and to what extent?
  - Are costs transferred abroad?
- *Trial question 6*: What is the result of comparing the cost and benefit effects determined above?

  For the actual norm addressees:

  - If the benefit effects are greater than the cost effects: The regulation can be further pursued, but the efficiency of the regulation must be taken into account, i.e. the information costs, for example, should be as low as possible.
  - If the cost effects are greater than the benefit effects, the regulation should not be further pursued, unless there is a substantial benefit effect on the social level, which cancels out this disproportion at norm addressee level. Of course, at the same time, taking account of the efficiency of the regulation: compliance should be at the lowest possible level.

  The following applies accordingly for the social level:

  - If the costs for the norm addressees are greater than the social benefit, then the regulation should not be further pursued.
  - If the costs for the norm addressees are less than the social benefit, then the regulation should be further pursued, at the same time taking account of the efficiency of the regulation.

With these trial steps, an improved transparency can be introduced to the entire process, based on initial rough estimates, at the same time taking recourse to the cost and benefit effect system.

18.5 Context-Related Implementation of Instruments

18.5.1 Leading Questions for Implementation

The purpose of linking the previous considerations with the methods coming into question and their specific strengths and weaknesses is to create a reliable and objective basis for decision-making for political principals. The goal is to assign the right method to the respective question (Benefit effects of a regulation, Cost effects of a regulation, or Alternatives of a regulation?).

The measuring methods used can be classified with the help of the following newly developed central questions:

1. What is to be measured? Which cost or benefit effects?
2. How does the measurement occur? Which process must be adhered to?
3. Who bears responsibility for the measurement and who performs it?
4. Which method is suitable for which situation in the decision tree sequence?
5. Which prerequisites must be in place for use of the method?
6. Which purpose is pursued with the measurement? Should existing regulations be measured ex post or new regulations be measured ex ante?
7. What are the limits of the individual methods?
8. How can the methods be linked together? What is their logical sequence?

The following brief overview assumes that the method types are already known in detail. Therefore, only a recapitulative brief description based on the central features will be provided at this point (Table 18.4).[7]

Table 18.4 Overview of methods

Measuring method	Focus on effects for norm addressee	Focus on effects for society
SCM modules – compliance costs and ex ante appraisal	x	
SCM modules – information costs and ex ante appraisal	x	
Surveys	x	x
Observation, laboratory, experiments		x
Business Impact Analysis	x	
Economic simulation models		x
Cost–benefit analysis		x

[7] See also Kip Viscusi, 1997.

18.5.2 Categorization of the Instruments to Costs and Benefits Effects

The result of this analysis is the following allocation of the measuring methods to the cost and benefit effects (Table 18.5):

It thus appears that the individual effects can be most expediently recorded with a special measuring instrument. Fundamental importance is attached to the right method in the decision tree sequence for appropriate application of the available methods. The allocation appears as follows: Direct financial effects can be determined without special methods, as the amounts or percentages are concretely specified in law by a defined basic principle. The compliance costs can be ascertained with the new EIM instrument, SIROCCO, a module of the Standard Cost Model, for precise determination of these cost effects See Chapter 5, Section 3. The information costs in turn, which are the focus of the current measurements, can be best determined with the Standard Cost

Table 18.5 Allocation of the measuring methods to the cost and benefit categories in the framework of the legislation processes for new laws (or adaptation of existing laws)

Measuring method	Primary effects			Secondary effects	
	Direct financial effects	Compliance costs and benefits	Information costs	Influence of competition, also: felt business decisions	Economic effects (costs and benefits)
No special method; directly measurable	x				
SCM modules – compliance costs		x			
SCM modules – information costs, ex ante appraisal			x		
Surveys		x	x	x	
Observation, laboratory, experiments				x	
Business Impact Analysis		x	x	x	x
Economic simulation models					x
Cost–benefit analysis	X	x	x	x	x

Model, its ex ante variants or one of the regulatory impact assessments. The influence of competition and felt business decisions can be measured with observations and laboratory experiments, although there is little experience with these at present. The values for felt business decisions are then added to the economic effects, but must be methodically determined in this way. The economic effects can be determined with economic simulation models, on the one hand, and on the other hand with a cost–benefit analysis. The Business Impact Analysis and the cost–benefit analysis can be used as recapitulative methods. However, these require knowledge of the other methods.

Benefit measurement is, from a methodological viewpoint, only in its infancy. Direct payments can be directly recorded without using a specific method. However, the targeted benefit requires a more detailed discussion with the norm addressee, with whom interviews must be conducted, comparably to the SCM measurements. This special measurement then becomes part of the cost/benefit analysis, as the exact benefit effect occurring for the norm addressee – which is also the (joint) aim of the regulation – occurs here. Finally, the provider benefit must be ascertained by means of an analysis of the regulation text and also discussion with the norm addressee. Only in this way is it possible to ascertain whether an external body (for certification etc.) must be called in, or whether a typical company requires a consultant, for example, in order to fulfill the regulation. Corresponding benefit is then created for the supporting service providers. The producer benefit can likewise be measured by means of the costs and frequency of the products to be used. However, further methodological development work still needs to be carried out for the benefit measurement. See Fig. 18.3 for an overview of the instruments.

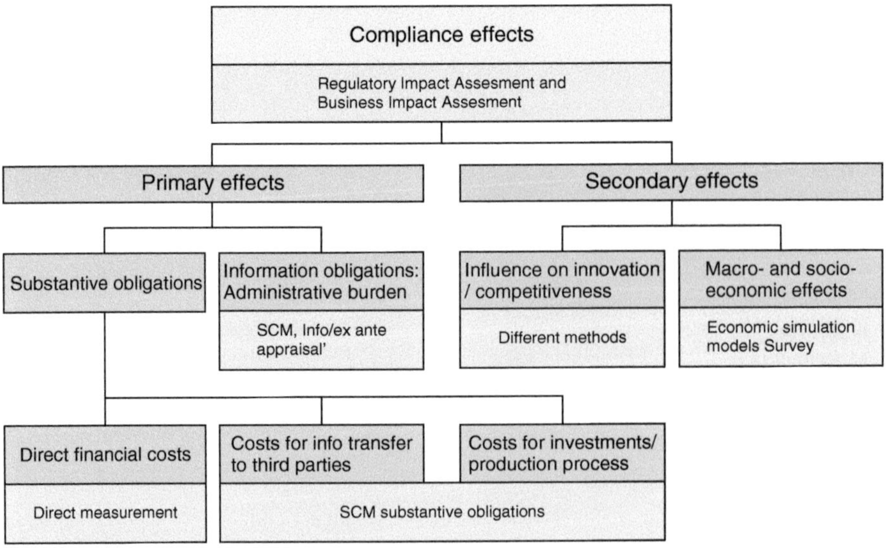

Fig. 18.3 Overview of instruments

18.5.3 Lessons Learned: Re-design of the Instruments

The current discussion on the introduction of a method to measure compliance costs highlights a number of points that must be taken into account during implementation. In addition, problems in comprehension can still be identified, which can be partly attributed to the fact that some models/proposals have been derived on a theoretical foundation, but others have been born more from practical use. The following 'Lessons Learnt' can therefore be derived for further implementation of the measurements:

1. The political and methodological concerns put forward by political and administrative representatives equate to a constant flow. New representatives repeatedly put the same questions in modified form, and these always produce new rounds of answers. For this reason, a transparent and systematic procedure is helpful.
2. An emerging interest can be observed amongst consulting firms, who see a promising future market segment in the 'Public Advisory' market. However, in many cases, the consultants have not developed their own methods, and to some extent, use the methods available on the market for quick training of their own staff. This sometimes causes considerable problems – as shown by international experiences – with regard to understanding and use of the methods. As a result, entire projects head off in the wrong direction and lead to tenuous results.
3. It can thus be stated that the behavior of market participants (can) leads to discrediting of the market for compliance costs and reduction policies, as the central topics take a back seat as regards content; and coalitions (can) form, whose own interests are opposed by this reduction. Such resistance comes particularly from the functional departments. The above-indicated, structured procedure with its systematized cost and benefit effects, trial steps and decision tree, also offers a neutral basis for making decisions for this reason. Further success factors for a long-term implementation of the initiatives of compliance costs and reduction policies can be found in the following points.
4. The skeptics/critics/opponents of such a reduction must be involved as early as possible. The arguments put forward should be subjected to an objective cost–benefit analysis in order to neutralize any ideological and purely politically motivated positions. One of the central problems in the reduction of compliance costs is the lack of transparency of the costs, processes and group-specific positions. A corresponding publicity must be generated in order to trigger pressure to act.
5. We must then ask: Who is against/can be against transparency of regulations? The following can be cited:
   - Politicians (with a special area of expertise), because they want to achieve their group-specific and campaign-strategical goals or because they do not have the strength for an opinion of their own.

- Officials/government employees, because the existence/purpose of their job is associated with the regulation.
- Experts/consultants, because they can advise businesses in matters concerning the regulation for a fee.
- Businesses or institutions profiting from the regulations (e.g. also professional persons (legal practitioners, chartered accountants, tax consultants, pharmacists), trades people or chambers of industry and commerce, who all profit from existing regulations in their markets and resist de-regulations and de-bureaucratization).
- Social groups, which benefit from the regulations affecting them.

6. The combination of social groups, politicians with a special area of expertise and competent authorities are described by Jann as 'iron triangles' or 'political networks'.[8] The corresponding theories of positive regulation should be indicated at this point, without discussing them in more detail. Important key-words in this regard are: consideration of the positions and power of interest groups in cost reduction; consideration of their level of organization and degree of mobility and therefore the potential for resistance of the interest groups; consideration of the possibilities for consistent and sustained communication of group-specific argumentation.The implementation of the measurement requires a clear management structure, a corresponding political will, tight project management and resource planning and an ambitious schedule. This is supported by the British experiences.[9] These also prove that sufficient time must be allowed for preparation of the measurement, a prioritization must occur (as is also the aim of the German Federal Statistical Office), a clear implementation plan must be present, the involvement of the functional department must be planned and the figures which it provides must be checked. The British functional departments discovered approximately 3,000 information obligations during their measurement, while the PWC consultants found approximately 21,000.

18.6 Summary and Conclusions

Measuring compliance costs of businesses e.g. administrative burden is hot stuff, from scientific view point as well from policy praxis. Also, the number of persons involved has increased considerably from a small inner circle of scientist and ministerial experts to rather big numbers of politicians, public

[8] Cf. also Jann (2006) and in his appraisal in Empter, S. et al. (Hrsg., 2005).

[9] Cf. Hill, K. (2006) The SCM in Great Britain, presentation by the Bertelsmann Foundation, 27.06.06, Berlin; these experiences were confirmed by Fischer T. (2006): The SCM Scan Brandenburg, ebenda presentation. It also appears that in Germany, less than 5% of national regulations concern the economy, and 95% can be ascribed to the Federation or the EU.

officers and private consultants, specialized in public advisory. Almost by consequence, the debate about concepts, definitions and methodology starts again, every time new participants are joining the debate.

In the debates, there are mostly two key questions:

- Are there arguments to introduce the public goals of regulations in the measurements or could the measurement be restricted to the costs of the regulated parties (businesses, citizens etc.) only?
- Which methodology is most appropriate to measure benefits and costs of regulations?

This chapter tries to bring more transparency in order to stimulate a more impartial discussion about the topic deregulation and its consequences. Important elements of this transparency are an adequate categorization of the separate cost and benefit effects, a systematic evaluation of these cost and benefit effects, and finally, an evaluation of the available techniques/methodologies. Such transparency could be guidance for all who are involved in the law making process and the measurement of compliance effects.

From the scope of deregulation, there are many methodologies to measure the cost of regulation. The international Standard Cost Model (SCM), which originates from the Dutch Mistral® Methodology and has its focus on administrative burden (costs of information transfers), is one of them. Besides, there are, among others, the well-known Regulatory Impact Assessment (RIA) from UK, and the 'Regulierungsdichte-Indikator' from Switzerland. More recently, a new module of the SCM was developed in the Netherlands with a focus on the cost of compliance with content obligations (e.g. the cost of investments to comply with legal obligations to adapt production process, products and services). One of the lessons learned is that, only a relatively small number of laws determines the majority of compliance costs for e.g. businesses and citizens. A second lesson is that the complexity of laws is one of the main features to reckon with, while measuring compliance effects.

Another relevant aspect is the variety of actors in the market of regulation, e.g. citizens, politicians, public servants, businesses. All these actors have different view points, depending on their different positions in the law making process: input, policy-making, output, impact and outcome. In the context of this chapter, the focus is on the political process of law making, the output of this process (the specific law) and the outcome of this law (cost and benefits for the society). The starting point of most discussions about compliance costs is the cost–benefits effects of the law. The problem is that costs and benefits mostly are not located with the same actors and in the same time period. Mostly, compliance costs are located with the actor who has to comply with the law, e.g. the regulated businesses, while the benefits are more at a generic level of the society as a whole. The basic idea of this chapter is that the regulated business should be the starting point of the measurement of compliance effects (bottom-up) and not the society as a whole (top-down). The ultimate goal of such an approach should not be to stop regulation anyhow, but to improve the quality of regulation in order to raise the level of compliance with the ultimate end, to achieve the intended public goal of the specific regulation. Of course, bad regulation – in the sense of low quality regulation – should not be continued.

In order to balance cost and benefits of law compliance for the regulated businesses, it is important to develop a conceptual system to arrange these different types of effects in a comparable way. One of the main features is the well-known distinction of primary and secondary effects (cost and benefits). Both primary and secondary effects can be subdivided into different relevant categories in order to understand what is really happening when regulated businesses have to comply with certain laws.

Such type of analysis should be implemented especially in case there is a new law to regulate businesses. Four different variants could result from such an analysis:

- Variant a: The compliance costs of the new regulation are higher for the regulated businesses than the compliance benefits for the same regulated businesses and, at the level of the society as a whole, there are no major benefits. This type of regulation should not be continued.
- Variant b: The same as variant a, but for the society as a whole there are major benefits (collateral benefits). In this case, regulation should be reconsidered again in order to check for unnecessary imbalances in compliance costs for the regulated businesses.
- Variant c: The compliance benefits of the new regulation are higher for the regulated businesses than the compliance costs for the same regulated businesses. In this case, the regulation should be checked for unnecessary costs for the regulated businesses in order to raise the quality of regulation and the level of compliance.
- Variant d: The same as variant c, but for the society as a whole there are major costs (collateral costs). In this case, the regulation should not be continued.

A major question is, which type of already existing methodologies (measurements) fits, reckoning with the different phases of the policy making process? The following methodologies are discussed briefly: Cost–benefit analysis, cost-effectiveness analysis, cost impact analysis (information obligations and content obligations), laboratory experiments and macroeconomic models. It appears that different effects (primary and secondary effects etc.) need different methodologies and should be applied in a proper sequence in order to optimize the quality of regulation and the realization of the public goals in question.

The chapter finishes with "lessons learned":

1. The political and methodological objections against regulatory impact assessments from the side of politicians and public officers look overwhelming and never ending. Transparency about the different methodologies might help to overcome this.

2. The market of policy advising seems booming and, by consequence, the number of commercial policy advisers. In many cases, policy advisers only implement already existing methodologies, without a full understanding of these methodologies and without developing new methodologies themselves. This could lead to questionable results and some risk of damage regarding the value of these methodologies.
3. By consequence, there is a risk of resistance within specialized departments of public administration against deregulation and the connected methodologies.
4. One of the core problems with deregulation is the lack of transparency about the costs of regulation, the regulation process and the different political position of the stakeholders. More transparency might stimulate the process of better law making.
5. The opposition against more transparency could arise from all parties which earn their money with keeping up a system of too complex regulations, viz. politicians, public servants, advisors, professionals like lawyers, accountants, fiscal experts, chambers of commerce and industry, etc.
6. To implement an efficient and effective system of regulatory impact assessments, one needs a strong political will at the highest possible level (prime minister), an excellent project management, the availability of financial resources and an ambitious time schedule.

References

Bertelsmann Foundation (2006): Das Standard – Kosten – Modell, Gütersloh

Bertelsmann Foundation, Kay, R. (2006): Draft: Handbuch zur Messung von Bürokratiekosten – Die Anwendung des Standard-Kosten-Modells in Deutschland, Gütersloh

DGME – Mesures et réduction des charges administratives, 2007

Empter, S., Frick, F., and Vehrkamp, R. (Hrsg., 2005): Auf dem Weg zu moderner Regulierung – eine kritische Bestandsaufnahme, Gütersloh

Fischer, T. (2006): The SCM Scan Brandenburg, presentation by the Bertelsmann Foundation, 27.06.06, Berlin

Fueglistaller, U., Schliesser, J., and Federer, S. with BDO VISURA (2007): Administrative Belastung von Kleinunternehmen – Analyze, Herausforderungen und Chancen, Solothurn

GEM Report (2006): Authors: Sternberg, R., Brixy, U., and Hundt, C., Global Entrepreneurship Monitor – Unternehmensgründungen im weltweiten Vergleich, Länderbericht Deutschland 2006, Hannover / Nürnberg, März 2007

Hedström, J. (2007): Cutting red tape for business, Stockholm, Rotterdam

Hill, K. (2006): The SCM in Great Britain, presentation by the Bertelsmann Foundation, 27.06.06, Berlin

Hopkins, T. D. (1997): Developing general indicators of regulatory costs, in: Regulatory Impact Analysis, Best Practices in OECD countries, OECD/PUMA, Paris

Jann, W. (2006): Die Deutschen können schlecht mit Unsicherheit umgehen, in: F.A.Z., 29.05.2006, no. 123, p. 15

Kip Viscusi, W. (1997): Improving the analytical basis for regulatory decision-making, in: Regulatory Impact Analysis, Best Practices in OECD countries, OECD/PUMA, Paris

Kip Viscusi, W. (1997): Improving the analytical basis for regulatory decision-making, in: Regulatory Impact Analysis, Best Practices in OECD countries, OECD/PUMA, Paris
Merk, R. (Hrsg., 2005): Bürokratieabbau und Bürokratiekostenmessung in der Bundesrepublik Deutschland – Strategien und Modelle unter besonderer Berücksichtigung ausländischer Erfahrungen, Bielefeld
Ministry of Finance Legislative Burden Department the Netherlands (2004): The Standard Cost Model – A framework for defining and quantifying administra-tive burdens for businesses
Mishan, E.J. (1998): Cost–Benefit Analysis (fourth edition), Unwin Hyman, London
Nijsen, A.F.M. and N. Vellinga (2002): Mistral®, A Model to Measure the Administrative Burden of Businesses, Research Report H200110, EIM, Zoeter-meer
Nijsen, A.F.M., van der Hauw, P.A., and Regter, G. (2005a): Kosten van inhoudelijke verplichtingen voor het bedrijfsleven; Definitie en ontwikkeling meetmethode, Zoetermeer
Nijsen, A.F.M., van der Hauw, P.A., and Regter, G. (2005b): Handleiding meetinstrument, inhoudelijke nalevingskosten bedrijfsleven' – Stappen, vragenlijst en toelichting, Zoetermeer
Nijsen, A.F.M. and Regter, G. (2006): Nalevingskosten Geldtransactiekantoren; Onderzoek Wet inzake de Geldtransactiekantoren, Zoetermeer
SCM Network (2006 Internet): International Standard Cost Model Manual – Measuring and reducing administrative burdens for businesses
World Bank Group (2007): Review of the Dutch Administrative Burden Reduction Program

Annex I Questions referring methodological requirements

	Compliance costs – SCM content	Administrative / information costs – SCM info	Variant of SCM info: Ex ante appraisal	Surveys / SME – compatibility test by Federal Government	Economic simulation model	Business Impact Assessment (BIA) or Regulatory IA	Cost–benefit analysis
What must be measured? Which cost or benefit category?	Compliance costs, and the additional costs in comparison to existing laws/ practice in the industry	Bureaucracy costs/ Information costs	Ex ante appraisal of the arising administrative costs, for planned laws as simple or complex variant	Influence/effects on innovation and competitiveness of companies	Economic effects of a new regulation, insofar as these can be presented as factor changes	Intended and unforeseeable effects of planned regulations for commerce	All cost and benefit categories for norm addressees and other affected parties
How does the measurement occur? Which process must be adhered to?	Standardized systematics and process according to EIM	Standardized systematics and process according to SCM by various providers	*Simple:* Administration performs appraisal without interviews, norm addressee known, database from SCM measurement available. *Complex:* External team of experts performs interviews, on basis of an SCM database orwithout	Classic surveys / interviews with companies e.g. in conjunction with SCM measurements	Use of economic simulation models	Process is oriented towards eight questions (see above) including questions on the cost effects, important: company as norm addressee is starting point for consideration in BIA	Systematic analysis of total cost and benefit effects, partially with assumptions to be made
Who bears responsibility for the measurement and who performs it?	In simpler cases, administration can perform the measurement itself. With large, complicated laws, an external body should be commissioned	In simpler cases, administration can perform the measurement itself. With large, complicated laws, an external body should be commissioned	*Simple:* Administration, if it lacks experience - preceding training by experts necessary. *Complex:* Department or as a rule a team of experts	Either administration and / or external team of experts in the course of SCM interviews	Simulation should be performed by an institute with a corresponding simulation model	Administration or, on account of the scope and the necessary expertise, an external team of experts.	On account of the complexity, delegation by administration to an external team of experts.

(continued)

	Compliance costs – SCM content	Administrative / information costs – SCM info	Variant of SCM info: Ex ante appraisal	Surveys / SME – compatibility test by Federal Government	Economic simulation model	Business Impact Assessment (BIA) or Regulatory IA	Cost–benefit analysis
Which method is suitable for which situation?	For all new laws before they enter into force	New and existing laws. Quick Scan at beginning for the '7;big fish'7;, then a detailed SCM measurement if required	Existing laws, and new laws, whose effects are to be assessed	For ex ante appraisal with deliberately explorative, qualitative character without detailed measurement.	Ex ante determination of the secondary effects based on an appropriate random sample.	BIA summarizes the methods on the left and provides a complete overview.	Cost–benefit analysis only comes into question if a cost analysis has resulted in substantial costs.
Which prerequisites must be in place for use of the method?	Focusing on the norm addressees: qualitative and quantitative availability of statistical data	Database with process steps, frequency and tariff parameters with assignable cost items; availability of companies/ experts	Specialists trained for assessments in SCM, database with SCM- and law-specific data	Trained interviewers, who must distinguish between individual case and generalization	Functional and realistic model	Methodological expertise for methods on the left must be available	Personnel and financial resources and time for the measurement as well as given quantifiability of benefits and goals
Which purpose is pursued with the measurement? Are existing regulations to be measured ex post or new regulations to be measured ex ante?	Ex ante measurement of a new regulation. Debate on contents of the regulation objective, thus preventing imposition of unnecessary costs on norm addressees. Measurement of existing regulation only useful in selected cases	Precise ex post measurement of administrative costs of existing laws on account of transparency and identification of inefficient administrative processes. Global ex ante measurements of a new regulation	Suitable for ex ante appraisals and in case of complex variant for examining different alternatives	Explorative ex ante appraisal for assessment of secondary consequential effects of different regulation alternatives	Assessment of macroeconomic effects	Particularly suitable for comprehensive ex ante studies of all consequential effects	Comprehensive ex ante and ex post measurement of all effects, the result must be meaningful from the perspective of the political goal.

(continued)

	Compliance costs – SCM content	Administrative / information costs – SCM info	Variant of SCM info: Ex ante appraisal	Surveys / SME – compatibility test by Federal Government	Economic simulation model	Business Impact Assessment (BIA) or Regulatory IA	Cost–benefit analysis
What are the limits of the individual methods?	Masking of the benefit and bureaucratic costs dimension; discussion of political goals is opened, enabling influence of interest group politics	Masking of benefit dimension as well as compliance cost dimension and secondary effects	*Simple*: Quality and acceptance of results, missing reference data, difficult alternative tests *Complex:* Training, time, costs	Accuracy is limited, as representativeness requires a high number of cases, also danger of influence of interests as well as non-standardized methodology (acceptance)	Further non-controllable variables in economic context influence the result (like psychology)	Prerequisites on the left must be fulfilled, comparatively complex	High expenditure, dependence on assumptions and estimations; openness in comparison to group-specific interventions
How can the methods be linked together? What is their logical sequence?	New regulation: Start with measurement of compliance costs	New regulation: Start with SCM measurement of administrative costs; Existing regulation: Start with Quick-Scan variant of SCM, then SCM measurement	New regulation: Detailed SCM measurement is replaced by either simple or complex ex ante appraisal	Perform in conjunction with SCM interviews	After determination of the effects for the individual norm addressees, the economic dimensions are determined	Comprehensive method for cost measurement, also possible as RIA, the regulation and not the company is then in focus	In case of substantial administrative costs and/or compliance costs, cost–benefit analysis is used
Assessment of criteria:							
Practicable	3	4	5	5	3	2	1
Easily comprehensible	4	5	5	5	3	4	3
Acceptance	4	5	5	2	2	3	3
SME reference	5	5	5	5	2	5	5
Methodological foundation	4	5	4	2	3	4	3
Efficient use	3	4	5	5	3	2	1
Selective	4	5	5	5	2	3	3
Pragmatic	4	5	5	5	2	4	3
Verifiable/ transparent	5	5	5	2	5	5	4

(continued)

	Compliance costs – SCM content	Administrative / information costs – SCM info	Variant of SCM info: Ex ante appraisal	Surveys / SME – compatibility test by Federal Government	Economic simulation model	Business Impact Assessment (BIA) or Regulatory IA	Cost–benefit analysis
Reliable and valid	5	5	5	2	5	4	4
Integration into regulation process	5	5	5	5	4	4	3
Internationally comparable	4	5	4	2	2	3	3
Easily enforceable	4	5	5	5	2	4	2
Without political interest	3	5	5	2	4	4	2
Comprehensive	3	2	2	3	2	4	5
Total score:	60	70	70	55	45	55	45

Index

B

T

MIX
Papier aus verantwortungsvollen Quellen
Paper from responsible sources
FSC® C105338

If you have any concerns about our products,
you can contact us on
ProductSafety@springernature.com

In case Publisher is established outside the EU,
the EU authorized representative is:
Springer Nature Customer Service Center GmbH
Europaplatz 3, 69115 Heidelberg, Germany

Printed by Libri Plureos GmbH
in Hamburg, Germany